THE
SIEGE

BY BEN MACINTYRE

The Siege

Prisoners of the Castle

Agent Sonya

The Spy and the Traitor

Rogue Heroes

A Spy Among Friends

Agent Zigzag

Operation Mincemeat

Double Cross

The Last Word

For Your Eyes Only

Josiah the Great

The Englishman's Daughter

The Napoleon of Crime

Forgotten Fatherland

THE
SIEGE

A SIX-DAY HOSTAGE CRISIS
AND THE DARING SPECIAL-
FORCES OPERATION THAT
SHOCKED THE WORLD

BEN MACINTYRE

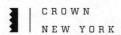

CROWN
NEW YORK

Copyright © 2024 by Ben Macintyre

Published in the United States by Crown, an imprint of the Crown Publishing Group,
a division of Penguin Random House LLC, New York.
crownpublishing.com

CROWN and the Crown colophon are registered trademarks of
Penguin Random House LLC.

Simultaneously published in Great Britain by Viking, an imprint of Penguin Random
House Ltd., London, and in Canada by Signal, an imprint of Random House Canada,
a division of Penguin Random House Canada Limited, Toronto.

Library of Congress Cataloging-in-Publication Data
Names: Macintyre, Ben, 1963- author.
Title: The siege : a six-day hostage crisis and the daring special-forces operation that
    shocked the world / Ben Macintyre.
Other titles: Six-day hostage crisis and the daring special-forces operation that shocked
    the world
Description: First edition. | New York : Crown Publishing, [2024] | Includes
    bibliographical references and index.
Identifiers: LCCN 2024021548 (print) | LCCN 2024021549 (ebook) |
    ISBN 9780593728093 (hardcover) | ISBN 9780593728109 (ebook)
Subjects: LCSH: Great Britain. Army. Special Air Service. | Iranian embassy siege,
    London, England, 1980. | Special forces (Military science)—Great Britain—
    History—20th century. | Terrorism—England—London—History—20th century.
Classification: LCC UA659.S67 M335 2024 (print) | LCC UA659.S67 (ebook) |
    DDC 356.1670941—dc23/eng/20240530
LC record available at https://lccn.loc.gov/2024021548
LC ebook record available at https://lccn.loc.gov/2024021549

ISBN 978-0-593-72809-3
Ebook ISBN 978-0-593-72810-9

Printed in the United States of America on acid-free paper

9 8 7 6 5 4 3 2 1

First US Edition

Book design by Aubrey Khan
Jacket design by Chris Bentham

FOR ALEXANDRA

CONTENTS

ILLUSTRATION CREDITS

Every effort has been made to contact all copyright holders. The publisher will be pleased to amend in future editions any errors or omissions brought to our attention.

Ben Macintyre would like to thank those individuals who lived through the siege and their families for generously contributing images from their private collections.

INSERT ONE

PAGE 1: (top left) Getty Images: Stuart Nicol/*Evening Standard*; (top right) Hoover Institution Library & Archives: (Poster IR 51); (center right) Shutterstock: Neville Marriner/ANL; (bottom) Report Digital: © NLA/reportdigital.co.uk

PAGE 2: (top left) Courtesy of Sim Harris; (Iranian Embassy) Historic England Archive: (© Adam Watson); (center inset) Courtesy of Faten Omary Karkouti; (bottom right) Private collection; (bottom left) Alamy: Trinity Mirror/Mirrorpix; (center left) © Telegraph Media Group: *The Telegraph,* May 1, 1980

PAGE 3: (top left) Historic England Archive: (© Adam Watson); (top right) Alamy: PA; (letter) Courtesy of Hannah Cramer; (bottom left) Courtesy of Sim Harris

PAGE 4: (top left) Courtesy of Sim Harris; (top right) *Impact International*: June 13–26, 1980; (center right) TopFoto; (bottom right)

Courtesy of Sim Harris; (bottom left) Courtesy of Anton Antonowicz; (center left) Alamy: PA

PAGE 5: (top, center, and bottom right) Private collection; (center right and center left) Courtesy of Sim Harris; (bottom left) Alamy: Keystone

PAGE 6: (top) Alamy: CPA Media Pte Ltd; (center) Alamy: World Politics Archive; (bottom) © Michel Setboun

PAGE 7: (top) Camera Press London: Reza; (center) Camera Press Long: Jacques Haillot; (bottom) © Michel Setboun

PAGE 8: (top left) University of Manchester, image from Javanan-i Imruz (Nov 1979, provided by UML); (top right) Getty Images: Alain Mingam/Gamma-Rapho; (center) Shutterstock: Rex; (bottom) Magnum Photos: A. Abbas

PAGE 9: (top left and bottom left) Alamy: Keystone; (right) Private collection; (center inset) Shutterstock: Rex

PAGE 10: (top left, center right, bottom left) Private collection; (top center) TV Times, March 14–20, 1980; (map) David Rumsey Map Collection

PAGE 11: (top row, center right, bottom left) University of Manchester, images from Tihrān Musavvar 20 (June 14, 1979, provided by UML); (Saddam Hussein) Shutterstock: Rex; (bottom right) Getty Images: Cristine Spengler/Sygma

PAGE 12: (top left) Courtesy of Caroline Probyn; (top right) Courtesy of Cherida Morgan; (bottom right) Courtesy of Bethan and Gail Parry; (bottom left) Private collection

PAGE 13: (top left) Private collection; (top right) Getty Images: Popperfoto; (center) Courtesy of Bethan and Gail Parry; (bottom) Shutterstock: Stuart Clarke

PAGE 14: (top left) Alamy: Homer Sykes; (top right) Mary Evans Picture Library: Keystone/ZUMA Press; (center upper right) Alamy: PA; (center lower right and bottom) Mirrorpix

PAGE 15: (top left) Private collection; (top right) Getty Images: Dominique Berretty/Gamma-Rapho; (center) News International: *The Sun*, May 1, 1980; (bottom) Mirrorpix

PAGE 16: (top left) Getty Images: N. Beattie/*Evening Standard*/Hulton Archive; (center right) Private collection; (bottom left) Getty Images: Fox Photos/Hulton Archive; (center left) Shutterstock: John Curtis

INSERT TWO

PAGE 1: (left row) Private collection; (top right) Getty Images: AFP; (center right) *Impact International*, May 2 to June 12, 1980

PAGE 2: (top row) Alamy: Homer Sykes; (center and bottom right) Alamy: Trinity Mirror/Mirrorpix; (bottom left) Getty Images: Jayne Fincher/Popperfoto

PAGE 3: (top, center right) Alamy: ZUMA Press; (bottom) Mirrorpix; (center left) TopFoto: PA

PAGE 4: (top left) Alamy: PA; (top right, center, bottom) Private collection

PAGE 5: (top and center) Private collection; (bottom right) © BBC

PAGE 6: All private collection

PAGE 7: (top left and bottom left) Private collection; (right) © Sim Harris

PAGE 8: (background letter) Private collection; (top right and center left) Mirrorpix; (bottom right) Alamy: Keystone

PAGE 9: (top) © Guardian News & Media Limited: *The Guardian*, May 5, 1980; (center) Alamy: PA; (bottom) Private collection

PAGE 10: (top left on film reel) Alamy: Trinity Mirror/Mirrorpix; (top right and bottom center) Mirrorpix; (bottom three on film reel) Private collection

MAPS AND FLOOR PLANS

MAPS

Khuzestan Province, Iran-Iraq border

Kensington, London

16 Princes Gate

FLOOR PLANS[*]

16 Princes Gate: Basement

16 Princes Gate: Ground Floor

16 Princes Gate: First Floor

16 Princes Gate: Second Floor

16 Princes Gate: Third Floor

16 Princes Gate: Fourth Floor

Front and back of the embassy, preattack on page 246

---

[*] In the United Kingdom, the floor you enter from the street is called the ground floor, whereas in the United States it's called the first floor. The next floor up in the United Kingdom is called the first floor, whereas in the United States it's called the second floor, and so on. To maintain the integrity of the story, the United Kingdom's floor numbering system is used throughout the text.

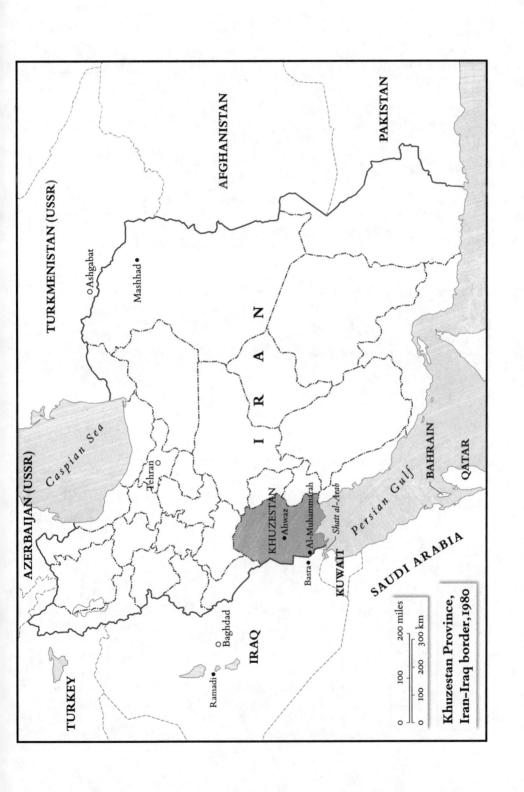

Khuzestan Province,
Iran-Iraq border, 1980

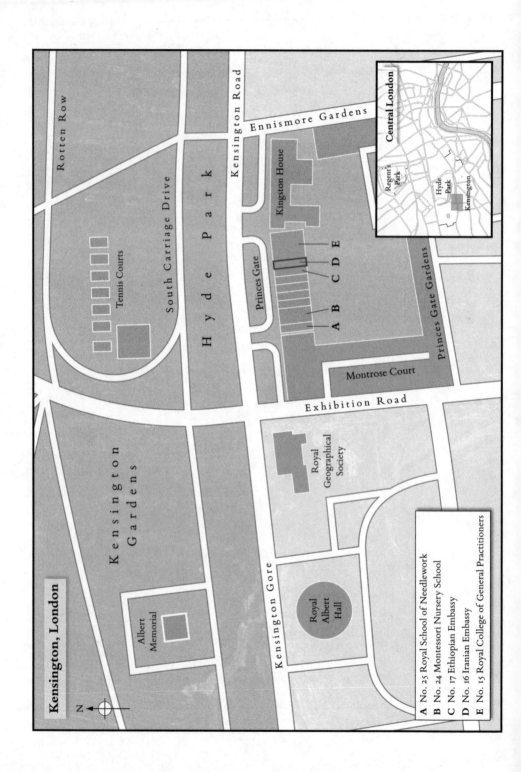

Kensington, London

Rotten Row

Kensington Road

Ennismore Gardens

Hyde Park

South Carriage Drive

Tennis Courts

Kingston House

Princes Gate

A B C D E

Princes Gate Gardens

Montrose Court

Exhibition Road

Kensington Gardens

Royal Geographical Society

Albert Memorial

Kensington Gore

Royal Albert Hall

N

Central London

Regent's Park

Hyde Park

Kensington

A No. 25 Royal School of Needlework
B No. 24 Montessori Nursery School
C No. 17 Ethiopian Embassy
D No. 16 Iranian Embassy
E No. 15 Royal College of General Practitioners

Situation: Day Six

RED

WHITE

GREEN

BLACK

A No. 24 Montessori Nursery School, Alpha and Zulu Controls
B No. 17 Ethiopian Embassy
C No. 16 Iranian Embassy
D No. 15 Royal College of General Practitioners

Ennismore Gardens

Road-works

Specialist Medical Teams, ambulances

Kingston House

▲ Sniper control
● Command point
△ 6th floor flat (Sunray)

South Carriage Drive

Kensington Road

Princes Gate

D

C

B

A

Reception area

Princes Gate Gardens

Lighting rig

Generator for smoke machines

Dog control

Lighting

Press enclosure

Exhibition Road

Outer cordon
Inner cordon
Barriers
++++ Caltrops, road spikes

Dogs
× Armed Diplomatic Control Group Officer
△ Snipers

16 Princes Gate: Basement

FRONT

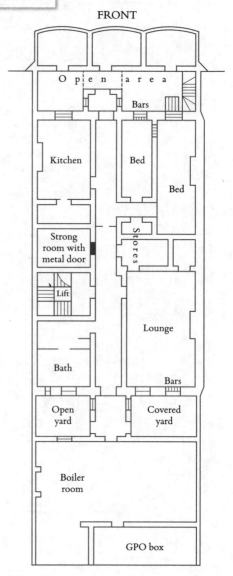

16 Princes Gate: Ground Floor

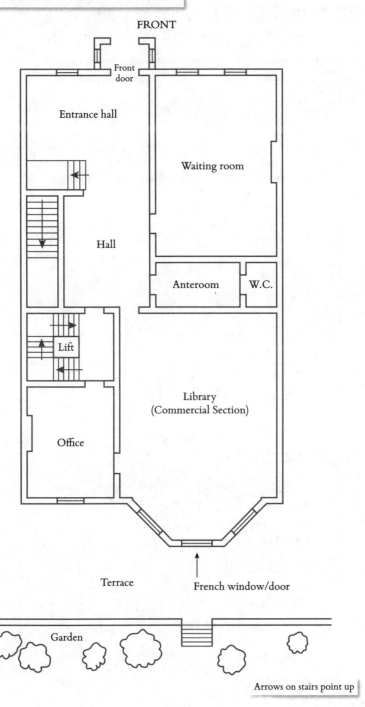

FRONT

Front door

Entrance hall

Waiting room

Hall

Anteroom

W.C.

Lift

Office

Library
(Commercial Section)

Terrace

French window/door

Garden

Arrows on stairs point up

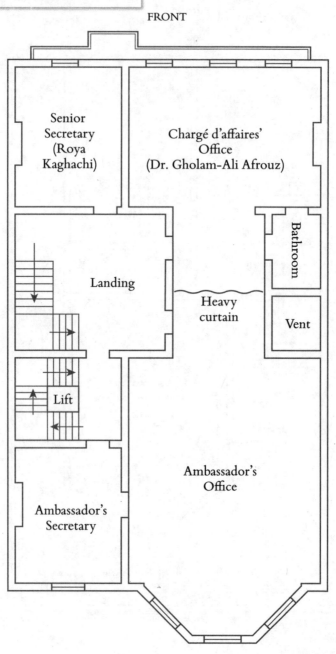

16 Princes Gate: First Floor

FRONT

Senior Secretary (Roya Kaghachi)

Chargé d'affaires' Office (Dr. Gholam-Ali Afrouz)

Bathroom

Landing

Heavy curtain

Vent

Lift

Ambassador's Office

Ambassador's Secretary

Arrows on stairs point up

FRONT

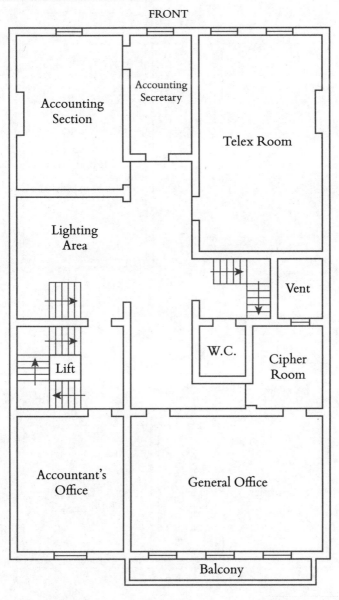

Accounting Section

Accounting Secretary

Telex Room

Lighting Area

Vent

W.C.

Cipher Room

Lift

Accountant's Office

General Office

Balcony

Arrows on stairs point up

16 Princes Gate: Third Floor

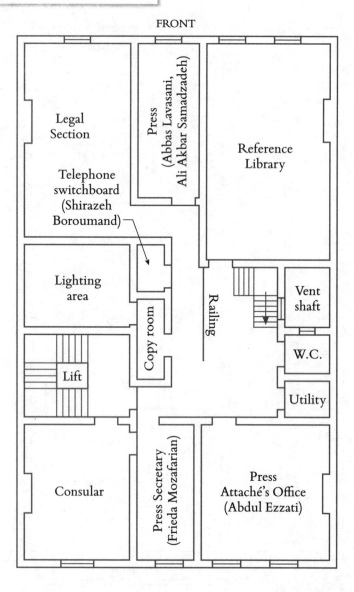

FRONT

Legal Section

Telephone switchboard (Shirazeh Boroumand)

Press (Abbas Lavasani, Ali Akbar Samadzadeh)

Reference Library

Lighting area

Copy room

Railing

Vent shaft

W.C.

Lift

Utility

Consular

Press Secretary (Frieda Mozafarian)

Press Attaché's Office (Abdul Ezzati)

Arrows on stairs point up

16 Princes Gate: Fourth Floor

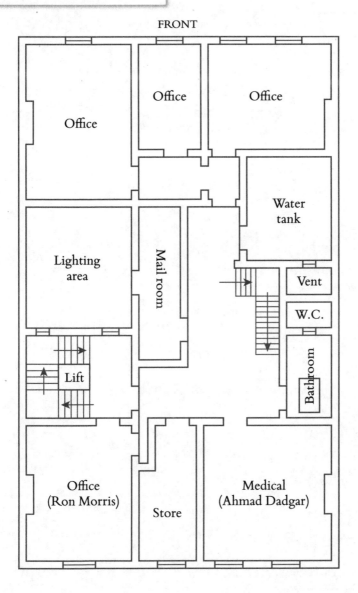

FRONT

Office

Office

Office

Water tank

Lighting area

Mail room

Vent

W.C.

Lift

Bathroom

Office (Ron Morris)

Store

Medical (Ahmad Dadgar)

Arrows on stairs point up

PREFACE

This is a true story of people thrust into a dangerous situation they could not control: a group of strangers who suddenly found themselves captive and besieged. As always in such circumstances, individuals reacted differently: with courage, cowardice, resilience, terror, desperation, or humor. Even the perpetrators were swept along by events, in ways they did not anticipate or fully understand.

The Iranian Embassy siege gripped the world, and immediately entered national mythology in Britain. For millions it became a historical watershed, a "Where were you when it happened?" moment, like the JFK assassination or 9/11. Via the new miracle of live television news, the drama was played out on screens in homes up and down the country, day by day, hour by hour, minute by minute; the first-ever hostage crisis to be relayed in real time, it marked a turning point in the relationship between breaking news and the viewing public. Like most legends, the episode was presented afterward as a straightforward morality tale of military daring, civilian bravery, patient police work, and wicked foreign terrorists bent on mayhem. But the siege was more complicated than that, and much more extraordinary.

This is not a simple black-and-white moral fable, in which the righteous triumph and the losers meet their just deserts. Rather, it is a tale of human error and unintended consequences, the self-replicating tragedy of man's inhumanity to man, and the collision of intolerant beliefs in an era of political, ethnic, and religious violence. The underlying forces that produced the crisis in London more than forty years ago still agonize and destabilize our world, from Gaza to Iran to Ukraine. Britain had never before faced an international hostage-taking incident on this scale, and the siege changed forever the way terrorism was perceived, and dealt with.

Everyone involved was tested to a limit invisible to them at the time: hostages, gunmen, police, journalists, politicians, and members of the Special Air Service. None knew how the story would end. These were ordinary people, making life or death choices based on instinct and character, for which no training is possible. There are few outright heroes or villains in *The Siege*, only humans, fallible and unpredictable, struggling to survive and subdue a sudden, terrifying storm.

This book offers just one universal truth: no one knows how they will respond to lethal jeopardy, until they have to.

DAY ONE

WEDNESDAY

1

16 PRINCES GATE

At 19:30, on Wednesday, April 30, 1980, a small, secret, and exceptionally well-equipped army rolled out of Bradbury Lines, the Special Air Service camp at Hereford.

Locals tended to be overly curious about the goings-on at the SAS camp, and so, to avoid attracting attention, the seven white Range Rovers departed at irregular intervals from the three exits, three men lying under blankets on the back seat, with two in the front. These were followed by two white Ford Transit vans and two large yellow furniture trucks.

This small convoy carried forty-five soldiers in civilian clothes, and enough weaponry to fight a medium-size war.

Each man had a green carryall packed with his personal weapons and gear: a submachine gun with four 30-round magazines, a 9mm semi-automatic pistol with two spare rounds of ammunition, a respirator, gloves, a balaclava helmet, body armor, boots, a belt, and a weapons-cleaning kit. In addition, each soldier had a prepacked long-stay bag with toiletries, sneakers, a tracksuit, and a sleeping bag. The vans carried extra ammunition, tear-gas launchers and canisters, stun grenades, frame charges, sawed-off pump-action shotguns, explosives, weapon-mount flashlights, food, water, radios, medical equipment, and spare weapons. The trucks contained the heavy gear: scaling ladders, ropes, and abseiling (rappelling) gear, lighting rigs, screens, thermal lances for cutting through metal, smoke machines, generators, and battering rams.

The SAS Special Projects team might have been setting out to repel the invasion of Britain—which, in a way, they were.

SHORTLY BEFORE 11:00 that morning, six young men had gathered beside the Albert Memorial, Queen Victoria's ornate tribute to her late husband, opposite the Royal Albert Hall in London's Kensington Gardens, west of Hyde Park. They were Middle Eastern, students or perhaps tourists, wearing smart new sneakers, clean hooded jackets, and backpacks. Around their necks each wore a keffiyeh, the traditional Arab cotton scarf with a red or black fishnet pattern. The PLO leader Yasser Arafat wore the keffiyeh, as did Westerners to signify sympathy for the Palestinian cause. The park was almost deserted on a weekday morning, with a handful of mothers wheeling strollers in the light rain and the occasional jogger. The men sat on the steps and listened intently as one of their number, a slim, wiry man in his late twenties with a goatee beard and thin mustache, spoke rapidly in Arabic.

At 11:12, the six men rose and picked up their bags. Then they split into two groups of three and headed for Princes Gate, a stuccoed terrace of large houses set back from Kensington Road, separated from the main thoroughfare by an eight-foot-high brick wall and a service road with parked cars. One group entered the road from the east, the other from the west. As they neared the door to Number 16, they wrapped the keffiyehs around their heads so that only their eyes showed. "*Yalla*," said their leader. "Go!"

TO SAY THAT Police Constable 469K, Trevor James Lock, was "guarding" the Iranian Embassy implies rather more focus and energy than the task demanded. Lock was an officer of the Diplomatic Protection Group, the Metropolitan Police unit responsible for security at the 138 foreign embassies and high commissions dotted around London. Most of these premises did not need protection. The DPG was largely diplomatic decoration, symbolizing Britain's duty to safeguard foreign dignitaries. Lock's primary function was to nod in a friendly but official manner to visitors and diplomats as they passed in and out of the building.

The job was one of the least stressful and most boring in British policing. This suited PC Lock just fine.

At forty-one, portly, patient, and placid, Lock was a far cry from *The Sweeney*, the popular 1970s TV show in which tough, gun-wielding cops screeched around London in fast cars apprehending villains. He was closer to *Dixon of Dock Green*, another policeman familiar to British television viewers, policing with common sense by standing around on street corners, being avuncular. Some join the police to fight crime and improve society; Lock became a policeman, as he put it, "to help old ladies across the road."

Born into a working-class East London family, Lock had spent most of his life in the borough of Barking, where he knew every road (and almost every old lady). During National Service with the army, he volunteered for deployment to Tripoli, in the mistaken belief that it was in Italy. In Libya, he learned how to handle firearms, and how to swear in Arabic. After a stint in the Ford Dagenham factory, he joined the police at the age of twenty-six. Lock worked out of Barking Station, patrolling the world he had known since boyhood. He was part of the street furniture, as familiar and unchanging as the lampposts: everyone knew Trev. Lock's first wife died in 1971, and he now lived in a council house with his second wife, Doreen, another native of Barking, and their six children, three from her first marriage and three from his. She was a devout Catholic. He worshipped West Ham United Football Club. He also believed in fair play, British cultural values (though he would be hard put to say what these were), and the police. Beneath his mild exterior, Lock was tougher than he seemed, or knew.

After fifteen years on the beat, in January 1980, Lock had requested a posting to the DPG, which was better paid: Trevor and Doreen were saving up for a holiday with the children on the Costa Brava. British police did not carry guns in 1980, but Diplomatic Protection officers were an exception. After three days of weapons training, Lock was issued with a Smith & Wesson .38 Regulation Police revolver, which fit into a leather holster on his belt. Lock was confident he would never have to fire it. "Police and guns don't go together," he said.

It was chilly and drizzling when Lock left his home in Dagenham that Wednesday morning, and Doreen insisted he dress warmly since he would be standing outside on the porch of the Iranian Embassy all day: he wore two pullovers and his police tunic, beneath a waterproof gabardine coat. It was Doreen's birthday, and Lock had planned a night out in town. After work they would go shopping at Harrods for perfume, followed by a surprise treat: two tickets for *Ipi Tombi*, the hit musical playing at the London Astoria Theatre in the West End. Doreen liked surprises.

At 11:18, the Iranian doorman Abbas Fallahi popped his head around the front door and offered Lock a cup of coffee. According to police regulations, a DPG officer should not be seen eating or drinking while on duty, and Lock was not supposed to leave his post on the front step. Besides, Fallahi's Persian-style coffee, strong, black, and sweet, was "a cup of yuk" in his opinion. But "to refuse might offend," and so Lock slipped into the space between the oak outer door and the inner security door of glass and wrought iron, and accepted the steaming cup.

Abbas Fallahi had worked at the Iranian Embassy for nine years. His first job, fresh from Tehran, was driving the ambassador around London in a gleaming Rolls-Royce Silver Shadow. His Excellency Parviz Radji represented the Shah of Iran, King of Kings, Light of the Aryans, and Sovereign of the Order of the Red Lion and the Sun. The ambassador lived a sumptuous life of parties and receptions, and he entertained lavishly at Princes Gate, where Fallahi doubled as a waiter, serving caviar and champagne.

The shah was then the West's favorite Middle Eastern despot, modernizing, cooperative, and oil-rich. He was also haughty, luxury-loving, and autocratic. The CIA and Britain's Secret Intelligence Service, also known as MI6, had conspired to strengthen his rule in Iran by overthrowing the democratically elected government in 1953, when it threatened to nationalize the oil industry. The shah's courtiers flattered and fawned over him, while many of his subjects loathed him; all opposition was suppressed with ruthless brutality by his secret police, the Bureau for Intelligence and State Security, known as SAVAK.

The embassy at 16 Princes Gate symbolized the shah's wealth and power: a huge Victorian town house built in 1849, with fifty-six rooms, five stories, and a basement, in an Italianate row of eleven houses overlooking Hyde Park to the north. It had thick Persian carpets, molded ceilings, marble flooring, swagged curtains, polished banisters, and an air of lofty grandeur befitting the monarch of the Peacock Throne. Former residents of Princes Gate included Joseph Chamberlain and Field Marshal Douglas Haig. The neighbors were illustrious: John F. Kennedy had lived next door when his father was U.S. ambassador; the Ethiopian Embassy was on the other side, at Number 17.

In 1979, the shah was toppled by the Islamic Revolution, an event that took him, his Western allies, and most of the rest of the world by surprise. Iran's proud monarch was forced into ignominious exile, and the secular Pahlavi imperial dynasty was replaced with an anti-Western, authoritarian, Islamist theocracy under the hard-line cleric Ayatollah Ruhollah Khomeini: a militant regime determined to spread Shia Islam across the Middle East and establish Iranian dominance.

Life at the Iranian Embassy in London was transformed overnight, and Ambassador Radji shuffled into exile like his king, replaced by a representative of the Islamic Republic of Iran. Dr. Gholam-Ali Afrouz was a new breed of Iranian diplomat: fanatically dedicated to the ayatollah, unshakable in his Islamic fundamentalism, and almost wholly inexperienced in the ways of international diplomacy. Afrouz had studied psychology and education at Michigan State University before returning to Tehran to join the Islamic Revolution. Arrested and imprisoned by SAVAK, he was released when the ayatollah swept to power and put to work enforcing strict ideological conformity as a senior official of the new Ministry of National Guidance. In September 1979, at the age of twenty-nine, he was sent to London as Iran's chargé d'affaires (deputy ambassador), the most senior Iranian diplomat in the country.

A sleek, self-satisfied opportunist with a paunch and a dignified air, Afrouz brought with him a new Islamic austerity and a cadre of like-minded men, young revolutionaries who mostly owed their positions to religious fervor. A devout Muslim teetotaler, Afrouz chose as his first and very public act to empty the embassy's outstanding wine cellar and pour every bottle down the drain. The embassy Rolls was sold off.

Abbas Fallahi was demoted to doorman, swapping his chauffeur's cap and waiter's tails for a blue suit. The parties ceased.

Contacts between London and Tehran hovered between frostiness and outright hostility, but diplomatic relations had not yet been severed, and PC Lock was the proof.

After handing the policeman his coffee, Fallahi poured seven more cups and took them on a tray into the ground-floor waiting room, where a handful of visitors sat beneath a large portrait of the white-bearded and beetle-browed ayatollah: two BBC journalists applying for visas to Iran, a student, a banker, two Pakistani tourists, and an Iranian rug salesman with an appointment to see the embassy's medical officer.

In his first-floor office, Afrouz was delivering a revolutionary lecture to a visiting journalist. In the press room two floors above, the press attaché chatted to another journalist. Seven female secretarial staff were dotted around the building. Ron Morris was the embassy majordomo and the only full-time British employee. He kept the place running; ensured sufficient stocks of telex tape, toilet paper, and tea; and checked the oil for the boiler. At this moment he was roosting in his small office on the fourth floor having a cup of tea—a ritual he performed with almost religious regularity throughout the day.

At 11:26, there were thirty-one people inside the embassy, none of them doing anything interesting or important.

"Just another Iranian student," thought PC Lock as he spotted a young man approaching the half-open front door.

Then he saw the submachine gun.

The first bullet smashed through the glass security door, sending shards flying into Lock's face. As he staggered backward, the gunman fired another volley of shots, shouting in Arabic. The coffee cup and saucer smashed on the marble floor. Blood pouring into his eyes, Lock was bundled backward into the hall as two more armed men, their faces masked by keffiyehs, burst into the building, firing into the air.

"Don't move!" shouted the leading gunman, in English. "Put your hands up! Against the wall!"

Instinctively, Lock reached for his lapel radio and pressed the emergency button. A second later the first intruder tore it off his tunic. Three miles away in Central London, an alarm sounded in Scotland Yard's information room.

Chris Cramer, a BBC news producer, was standing in the main hall-way when the attackers stormed in through the front door. He stumbled back into the waiting room, where the other visitors were already on their feet. "There are gunmen out there," he gasped. Two of the attackers charged up the stairs, firing pistols into the air and shouting. Lock raised his hands and backed against the wall of the reception area, where Fallahi was already standing, wide-eyed, the coffee pot still in his hand.

The gunman pulled down his keffiyeh. "Please do not be afraid," he said. "We get everyone in the building together, make a few speeches, and then we go."

Lock could barely see him through the blood.

The voice was clear, and oddly calm. "Don't worry, nothing is going to happen to you. You are all our friends."

But, as he spoke, a second gunman, taller than the first, took a green hand grenade from the pocket of his jacket and placed his finger through the ring holding the firing pin in place. His hands were shaking.

Hearing the commotion below, Afrouz rushed to his office door and locked it just as the attackers reached the landing. The chargé d'affaires and his interviewer stared at each other, speechless, as the intruders hammered on the door with their guns, shouting for the occupants to open up. Afrouz knew enough Arabic to understand what they were saying: "This is his office, Ali Afrouz . . . Don't let him escape." Then the sound of feet thundering up the stairs to the floor above.

"There's a lot of noise out there today," Ron Morris thought idly. "Is it another student demonstration? I think it is. Someone has fired a blank cartridge . . ." He emerged from his office and peered down into the stairwell to see the policeman and doorman being herded up the stairs by a man with a sub-machine gun. He swiftly backed into his room and closed the door.

Morris was not a man who ruffled easily, but nor was he a swift thinker. In his twenty-seven years at the embassy, nothing remotely like this had ever happened before. A man of hobbies, Morris collected replica and toy guns. He had several in the drawer of his desk, including a

Diana .177 air pistol, which looked a little like a Browning. Morris took it out, then thought better of that idea and quickly put it away again. The air pistol was useful for killing rats in the embassy basement; it would not be an effective weapon for repelling heavily armed terrorists. Instead, he picked up the telephone and dialed 999.

"Fire, police, or ambulance?" said a voice.

"Police, please," he whispered. The shouting and shooting were coming closer. Morris put down the receiver. "Is it better not to be caught with the phone in my hand?" he thought. "Yes. And better to stay sitting down? Yes." So that is what he did.

All over the building, terrified people tried to escape; five succeeded. Two women opened the front door and rushed into the street, screaming. The chief medical officer seized an elderly Iranian clerk by the arm, and together they climbed out of her office window at the back of the ground floor. The Iranian consul general clambered onto the rear balcony and then jumped over to the balcony of the Ethiopian Embassy next door, and went in through the window.

For a moment, those in the waiting room were left unguarded. Among them was a BBC sound engineer, Simeon Harris, known as Sim. Harris was a veteran journalist, one of the unsung but vital technicians who record the soundtrack to the news. For fifteen years he had traveled the world covering wars, conflicts, and upheavals, as well as domestic news. The previous year in Tehran he had been part of the BBC team reporting on the return of the ayatollah from exile, and the street fighting that accompanied it. When he first heard the shouting, Harris assumed that Khomeini supporters were mounting some sort of demonstration. "They are always doing odd things," he reflected. While his colleague Chris Cramer struggled to open the window onto the street (which was sealed shut), Harris was disinclined to fuss. "They will dash in and run around shouting," he thought, "and eventually be removed by police."

Another gunman burst in. "Don't move," he said, pointing his machine gun at Cramer's head. "You'll be killed if you move."

A group of eight or nine embassy staff rushed up the stairs ahead of the gunmen and dived into a small, unused top-floor room. The most senior secretary, twenty-five-year-old Roya Kaghachi, locked the door.

They huddled against the wall as the yelling grew closer: "Find the ambassador! Make sure all rooms are carefully searched." Frieda Mozafarian, another young secretary, suddenly began to scream uncontrollably. Roya slapped her hard, but it was too late. The door was kicked open with a crash, and a gunman fired into the ceiling. "*Dasta bala*," he shouted in Farsi, the language of Iran. "Hands on your heads! Stand against the wall!"

Frieda screamed again and fainted.

Then, in a surreal moment, one gunman turned to the other and, switching from Farsi to Arabic, asked: "What do we do now?"

Gholam-Ali Afrouz unlocked his office door and opened it a crack. The landing was empty. He sprinted to the back of the building and threw open the window facing the garden. Twenty feet below him was a stone-paved terrace, and the basement stairwell with an iron railing. Afrouz paused on the ledge. He was overweight and out of condition, already panting from the exertion. Then he jumped.

Ron Morris was still sitting down when his door crashed open. "What's the matter?" the Englishman asked. "What's going on?"

The tallest gunman had now abandoned his keffiyeh to reveal a bushy, almost Afro hairstyle, and wild eyes. Morris noticed he was wearing cowboy boots. The man pointed his submachine gun at Morris's forehead.

"English, English. You my friend. Come."

SECONDS AFTER LOCK pressed his emergency button, the duty sergeant on the console at Scotland Yard sent out a radio alert to every armed Diplomatic Protection Group unit. Within three minutes, four DPG officers on motorbikes stationed at nearby embassies had converged on Princes Gate. Another five appeared in two squad cars, two minutes later. All were armed with .38 revolvers.

An announcement swiftly followed on the main Metropolitan Police radio frequency: "Armed terrorists have attacked and taken the Iranian Embassy." A second announcement reported that Lock had initiated the emergency-call signal and was not responding to his radio: "The Iranian Embassy's direct emergency link to Scotland Yard has been activated. All available units attend immediately." Every police car in the area was soon hurtling to the scene, sirens screeching. The police log reported: "Unconfirmed reports that embassy staff are jumping out of the back window to escape."

The writer and journalist Rebecca West was idly staring out the window of her flat in Kingston House North, overlooking the embassy gardens, when she saw a chubby man climb onto the window ledge of the building opposite and leap off. He bounced off the cast-iron railing and landed with a shocking crunch, spread-eagled on the flagstone patio. Dame Rebecca was eighty-seven years old. She had reported on prewar Yugoslavia, the Nuremberg trials, and apartheid South Africa. "Tremendously excited at the drama being enacted not 50 yards away," she later wrote, the veteran reporter pulled up a chair, opened the window to hear clearly what was going on, and started taking notes. The threat of nearby violence, she continued, "caused a sensation in the stomach and bowels which is similar to the kind of seasickness that does not relieve itself by vomiting. This is a malaise that can only descend on one in peace. War prepares one's nerves for horror. In peace it comes to one uncooked." Raw drama was playing out under her very window, and she was not going to miss a minute. Two men in Arab headscarves emerged from the basement, picked up the inert body, and dragged it inside.

PC Dusty Gray was on duty in West London when he picked up the emergency signal on his radio. Gray had served nineteen years in D Squadron of 22 SAS (the regular component of the regiment, as distinct from the reserves), including two years in the anti-terrorist team, before joining the police as a dog handler. He made his way to the embassy, conducted a swift and unauthorized reconnaissance of the area, and then found a telephone booth, from which he called Bradbury Lines, the Hereford SAS headquarters, also known as "the Kremlin." At 12:07, the operator put Gray straight through to Lieutenant Colonel Michael Rose, commanding officer of 22 SAS.

"I'm standing outside the Iranian Embassy in London and some armed terrorists have just taken it over."

"Are you taking the piss, Dusty?" the colonel demanded. "Are you absolutely certain?"

"Boss, I've seen armed terrorists moving about the building. This is really serious."

Rose immediately put a call through to Brigadier Peter de la Billière, director of special forces at the Ministry of Defense in London. He then ordered Major Hector Gullan, officer commanding, B Squadron, to gather whatever information was available and give an initial briefing once the men had assembled. "Tell them all to step on it, in case we have to move fast." Without waiting for official authorization from the Ministry of Defense, Rose ordered the squadron to deploy to London immediately.

B Squadron was the current Special Projects team at Hereford, the standing counterterrorist force; it was subdivided into two teams, the Red and the Blue. Each team was made up of twenty men: twelve trained in assault and eight snipers (the latter also cross-trained as assaulters), plus officers and others. The Red Team was undergoing firearms training, but by lunchtime most of the men were in the cookhouse. The men of Blue Team were outside the camp, at home relaxing, or, in several cases, in the pub. At 11:48, approximately twenty minutes after the gunmen first entered the embassy, the live operation code 9999 flashed up on dozens of electronic pagers, followed by a message: "This is the real thing."

RON MORRIS WAS marched down two flights of stairs and into the small cipher room at the back of the second floor, where confidential incoming and outgoing messages were encrypted and decoded. It contained just two metal desks, for the cipher clerk and his secretary. Now it was packed with twenty-two cowering hostages, guarded by three armed men. The air was electric with shock and fear.

Chris Cramer tried to wipe the blood off PC Lock's face with a crumpled tissue.

"Don't worry," the policeman kept repeating, as much to himself as anyone else. "I'm all right. We hope things are going to be all right."

Morris paused in the doorway, and the muzzle of a gun jammed hard into his spine.

"Put your hands up! Stand against the wall."

He joined the other British hostages: Lock, Cramer, and Harris.

At this moment, three more male hostages were pushed into the crowded room, including a young man clad in a bright yellow cardigan. "Afrouz has jumped," he wailed. "I saw him on the ground outside. Dr. Afrouz is dead. He is just lying there dead!"

Some of the women began weeping.

PC Lock, back to the wall with his hands up, addressed the room: "Let's all keep perfectly quiet, especially you, ladies," he urged. "They're only firing blanks. Nobody's going to get hurt. Let's keep quiet."

The policeman was ashen, blood dribbling down his face from dozens of glass cuts. Harris thought he "looked like he'd been shot with a pellet gun." The BBC soundman's earlier insouciance had now evaporated. He saw that his own hands were shaking.

All the gunmen had removed their keffiyehs, and the hostages saw their captors' faces for the first time. There was no doubt who was in command. The leading terrorist was slim and slight, with a neat goatee beard, "in his late twenties, with a round, almost serene face and heavy eyebrows. He moved casually on his feet and cradled a machine pistol in both hands." Harris possessed an extraordinary knack for spotting details others might miss: he noticed how well-dressed the intruders were. Their leader might have emerged from a high-street fashion shoot, with fresh blue jeans, a crisp black cotton shirt, and expensive-looking red-and-white sneakers. The other gunmen listened intently to "every word he uttered and every movement he made. No one disputed his orders." They called him Salim. (Sometimes he called himself Oan.)

Chris Cramer was the thirty-two-year-old son of a policeman, and a man whose outward self-confidence concealed an inner anxiety. He looked like a burly hippie, over six feet tall with long hair and a beard. Cramer chose this moment to approach the leader, proffering an open packet of cigarettes: "What do you want us to do? How can we help you?"

The lead gunman flinched and raised his gun: "Get back across the room," he snapped in perfect English. Then, more gently, he added: "Please do not talk. I think it is best you keep quiet. Yes?" Then he switched to Arabic. "Is this all the hostages?" he asked.

"Yes, I believe so," answered the tall gunman beside him, his number two.

The voice of the third came from the hallway. "Salim, come here. There is no ambassador. His office is empty."

Salim shouted back: "I am coming, be careful, go back to the top and check all rooms one by one, no shooting . . . no shooting, okay?" He turned to his deputy: "Faisal, search them." There was a peculiar formality to the way the gunmen addressed each other. These were evidently not their real names.

Faisal patted down Harris, and the BBC soundman got a closer look at him: "A type-cast desert Arab" was Harris's assessment, with "fine features and a slightly hooked nose, an 'Afro'-style haircut of black hair and droopy mustache."

The gunman found Harris's electronic pager clipped to his belt and examined it suspiciously.

"What is this?" he demanded.

"It's my work bleeper."

"Is connected to police?"

"No, of course not."

Faisal tossed it onto a desk. He pulled Ron Morris's glasses case from his jacket pocket and threw it onto the floor, where it snapped open, sending the spectacles skidding over the green carpet. "Hey, go easy. That's my glasses," said Morris.

Lock was next. The tall gunman patted his pockets, felt the bulge of the gun on his side, and looked up at the policeman in inquiry. "Notebooks, maps, and the like," said Lock quickly. He drew a pad halfway out of his pocket, an instinctive deception that may have saved his life. He had not planned to hide his police revolver. He immediately wondered if, by concealing it, he had placed them all in even greater danger.

Without explanation, the hostages were hustled into the larger adjoining room, the general office, with windows facing the rear garden.

"Close curtain," the lead gunman ordered Cramer and Harris before switching on the overhead fluorescent strip lights, bathing the room in a gloomy yellowish glow. They began dividing the hostages into groups. Women in one corner, Iranian men in another, and a third group consisting of the seven non-Iranians: two Pakistanis, a Syrian, and four British citizens.

Moments later, Afrouz was dragged in by two of the other gunmen. Blood poured from a gash to the side of his face, and his left eye was swollen shut. The diplomat staggered a few feet, the leg of his dark brown suit trousers flapping where the seam had ripped, and collapsed heavily on the floor. Frieda Mozafarian screamed and passed out again. In his failed escape attempt from the window, the chargé d'affaires had broken his jaw and several ribs. He was still alive but too concussed to speak.

Ron Morris knelt to take his pulse. "Oh, guv, no . . . What have they done to you, sir?" He then turned on the gunmen. "What have you done to him? Call a doctor at once! This man is very sick."

Salim briefly conferred with Faisal before answering: "It is not possible. He is all right."

"Get a doctor. He might die," Morris pleaded.

"Please be quiet." The voice was firm.

Lock spoke again. "If you bring me my radio telephone, I can talk to the police and arrange for a doctor."

Salim smiled. It was not an unpleasant smile. "You're being smart," he said softly. "Please be quiet. I want all to be quiet."

The youngest of the intruders appeared with a vase filled with water from the bathroom across the corridor and offered it to Morris with a wobbling grin. Barely more than a boy, he seemed almost as confused as the hostages.

"It's going to be all right, sir," Morris said gently, wiping the blood from the injured man's face. "Don't worry, guv. We'll all be okay."

Afrouz stirred and seemed to revive a little. Morris propped a chair cushion under his head. Roya Kaghachi began to bathe his face, speaking softly in Farsi.

From below came the sound of heavy furniture being dragged across floors: the attackers were barricading themselves in.

The general office was seldom used and sparsely furnished with empty gray filing cabinets and three steel desks. The hostages sat on the faded green Wilton carpet, stared at the walls in shock, or conferred in small groups. The tall gunman guarded the door. The lacerations to the policeman's face had stopped bleeding, but his eye was swelling. Cramer moved over to him and whispered: "What's your name?"

"PC Trevor Lock."

"How did they get in?"

"I couldn't get my gun out in time." Lock looked around and dropped his voice further. "They haven't got it. They missed it."

The discovery that the policeman was still armed was encouraging, and also terrifying.

"Do you intend to use it?" asked Cramer.

"Not at the moment. I've thought about that. I can't take out more than two of them, at the most."

Cramer was struck by another alarming thought. What if Lock himself were to be shot?

"I don't want to be morbid, but, in case anything happens, where is it and how do I use it?"

Lock nodded toward his hip. "It's under my jumper. There's no safety catch. Just pull the trigger."

Suddenly a telephone rang. Everyone in the room jumped. No one moved.

After several rings, Salim gestured to the nearest hostage to answer it: a burly, swarthy man of thirty-five with a substantial mustache, a fat tie, and a worldly air.

Mustapha Karkouti was a Syrian journalist who spoke Arabic by birth, perfect English by adoption, and a decent smattering of Farsi, making him the only person in the embassy able to communicate in all three languages. He also understood the complexities of Middle Eastern politics better than anyone else in the building; indeed, he had lived through them.

At the age of seventeen, Karkouti had been arrested for breaking into his school and daubing the walls with graffiti condemning Syria's military regime. The son of a grocery-store owner, he was thrown into prison, beaten up by the secret police, and then ordered to leave the country. He moved to Lebanon, attended university in Beirut, worked as a teacher and journalist, and became a lifelong supporter of the Palestine Liberation Organization, the militant group fighting for Palestinian statehood. A left-leaning Arab nationalist, Karkouti joined the

Marxist-Leninist Democratic Front for the Liberation of Palestine, spent his summers working in Palestinian refugee camps, and underwent weapons training in Jordan. After helping to found *As-Safir* (The Ambassador), a popular left-wing Arabic newspaper, he was posted to London in 1974 as the paper's chief foreign correspondent, reporting on Middle Eastern politics and religion, specializing in Iran. He adored Britain, a country he had first visited for the World Cup in 1966, and vowed never to leave, but he also remained an active PLO supporter, vehemently opposed to Israel.

In a situation involving Arabs, Iranians, and British citizens, Karkouti's politics, language, and personality made him the ideal go-between: a role he would have done anything to avoid.

That morning, Karkouti had an appointment with the Iranian press attaché to discuss a visit to Tehran, but he was late, due to a domestic spat. His wife, Faten, five months pregnant with their second child, was insisting they go out to dinner with her newly married niece. Mustapha wanted to stay at home in Ealing. The row had escalated, and he was still trimming his mustache in a rage when Faten stormed out of the house and slammed the door. Driving his white Renault 11 around the embassy searching for a parking place, Karkouti spotted several men in keffiyehs on the corner, "the hoods of their anoraks covering their heads, wearing identical dark sunglasses," although the day was overcast. Their appearance struck him as odd, but he gave it no further thought. He parked on Rutland Gate, fed the meter with enough coins for two hours, and ran to the embassy, his yellow shiny plastic briefcase clamped under one arm. The chubby policeman on the doorstep smiled and nodded. The doorman escorted him to the third-floor press office. "Sorry I'm late," he panted as the press attaché offered him a seat. "Terrible traffic." He spent the rest of his life wishing his argument with Faten had continued for three minutes longer.

In the general office, Karkouti gingerly picked up the receiver.

"Hello, who is there, please?"

The gunman Salim cocked his pistol and held it to Karkouti's head. With the cold barrel pressed against his temple, the journalist felt his stomach lurch, as if "deeply hit inside my guts."

Trembling, Karkouti replaced the receiver and stammered: "It was a wrong number, I think."

The gunman was astonished to be addressed in Arabic.

"What? An Arab? What are you doing here among Persians? *Jasus?*" Spy?

"I am a journalist and write for a Lebanese newspaper."

"How come you are here? How can we be sure you are not lying?"

Karkouti fumbled in his wallet for his National Union of Journalists membership card. "I am here to meet the press director, Dr. Ezzati." He pointed across the room to a balding Iranian, who nodded vigorously.

"Yes, this is correct," Abdul Ezzati said in Farsi.

Salim studied the card for a moment and put it in his pocket. "We'll talk later."

Karkouti pointed to the telephone and spoke in English for the others. "Wrong number: just a man's voice."

"Probably the police," Cramer whispered to Lock. "At least they know we're here."

The police did not know who was in the embassy. They knew only that armed men had entered, shots had been fired, and hostages were inside, including a policeman. One person had been injured jumping from a window and then dragged back inside by masked men.

But these few sketchy details were enough to trigger one of the most dramatic anti-terrorism operations London has ever seen.

2

THE GROUP OF
THE MARTYR

John Albert Dellow was the chief troubleshooter of Scotland Yard. As deputy assistant commissioner of the "A" Department in command of operations, his job was to handle live crime situations and bring calm to crisis, a role to which his reassuring personality was perfectly suited.

Dellow had been a policeman for nearly thirty years and never seriously considered being anything else: his father was a policeman; he was married to a policeman's daughter; and, by the time he found himself parked outside the Iranian Embassy, he had performed just about every form of policing, from investigations to traffic control, in four different forces. Precise, focused, disciplined, calm, always immaculately uniformed, crisp of hair, and brisk of manner, Dellow had a favorite phrase: "Say what you mean, mean what you say," often the mantra of people who do not understand nuance. Dellow was rigorously clear-cut. He wore handmade shoes from Poulsen Skone in St. James's, which he polished to a dazzling shine every Sunday.

No one was ever in any doubt about what he meant to say. The word most often used to describe him was "straight." The fourth-highest-ranking officer in the Metropolitan Police, he was not exciting, but neither was he impulsive. And, as the first police officer ever to attend the National Defense College for military personnel, he knew how to talk to soldiers. Dellow of the Yard played everything by the book, and always seemed to be in control, at least from the outside.

By 11:31, four minutes after Lock pressed the emergency button, ten Diplomatic Protection Group officers were on the scene, as well as the chief superintendent of the DPG, Roger Bromley, who was nearby when he picked up the emergency signal. Guns drawn, they took up positions behind cars parked in front of the building. Bromley and another officer worked their way to the rear, through the passageway leading to Kingston House.

From her window Rebecca West watched as Bromley moved cautiously across the lawn to the terrace, and then pointed a gun at the upstairs windows. "What do you want?" he shouted. "What is this all about?"

A voice immediately responded in accented but precise English: "If you take one more step you'll be shot." Bromley backed away hastily.

Dellow arrived at midday, smoothed down his hair, adjusted his cap, conducted a brief reconnaissance of the building, and set up a forward command post, Alpha Control, in a blue police van parked at the west end of Princes Gate. He then instructed the DPG officers to form a "tight inner cordon" around the embassy, and gave orders that no messages should be relayed on the DPG radio channel: if the gunmen had Lock's radio, they might be listening in. According to the rulebook on hostage situations, Dellow now needed a negotiator to establish contact with the perpetrators before any blood was spilled. By chance, one happened to be on duty less than a mile away.

Chief Superintendent Fred Luff, the commander at Gerald Road Police Station and one of a select team of officers trained in hostage negotiation, heard the emergency call and arrived minutes after Dellow. At 12:06, wearing plain clothes and with hands raised above his head, Luff walked to the front of the building and shouted up: "I am superintendent of police in charge of this area. Will you please answer me?" Given that the gunmen had already threatened to shoot one of his colleagues, Luff was taking a major risk. As he would probably have put it, he was Daniel entering the lions' den.

After about a minute Luff spotted a figure, head swathed in a keffiyeh, observing him through the curtains of a first-floor window. "The building is surrounded," shouted Luff. "As long as no one is harmed, there is no problem. Will you tell me what you want?" The window opened a crack, and some sheets of paper fluttered down to the pavement. Luff trapped one with his foot. On it were several paragraphs typed in Arabic.

He waved the paper up at the window. "What does this mean?"

Luff picked up another sheet from the pavement, this one written in English.

INSIDE THE GENERAL OFFICE, its meaning was dawning with horrible clarity. Minutes before, Salim had entered with two typed sheets in his hand: one, in Farsi, he began reading aloud to the Iranian group. The other, translated into garbled English, he handed to Cramer.

The non-Iranians clustered around as Cramer took a deep breath and began to read aloud.

Dear Britishs,

May you excuse us for the armed operation that we committed on yours land after the racial regime of Iran had closed the legitimate ways for obtaining the simplest right.

The Iranian peoples were pleased after the overthrow of the Shah's regime as a result to huge sacrifices rendered by all the Iranians. The new Iran rulers pretended an adherence to Islam and its great principles, but few days later the game was uncovered and the faces unmasked. Their agents drawn the whole of Iran into a bloodbath with no distinction. They also allowed their followers to purge the non-Persian nationalities who played the main role in overthrowing the ex-regime, hoping to obtain their legitimate national rights, their freedom, and their longing generous life.

So, all we tried to do through our operation is to carry the voice of these oppressed peoples to the whole world, continuing the struggle against this regime whose fate would not be better than the previous one.

We are fully convinced that the Britishs and their government would greatly recognize our claimed most important of which are:

1. Setting free "91" prisoners of our friends, who are imprisoned by khomeini, and whose names are mentioned in the distributed list, these prisoners are exposed to the savage means of torture, terrorism and liquidation at the hand of the new "Savak" system agents.
2. Iran's recognition of the legitimate national rights of the Iranian peoples, halting the liquidation campaigns and the daily mass extermination to which people are exposed.
3. Providing a special plane for carrying the group with the hostages outside England, following the achievement of khomeini's authorities to the first above mentioned article, "24" hours after the distribution of this statement.

We also warn against any action aiming at ending this operation without carrying out its goals, otherwise we would kill the hostages and explode the building and the group as well.

We hope you would cooperate with us so as not to disfigure the human ends of the operation.

Glory and eternity for Arabistan Martyrs. Long live Arabistan as an Arab free region. Glory and Eternity for the martyrs of the Iranian peoples.

This was followed by a long list of Arab names.

The document was signed "The leader of the Martyr Muhyiddin Al Nasser Group."

Cramer and Harris had both traveled extensively in the Middle East, but neither had ever heard of a country called Arabistan. Even Mustapha Karkouti, an Arab expert on the Middle East, had only a vague understanding of where the place was, and the name of the group meant nothing to him. The note seemed bizarre, almost poetic, a mixture of politeness and menace. The English was torturous, but the meaning was clear: the intruders were threatening to destroy the embassy, and everyone in it, if they did not get what they wanted.

THE STATEMENT, opaque as it was, contained enough information to trigger a flurry of police actions, and a flicker of anxiety inside John Dellow. The scale of the problem was starting to dawn on the deputy assistant commissioner of operations. This was not just some domestic incident, but rather a hostage situation with international political implications. In the diary he maintained scrupulously throughout the siege, Dellow wrote: "HM Government will have immediate interest in the matter." At 12:13, he informed the Home Office. Dellow then summoned additional forces, established observation posts around the embassy, and instructed that all telephone lines into the embassy be cut off, "to commence the isolation of the terrorists and enforce communication with police negotiators." He also alerted the Anti-terrorist Branch (C13) and requested an officer with "a knowledge of Arabic matters" to come to Princes Gate, along with Arabic and Farsi interpreters.

Within an hour an outer cordon was in place: a square bounded by the roads to the east and west of Princes Gate, Hyde Park south of Rotten Row (the sandy bridleway running across the park), and the communal gardens behind the embassy. The area was sealed off by lines of white tape, mobile crash barriers, and an expanding horde of uniformed officers. No one was to be allowed in or out without authorization. All traffic was diverted, causing spectacular jams as police cars, ambulances, and fire trucks poured into Kensington from every direction.

At 13:01, Dellow sent "an informal message alerting the 22nd SAS Regiment," exactly fifty-four minutes after Dusty Gray had done so.

SALIM WAS GRATIFIED by the hostages' shocked reaction to his declaration. He had spent several days composing the message in Arabic and translating it into English, and then laboriously typing it out with one finger on two old typewriters, left to right in English and right to left in Arabic script. Soon the oppression of Arabistan would be known to the world, and they could all go home.

Before setting out on this mission, he had adopted the nom de guerre Salim. He was not a religious man, but he liked the sound of this Koranic name meaning "pure" or "righteous." Like most extremists, he was convinced of his own righteousness.

Terrorist schemes are usually plotted by clever people, and then carried out by manipulated morons. This man was highly intelligent, well educated, multilingual, damaged, and determined. He was also volatile and sensitive. He wept easily. He was also capable of self-righteous murder.

Salim's real name was Towfiq Ibrahim al-Rashidi, and he was an unlikely terrorist.

THE REASON WHY this bright and dangerous twenty-seven-year-old university graduate was pointing a submachine gun at twenty-six innocent people in a Victorian mansion off Hyde Park lay five thousand years in the past, in the southwestern corner of Iran.

The region abutting the Persian Gulf known to its Arab inhabitants as Arabistan, or Ahwaz (which is also the name of the region's capital), was once the center of an ancient civilization. The majority of its inhabitants are Arabs, Shia Muslims, but they are ethnically distinct from the Aryans of Iran, or Persia, as it was traditionally known ("Iran" is the Farsi word for "Land of the Aryans"). By the mid-nineteenth century, the region had been absorbed into Persia, but its sheikhs enjoyed semi-independence from Tehran. When the shah's father, Reza Shah Pahlavi, took power (with British backing) in 1925, he set about "Persianizing" the region, a policy his son intensified: Farsi replaced Arabic as the official language, Iranian nationalists settled in the thousands, and senior official positions were filled by Farsi-speaking Persian Iranians. The province was renamed Khuzestan, an Iranian name. Arab opposition was suppressed. This Persianizing policy was motivated by power politics and ethnic prejudice but mostly by greed: for beneath the region's desert sands bubbled a vast ocean of oil. Had fate dealt differently with the region, it might have become another Gulf oil state, like Qatar or Kuwait, with a small Arab population, and a lot of money. Instead, its oil riches bankrolled the shahs, exploited in concert with the British, then with the Americans. The expensive rugs and chandeliers in Iran's London embassy were paid for with Khuzestan's oil. At the height of the shah's power, some five million barrels were being exported from the province daily, about one-tenth of the world's entire oil trade.

The Arabs clung to their culture and language. Resistance spread, under a bewildering variety of names: the Arabistan Liberation Front, the Popular Front for the Liberation of Ahwaz, and the Democratic Revolutionary Movement for the Liberation of Arabistan. The more militant groups—"terrorists" or "freedom fighters" depending on perspective—launched a campaign of violence, with backing from neighboring Iraq. By 1978, the shah was facing a wave of popular rebellion across the country. The coup de grâce came from Khuzestan, where oil workers mounted crippling strikes, cutting the flow of cash to the royal coffers: the shah went bust.

Many Iranian Arabs greeted the fall of the Pahlavi dynasty with unbridled joy. Towfiq Ibrahim al-Rashidi was one of them: the ayatollah had pledged to recognize Arabistan's autonomy and the rights of its oppressed people. Freedom was at hand.

Except it was not: a disappointment that would carry Towfiq on a wave of anger and violence all the way to Princes Gate.

By Iranian Arab standards, Towfiq was a child of privilege. The al-Rashidis were a notable family in the inland port city known as Al-Muhammarah in Arabic, renamed Khorramshahr by the Iranians. His father was in the shipping business, his mother an educated Iraqi woman from Basra, across the Shatt al-Arab waterway. Towfiq grew up in a comfortable middle-class home in Al-Manuhi, a small town south of the city of Abadan, with six half siblings by his father's first marriage, and one elder, full brother, Naji, whom he idolized.

Naji had lived in Kuwait in the 1970s, where he absorbed the politics of Arab nationalism. The brothers joined a moderate wing of the Arab liberation movement, demanding greater autonomy for Arabistan within Iran, Arabic-language teaching in schools, and equal opportunities for Arabs. Some sought Islamic revolution, while others wanted full independence. The al-Rashidi brothers campaigned only for an end to discrimination in their homeland. Most of his fellow Arabs were illiterate, Towfiq complained, workhorses made to toil for their Iranian bosses: "We are very rich in resources, but it is taken away from Arabistan." Only a handful of Arabs worked in the Iranian civil service; no Arab rose above the rank of captain in the armed forces.

Fascinated by foreign culture, hungry for learning, Towfiq won a place to study English language and literature at the University of Tehran. "I am a rare case," he said. "Out of four million people, we are only four thousand university graduates." There he eagerly joined the students demonstrating against the shah. The university was riddled with spies working for SAVAK, the shah's secret police, and, as opposition to the regime mounted, repression grew more extreme: imprisonment without trial, torture, and summary execution. Towfiq was arrested, thrown into the notorious Evin Prison, and thrashed with an iron bar before being released without charge. He was deeply traumatized, enraged by the injustice. The beating left permanent scars across his back and shoulders, and on his heart. "These hardships and the racist policy of the Persians have made us into fighters and strugglers," he said. Towfiq and Naji joined the Democratic Revolutionary Movement for the Liberation of Arabistan, a more radical Marxist-Leninist splinter group. His lifestyle, however, remained cosmopolitan. Towfiq drove around town in a two-seater Toyota with his Persian Iranian girlfriend. He recited poetry in Arabic, Farsi, and English.

With the fall of the shah, the Arab liberation movement placed itself under the control of the new regime, awaiting the moment when the revolutionary Islamic government would fulfill its promises to Arabistan.

But the ayatollah was no more willing than the shah to countenance self-government for oil-rich Khuzestan. Arabs were not the only ethnic minority agitating for greater self-determination. Kurds, Turkmens, Azeris, and Baluchis all sought to loosen Tehran's grip, some by democratic means, others through violence. If the Arabs won autonomy, other groups would demand the same, threatening the very integrity of the country. "The new leaders forgot all their promises," said Towfiq. The ayatollah clamped down on the Arabs, just as the shah had done. In a familiar vicious cycle, repression met with increasing resistance. More radical Arab separatists resorted to violence, urged on by a man whose machinations would disfigure the rest of the twentieth century, and spill into the twenty-first.

Saddam Hussein, de facto ruler of Iraq since 1968 and president since 1979, spotted an opportunity in the unrest. A secular nationalist with pretensions to lead the Arab world, Saddam saw Iran's aggressive new theocracy as a threat to his power and ambitions. Inciting rebellion among the Arabs of neighboring Khuzestan was an easy and cheap way to undermine the ayatollah and destabilize Iran, while also demonstrating Saddam's credentials as an Arab champion. Bands of Iranian Arabs were trained in Iraq, armed, and sent back across the border to attack police stations, military checkpoints, roads, bridges, and above all the oil pipelines carrying Iran's economic lifeblood. These Arab guerrillas saw themselves as fighters for independence, but they were dependent on Saddam Hussein, pawns cynically manipulated by the Iraqi leader for his own ends.

Popular unrest in Khuzestan escalated. Towfiq and other young Arabs staged noisy street protests and sit-ins at the Arab Cultural Center in Al-Muhammarah. The Iranian authorities responded with extreme brutality, the hallmark of the Islamic Revolutionary Republic. Admiral Ahmad Madani, the regime's first defense minister and a ruthless hard-liner, was appointed governor of Khuzestan. Hundreds of suspected Arab "subversives" were rounded up, imprisoned, tortured, and killed. An uprising in April 1979 was suppressed by units of the Islamic Revolutionary Guard Corps. Iran accused Iraq of supporting the Arab insurgents. Towfiq was at the center of the demonstrations, angry, loud, but still nonviolent. "He was a peaceful, progressive nationalist," a friend and fellow protester recalled. "He still believed in political struggle and was not in favor of complete secession from Iran, although these ideas were spreading in the region."

On Wednesday, May 30, 1979, blood ran in the streets of Al-Muhammarah. Shortly before dawn, the security forces and armed militiamen attacked demonstrators camped out in the cultural center and the recently abandoned American Consulate. Members of the Revolutionary Guard fired into the crowds with machine guns mounted on surrounding buildings, killing dozens. Madani declared a state of emergency and imposed a curfew. Arabs attempting to flee across the bridges into Iraq were stopped at roadblocks by men wearing white hoods (eerily resembling Ku Klux Klansmen), interrogated, and frequently killed, their bodies tipped into the river. The conflict was racial as well as political, an ethnic confrontation between indigenous Arabs and Farsi-speaking Iranians introduced by the shahs to Persianize the region. Iranian militiamen flown in from Tehran roamed the streets in search of insurgents. Some fought back. Armed Arabs attacked a naval base, the central police station, government buildings, and shops. Three days of street fighting left 220 people dead and 600 wounded. The ayatollah's secret police, the successors to SAVAK and no less vicious, set about hunting down Arab activists, many of whom were tried in hastily convened Revolutionary Courts and summarily executed. Ayatollah Sheikh Muhammad-Taher al-Khaqani, spiritual leader of the region's Arabs and Khomeini's former teacher, was arrested, along with hundreds of others. Those who escaped fled to Iraq or went into hiding.

The "Black Wednesday" massacre was the darkest day in Arabistan's history. Towfiq witnessed the carnage with horror and disbelief: "That bloody incident was the breaking point in our relations with the central Iranian government."

Towfiq and Naji al-Rashidi were identified as counterrevolutionaries, wanted men pursued by the secret police. The brothers fled to the city of Mashhad in northeast Iran, adopted different names, and went to ground. A few months later, Naji announced he was going home to continue the struggle. Towfiq begged him not to go.

Just a week after returning to Al-Muhammarah, Naji was arrested by the secret police. His wife's brother had been caught with an arms stash in his boat, which he claimed belonged to Naji. Under duress, he revealed his brother-in-law's whereabouts. Naji was tortured for a week, then taken into the desert and shot. Naji al-Rashidi's execution was announced on the same day as that of Safar Weisi, a notorious former SAVAK officer, to give the false impression that Naji had also been an informer for the shah's hated security apparatus.

Devastated by Naji's excruciating death, traumatized, and terrified, Towfiq headed for Iraq to take up arms against the ayatollah. "The execution of his brother was the catalyst that pushed him toward armed struggle," said his closest friend, who tried to remonstrate with him.

"Believe me, it's not revenge," insisted Towfiq. "It is self-defense. After Naji's execution and the dangers I am facing, I see no other way." In the space of a year, Towfiq had been transformed from a gentle, poetry-loving moderate into a violent, brutalized extremist, bent on revenge.

On arrival in Basra in January 1980, Towfiq was met by a plump, balding Iraqi in his midthirties with a scar running down his left cheek, who introduced himself as Sami Muhammad Ali, a name so common it had to be false. He preferred to be addressed by another nom de guerre: Al-thaalab, "the Fox." Sami the Fox was an officer in Directorate 4 of the Mukhabarat, the branch of Iraq's intelligence service dedicated to infiltrating foreign governments, unions, and embassies; undermining opposition groups; encouraging terrorist actions against Iraq's enemies; and undertaking assassinations.

According to an Iraqi spy who defected in 2003, the man who actually "trained, equipped, and directed" the operation was a senior officer in Directorate 4 of the Mukhabarat. His name was Fowzi al-Naimi.

The Fox escorted Towfiq and a score of other young Arab militants to Ramadi, a training camp outside Baghdad run by Palestinian guerrillas. Over the next three weeks they learned to handle pistols and submachine guns, and practiced detonating hand grenades. From time to time, al-Naimi would appear on horseback, wearing a military uniform, to monitor progress.

Here Towfiq was introduced to Jassim Alwan al-Nasiri, another young radical, who fought under the name Faisal. A key figure in the militant wing of the movement, Jassim was an experienced fighter who had led several daring raids against oil installations inside Iran. He too had been tortured by SAVAK. Two years older than Towfiq, Jassim was a tall, rangy figure who favored communist rhetoric and cowboy boots. While it had taken Towfiq many years and the trauma of his brother's murder to embrace armed struggle, Jassim had long advocated the use of force in pursuit of the movement's aims. He was no stranger to violence.

Al-Naimi selected four more men from the Iranian Arab group for a "special operation." Each had suffered horrifically at the hands of the Iranian security forces.

Shaye Hamid al-Sahar (alias Hassan) was a twenty-two-year-old from the village of Ghajaria near Ahwaz. His father, Sheikh Hamid Saleh al-Sahar, had been a prominent leader of the liberation movement. In the crackdown after Black Wednesday, Shaye's father, brother, cousin, and brother-in-law had all been executed. Other members of his family, including several women, were still in prison.

Makki Hanoun and Abbas Maytham were both semi-literate, obedient foot soldiers from poor families, radicalized by the carnage that had engulfed their homes and families, and easily manipulated. Abbas was psychologically unstable, given to fits of sudden rage. Makki's father was in prison facing a death sentence. His young wife back in Al-Muhammarah was pregnant with their first child. Abbas and Makki did not adopt pseudonyms.

The last and youngest of the group was also the most incongruous. Twenty-two-year-old Fowzi Badavi Nejad (alias Ali) was a product of one of the most prominent tribes in Al-Muhammarah. His father was a businessman; his uncle had been a member of parliament at the time of the shah. With a shock of dark hair, aquiline features, and deep-set brown eyes, Fowzi was extremely handsome, and knew it. A feckless youth, he left school at fifteen, spent two years on National Service in the Iranian army, and then returned to his hometown, where he worked on the docks and drifted into the liberation movement. The story was that Fowzi was in the Arab Cultural Center when the Iranian security forces attacked. Running into the street, he saw four of his friends hacked down by machine-gun fire. Fleeing, he spotted a girl, perhaps five years old, lying on the pavement covered in blood. He picked up the child and ran to the hospital, her blood soaking into his shirt. In the hospital-entrance corridor, corpses were piling up. That evening, trying to escape across the bridge into Iraq, he was stopped by hooded militiamen. "Long live Khomeini!" he shouted. They let him pass. A week later, he reached the Ramadi training base. Fowzi never discovered if the little girl survived.

In Mukhabarat headquarters in Baghdad, al-Naimi introduced Towfiq to a small and intense Palestinian, a man with "experience of guerrilla war" who spoke rapidly and with authority. The Fox and the other Mukhabarat officers treated him with elaborate respect, deferring to him and refilling his whiskey glass. They almost seemed to fear him, this nameless little man with eyes like bullet holes.

Towfiq knew exactly who this man was and what, by reputation, he was capable of.

The Palestinian laid out the plan. The freedom fighters would fly to London, accompanied by Sami the Fox. Towfiq assumed the Palestinian would be leading the operation in person. There they would occupy the Iranian Embassy, take the ambassador and other diplomats hostage, draw worldwide attention to the cruel treatment of Arabs in southwestern Iran, and force Tehran to set free ninety-one Arab activists languishing in Iranian jails, including their spiritual leader, Ayatollah al-Khaqani. "This will force Khomeini to release our Arab brothers from captivity," al-Naimi declared. The hostages would then be released unharmed in exchange for safe passage on a flight back to the Middle East. The six would return as heroes.

The Mukhabarat had carried out illegal terrorist actions in Britain before. Two years earlier, General Abdul Razzaq al-Naif, the former Iraqi prime minister deposed by Saddam Hussein in 1968, was assassinated as he left the InterContinental Hotel in Park Lane. The Iraqi Embassy in London housed an intelligence cell of four Mukhabarat spies running a network of informants that included journalists, businessmen, and Iraqi students. When the time came, they would furnish weapons for the operation.

The plan was undoubtedly risky, but terrorist hostage-taking could yield spectacular results, and there was a precedent. Five years earlier, the Venezuelan terrorist Ilich Ramírez Sánchez, known as Carlos the Jackal, led a group of pro-Palestinian militants, the Arm of the Arab Revolution, in an assault on a meeting of OPEC leaders in Vienna. They took more than sixty hostages and killed three people. Ramírez Sánchez threatened to kill a hostage every fifteen minutes unless the Austrian authorities read a communiqué on the radio and television networks every two hours. After complex negotiations and a two-day standoff, the authorities agreed to broadcast the terrorists' statement, and allowed the gunmen to fly to sanctuary in Algeria and Libya, having secured a large ransom and global publicity for the Palestinian cause. All the terrorists and hostages walked away. The United Nations

Convention on the Prevention and Punishment of Crimes Against Internationally Protected Persons subsequently forbade granting safe passage to anyone killing, kidnapping, or attacking a diplomatic official, but, in practice, governments were prepared to negotiate. The assault on the Iranian Embassy was directly modeled on the OPEC siege.

For reasons both symbolic and practical, London was selected as the ideal target. Many Iranian Arabs held Britain responsible for their plight: the British government had supported the semi-independent sheikhdom of Arabistan before switching allegiance to Reza Shah in 1925. The group would pass unnoticed among London's large Middle Eastern population. "British police are not armed," the Fox assured Towfiq. "They will not attack you." London was packed with journalists and other members of media organizations, domestic and international, who were not controlled by the government. News coverage would be huge. With his command of English, Towfiq would manage negotiations with the police and the press.

"Britain is the seat of democracy and it's the right place, where you can get a fair hearing," said the Fox. "You can be sure that you'll get good publicity for your cause."

The team selected a name that was also plucked from the troubled history of southwestern Iran: the Group of the Martyr Muhyiddin al-Nasser. This was a reference to an earlier activist, Muhyiddin al-Nasser, executed in 1953, the first Iranian Arab to die at the hands of SAVAK. The word "martyr" would later be interpreted as evidence that the group was a suicide squad, intent on self-destruction. It was not. "The martyr" was a person, not a purpose; this was a political operation, not a religious mission; and Towfiq planned to emerge from it a living hero, not a dead martyr. The group was prepared to kill and be killed, if necessary, but it had no desire to do either. The operation should take twenty-four hours, forty-eight at most. There would also be plenty of time for shopping.

At the last moment, al-Naimi explained that he and the Palestinian organizer would not be coming. Towfiq would be in command, with Jassim as his deputy.

Traveling on Iraqi passports with fake names, Towfiq, Makki, Shaye, and Abbas arrived in London on March 31 and rented a rundown flat in Earl's Court for seventy pounds a week, telling the landlord they were students. Jassim and Fowzi, the youngest, flew into Heathrow a week later, accompanied by Sami the Fox. None of the Iranian Arabs had set foot in Europe before. The weapons were being assembled, the Fox told them. While they waited, the group watched a lot of British television, drank at the Duke of Richmond pub, and visited the tourist sites. They joined an anti-Khomeini march in Hyde Park. One night, neighbors heard voices raised in what sounded like an altercation with a prostitute. Middle Eastern men sometimes gathered at the flat. In the morning, there were empty whiskey bottles in the trash. After a fortnight, the landlord said they were making too much noise and told them to leave. The group moved into nearby 105 Lexham Gardens, a larger flat with three bedrooms, at twice the rent; from there it was a short walk to Princes Gate. The Fox paid for everything but stayed in a different flat, at 24 Queens Gate, just two doors down from the office of the Iraqi military attaché. He was often accompanied by a dark-haired woman later described by the police as having "a good figure." One evening, in Lexham Gardens, the Fox switched on the television news: the most important Iranian diplomat in London had given an interview to the BBC. A short, tubby man in a suit, Dr. Gholam-Ali Afrouz, the chargé d'affaires, duly appeared on-screen. "Remember his face," the Fox instructed.

On April 25, the Iraqi officer presented each man with seven hundred pounds in cash (over three thousand pounds in today's money). The Group of the Martyr returned from Oxford Street laden with luxury merchandise: suits, ties, shoes, children's toys, and women's cocktail dresses and lingerie. Towfiq bought a pair of fashionable red-and-white leather sneakers, the colors of the flag of Arabistan. "These will bring me luck," he said. "I will not take them off the whole time I am in the embassy."

On the evening of Tuesday, April 29, the Fox and Towfiq arrived at Lexham Gardens with a sack containing two 9mm Polish-made WZ 63 "Skorpion" submachine guns (also known as machine pistols) with twenty-five-round magazines capable of firing six hundred rounds a minute; three Browning 9mm semi-automatic pistols loaded with thirteen Winchester hollow-point bullets; an Astra .38 five-shot revolver;

and six Russian RGD-5 hand grenades, containing four ounces of TNT apiece. A gun and a grenade for each man, with five hundred rounds of ammunition. These were the weapons they had trained with in Iraq. The arsenal had been smuggled into Britain, via Kuwait, in the Iraqi diplomatic bag, the container used to carry official items between a foreign country and its diplomats without being searched. The Fox also brought a floor plan of the embassy.

"How did you get that?" one of the recruits asked innocently.

The Fox gave him a sharp look. "None of your business. Your job now is to make sure that you know every room by memory." They should take hostage all the Iranian diplomats, most importantly Afrouz, and then start negotiations. "Do not tell the police you have come from Baghdad," he instructed. "Say you are from Tehran, or Lebanon."

Some might not return from the battle, the Fox warned, so they should each leave a short will or testament. Makki and Abbas dictated theirs, in the clichéd language of the heroic freedom fighter: "We must take revenge till the last drop of our blood." Makki requested that his unborn child be named Ahwaz, the other name for Arabistan/Khuzestan. "One day Arabistan will be liberated," wrote Jassim. In his statement, Shaye recalled his slaughtered family: "Our father, our brother, our cousins and many of our compatriots have shed their blood on this road, if I die I will die remembering our abandoned occupied house in the city of Ahwaz on Danish Street, Number 24."

Towfiq asked his comrades to care for his elderly mother if he died, but his thoughts were with the brother tortured and murdered just six months earlier: "Transfer my body to the land of Ahwaz and bury me in the cemetery of the city of Abadan, next to my martyred brother Naji."

Fowzi left no will. He did not intend to die.

The Fox paid off the landlord in cash, explaining that he and his friends were visiting Bristol before flying home. He also instructed him to ship their shopping to Iraq: nine large suitcases and boxes, weighing 203 pounds in total, including a color TV and a VCR, to be sent to Sami Muhammad, PO Box 767, Baghdad, Iraq. The landlord was unsurprised: wealthy Middle Eastern tourists often went on extravagant buying binges.

Before dawn on April 30, the group posed for a photograph in the flat, brandishing their guns, grinning at the camera, and flashing "V for victory" signs. Towfiq kneels at the center of the picture, hard-faced and staring into the distance. Jassim is standing on the left, an unnervingly broad grin on his face. Fowzi has forgotten to look at the camera.

The Fox collected the false passports they no longer needed. In a few days they would be flying out of the country, courtesy of the British government. He had one final instruction. The operation must not be launched before 11:00 at the earliest. "Not a minute before, do you understand?"

He then kissed each man solemnly on both cheeks and declared, "Your brothers and sisters back home are counting on you. God be with you all." He added, "I will be closer to you than you think." And then he was gone.

By the time the Group of the Martyr stormed into the embassy, the Fox was safely aboard the 11:00 flight to Paris.

3

COBRA

Superintendent Fred Luff and his boss, John Dellow, read and reread the English translation of Towfiq's declaration in bafflement. Most hostage-takers have quite straightforward demands: this group seemed to want freedom for people in a distant land the two policemen had never heard of. Dellow sent the note by police courier to the Home Office, thereby plunging the British authorities into a frantic crash course on Iranian politics, made doubly confusing by another, different embassy siege taking place in Iran itself.

Six months earlier, on November 4, 1979, armed Islamic students took over the U.S. Embassy in Tehran, presenting Jimmy Carter with the worst crisis of his presidency. Some fifty-two Americans, including diplomats, were still being held hostage inside the building, in the name of the Islamic Revolution. The United States had broken off all formal diplomatic ties with Iran, and Britain was contemplating doing likewise. Carter condemned the hostage-taking as an act of "terrorism and anarchy." In Iran, it was welcomed as a righteous blow against infidel America for supporting the shah and granting him asylum. The next day Khomeini described the United States as "the great Satan, the wounded snake."

The Americans demanded the release of the hostages; Iran refused. The Iranian government insisted the shah be returned to stand trial; America refused. Negotiations were going nowhere, and an attempt to liberate the hostages by force had recently ended in disaster. The Group of the Martyr chose to attack the Iranian Embassy in London, in part, as a parallel to the hostage crisis taking place in Tehran: Iranian militants had taken over the American Embassy in Iran, so Arab gunmen would occupy the Iranian Embassy in the United Kingdom.

The U.S. Embassy siege in Tehran was front-page news in Britain, but the ayatollah's other conflict, with the Arabs of Khuzestan, was virtually unknown in the West, and certainly news to John Dellow.

The deputy assistant commissioner was a keen follower of cricket, a sport with complicated but logical rules. Now straight-batting Dellow had been bowled a tricky political googly. It is hard to negotiate with someone if you have no idea who they are.

From the first, Dellow found himself adrift in a blizzard of guesswork as wild theories swirled around Scotland Yard. Could this be retaliation for the U.S. Embassy siege? Might these be American radicals, attempting some form of reprisal? Had the Iranians occupied their own embassy? Was this a fresh outrage by Iranian fundamentalists? When it emerged that the gunmen were actually opposed to the Iranian government, many assumed they must be the ousted shah's supporters, or Iraqis, the sworn enemies of the Iranians. Every conjecture was wrong. From her kitchen window, Rebecca West overheard a confused conversation between two police officers crouched behind a wall as they struggled to comprehend who and what they were dealing with: "They looked puzzled from their caps to their boots, and their dialogue confirmed this impression: 'Not the Ayatollah lot? They're the other lot that get into fights with the Ayatollah lot on Sundays in the park . . .'" In fact, this was a different lot altogether, opposed to both the shah *and* the ayatollah.

The Metropolitan Police had experience with hostage situations. In September 1975, during a botched attempt to rob the Spaghetti House restaurant in Knightsbridge, thieves seized six hostages, leading to a six-day siege. Three months later, four members of a fugitive Irish Republican Army gang took an elderly couple hostage for six days in their

Balcombe Street flat near Regent's Park. Both episodes ended blood-lessly, with the hostages released and the gunmen arrested.

But criminals and IRA thugs were familiar foes. This situation was unprecedented: a group of heavily armed foreigners with a planned operation, taking dozens of hostages and making political demands coupled with the threat of mass murder. All to further an obscure cause in a faraway place.

WHILE JOHN DELLOW struggled to locate Arabistan on a map, rein-forcements and specialist units converged on Princes Gate: a combina-tion of muscle, technology, weaponry, snipers, listeners, talkers, and animals.

Police marksmen, known as the Blue Berets, took up sniper positions on the ground and first floors of the Ethiopian Embassy, and the fifth and sixth floors of Kingston House overlooking the gardens, their high-powered rifles with telescopic sights trained on the windows and doors of the building. The snipers operated on an independent-radio network, feeding information into Alpha Control. The Special Patrol Group, a mobile tactical unit of thirty police officers, arrived in unmarked blue vans, parked up a nearby side street, and conducted a sweep search of the area, checking parked cars against the Police National Computer in case of car bombs. The SPG was the closest thing to a police paramili-tary force, formed to fight violent crime, public disorder, and terrorism. They brought with them pistols, riot shields, gas grenades, and a grim reputation for excessive force. Next came C13, the anti-terrorist detec-tive unit forged during the long conflict with the IRA, with wide experi-ence in preventing and investigating terrorist activity. This force, which would swiftly expand to twenty-six officers and five typists, was tasked with executing John Dellow's orders, logging all actions taken, and gathering evidence. They were joined by a ten-strong team from Spe-cial Branch, responsible for national security policy, helping to gather intelligence and liaising with the Security Service, also known as MI5. The "hard dog" section arrived from its base at Heathrow, and the handlers and their Alsatians took up strategic points around the inner cordon: two dogs at either end of Princes Gate, and another three guarding the mews exits from the gardens. The anti-terrorist dog team was brought in as a reserve. The army's Explosive Ordnance Disposal unit, better known as the Bomb Squad, was placed on standby.

John Dellow deployed a mass of uniformed "foot duty" police to man the outer cordon, keep the public at a distance, and form a "sterile and safe" area around the building. Traffic Division officers set up filter diversions to try to clear the jams. Hundreds of metal barriers arrived by truck. The closed roads through Hyde Park became police car parks. Residents and workers in the immediate vicinity of the embassy were evacuated. The Ethiopian ambassador, His Excellency Ayalew Wolde-Giorgis, was extremely unwilling to leave his residence, and the Foreign Office had to intervene. The dismayed ambassador, "with a train of children and servants," was asked to decamp to a hotel.

The Metropolitan Police commissioner, Sir David McNee, Dellow's overall boss and Britain's most senior police officer, abandoned a holiday in his native Scotland and caught the first plane south to London. A fleet of mobile police catering vans set up shop several streets away and began dispensing tea and sandwiches. Within twenty-four hours, more than a hundred police caterers would be deployed in different locations, feeding members of the police, army, fire brigade, and medical services.

Behind the catering vans were the ambulances, with two dozen doctors and nurses in readiness. A peculiar midafternoon stillness descended on Princes Gate, broken only by birdsong from the park. The siege was under way.

The most potent force at Dellow's disposal was armed not with guns or gizmos, but with a more subtle weapon: the art of persuasion.

HOSTAGE NEGOTIATION IS a strange and difficult dance with complex patterns, small movements, and evolving rhythms, a lethal tango that culminates in either harmony or chaos. If the dance gets out of step, the results can be fatal.

Throughout the 1970s, terrorist activity had been growing across the world as violent groups sought political results through bombing, kidnapping, assassination, and armed robbery. Hostage-taking was an increasingly popular weapon in the terrorist arsenal. In 1972, Palestinian terrorists of the Black September group seized Israeli athletes during the Munich Olympic Games. The West German handling of that incident had been a disaster, ending in the deaths of all the hostages and most of the terrorists. This prompted the British government to draw up contingency plans for a similar incident in the UK, along with a set of basic principles: terrorism should be treated as a crime and prosecuted in Britain; police would handle tactics during any hostage-taking incident, but the controlling, strategic role would be exercised by the government, through the home secretary. If all else failed, the incident might be terminated with an assault by an armed force, trained and equipped specifically for the purpose: the SAS.

For seven years, Scotland Yard had been studying terrorist groups and training specialist police officers to negotiate with the aim of achieving two often incompatible goals: securing the release of hostages and conceding as little as possible.

As hostage negotiator, Fred Luff would first need to introduce composure into a highly tense situation, by communicating in a measured and balanced way. But these hostage-takers were neither calm nor stable, and nor was he.

Luff was a committed conservative Christian with piercing blue eyes and an unshakable aversion to the permissive society. He was opposed to sex, drugs, and rock and roll, and had policed all three, with extreme moral rigor. In 1970, as head of Scotland Yard's Obscene Publications Squad, he raided a Mayfair art gallery and confiscated fourteen artworks painted by John Lennon, in which the Beatle depicted himself performing sex acts with Yoko Ono. To Luff's straitlaced mind, an image of a famous pop star engaging in oral sex would violate public morality and invite anarchy. "Many toilet walls depict works of similar merit," Luff proclaimed. "It is perhaps charitable to suggest that they are the work of a sick mind." (The case was thrown out on a technicality.) In his next position, as head of the Drugs Squad, Luff hunted down dealers and celebrity drug users with crusading zeal, and notable success. A Chinese Triad drug syndicate took out a contract for Luff's murder, a threat he embraced with the pride of a martyr. A colleague described him as "very intense, very single-minded, and very, very opinionated."

Luff had taken the police hostage-negotiation course, which sought to instill a series of complex and overlapping principles. Having set up a channel of interaction—by telephone, loudspeaker, or face-to-face—the negotiator then works to gather information about the personalities, motivations, intentions, weapons, hopes, and fears of those holding the hostages and, in the process, to establish a level of trust. A hostage negotiator is not a decision-maker but an intermediary. He or she cannot offer to meet terrorists' demands, only to pass them on to a higher authority and relay the answers, keeping the conversation afloat by bargaining over food, cigarettes, or publicity. That way the negotiator can appear evenhanded, even sympathetic, and blame delay or lack of cooperation on the bosses. Prevarication is the core of hostage negotiation, because the longer a standoff continues, the more likely it is to end without violence. Once terrorists become tired, hungry, or bored, the dynamic changes quickly. If hostage-takers sense they are being manipulated, frustration mounts, and with it the probability of a violent reaction. Negotiators need to be thick-skinned, since they may have to put up with abuse or tiresome preaching from volatile and self-righteous people. Humor can help the process. The negotiator must appear constructive while actually being noncommittal, helpful, and understanding to violent people he does not want to help and does not necessarily understand. The negotiator must tell the truth to maintain his or her credibility with the hostage-takers, while at all times deceiving them; be an honest broker and an excellent liar; play good cop and bad cop.

The characteristics of a successful hostage negotiator include patience, stamina, humor, deviousness, composure, compassion, sensitivity, and tolerance for alternative points of view. These qualities seldom coexist in one individual, let alone one policeman.

Fred Luff and Towfiq al-Rashidi were both true believers. They just believed, with equal passion, in very different things.

ABOVE ALL, the Group of the Martyr wanted media attention, and, by chance, no fewer than five of their hostages happened to be journalists: the two BBC men and the Syrian-born Mustapha Karkouti, but also Muhammad Hashir Faruqi, the Pakistani British editor of the Muslim magazine *Impact International,* and Vahid Khabaz, a student correspondent for the conservative Iranian newspaper *Kayhan.* Three of the Iranian captives were press officers. By accident, the gang had kidnapped a group of people with exactly the right expertise to disseminate their message.

Sim Harris was still assessing the situation when his colleague Chris Cramer approached the lead gunman again: "I work for the BBC. If there's anything I can do to help, please ask. Why don't you let me call the BBC and pass on your demands?"

Towfiq considered this suggestion, then nodded. With a submachine gun pointed at his back, Cramer was marched to a small anteroom off the ground-floor hallway that had a telephone. He dialed his own number at BBC Television Center.

An official-sounding voice answered: "Hello, this is Scotland Yard. Can I help you?" Some of the lines out of the embassy had already been either cut off or routed to the police.

With the gun pointed at his head, Cramer could barely get the words out: "I would like to talk to the BBC. Can you put me through?"

"No, I can't do that. What do you want?" said the policeman, clearly thinking he was speaking to a terrorist.

"This is Chris Cramer, of BBC Television News. Get me the BBC."

"I can't do that."

The Scotland Yard voice then asked whether Cramer could "pass on any vital information."

Cramer took a deep breath, and did something brave, and very stupid: "Well, I just want to say that the twenty men and six women being held here in the Iranian Embassy are safe and well, and—"

Furious, Towfiq snatched the receiver and slammed it down. "You trick me, you trick us all," he shouted, cocking his gun ominously. "Just get out." Terrified, Cramer was hauled upstairs and roughly shoved into the general office with the rest of the hostages.

"What happened?" whispered Karkouti.

"I wasn't very clever," said Cramer, sheepish and shaking. "I got Scotland Yard and I tried to pass on a few bits and pieces."

His colleague Sim Harris made a mental note not to take such a risk: any attempt to fool these unstable people was an invitation to die. Whatever information came out of the besieged embassy, Towfiq intended to ensure it focused exclusively on the liberation of Arabistan.

But the news was emerging anyway, at high speed.

The first report was an LBC radio bulletin at 12:10, sent in by a breathless reporter who had become stuck in the traffic around Princes Gate, abandoned his car, asked a few questions of the nearest policeman, and dashed into the Thai Embassy to borrow a telephone: "A policeman is being held hostage at the Iranian Embassy in London. It's understood that a man armed with a rifle walked up to the policeman who was guarding the embassy and forced him inside . . . I gather he's not English." That first report was sketchy, but in one respect it was perfectly accurate: "It has all the appearance of a siege."

The breaking news sparked a media stampede. Kate Adie, a young BBC reporter, joined the exodus from Television Center when word flew around the newsroom: "There's trouble down near Hyde Park." Margaret Thatcher had just finished recording an interview on the *Jimmy Young Show* for Radio 2 when the news broke. As she was being escorted from the building, the prime minister spotted an excited gathering around the news desk and asked what was happening.

"It's the hostages at the embassy, Prime Minister," a BBC reporter told her.

"Yes, isn't it terrible?" said Mrs. Thatcher. "The government seems to have lost all control of the situation."

This remark was greeted with stunned silence. Was the prime minister really admitting that her government was already floundering? Then it dawned: Mrs. Thatcher had been chatting on air when the story broke and knew nothing of the drama unfolding at Princes Gate. She was referring to the *other* embassy siege, the one in Tehran, and the Iranian government's refusal to liberate the American hostages inside. She was swiftly brought up to speed and rushed to Downing Street.

As reporters and camera crews converged on the area, they were corralled into an enclosure erected inside the park on the corner of Exhibition Road, some two hundred yards west of the embassy. Pressville, as the fenced area was dubbed, grew more populous by the minute. "The police have clammed up," one journalist complained. "Nobody is speaking to anybody." While some journalists hastened to the scene and others called their contacts in the police and government, John Hooper of *The Guardian* simply dialed up the embassy telex

machine—the accepted method of sending written messages electroni-
cally via teleprinters, soon to be rendered obsolete by the fax machine.

Hooper called the embassy telex number seven times, without response, but on the eighth attempt, to his astonishment, the machine
responded: "Answer Back."

Seconds earlier, Mustapha Karkouti had entered the telex room on
the second floor, accompanied by Towfiq, who had agreed to let the
Syrian journalist contact his newspaper, on condition that he conveyed
the statement in full. Karkouti, drenched in sweat, had loosened his tie
and was about to dial Beirut when Hooper's incoming message clicked
out of the teleprinter.

What is happening?

Towfiq took Karkouti's place at the telex keyboard. With his gun
trained on the journalist, he slowly typed with one finger of the other
hand:

The Group of the Martyr has occupied the embassy

Hooper responded:

How many people are occupying the embassy?

Towfiq was not about to reveal the forces at his disposal. He did not
reply. Hooper tried again.

HOOPER: Are you the spokesman for the group occupying the
embassy?

TOWFIQ: Yes

HOOPER: Why did you occupy the embassy?

TOWFIQ: For our human and legitimite [sic] rights.

HOOPER: What are your rights?

TOWFIQ: Freedom, autonomy and reconition [*sic*] of the Arabistan people.

HOOPER: How do you intend to secure your rights with this occupation?

TOWFIQ: This is only one mean [*sic*] to make public opinion know and hear us.

Then the line went dead. Towfiq was not prepared to get into a debate: the media should publish his demands, in full, now.

Karkouti was led down the corridor to join the others.

Back in the general office, the hostages, wide-eyed with the alertness of profound alarm, huddled in groups. Jassim stood guard in the doorway. In his new boots and jeans, Karkouti reflected, he looked "as if he had just left a retail outlet." Afrouz sat propped in the corner, concussed and silent, only foggily aware of what was happening around him. By the door lay twenty-six-year-old Frieda Mozafarian, weeping and repeatedly fainting. The other women gathered around the stricken secretary, fanning her with copies of *Aviation News*. Sim Harris laid his blue jacket over her, to stop the shivering. As Towfiq came back into the room, she regained consciousness, screamed, and vomited into a gray metal wastepaper bin. Suddenly her body arched. Roya Kaghachi turned to Towfiq and pleaded in a mixture of Farsi and English: "Please let her go! She's having contractions. She may lose the baby. This woman urgently needs medical attention."

Frieda was not pregnant (though another of the hostages was); she was just petrified.

"Please send for a doctor," demanded Roya. "You don't want her to die here, right?"

"No, of course not. She is not going to die," said Towfiq, a little uncertainly.

Roya's tone to the gunmen was gently admonishing rather than confrontational, like an older sister ticking off her errant siblings. If she was scared, she was not about to show it.

Ron Morris now got to his feet and joined in: "Can't you see this woman is seriously ill? Why don't you let all the women go?"

As the longest-serving employee in the embassy, Morris was propri-etorial about the place. His Iranian employers had always treated him well. He and his wife had made a trip to Iran in 1970, as a reward for long service. They found it "nice, but a bit too bloody hot." Ron had a knack for stating the obvious, usually accompanied by a reinforcing expletive. His preferred method of communication was to ask himself a question, and then answer it. He knew nothing and cared less about Iran's political upheavals. The new regime struck him as similar, in all important respects, to the old one. "Am I above politics?" he liked to say, with mock grandeur. "Yes, I am." From his father, the stationmaster at Waterloo, he had inherited habits of strict punctuality and respect for order. His home in Battersea, where he lived with Maria, his "good lady wife," and their cat, Gingerella, was a model of tidiness. Every day he came to work, on his moped, arriving at exactly 09:00, wearing the same dark blue suit, white shirt, and tie. His replica-gun collection at home was neatly arranged in drawers and labeled. Ron Morris liked everything to be just so.

And now these people had barged into his embassy and mucked up its orderliness. He was suddenly quite cross. "Not very brave, are you?" he bellowed, moving toward Towfiq. "At least call for a doctor." Jassim lurched forward to intercept him, raising the butt of his gun.

The other hostages pulled Morris back. "Cool it, mate," urged Harris. "It's no good shouting at them."

"You're only making them angry," added Karkouti.

Morris's rage subsided. "Okay," he said meekly. "I won't say a word."

In his own mind, Towfiq was a noble warrior for a sacred cause. He did not see himself as a kidnapper of pregnant, hysterical women, and the possibility that one of his hostages might go into labor on the em-bassy floor gave him pause.

He took Lock aside. "How do I get a doctor?" he asked.

"You dial 999," said the policeman.

"But make sure you dial 9 first, to get an outside line," Morris chipped in.

"Why don't you let me phone and get a doctor?" Harris suggested.

"No, no. Leave it to me, I'll do it myself."

———

AT 14:03, a call to the emergency services from inside the embassy was rerouted to the information room at Scotland Yard.

"Get me a doctor," said Towfiq, explaining that a woman had been taken ill. "Woman doctor."

The police switchboard operator told him to hold the line and relayed an urgent message to John Dellow.

The police commander thought quickly. A doctor could be taken hostage. Better to withhold medical assistance until the gunmen made some concession. "This request is not to be met," he instructed. "Nobody, including doctors, is to enter the embassy. This request is to be used as a bargaining issue."

Towfiq returned to the hostage room with an announcement: "We are doing our best to get a doctor, but the police are saying no. Obviously they don't give a damn about you."

AT 15:00, Margaret Thatcher convened a meeting of the Civil Contingencies Committee for the first time.

This was the government equivalent of the emergency button on Lock's radio, bringing together top officials from the Home Office; the Foreign Office; the police; the intelligence services including MI5 and MI6; and the army and special forces, with some twenty-five other specialist advisers on standby. Formed to handle national emergencies and major disruptions, this crisis committee met in the Cabinet Office at Number 70 Whitehall, located immediately behind Number 10 Downing Street. It is technically the COBR committee, the acronym for Cabinet Office Briefing Room, but is usually referred to as Cobra, particularly by politicians who favor an emotive word suggesting a government striking back when serious trouble rears its head. Cobra began life as a top-level response to the 1972 miners' strike. It had last been convened in 1977, amid reports that the Ugandan dictator Idi Amin might land with two hundred bodyguards at Heathrow and attempt to gatecrash the queen's Silver Jubilee. The committee was stood down when the false alarm was traced to an Aer Lingus flight with the call sign "Uganda One."

The prime minister was present at the first Cobra meeting on the embassy siege and would attend in person twice more. She would be kept abreast of every development, and act as the final arbiter on decisions; but it would be run by the home secretary, William Whitelaw. Before the meeting began, Commissioner McNee briefed Whitelaw and Douglas Hurd, the foreign minister standing in for the foreign secretary, Peter Carington, who was traveling abroad. McNee was a tough, vain, no-nonsense copper who gloried in the nickname Hammer. He laid out the situation with Glaswegian bluntness: "The basic issue is whether to capitulate or stand firm. In my view the right course is one of no concession." This was also the view of the home secretary.

William Whitelaw was one of Thatcher's most trusted advisers. As a former officer in the Scots Guards who had won the Military Cross commanding a tank unit in Normandy, he knew his way around a crisis. He was Thatcher's acolyte, fixer, and de facto deputy. "Every prime minister needs a Willie," she is said to have remarked, with a smirk. Beneath his jovial exterior and rheumy eyes, Whitelaw was a stickler for law and order with little sympathy for young offenders, striking miners, and protesting ethnic minorities, and none whatsoever for terrorists. In the policing of domestic disorder and criminal behavior, he was a heavily armored political tank. But Whitelaw also knew that the situation in Princes Gate would need subtle handling, a domestic crisis with major international implications.

The U.S. government would be watching closely, because just six days earlier America had tried, and spectacularly failed, to end its own Iranian hostage crisis.

After four months of negotiations, President Carter had finally declared it was "time for us to bring our hostages home" and ordered the U.S. military to carry out a top-secret rescue mission. Operation Eagle Claw, launched on April 24, was daring and doomed. Helicopters would rendezvous with transport planes on a remote salt flat in the desert southeast of Tehran, and then ferry special forces to a mountain location closer to the capital. From there, Delta Force combat troops would launch a raid into the city with the support of the CIA operatives who were already in place, storm the U.S. Embassy, rescue the hostages, transport them to an airport captured by another unit of U.S. troops, and, finally, fly them to Egypt. The operation never got off the ground. Three of the eight helicopters were crippled before reaching the first rendezvous due to mechanical problems, a sandstorm, and a cracked blade. Carter aborted the operation, but, as American forces prepared to withdraw, one of the remaining helicopters crashed into a transport plane in the desert, killing eight soldiers and one Iranian civilian, and destroying both aircraft. When news of the botched raid reached Tehran, it was hailed by Ayatollah Khomeini as divine intervention: "Angels of God" had foiled America's evil plot and protected the Islamic Republic. Carter's presidency never recovered from the debacle.

Thatcher, Whitelaw, and everyone else in the Cobra meeting was acutely aware that America's attempt to liberate its hostages had ended in abject failure. If another rescue attempt went wrong, the West would be humiliated again, and the ayatollah doubly triumphant.

The two situations were quite different. The Americans were being held in the capital city of a hostile country; the hostages inside the Iranian Embassy were captives in leafy Kensington, and surrounded. The Americans were prisoners of Iran's Islamic regime; most of the hostages in London were representatives or employees of that regime. But in the popular mind (the steering force of most politics), the parallels were obvious: another outrage by Middle Eastern fanatics. How would Iran respond to seeing its citizens kidnapped, in a foreign country, by Iranian Arabs? If the Iranian diplomats in London could be rescued, might that be used as leverage to liberate the Americans held in Iran?

Margaret Thatcher had been in power less than a year. IRA terrorists locked in bloody battle with the British state would judge her resolve by what happened in Princes Gate. The next few hours and days would be a test of the Iron Lady's mettle.

Peter de la Billière, the swashbuckling SAS director who had seen action in Malaya, Oman, and Borneo, was among the first to arrive at the Cabinet Office. He had no automatic right to be there but had angled for a seat in the room, sensing the SAS might soon be needed. He described the scene as the prime minister and two dozen of the country's most powerful officials arranged themselves around a long table in the windowless room, and took stock of the crisis. The police and army officers sat at one end, the Foreign Office and the spooks at the other;

the ministers of state and their advisers were ranged down the sides, with the home secretary and prime minister side by side in the middle.

De la Billière was impressed by Thatcher's forthright manner. "She was very good," he observed. "She set the overall direction of policy, and left it to Whitelaw to execute." But the situation also brought out her intransigence and high-handedness. John Chilcot, Whitelaw's principal private secretary, described her first Cobra performance as "frankly dreadful"; she was overbearing and underinformed, "trying to dominate the occasion without really being on top of the detail."

As always, Thatcher made her opinions abundantly clear: she had "no intention of allowing terrorists to succeed in their hostage-taking," as she wrote in her memoirs. "This was no less an attempt to exploit perceived Western weakness than was the hostage-taking of the American Embassy personnel in Tehran." The Iron Lady was not for turning, in this or any other way, and her mind was already made up. "My policy would be to do everything possible to resolve the crisis peacefully, without unnecessarily risking the lives of the hostages, but above all that terrorism should be—and should be seen to be—defeated." In any case, the gunmen were demanding something she could not deliver: the release of political prisoners in another, hostile country. The terrorists, whoever they were and whatever the eventual outcome, had committed a crime on British soil, and would be tried under English law.

Mrs. Thatcher would not have made a good hostage negotiator.

Peter de la Billière left the first Cobra meeting with a grim premonition that, despite the prime minister's stated desire for a bloodless conclusion, such a prospect was already remote. The terrorists would not get what they wanted. Mrs. Thatcher was not going to allow the gunmen to walk free, and she was prepared to put hostages' lives at risk in her determination to defeat terrorism. "The police were not equipped to deal with what amounted to a military force of half a dozen fanatics armed with automatic weapons, hand grenades, and possibly explosives," de la Billière observed, predicting that eventually "there would be a confrontation and a shoot-out. Sooner or later the SAS would have to be involved."

Dellow shared that foreboding. Thatcher had left him little to negotiate with.

4

GRAPPLERS

John Dellow could not run a siege from the back of a van. The police needed to establish a center of operations, somewhere sufficiently spacious to accommodate a shifting force of several dozen officers and an array of communications equipment. The huge Royal Albert Hall, five hundred yards to the west, was briefly considered as a headquarters, but then rejected in favor of a building that was closer, less public, and even more unlikely.

The Royal School of Needlework at 25 Princes Gate was the national nucleus of British embroidery, home to more than four thousand beautiful handmade objects crafted with needle and thread: gowns, robes, psalters, samplers, and regimental colors. Here expert stitchers made the velvet cushions on which the crowns for George VI's coronation were carried, and the gold embroidery on the purple Robe of Estate worn by Queen Elizabeth II. A gentle, refined place of craftwork since 1872, the needlework school was just about the last place in London that might expect to be involved in a violent terrorist incident. But it was large and empty.

The police moved in among the fabrics: Alpha Control, managing the immediate area of the incident, occupied the first floor, while John Dellow and Zulu Control, the base for overall command of the operation, took up residence on the ground floor, beside a glass wall cabinet housing the world's largest collection of antique thimbles.

The SAS would not be ready to deploy for several hours, so Dellow drew up some contingency plans. If the gunmen started shooting hostages, armed police and snipers would attack the building using automatic weapons. Dellow's second-in-command, Deputy Assistant Commissioner Edgar Maybanks, also framed a set of instructions in case the gunmen tried to escape. If the terrorists ran from the building leaving the hostages inside, they should be chased down ("pursuit will be by dogs"); if they came out shooting and dragging hostages with them, the Blue Berets would open fire "under direction of sniper chief"; if they surrendered, the Special Patrol Group would move in and arrest them. Maybanks added a footnote: "All officers should be aware of the possibility that a hostage might attempt an escape from the building." He did not explain how even the most highly trained police dog would be able to distinguish between a fleeing hostage and an escaping terrorist. Dellow fervently hoped the SAS would arrive before such drastic action was called for: a shoot-out between police and gunmen would likely end in a bloodbath, as at Munich.

Professor John Gunn was working in his office at the Maudsley, Britain's leading psychiatric hospital, when a call came through from Scotland Yard: "Come immediately. A car will pick you up." A professor of forensic psychiatry since 1978, Gunn was an expert on the psychiatry of criminal behavior. Few knew more about the workings of the terrorist mind. For a year Gunn had been helping to train police hostage negotiators. He was escorted into the Royal School of Needlework. "It was bizarre," he recalled. "There were flat-footed coppers everywhere, surrounded by these delicate tapestries on every wall. The team was entirely composed of men, except for one woman police constable, who was there to make the tea." Gunn's task would be to try to understand the psychology of the hostage-takers and, if possible, the hostages, and advise the police on tactics. His secondary role would be to monitor the psychological impact on the negotiators themselves, since the siege might continue indefinitely and "the stress could be beyond their ability to cope." The police, gunmen, and hostages were all, in a sense, Gunn's patients.

Major news events tend to bring out a wide range of troublemakers, protesters, publicity seekers, and crackpots. An idiot with an English accent telephoned Scotland Yard threatening to blow up the Iran Air office in Piccadilly. Another bomb scare emptied the Brazilian Embassy in Mayfair. Anticipating unruly crowds, police erected metal barriers between the Albert Memorial and the park. Sure enough, by midafternoon demonstrators started to appear. Supporters of the Iranian regime (assuming, like everyone else, that this must be a tit-for-tat response to the U.S. Embassy siege in Tehran) marched in a circle chanting Islamic slogans and bearing placards reading: DEATH TO CARTER and DOWN WITH THE CIA. A smaller but no less vocal group of anti-Khomeini protesters arrived to taunt and heckle the Iranians. The police moved in to keep them apart.

The sounds of police sirens and shouting wafted down the empty street, faintly audible from inside the embassy, noises from another, distant world.

SUDDEN INCARCERATION without warning is a rare and deeply traumatizing experience. Civilian prisoners, soldiers captured in battle, and others deprived of liberty can usually see captivity coming, and brace for it. Karkouti, Towfiq, and Jassim had each imagined what it would be like to be arrested by the secret police long before it happened. Kidnapping is quite different, an eventuality for which preparation is impossible. A few hours earlier, the people in the general office had been enjoying a freedom as natural and unremarkable as the damp spring weather. Now they were imprisoned in a gloomy cell they could not leave; and, if the gunmen went through with their threat, they never would.

The hostages all had very different reactions, as ordinary people do when faced with unexpected circumstances beyond their control: panic, resignation, bafflement, anger, and a flicker of resistance.

The only substantial piece of furniture in the room was a large and ugly Queen Anne chair, with a high back and arms, another remnant of Iranian royal grandeur. Trevor Lock placed himself in it, instinctively assuming a position of authority. The policeman never sought to lead from the front. The most demanding management role he had ever undertaken was organizing the Jubilee festivities in Warley Avenue, Dagenham. But somehow the moment, and his uniform, required that he occupy the largest chair. "I had to preserve my image," he said. The hostages were looking to him for guidance.

Ron Morris's earlier bravado had given way to anxiety. "It's all going to be okay, isn't it?" he whispered to Lock. "I mean, this is nothing to do with us, is it?"

Lock nodded, trying to exude a confidence he did not feel.

"Every ten minutes or so," Harris observed, "Trevor stood up from his chair and rebuttoned his coat. He would straighten his peaked cap on his head before sitting again." The rest of the time he spent "gazing vacantly ahead," occasionally touching his face where the flying glass had gashed him, wondering, worrying, and attempting not to show it. The feel of the gun strapped to his side was a reassurance but also a liability. Only Cramer and Harris knew he had it. What would the gunmen do if they discovered he was armed? If he tried to use the revolver, he would surely die. And if, by some miracle, he did survive, he would be in deep trouble for drinking coffee that morning when he should have been guarding the front door. "The bosses aren't going to like it," he reflected grimly. "My police days are over." His wife would be worried when she heard the news. She had been looking forward to going out tonight. "This *would* happen today," he thought.

DOREEN LOCK WAS dressed in her best trouser suit and preparing to leave the house, when she received a telephone call from the sort of friend who likes to be the first with bad tidings.

"Have you heard the news?"

"No, what?"

"They've taken a PC hostage at the Iranian Embassy—they've either shot him or are going to shoot him, and I think it's Trevor."

Doreen's hell began. She sent the children to stay with their grandparents around the corner. The police arrived at 14:30, two constables from the Dagenham Station.

"Has his gun gone?" she asked. "Has he lost his gun?"

They were reassuring, and misleading. "He doesn't have his gun. Don't worry about it."

The journalists would be coming soon, they warned, before string-ing yellow tape between the lampposts on Warley Avenue. "Don't an-swer the door to anyone but the police," they said as they left.

Doreen sat on the sofa and waited.

FATEN KARKOUTI FOUGHT her way through the banner-waving dem-onstrators until she reached a policeman manning the cordon.

"My husband is inside the embassy," she said.

"Just a minute, please." The policeman spoke into his radio.

Faten was rushed to the Royal School of Needlework, and into a basement full of policemen.

"So sorry for what's happening," said a young man in plain clothes. "Your husband is inside the embassy?"

"Yes, he is."

"Is he a diplomat?"

"No, he is not; he is not even an Iranian."

"What is he doing in the embassy?"

"He is a journalist working for a Lebanese newspaper."

"Do you know why he went to the embassy or whom he was meeting?"

"No, he did not tell me when we left the house this morning."

"Do you have a photo of your husband?"

Faten fished into her handbag for a small black-and-white photo-graph of Karkouti.

"I want you to go home," the policeman told her. "And stay there until you hear from us."

An unmarked police car drove Faten back to Ealing.

Mustapha Karkouti's name was already known to the British au-thorities, and the discovery that he was inside the Iranian Embassy raised a small but piercing alarm bell in some quarters of MI5. An Arab PLO sympathizer, it seemed, had been inside the Iranian Em-bassy at the precise moment it was attacked by Arab terrorists. Was this an inside job?

"HAVE YOU GOT a piece of paper?" Chris Cramer whispered to his colleague.

In his pocket, Sim Harris found a crumpled BBC briefing note on the story he had covered the day before, about female wrestlers in West London. It was headlined "Grapplers" and asked: "What makes ordinary Acton housewives take it up for a hobby?" Twenty-four hours earlier Harris had been on a fluffy story about wrestling housewives, and now he was at the center of one of the biggest news events of the decade.

Cramer smoothed the sheet, took out his pen, and began writing a letter to his parents, something he had never done before. In a rushed scrawl, fearful of being spotted, he scribbled:

Dear Mum and Dad,

This seems most strange sitting on the floor here in this strange office in the embassy writing to you. Just think—I had no particular reason to come here this morning. Another few minutes and I would have been out of the place.

My feelings now are difficult to describe. I'm obviously frightened but I figure the gunmen are as well. None of us is saying much really.

God knows how this will all end—all I can think about is when [*sic*] I can tell the lads in the bar when this is all over. The trouble is I can't see an end to it. *They* have their demands and we know that they will *never be met*.

I think the reason I am writing this is to say that I love you all deeply although I've probably not showed it too much. I know how really good you have been to me always. Please take care of all yourselves. I am thinking of you the whole time. God bless.

Chris

Cramer folded the paper into a small square and tucked it into his wallet. If he was killed, the police would find it.

Like many senior journalists of that era, Cramer liked to give off an aura of extreme toughness, stomping around the newsroom, shouting and swearing. His nickname was Crusher Cramer. But beneath the bullish exterior was a sensitive man who masked his lack of confidence with loud bluster. He was petrified.

At 15:35, raised voices floated up from below. Through the half-open window of Roya Kaghachi's first-floor office, a shouted conversation was taking place between the leading gunman and the police negotiator.

Fred Luff stood on the pavement, now with an Iranian interpreter, introduced to him only as Mrs. Shadloi, crouched nervously behind him. She was wearing an incongruous fur coat; beneath it was a flak jacket, and beneath that was a tape recorder, attached to the radio microphone on Luff's lapel.

"Who are you?" demanded Towfiq.

"I'm the police officer in charge of this area. You may call me Mr. Luff. Who are you?"

"Mr. Luff, I am Salim. We apologize to you and people of your country for this intrusion. We mean no harm to you or to any of the hostages, and I promise that no harm will come to any of the British people in the embassy. We have no argument with your democratic country. I promise you that this is the case."

"Salim, I'm pleased to hear you say that," said Luff. (Repeating a hostage-taker's name is a basic rule of negotiation.) "I can promise you that no harm will come to you whilst your hostages are safe. Do you understand?"

"Mr. Luff, we have no argument with you. Our protest is against Khomeini."

So far, Luff had not needed the interpreter. The man at the window spoke excellent English. Luff attempted a gamble.

"Will you please allow my officer to come out now, Salim?"

"He's all right and we promise you we will release him. He will not be harmed but he must stop with us for a while."

Luff pressed again: "Salim, if you have no quarrel with us, the British people, why do you not prove it by releasing all the British people?"

"There is no difference between the British people or Iranians," Towfiq replied. "No harm will come to any of them." There was an ominous pause. "But you understand we will kill them all if you attack us."

Luff's instructions and training told him to keep the hostage-taker talking, but he was becoming irritated: the man was contradicting himself. Luff liked clarity. And he was better at preaching than listening.

"I'm sorry to hear you say that," he said sharply. "If you have a political message it will be destroyed if you kill one hostage, British or otherwise."

Towfiq shook his head. "There is no difference between British and Iranian hostages. They are all people—" Suddenly his tone changed, and he pointed furiously to a spot behind Luff's head. "You are lying, Mr. Luff. You are trying to trick us."

The policeman turned and saw with horror that three armed policemen from the forward response unit had maneuvered a large mirror into a position, behind the wall, where they could observe the front door without being shot at.

From Towfiq's position at the first-floor window, this looked like the prelude to an attack. "You are a liar, Mr. Luff!" The window banged shut and the curtain closed.

HEARING THE SHOUTING BELOW, the hostages exchanged terrified looks. Lock stood up, straightened his cap, and sat down again.

Back in the general office, Towfiq shoved a portable radio into Harris's hands: "Get news." Harris turned the knob until he found a news report—which was sensational, and mostly wrong. "An armed man" had entered the embassy and taken hostages, said the newsreader. "The intruder is reported to be an Iraqi." Another station reported that "Iraqi terrorists" had stormed the embassy. This made Towfiq even angrier. The police had received his statement three hours ago. Why had it not been broadcast?

"They are calling us Iraqis and terrorists, and we are not Iraqi or terrorists."

He seized the radio and shook it angrily.

"Why this radio doesn't pick up BBC Arabic?"

Towfiq's father had listened to the Arabic service of the BBC back in Al-Muhammarah, and, like many people living under dictatorships, he regarded "Huna BBC," as it was known in Arabic, as the only objective source of news.

"Why not let me contact the BBC World Service?" Karkouti suggested. "Once it is put on the main English service you will get your statement on air in thirty-six languages."

"Do it," said Towfiq. "But don't trick me and don't make any mistakes. When I say speak, you speak. When I say stop, you stop."

At 15:50, Karkouti called the switchboard at Bush House, headquarters of the BBC's international service, on one of the working telephone lines in the telex room. He was put through to the news desk.

"I have next to me the leader of the group that has occupied the embassy," Karkouti explained breathlessly, before reading out the prepared statement.

To this, Towfiq added a new and highly sinister element: unless the demands were met within twenty-four hours of the initial assault, midday the next day, the building would be blown up.

"How many are in the embassy?" the desk man asked.

Towfiq cut off the call.

"Good," he said to Karkouti. "We don't have much time. We are here only for twenty-four hours to finish the siege."

Karkouti was astonished. The gunmen seriously expected their demands to be met in a single day.

"The time margin you are giving here is very tight," he said.

"I know what I am doing," Towfiq snapped, and walked out. "Just do what I tell you to do."

Karkouti was left alone with Jassim. The tall, bushy-haired gunman they called Faisal was in no hurry to join the others. He radiated a violent energy but seemed inquisitive. "He looked like any attractive young man you might see in any West End nightclub, save for the machine gun in his lap."

Jassim began to quiz the Syrian journalist, in Arabic, about his life in Britain, addressing him by the honorific title *ustaz* (teacher).

"Are you happy here?" the gunman asked.

"Of course, good living, good job, free to do what you want and to think what you want."

"When did you come to London?"

"About seven years ago."

"Obviously you like it here."

"I love it." Karkouti ventured a question in return: "How long have you been in London?"

"Long enough," said Jassim cagily.

"Enough to go shopping? You have a nice shirt and trousers. They look new."

"Yes, we went shopping, and we already sent our shopping back home."

Karkouti took a gamble. "Look, Faisal, you'll do me a great favor if you allow me to phone my wife. We had an argument this morning before I left for work and I really feel horrible about it. She is pregnant. We may never see each other again."

Jassim glanced at the door. "Okay, do it quickly before anyone comes. I trust you, Ustaz Mustapha. Please don't trick me."

With shaking fingers, Karkouti dialed his home number.

Mustapha and Faten Karkouti had met in London seven years earlier. Theirs was a love match, stormy and secure. They now spoke, in Arabic, for what both knew might be the last time.

"Hey, *habibi*," said Faten, using an Arabic term of endearment. "Where are you?"

"I am still inside the embassy and I am sitting next to a very nice man from the group controlling the embassy who has allowed me to phone you."

"How are you coping?"

"Listen, about this morning, please forgive—"

"Of course, *habibi*, don't worry. Are you treated well? Are you injured? Are you okay?"

"How is our baby daughter?"

"She is fine—"

"I am really worried that the police may mistake me for a gunman or an associate—" Karkouti broke off with a sob.

"How many are you?" Faten asked.

Karkouti switched to English: "More than two dozen."

"And how many of them?"

"Your hand's fingers."

Jassim was now alert and suspicious.

Karkouti addressed him in Arabic: "Sorry, it was a slip, really sorry."

"Hurry up and get off the line."

"Just one more second, please," Karkouti begged, then gabbled to Faten: "I love you so much. Please take care, and look after our little baby. Pray for us, *habibti* . . ."

"That is enough," said Jassim, reaching for the telephone and hanging up.

Overcome by the tension, Karkouti laid his head on the desk and wept.

The gunman patted his shoulder: "Don't worry, everything will be all right."

IN THE GENERAL OFFICE, Frieda Mozafarian had regained consciousness and was wailing. Towfiq eyed her chalk-white face apprehensively.

"Look, you won't do your cause any good by hanging on to a sick, pregnant woman," said Trevor Lock, in the same reasonable voice he used for rowdy soccer fans after a match.

Their conversation was interrupted at 16:09 by the voice of Fred Luff, calling up from the pavement.

Towfiq returned to the first floor and opened the window.

"Salim, I've conveyed your message to my senior officers," said Luff. "I've told them you don't intend to harm the hostages. Why don't you let us pass in a telephone connected to the police? Then you'll be able to communicate directly with the authorities."

"No," said Towfiq. "I do not trust you, Mr. Luff. You have tricked us. You have surrounded us with armed men. You are going to attack us. We are prepared to die, but I tell you, if you shoot any of us, all the hostages will die."

"Salim, we are not going to attack you," Luff insisted. "I wouldn't be standing here like this if that was true, would I? You have my word that we won't attack whilst the hostages are safe—"

Towfiq interrupted him. "We are going to release a sick hostage. This is a humanitarian act and should not be seen as weakness." He closed the window.

Luff was puzzled. The man Salim appeared calmer. But he was hard to read: one moment polite and apologetic, then suddenly aggressive; in one breath threatening to kill many innocent people, and in the next describing himself as a benevolent humanitarian. He was clearly intelligent but volatile, lurching from one emotional pole to the other. The training course had done nothing to prepare him for someone so unpredictable.

Luff discussed the latest exchange with Professor Gunn. "Are these people serious terrorists, or nuts?"

The psychiatrist replied that, as far as he could tell, the gunman appeared to be sincere, sane, and extremely dangerous. He also warned that this situation was a medical and psychological time bomb, in which both gunmen and hostages would react to the stress in different ways. One hostage was already ill. Most would experience some sort of physical reaction. "Symptoms will vary widely between individuals and may begin with obvious signs of distress such as weeping, screaming, and running about, but they may also include pains, particularly in the chest and abdomen, palpitations, diarrhea, dysmenorrhea, and heavy menstrual bleeding. Psychological features, such as depression, paranoid states, and anxiety, may also be exacerbated or even induced by the circumstances. Overactivity, overtalkativeness, and grandiosity are quite common."

Luff himself was exhibiting some of those symptoms.

Negotiators in a siege situation, Gunn warned, "feel the pressure of publicity and immense responsibility, and added to their problems is the unusual loss of authority and autonomy, which is in itself stressful."

At 16:20, Roya Kaghachi finally convinced Towfiq that, unless he released Frieda Mozafarian at once, the panic-stricken woman would give birth prematurely on the floor.

With the help of the switchboard operator, Shirazeh Boroumand, Roya half carried, half dragged Mozafarian down the two flights of stairs into the hall. The front door was opened by Towfiq, and she staggered onto the doorstep, shrieking. Two policemen rushed forward and led the distraught woman to a waiting ambulance.

"Now, there is hope," said Roya.

Not for the first time, Sim Harris was struck by the young woman's poise.

The release of a hostage was an important breakthrough. But, as a source of information on the situation inside the embassy, Frieda proved wholly (and permanently) useless. The experience of the previous five hours induced complete traumatic amnesia. "I don't remember anything," she insisted. She was sedated, in the hope that when she came around she might recall something useful.

The atmosphere inside the hostage room relaxed. Frieda's screaming and fainting had scrambled everyone's nerves. "I am very happy she is out," Shirazeh told the other hostages, laughing and crying simultaneously. "What a lovely breeze there was when the front door was opened."

Gholam-Ali Afrouz slowly emerged from his concussion-induced trance. The gunmen seemed less agitated, handing out cigarettes and smiling diffidently. The hostages were permitted to leave the room to get water, in conical paper cups, from the water fountain in the corridor, and to visit the lavatory. The women were allowed to close the door to the toilet; the men were not.

Towfiq tapped gently on the doorframe to get attention. "Ladies and gentlemen, we would like to get to know each other. Now, I want you to say your full name, status, and brief background about your life. Let us start with the ladies first."

Roya Kaghachi found a large brown envelope behind a filing cabinet, and a pen.

Towfiq continued: "I want you to first write your name, job title, and address, and then pass on to others. And I want you to say it out loud while you are writing." Towfiq wanted to know who he was dealing with. He was also gathering information for negotiation.

Having introduced themselves, the captives in the general office began to mix and mingle, as if at some surreal diplomatic gathering.

The senior Iranian Embassy staff were all newcomers, Islamic radicals brought in since the Revolution. "They represent the face of the new Iran," Ron Morris explained to the other British hostages. "They are straight guys and they fear God, unlike the shah's lot." The rest of the embassy employees were "old guard," support staff, including secretaries, local hires, medical and consular officials, accountants, clerks, and others who, like the doorman Abbas Fallahi, had transferred to employment under the new regime.

"Which of you is Ezzati?" asked Chris Cramer, remembering the name of the press attaché responsible for issuing journalists' visas.

A balding man detached himself from the Iranian group. Abdul Ezzati smiled and extended a hand. "You're not *reporting* the news now, Mr. Cramer," he said, in excellent English. "You're *making* it." A devout supporter of the ayatollah, the forty-nine-year-old Ezzati was a former lecturer at Tehran University and one of the newest ideological appointees at the embassy. He beckoned over one of his colleagues in the press department, a man in his late twenties wearing an immaculate blue three-piece suit. Ali Akbar Samadzadeh had lived in Britain for eight years, spoke fluent English, supported the soccer team Arsenal, and had an Irish girlfriend called Mary. He worked part-time in the embassy while finishing a PhD in computer science. Thoroughly Westernized, Samadzadeh was in no hurry to return to an Iran ruled by mullahs. "He was no fanatic," Karkouti observed. They were joined by Ali Asghar Tabatabai, a besuited figure from a similarly cosmopolitan background. The scion of one of Iran's grandest families (the Tabatabais are thought to be descendants of the Prophet) and an employee of the Bank of Iran, he had come to Britain a few months earlier to take a scholarship course at Midland Bank. He was visiting the embassy to pick up some maps for an illustrated lecture to his fellow students, and through sheer bad luck had just sat down in the waiting room when the gunmen burst in.

Roya Kaghachi, Afrouz's secretary, was another who straddled the old Iran and the new. A product of the Iranian middle class, she had joined the staff at the age of nineteen as secretary to the shah's ambassador, Parviz Radji, when her family moved to Britain. She spoke flawless English, as well as French, German, and some Italian, and mixed with the wealthy young Iranian expatriates of London, "having fun, driving sports cars and organizing parties," in Karkouti's words. Roya did not disguise her opinion that the dreary new fundamentalist Iranian regime couldn't hold a candle to its flamboyant predecessor. She had already been warned that she'd be sacked for refusing to wear the hijab outside the embassy, a stricture she ignored. Forthright and highly intelligent, from the first gunshot Roya assumed a position of authority, and not just among the women hostages. Karkouti (who considered himself a connoisseur of female beauty) was in awe of her good looks: "Her greenish eyes were irresistible." But Roya Kaghachi did not suffer fools gladly, a category in which she included most of her male Iranian colleagues. Afrouz, her boss, was slightly scared of her. So was Towfiq; he had never been shouted at by a woman before.

The four other women were Shirazeh Boroumand, the switchboard operator and secretary ("exceptionally pretty with an ever-naughty smile": Karkouti); secretary Nooshin Hashemenian, at twenty-one the youngest hostage ("stunningly beautiful Sophia Loren-esque black eyes": Karkouti); and Zahra Zomorrodian, the assistant telex operator, and secretary Hiyech Sanai Kanji (neither of whom was considered pretty enough by Karkouti to merit a description). Kanji was married to a Tanzanian Asian civil servant, and three months pregnant with their first child.

The strange socializing was briefly interrupted when a large, heavy-bearded man in a baggy brown suit and topcoat with a dark shawl over his shoulders called for silence, and then grandly declared himself to be Nawabzada Ghazanfar Ali Gul from Pakistan, an "agriculturalist, economist, educationalist, and gentleman farmer." Distinctive in his furry karakul hat known as a "Jinnah topi," Gul was from a wealthy, landowning Gujarat family, and passing through London on his way home from a visit to Canada. That morning he had pondered whether to visit Kew Gardens or the British Museum, but instead chose to accompany his friend and fellow Pakistani, the journalist Muhammad Hashir Faruqi, who had an appointment to interview the Iranian chargé d'affaires. Gul was less worried by the death threat hanging over them than by whether he would catch his flight to Lahore on Monday morning. "I have an important business appointment," he declared.

Only one of the Iranian diplomats held aloof from the throng. He declined to introduce himself or to shake hands. Karkouti immediately spotted that he was different from the rest, "a slight figure with a long-haired beard, fair skinned, European-looking rather than Asian, with curly hair." The other members of staff kept their distance from him, and with reason.

The young man in the yellow cardigan with the intense expression was the embassy's resident Revolutionary Guard member, moral authority, and spy.

5

REVOLUTIONARY GUARD

Twenty-nine-year-old Seyyed Abbas Lavasani was not just a representative of the Islamic Republic; he was a living incarnation of the revolution that had brought it to power.

The least experienced of the new diplomats, he was also the oddest dresser. In addition to his bright yellow woman's cardigan, he wore green trousers tucked into his socks, a black-and-red tie, and "a pair of dark-color slippers through which one could see at least four of his toes of each foot." But if his costume was comical, his political and religious beliefs were deadly serious. His revolutionary credentials were impeccable, his religion extreme, and his devotion to Khomeini obsessive. Lavasani was a fundamentalist fanatic.

Abbas Lavasani was the twelfth and last child of Ayatollah Seyyed Hassan Lavasani, a distinguished Shiite scholar and theologian from Najaf in Iraq. The young Abbas Lavasani was educated at religious schools, studied engineering at Beirut University in Lebanon, and then took a course at the London School of Economics before returning to Tehran and hurling himself into the Revolution. One of his classmates, his closest friend, was tortured and killed by SAVAK, a trauma that entered Lavasani's soul, turning him from revolution to revenge. The fall of the shah had been the happiest moment of his life, but the most exciting one had occurred the previous November, when he took part in the storming of the American Embassy in Tehran. With his friend and contemporary Mahmoud Ahmadinejad (who would go on to become Iran's president), he had joined the surging crowd as they burst through the embassy gates and occupied the building, taking its American occupants hostage. To Lavasani's delight, Khomeini supported the takeover of the "American spy den in Tehran," calling it "a second revolution." Lavasani took no part in the ensuing drama, but he was intensely proud of the minor role he had played in capturing the hated outpost of American power: he had firsthand experience of an embassy hostage situation, from the other side.

The Lavasani family was large and influential, with close ties to the new regime. One of Abbas's uncles, Muhammad Lavasani, had attended the same madrasa as Khomeini and introduced the future ayatollah to the woman he married in 1929. Another relative was the foreign editor at Iran's state news agency, and yet another was Iran's ambassador to Canada. Abbas Lavasani was seen as a rising star of the diplomatic corps, and the young zealot had been appointed deputy press attaché in March 1980, barely a month earlier. But that was not his most important job. Lavasani was also an officer in the Islamic Revolutionary Guard Corps or Sepah-e Pasdaran, the branch of the Iranian armed forces established to defend the integrity of the republic by crushing internal dissent, preventing foreign interference, and protecting the religious legacy of the Islamic Revolution. Guards were discreetly deployed in embassies around the world, with a direct line of communication back to the regime that bypassed normal diplomatic channels. As Karkouti observed, these postings "had two main objectives: to reflect the new religious image of Iran after the shah, and to present the various diplomats with a permanent reminder that the mullahs were watching." Lavasani was in London to monitor exiled subversives, gather evidence of foreign plots, and enforce ideological conformity among his colleagues. The Iranian upheaval of 1979 had forged countless people like Lavasani: religiously rigid, authoritarian, and paranoid.

MANY OF THE HOSTAGES, and all the hostage-takers, were heavy smokers. Chris Cramer, Ron Morris, and Mustapha Karkouti had been chain-smoking steadily for six hours. The ashtrays were brimming, empty cigarette packets littered the floor, and the air reeked. Some of the women objected. "You can't smoke that much in such a confined space," Nooshin Hashemenian complained.

Shirazeh agreed: "I can't open my eyes because of the smoke. It is too much."

Roya chimed in: "If only they would stop, or allow us to open the windows."

Nooshin grinned. "Perhaps they will let us go out to the balcony for some fresh air." This impossibility set off a fit of giggling.

But this was 1980. Passive smoking had not been invented. The men continued to puff away, ignoring all entreaties. And now they were running out of cigarettes. Morris remembered that he had a carton in his office and asked for permission to fetch them. Young Fowzi escorted him upstairs, his Browning leveled at Morris's broad back. The embassy factotum returned a few minutes later with two hundred Kent cigarettes, several packets of biscuits, and a box of raspberry truffles. "I always like to have one of these truffles before I light a cigarette," explained Morris.

The gunmen had erected a barricade of desks and tables on the stairs to the fourth floor, he reported, sotto voce. "They're obviously expecting the police to storm in from the roof."

Comedy tends to surface, unbidden, at moments of extreme tension, and, as Morris moved around the room offering cigarettes and truffles to captives and captors alike, a brittle humor took hold.

Nawabzada Gul, the hefty Pakistani farmer, yet again brandished his British Airways ticket and addressed himself to Towfiq. "I have to catch a plane on Monday—do you think you can let me out as well?"

"Sit down, please, no time for jokes, okay?"

Gul was not joking. "I am here by sheer coincidence and I could have been somewhere else when all of this happened."

"Sit down, please."

At this, the banker Ali Asghar Tabatabai produced a ticket for the London Underground and remarked: "Perhaps they'll let me go as well." Everyone sniggered. Sim Harris joked that, like Karkouti, he had left his car parked outside: "Could I pop out and feed the meter?"

Trevor Lock emerged from his reverie and began telling dirty jokes, recalled from long hours spent waiting on police buses at demonstrations. "Have you heard the joke about the man who only had twenty-four hours to live?" he asked, and proceeded with the story of that unfortunate man, who pestered his wife for sex until she told him, "I have to get up in the morning. You don't." Somehow this seemed hilarious. Even Towfiq was "struggling very hard to restrain a smile."

These Arab terrorists appeared to be both fierce and solicitous, eager to please but ready to kill. "They keep telling me they're sorry about your injuries," Karkouti told Lock. "They didn't mean to hurt you."

In the corridor, Karkouti overheard an exchange, in Arabic, between Towfiq and his deputy.

"There are a lot of foreigners. We did not take that into account."

"*Esh hal balwa,*" Jassim replied. "What a disaster."

Karkouti relayed the conversation to Lock. "I think the gunmen are in deep shit, God help us. I don't think they expected there to be so many of us."

Lock agreed. "They're a bit strange, aren't they? I don't understand them. They take over an embassy and take people hostage, and then apologize. They're a complete contradiction."

The one called Salim was in charge, but Faisal seemed the toughest of the gang, coiled and edgy. On guard duty, he kept one finger hooked through the ring of a grenade. He plainly understood some English and treated the foreign hostages with courtesy; but the Iranians he addressed with a sneer. The other gunmen spoke Arabic to each other, and Farsi to the Iranians.

Abbas Maytham, the jumpiest of the gunmen, was, according to Harris, "thin and short in his early twenties, with tiny bloodshot eyes and a thin hooked nose." Acne scars mottled both his cheeks. (The hostages secretly nicknamed him Ugly.) Harris noted his "rugged, rough, tough-looking features," and the way he would "nervously walk round the room behind the hostages, almost touching them, with a pistol in his right hand and a grenade in the other." Yet he had "a nice smile." Shaye Hamid al-Sahar, alias Hassan, was the shortest, at about five foot three, and visibly nervous, his "eyes darting around the room," knuckles white where he gripped his pistol. Makki Hanoun guarded the ground floor and seldom entered the room with the hostages. When he did, he seemed almost overcome with shyness.

The youngest, Fowzi Badavi Nejad, calling himself Ali, had an alarming habit of waving his gun about. "Very good-looking," Harris observed, with a journalist's eye for detail. "Straight black hair, paler complexion than the others . . . didn't show any particular aggression." When the other gunmen were out of the room, his expression changed completely: young Fowzi looked utterly bemused, and quite lost. The London pubs and the shopping had been fun, but the operation was not going as they had expected. They were here to capture Iranian diplomats. Instead, they had rounded up foreigners and civilians, including two accountants, five journalists, a Pakistani tourist, a policeman, a banker, and five women. These were hardly the enemies of Arabistan. In Iraq, they had been told they would be striking a blow against the ayatollah and the Revolutionary Guard members who had massacred Arab children on Black Wednesday, but the people in this embassy, particularly the women, seemed perfectly friendly.

The hardest to read was Towfiq himself. Karkouti was struck by his "enigmatic, courtly, controlled manner" and the way he spoke "precisely and without any trace of tension in his voice." The leader addressed the non-Iranians as "Mr. Trevor," "Mr. Sim," "Mr. Mustapha," and he treated the women with elaborate courtesy. When Shaye made a lewd remark about Roya Kaghachi's attractive figure, Towfiq snapped at him: "You have sisters, and you have mothers. Is that how you treat them? Show some respect." Shaye blushed to his roots.

From a pocket, Towfiq produced a packet of Valium, a drug used to treat anxiety, and handed one to the concussed diplomat Afrouz, before "offering them around the room." Several hostages gratefully accepted. This man had stormed the embassy armed with guns and explosives but also with pharmaceuticals to reduce the stress of his captives. Terrorists are supposed to inspire terror, not treat it. Towfiq did both.

IT WAS ROYA KAGHACHI who came up with the idea of passing the gunmen's demands directly to the Foreign Ministry in Iran. "Maybe Dr. Afrouz can talk to the foreign minister himself?" The diplomat might be able to convince Tehran to liberate the ninety-one activist prisoners and secure their release.

Towfiq nodded enthusiastically. "I welcome this idea."

Roya might be a secretary, Harris reflected, but "she seemed to be in control of the situation."

The telexed response from the Iranian Foreign Ministry stated that the minister was traveling in Abu Dhabi, and unavailable. "Reach him, please, as soon as you can. Get him to call us back," Roya instructed the telex operator in Tehran. "It is very urgent; he must talk to us before we all die."

Towfiq was gratified. He liked the idea of negotiating directly with the Iranian government. But a moment later, he spotted Morris chatting amiably with the Iranians and his mood swung again. Angrily, he ordered him to join his British compatriots.

"You join the other group," he insisted.

"I am a member of the Iranian Embassy staff," Morris protested.

"But you are not Iranian; you are not allowed to stay with them."

"I belong with these people. I have been working here for more than thirty years."

"Okay, listen, mister, do you want to die? Then stay with your people."

Morris reluctantly returned to the other side of the room.

"Be careful," Karkouti whispered to him. "You don't talk like that to people with guns in their hands."

"Okay, I won't say a word," said Morris huffily.

A little later, Karkouti approached Abbas and asked him, in Arabic, why the Iranians and non-Iranians were being kept apart.

"Because when we decide to kill, we'll shoot in the direction of Iranian hostages first," said Abbas.

"You can't be serious?"

"Wait and see," said Abbas, with "a smile in the corner of his mouth" that made Karkouti's stomach lurch.

Towfiq kept the radio pressed to his ear, changing stations repeatedly, searching for news that his message had gotten through. The siege was being reported, but not his statement. His temper was fraying.

If the BBC World Service was dragging its heels, suggested Chris

Cramer, why not use him to send a message directly to the BBC by telex? "You can check before I send it, Salim," said Cramer. "If you don't like anything, I can change it."

Towfiq slowly read the message Cramer had written in his notebook, and then amended it. "Okay. You can send it. But any tricks this time and I kill you."

With the barrel of Towfiq's machine gun pressed to his ear, Cramer typed:

> After six hours the siege at the Iranian Embassy is still on. Together with a group of men and women I was held after an Arab group who call themselves Mahealdin al Naser Martyr Group [sic] burst into the building, overpowered a policeman inside and took over the embassy. They are demanding the release of 91 Arabs held in prison in Arabistan, a southern region of Iran. They have given the Iranian government 24 hours to release the 91 and fly them to London. Once the plane is in London they say they will fly with the hostages to an unknown destination. The Arab group spokesman told me that they were also demanding autonomy for Arabistan and recognition for the region. The Arab group are at pains to say that all the hostages are safe and they will not be harmed if their demands are met. If they are not they will blow up the hostages and themselves.

Towfiq intervened to dictate a further paragraph, while Cramer typed.

> I have been instructed to say that the police should not try to put an end to this siege until the demands are met. Thanks a lot. I am fine.

The telex machine clicked out a response:

> Can you answer a question? Is Sim there and how many hostages are there?

"Sim is here," Cramer typed, and turned to Towfiq, wondering if he should answer the second question. The gunman shook his head, and dictated:

The group apologize to the British people and their government.

Towfiq saw the anguish on Cramer's face, and asked him what was the matter.

"I'm frightened of dying," said Cramer.

"Don't worry," said Towfiq. "So are we."

JOHN DELLOW HAD grounds for both satisfaction and disquiet, neither of which he manifested.

No one had been killed, and the gunmen were talking, not shooting. The embassy was encircled and the hostage-takers wanted to leave the country, which raised the odds on the hostages getting out alive too. One had already been set free.

But there were also worrying signs. The gunmen might seem amateurish in some respects, but they had a clear agenda. The leader, Salim, seemed to be fully in control, and Dellow was working with very little information: he still had no idea how many gunmen were inside, who they were, or what weapons and explosives they had. The World Service interview was disturbing, underlining the twenty-four-hour deadline. Margaret Thatcher's insistence on complete surrender gave him little room to maneuver. Whether the hostage-takers would really blow up the building at noon the next day if their demands were not met remained unclear. Even the precise number of hostages was unknown, let alone their identities.

One of the first objectives in a hostage situation is to isolate the perpetrators and ensure they can communicate only through the negotiators. To Dellow's mounting (though invisible) irritation, although most of the phone lines in and out of the embassy had been cut off, some were plainly still working, along with the telex. For a second time, he ordered that "all telephone and telex links to the stronghold be cut." So long as they could speak to the outside world, the gunmen had the upper hand.

IN THE HANGAR, the Special Projects team's secure garages and stores, Major Hector Gullan, officer commanding of B Squadron, presented the briefest of briefings: a London embassy was under occupation by a group of armed foreigners, no casualties yet, and an unknown number of hostages, including at least four British citizens.

"Get your kit," said Gullan. The men of B Squadron trooped off toward the Range Rovers, wondering whether this would turn out to be a real emergency, "no duff" in army parlance.

By chance, the squadron had spent the previous few days preparing for an anti-terrorist training exercise in the north of England. This was to be a hostage-taking incident with an international component, staged in a derelict warehouse near Newcastle. Such exercises were staged every few months in different parts of the UK, and the various participants, including the Home Office, Foreign Office, police, and SAS, were all familiar with the procedures involved. Sometimes Mrs. Thatcher attended in person, as did members of the royal family.

As the SAS convoy rumbled toward London, Lieutenant Colonel Michael Rose, commanding officer of 22 SAS, climbed into a Scout helicopter with his operations officer, Jeremy Phipps. Both had changed into civilian clothes, which, for many senior army officers, is also a uniform: tweed jacket, tie, corduroy trousers, and polished brogues. They landed at RAF Northolt, and climbed into an air force staff car. "We've got to get there PDQ," Rose told the young driver. "We're going to jump every traffic light and go the wrong side of every bollard." They set off down the A40 "like a rocket" and pulled into Princes Gate at 17:52.

Only Dellow knew that the SAS "head shed" had arrived. The other policemen assumed that the new arrivals must be a pair of plain-clothes detectives. The negotiating strategy, Dellow told Rose, was to "play it long and play it cool." Rose was a Coldstream Guards officer described as having "the hawkish good looks Hollywood might impose upon a CO of the SAS." As the stepson of the novelist John Masters, a regular British Indian Army officer who served behind the lines in Burma during the Second World War, he had grown up on stories of covert military operations. Rose now set about framing plans for "immediate action and full stronghold assault." A swift reconnaissance established that the embassy rear gardens were accessible via a narrow passageway at the east end of Princes Gate; from there, a communal walkway ran at basement level behind the houses for the length of the terrace, virtually invisible from the upper floors. In Victorian times it had been used by tradesmen and servants to enter the buildings without being seen by the grander inhabitants and dignitaries inside; now, it offered a concealed route to access all the Princes Gate properties and, if necessary, to enter the embassy from the back.

The Royal College of General Practitioners occupied the adjoined buildings to the east of the embassy, collectively Number 15, and was to British doctors what the Royal School of Needlework was to embroiderers. One of the most imposing private residences in London, it was once home to the American banker J. P. Morgan before becoming the official residence of eight successive U.S. ambassadors: to symbolize its role in U.S. diplomacy, an architect added the heads of Native Americans to the keystones on the arches of the front windows. In 1962, the building became headquarters for the professional body representing Britain's doctors, with offices, a library, a museum, conference rooms, and residential accommodations for members. It had been evacuated when the siege started, save for its administrators, two naval officers who remained on-site insisting that, if necessary, they would go down with the ship. The "Doctors' House," as the SAS dubbed it, was designated the forward holding area, immediately next door to the Iranian Embassy, the springboard for a potential armed assault.

Rose and his men faced another, more practical problem, of the regiment's own making. Two years earlier, with opposition mounting, the Iranian government sought British advice on securing its embassy against possible attack from the shah's enemies. The SAS was brought in to provide expert guidance, and suggested that the Iranians install reinforced, armored-glass windows on the ground and first floors facing the street, and a second glass-and-steel security door inside the front door. Whether this guidance had been implemented was unknown.

The immediate action plan, to be executed instantly if the gunmen started killing hostages, was basic. From the roof of the Doctors' House, the SAS assault team would climb onto the adjacent roof of Number 16, and then "smash through the windows of the top floor and fight their way downwards" with firearms and tear gas, in the hope of rescuing at least some of the hostages before they were massacred. Another team would attack from the rear. Peter de la Billière conceded that the scheme was "relatively crude" and extremely dangerous. "Inevitably," he said, "it would lead to high casualties."

BY EVENING, the hostages and their captors were hungry. No one had eaten since breakfast. Roya Kaghachi asked Towfiq if she might look for some food.

"Of course, *khanum*," he said, addressing her as "lady" in the politest form. "Where is the kitchen?"

Roya and two other women were escorted downstairs. The basement flat was occupied by a caretaker, who happened to be on holiday but had left behind some food. They returned with water, a bowl of rice, cheese, fruit, two tomatoes, one green pepper, and some figs in syrup. The gunman Makki discovered some sealed packs of pita bread, along with three oranges, which were peeled and passed around: each person took just one segment. Knowing how long the U.S. Embassy siege had already lasted, Harris warned: "You'd better keep some food. It may be the last we get."

Lock declined to eat anything and drank only a few sips of water. The policeman had reached an odd but highly significant realization: if he ate and drank, sooner or later he would need to go to the lavatory. Urinating was fine. He could do that with his back to the accompanying gunmen, keeping his gabardine jacket on. But defecating was a different matter. He would need to unbuckle his belt, to which his gun holster was attached, and sit facing the open door. Whichever gunman was on guard would surely spot the gun. And if, by some miracle, he managed to hide it with his trousers around his ankles, his behavior would still seem highly suspicious. Nobody shits with an overcoat on.

Bravery comes in different forms: in the case of the besieged policeman Trevor Lock, it meant fighting off the call of nature for as long as possible, in a heroic feat of self-imposed constipation.

Meanwhile, Towfiq's demands had still not been broadcast on the radio. "Mr. Chris, you help me," he said, beckoning to Cramer. "I must have BBC. Get me BBC."

Richard Ayre, the BBC's home news editor, was astonished to find himself speaking to Chris Cramer, inside the embassy, at 19:22. He had been calling various numbers at the Iranian Embassy all afternoon with no response.

"Are you okay, Chris?" asked Ayre, pressing the record button.

The conversation that ensued was clipped in the extreme. Cramer was speaking with a gun pressed to his head.

"We're fine. We're okay. We're safe."

Then he handed the phone to Towfiq.

"Can I ask what is happening in the embassy?" said Ayre.

"Nothing happen," said Towfiq.

"You have a number of hostages?"

"Yeah."

"Why have you taken hostages inside the embassy?"

"Because we have some demands and we just took them to get what we want."

"What is it that you want?"

"The free of ninety-one prisoners."

"You want ninety-one prisoners in Iran to be set free?"

"Yeah. And the recognition of our region as an autonomy."

"What makes you believe that taking over the embassy in London will force the Iranian government to carry out your demands?"

"You know it is one of the means that we want to send our voice to the world."

"Tell me a little more about the group that you represent in Iran?"

"You know that group who are fighting for the autonomy of Arabistan."

"Does that mean you are opposed to the new regime?"

"We are against every leader who don't want to give us our legitimate rights. Any leaders, it makes no difference for us."

"Are you saying that all the hostages are safe tonight?"

"Yeah."

Back in the general office, Karkouti was upbeat. Towfiq seemed a "reasonable man," he whispered to Lock. The entire episode might be no more than a "publicity stunt." The gunmen were well-dressed. "It's obvious most of their clothes are brand new," said Karkouti. "Have you noticed they're wearing new digital watches and bracelets?" Suicidal fanatics do not tend to invest in expensive wristwear. Karkouti had known PLO gunmen back in Lebanon, and by comparison this crew struck him as amateurs.

Lock was anxious about Doreen. "We were going to see *Ipi Tombi*," he said wistfully. "We don't get out very often."

Ron Morris was concerned for his elderly mother in Battersea. "She's very highly strung. I am not sure she'll cope when she discovers I'm in here." Morris had another, more practical concern: more than two thousand pounds in cash was hidden at the back of his desk drawer. If these men blew up the embassy, they would destroy his life savings, earned from a sideline in catering. To take his mind off this disturbing financial risk, Ron Morris tried to interest himself in an old copy of *Horse & Hound.*

Lock took careful note of the gunmen's weapons. The two submachine guns carried by Towfiq and Jassim looked particularly deadly. "We don't stand a chance if they spray us with those," he said.

Karkouti was more concerned about the hand grenades. "Those are really deadly weapons. I saw them when I went to do training in Palestinian guerrilla camps in Jordan back in 1969," he said.

Lock was surprised to discover the Syrian's PLO background.

"It was fashionable among Arab youth to be revolutionary in those days," Karkouti explained. "Lots of young men and women joined guerrilla organizations after the defeat of Arab armies during the Six-Day War with Israel in 1967. I was simply reacting to the call to fight for a just cause, the Palestinian cause."

Lock had been suspicious of Karkouti at the beginning. The presence of an Arab journalist in the embassy at the precise moment Arab gunmen attacked it struck him as uncanny. But trust was gradually building between them.

"Did you get training on those kinds of weapons?" Lock asked Karkouti.

"Some, but I am no expert," Karkouti replied.

"Your knowledge may come in handy."

"Don't count on it."

SIM HARRIS WAS becoming concerned about his BBC colleague, who had started to complain of violent stomach pains. Back in March, covering elections in the new Zimbabwe, Cramer had contracted a mild strain of dysentery, and the tension seemed to have retriggered the symptoms. His fear and pain erupted in sudden gusts of temper. When one of the Iranians took more than his share of their meager meal, the BBC producer swore furiously at him. Gul, the portly Pakistani, was still yammering on about the plane he wanted to catch. "My God, that man is so fucking annoying," Cramer snapped.

Conversation dwindled, and the room fell silent as each retreated into private fears.

The last working telephone rang in the telex room at 22:12.

Every other line, and the telex, had now been severed. This one remained live because it was the telephone used by Iranian intelligence officers to contact Tehran directly, bypassing the main switchboard. It was not listed on the embassy directory. The GPO (the state-owned telephone service) did not know it existed. But MI5 did.

Astonishingly, the foreign minister of Iran was on the line, demanding to speak to his chargé d'affaires, Dr. Gholam-Ali Afrouz.

Sadegh Ghotbzadeh, the Iranian foreign minister, was one of the more lurid figures spawned by the Islamic Revolution. Educated in the United States and Canada, he was thrown out of Iran for plotting against the shah, and then reemerged as one of Khomeini's closest aides. He accompanied the ayatollah on his triumphant return from exile in 1979. A brutal fanatic with round, clean-shaven features and a broad smile, Ghotbzadeh ruthlessly purged anyone deviating from the regime's rigid ideology. As Iran's newly appointed minister for foreign affairs, this cherubic enforcer was the international face of the Revolution, preaching a ferocious brand of Islamism to the world. He was closely involved in the deadlocked negotiations over the American hostages in Tehran (Jimmy Carter's failed rescue mission was an "act of war," he said). He too had leaped to the erroneous conclusion that this embassy hostage-taking must be in retaliation for that one. Ghotbzadeh had no intention of giving in to terrorists' demands. This was the only thing he had in common with Margaret Thatcher.

Afrouz was hauled to his feet by two of the gunmen and frog-marched to the telephone. Dazed as he was, the diplomat was in a delicate position. "Be careful, otherwise I will shoot you," Towfiq warned him. "You tell him exactly what we want, our demands, and that's it." But if Afrouz put the Arabs' case to his boss too enthusiastically, Ghotbzadeh might suspect him of disloyalty.

Afrouz mumbled through his injured jaw, "Sir, thank you very much for phoning back. I am the chargé d'affaires—"

Ghotbzadeh cut him off. "Yes, I know who you are."

"The situation is very serious, sir, and we would be very grateful if you could help us by responding favorably to the group's demands, particularly by releasing the ninety-one prisoners in Khuzestan as soon as possible."

"We make no bargains with terrorists," Ghotbzadeh retorted.

"Sir, we will all die if you don't look into the demands."

"I told you we don't bargain with terrorists."

"But, sir—"

"These people are agents of President Carter and the CIA," said Ghotbzadeh, before launching into a prepared speech. These terrorists were Iraqi mercenaries in the pay of the Americans; no prisoners would be released in Iran; no concessions would be made to the treacherous rebels of Khuzestan.

Towfiq had been listening in to the conversation with mounting fury. He now began shouting into the mouthpiece at the same time as Afrouz: "You better listen to us—"

But Ghotbzadeh was listening only to the sound of his own voice.

"We think highly of you and the other Iranian hostages, and we salute you for being ready to die as martyrs for Islam and for the Revolution."

Towfiq seized the telephone. "Okay, listen to me, you bastard, if you don't want to save your hostages, we will kill them all—"

"Do what the hell you like," Ghotbzadeh sneered. "You are American agents."

Towfiq hurled a torrent of abuse at Iran's foreign minister and smashed the phone down.

Afrouz was shoved roughly back into the hostage room. The scar-faced gunman Abbas moved to hit him, before being restrained by Jassim. They seemed to blame Afrouz for Ghotbzadeh's intransigence. The room crackled with fear and fury. Several of the women began to weep. It was, thought Harris, "the worst moment so far."

It was nearing midnight, and Towfiq ordered the room cleared of desks so that the hostages could lie on the floor. "I think it is time to sleep," he said. "There is no more action tonight and you must be very tired." Furious a moment earlier, he now seemed determined, in Karkouti's words, "to calm everyone down." Islamic decencies would be observed. The women would not sleep alongside the men. "Please, ladies," he said, addressing Roya, "go to your room." Fowzi herded the women into the adjoining cipher room, and stood at the door like a sentry, "with a very big smile on his face." The youngest gunman seemed pleased to be appointed the women's designated guard.

The Muslims were permitted to perform ablutions in the bathroom before praying. Then the Iranian hostages stood facing Mecca and recited the Isha, or night prayer. The ancient ritual seemed to lay a fragile sheet of stillness over the room. Several curled up on the green carpet. Soon Gul was fast asleep, apparently oblivious to the peril, and snoring loudly. Afrouz accepted another Valium.

An hour later Lock was still wide awake, sitting upright in his Queen Anne chair, when Towfiq drew near.

"Are you hungry, Mr. Trevor?"

"No."

"Are you tired?"

"A little."

"Why not lie down and rest?"

"Because I am a policeman and must make sure everyone else is okay."

"Do you want anything to eat?"

"No."

"We are very sorry about your face; do you want anything?"

"No, I'll be okay."

TOWFIQ ISSUED A last flurry of orders to his men in Arabic: "Make sure windows are locked, ensure the top floor is blocked, switch off all lights on the stairways . . . I am coming shortly to check every corner of the building myself."

With half of Towfiq's twenty-four-hour deadline expired, a precarious peace descended on Princes Gate. Some of the hostages drifted into semi-sleep or lurched between sleeping and waking, at once terrified and exhausted. Towfiq and Jassim stood guard at the front door, watchful, alert. Fowzi positioned himself between the two rooms, with his head in the cipher room, where the women were. Occasionally a sob broke the silence. In the Royal School of Needlework, the police night team remained glued to the closed-circuit screens, while uniformed police patrolled the perimeter, fueled by sandwiches and tea from the catering vans. Rebecca West abandoned her window overlooking the embassy gardens and went to bed.

AT 01:30, the hostages were jolted awake by a single shot from the floor below.

"Oh, blimey, what the fuck was that?" said Ron.

Seconds later, Towfiq entered the room, looking rueful. "It was just an accident," he explained. Makki had been fiddling with his Browning and accidentally fired a bullet into the ceiling.

"Don't worry," Towfiq repeated. "Nothing is happening."

He might have been a hotel manager, apologizing for the rowdiness of the other guests.

Harris drifted off, head on his rolled-up jacket. He came to with a jolt at around 03:00 and sat up, "trembling from cold and shock."

Lock was still sitting upright and alert in his chair. He nodded to Harris, a guard on night duty, a Diplomatic Protection Group of one.

HALF AN HOUR LATER, two vans pulled up at the east end of the terrace. In the deep predawn darkness two dozen men emerged, each with a large carryall, and slipped silently along the walkway behind Princes Gate, hopped over the low wall, and entered the basement back door to Number 15, the Royal College of General Practitioners. They wore jeans, sneakers, and checked shirts, and might have been taken for noc-turnal "tourists, or a brass band off duty," as one observed. A police-man led them into a reception room of plush red carpets and mahogany furniture, "with chandeliers throwing circles of light on the walls." Many of the SAS troopers had never been anywhere so grand before. Underneath the great polished conference table, they rolled out rubber mats and sleeping bags. The ammunition boxes were stashed under a glass cabinet containing nineteenth-century scalpels and forceps. Three men climbed five flights of stairs to the top floor, and through a skylight onto the roof to look for abseiling points. If the immediate action plan was activated, the Red Team of B Squadron would be ready to fight in under ten minutes.

They changed into black combat gear, checked their weapons, and put the kettle on.

DAY TWO

THURSDAY

6

EAVESDROPPERS

I n the middle of the SAS training base in Hereford stood a nonde-
script, single-story brick building known as the Killing House. It
had furniture, carpets, and pictures on the steel walls, which were
lined with thick rubber drapes to absorb bullets and prevent "splash-
back" from ricochets. Extractor fans removed gunshot fumes when
the shooting stopped. The floor was black stone chippings, covered in
old carpet.

The Killing House was built in 1973, for the SAS to train in hostage
rescue.

In later years, members of the royal family were brought here to
taste the experience of being kidnapped and then liberated by the most
elite force in the British Army. Before one such training session, Prince
Charles (now King Charles III) sent a jocular note: "Should this demonstration go wrong I, the undersigned Prince of Wales, will not commit B Squadron 22 Special Air Service Regiment to the Tower of
London. Charles." He was accompanied by his then wife, Princess
Diana, whose hair was slightly singed by a thunder-flash grenade during the demonstration. "Hope you're not going out tonight, love," said
one of the soldiers. "Your hair is a bit of a mess."

In a typical close-quarter battle exercise in the Killing House, life-size cardboard targets clearly identified as "terrorists" or "hostages" were arranged around the building. Using live ammunition and operating in pairs, the soldiers had to burst in, swiftly distinguish between friend and foe, and shoot each of the terrorist targets with two controlled bursts of fire to the head, a "double tap," from a Heckler & Koch MP5 submachine gun. The room layouts, windows, doors, and furniture were altered; obstacles were placed in the corridors; the hostages were mixed in among the gunmen. Electricity might be cut off while the exercise was in progress, plunging the building into darkness, and the rooms filled with smoke; loudspeakers blasted shouts, screams, and explosions. There could be multiple hostage-takers, or a lone gunman. Each trooper might fire a thousand rounds in a single morning. Inside the Killing House, one SAS soldier remarked, "you could taste the lead." Snipers also trained on the range, picking off human-size targets from up to five hundred yards.

The equipment in the Killing House had greatly evolved since it was initiated in the wake of the Munich massacre, but the object of the exercise remained unchanged: to rescue hostages, without shooting them or each other, and neutralize the gunmen.

The SAS practiced inside the Killing House using machine guns and handguns, gas masks, body armor, stun grenades known as flashbangs, explosives, and devices to pinpoint the locations of those inside. By 1980, the counterterrorism teams of the SAS had spent seven years undergoing close-quarter battle training, and a team of forty-five men was placed on standby around the clock, each with a packed carryall and a bleeper, prepared for immediate deployment.

There was only one sort of hostage-taking situation the SAS had never experienced: a real one.

NO ONE SLEPT much in Princes Gate that night: Zulu Control watched intently from one side of the embassy, while the SAS assault team remained poised on the other; the media mounted an all-night vigil; the hostages fidgeted and turned on the hard floor, never more than half-asleep. The exception was Nawabzada Gul, the large Pakistani tourist, who slumbered soundly, and very loudly, for eight hours.

As dawn broke and the light morning rain cleared, a message came into Alpha Control from the police surveillance position in Hyde Park: "Slight movement at embassy window, otherwise nothing."

The media awakened with a hungry roar. Broadsheet newspapers, TV, and radio had all complied with a police request not to publicize the gunmen's demands or the looming deadline, but the tabloids could not resist the juiciest story in a decade. THEY DIE AT NOON blared the front page of the *Daily Mail*. HIGH NOON FOR LONDON HOSTAGES salivated the *Daily Mirror*.

Overnight, Sadegh Ghotbzadeh, the Iranian foreign minister, issued a statement: "Iran will not give in to blackmail either from the superpowers or a small number of terrorists." He accused Iraq of organizing the attack and rejected any parallel with the siege of the U.S. Embassy in Iran. "The occupation in Tehran is in reaction to twenty-five years of oppression and killings in Iran. This is totally different from a few mercenaries who are being employed by another government . . . We condemn the occupation of our embassy." He accused the CIA of plotting the attack in league with Iraq, and called on the British authorities to end the siege as swiftly as possible, pointing out that the embassy was sovereign territory under diplomatic law ("totally a foreign land of foreign people"). More chilling yet, Ghotbzadeh added that if any Iranian hostages were harmed, Arab insurgents held in Iranian prisons would die.

MUSTAPHA KARKOUTI WAS roused by Fowzi gently tapping his shoulder.

"Mr. Mustapha, wake up, please. Salim wants you in the other room."

"Why, what's happening?"

"Go and see him; he wants you immediately."

Ron Morris was awake: "Don't worry, Mustapha, maybe they decided to release everyone at the deadline."

Towfiq and Jassim had established their headquarters in a small room off the corridor.

"Sorry, Mr. Mustapha, for waking you," said Towfiq. "We need you for very important mission. We want to speak to the BBC again."

Towfiq was angry with the British media. All night, he had listened to the radio, in English and Arabic, expecting to hear his statement read out, and becoming increasingly cross when it was not: the siege was top of the news, but his demands had not been mentioned.

Colin Thatcher, an editor at BBC Radio Newsreel, was astonished to receive a call at 07:02 from a foreign voice offering to read a statement from the gunmen inside the embassy. It was Karkouti, on the last working telephone in the telex room. Towfiq's gun was held to his head once more: the gunman might seem friendly and apologetic, but Karkouti knew that one wrong word or any attempt at trickery, and Towfiq would pull the trigger. His bowels lurched as he cleared his throat and read:

> The Group occupying the Iranian Embassy would like to assure
> the British public opinion that the British hostages, as well as all
> other non-Iranian hostages, will not be harmed. But the
> deadline for the safety of the other hostages, and the others as
> well—which is twelve o'clock noon—is still valid.

In the first sentence, Towfiq promised that the non-Iranians would be unhurt, and in the next he vowed to kill them all, along with everyone else.

Before Karkouti could hang up, Thatcher asked: "May we ask you a question about conditions inside the embassy at the moment?"

"The gentleman here doesn't want me to answer any questions," said Karkouti.

Putting his hand over the mouthpiece, he spoke to Towfiq in Arabic. "This is a great opportunity for you to speak with your own voice to the world."

Towfiq took the telephone. "Good morning," he said, brightly.

Thatcher was momentarily stunned, and then regained his composure. "Good morning to you. What are the conditions inside the embassy at the moment? Are the hostages well?"

"All well. And everything all right."

"You asked yesterday for a doctor to come to the embassy."

"Nobody has come."

"When were you last speaking to the police?"

"I'm not sure exactly."

"Have you received a message during the night from the Iranian Foreign Minister, Mr. Ghotbzadeh? What was the message?"

"The message I think he says was: 'We will not yield to the demands of the group.'"

"What was your reaction to that message?"

There was an ominous silence.

"I think he will regret it."

"What do you mean he will regret it?"

"I mean—after the deadline—I will kill everybody here. All the hostages."

"And the deadline is twelve noon today?"

"Twelve noon today," Towfiq repeated. "That is what Ghotbzadeh wants—because they are nothing to him. He doesn't care for the Iranian hostages."

This was undoubtedly true.

Thatcher pressed on. "Do you know Mr. Ghotbzadeh has issued a warning that if anyone in the Iranian Embassy is harmed, then the people in Arabistan will be harmed?"

"Okay. That doesn't matter."

"That doesn't matter?"

"Yes."

"You are not concerned about that? I thought you wanted the release of these people?"

This was all getting more complicated than Towfiq had anticipated. He wanted to state his case. He did not want to be interrogated.

Sensing his discomfort, Thatcher switched the subject. "Can you tell me how many hostages you're holding?"

"No, sorry."

"Are they being held in one room? Are they tied up? Are they allowed to move about?"

"Sorry, I can't answer this question."

"Would it be possible for us to speak to one of them on the telephone?"

"No, sorry. We are very sorry."

"Is it possible to speak to one of the English people there?"

"No. But they are all right. And will be all right."

"Will they be released before the deadline at midday?"

"No."

"Then how can you guarantee they will be unharmed?"

There was a pause while Towfiq digested this conundrum: he could hardly guarantee the safety of the hostages while simultaneously threatening to kill them.

"I will think about that," he said, and rang off.

AT 08:05, the last telephone line into the embassy was severed. The reason it had remained uncut for so long was simple: unbeknownst to Iranian intelligence, MI5 was tapping their dedicated telephone line. When John Dellow found out that "the security services had independently requested that one telephone remain operative," he lost his temper. The spies were listening in without telling the police, thereby enabling the gunmen to maintain contact with the outside world. Dellow was playing by the rules, as always, but MI5 was tampering with the ball: this was just not cricket. Dellow's rage was not like that of other men. He did not shout or bang the table. Instead, with his color slightly raised and his voice taut, he ordered the phone to be cut off immediately, and dispatched a fizzing note of protest to MI5. Twelve minutes later, the line went dead.

The hostages and their captors were now cut off.

Back in the general office, the men rubbed their eyes and stretched aching limbs. In the cipher room next door, the women tried to make conversation with their guard, the young handsome one. Bashful, he said his name was Ali. At around 08:15, he led them next door to rejoin the men.

"Their presence with the male hostages added a strange relief to the overall tension, a reassuring and positive sign," Karkouti reckoned. Some of the women had been weeping.

"They are frightened," said Roya Kaghachi, applying makeup. "Nooshin has a one-year-old baby; she kept talking about that last night and went on crying for a long time." She paused and sighed. "Let us hope we all get out today and go back home."

Karkouti was struck again by the young woman's uncanny poise. He asked her, "How long have you been working for the embassy?"

"More than six years."

"So you worked, then, for the shah's ambassador?"

"Yes, Ambassador Parviz Radji. He was a friend of the shah."

"Working for him was different to Dr. Afrouz, I guess?"

Glancing across at the injured chargé d'affaires propped in the corner, she sniffed: "There is no comparison whatsoever. Mr. Radji was representing a royal family, not like these . . ." Her words trailed off.

"Why are you still working for the embassy?" Karkouti asked, lowering his voice.

"I almost left a few times. After this, I am most certainly quitting, and never coming back to this building, or near it," Roya laughed.

Afrouz's face was a livid mass of bruising, his breathing labored through broken ribs. But he was now conscious and speaking more clearly. The gashes to Lock's face and forehead were healing. His left eye was still half-closed, but the swelling had subsided. Chris Cramer, however, seemed to be dying.

At around midnight, his stomach cramps dramatically worsened, accompanied by repeated bouts of diarrhea. The gunman Shaye, the one they called Hassan, helped him to hobble along the corridor to the bathroom. Towfiq urged Cramer to take a Valium. The BBC journalist lay doubled up on the floor, groaning and sweating profusely. Harris and Karkouti took turns bathing his face with water.

It is unclear how ill Cramer really was. He may not have known himself. As Professor John Gunn had warned, being held hostage can cause, or exacerbate, any number of health issues. Stress takes many forms, and Cramer's distress may have provoked genuine symptoms.

But Cramer was certainly less sick than he appeared. He later conceded that he had become "rather conveniently ill," and that his suffering was partly pretense, a deliberate ploy: "I ramped it up." From time to time, Cramer caught the lead gunman eyeing him anxiously, "genuinely concerned for his welfare." The gunmen seemed sympathetic. If he could convince them he was truly at death's door, he might be the next one out the front door.

AT 08:30, Fred Luff's voice wafted up from the pavement again, calling for Salim. The police negotiator had returned home to Shepperton in

Surrey, slept fitfully, woke early, prayed, and returned before dawn. He looked haggard.

Towfiq appeared at the window, visibly angry. "Why have you cut off the telephone?" he demanded. "Reconnect it or we will kill a hostage."

Luff played for time. "I will refer it to the higher authorities," he said. "What are your telephone numbers? I will try to get them restored."

Towfiq was incredulous. How could the police not know the embassy numbers? Nonetheless, he agreed to find them.

Luff offered again to provide a field telephone: "That way you can speak to us whenever you want."

Once again, Towfiq refused. "One of the British people is very sick," he said. "We need a doctor."

Luff agreed to pass on the request.

DELLOW'S EQUANIMITY was returning. The telephones were cut off, Luff seemed to be establishing a personal dialogue with the gunman Salim, and the terrorists had made some realistic demands that could be manipulated into bargaining tools. The deadline was just over three hours away, but an artificially prolonged discussion over doctors and telephones could buy valuable time. The lead gunman was threatening death, while demanding medical attention for his captives.

A few minutes later a small, rolled-up piece of paper was poked out through a bullet hole in the front door: on it was a list of the embassy telephone numbers. Towfiq was negotiating.

NINE DOORS DOWN, at Number 25, John Dellow was wrestling with a health-and-safety issue. Smoking was strictly forbidden in the Royal School of Needlework to protect the delicate hand-stitched wall hangings and to conform with insurance provisions. Some of the police were heavy smokers.

It is hard to run a siege when half your force, fidgety from nicotine withdrawal, keeps nipping out to smoke.

Number 24 Princes Gate, one building closer to the embassy, housed a nursery school, the St. Nicholas Montessori Center. The school gave permission for the premises to be commandeered on two conditions: the police must look after the pet gerbil, Nibbles, left behind in the evacuation, and they should not disturb a duck nesting on the first-floor window ledge. Police put the move down to the "fire risk and potential danger of damage to valuable tapestries." In reality, they were just desperate to smoke.

The Police Engineers Department, the Architects and Surveyors Department, and the Catering Department prepared the building for occupation.

The front rooms of the ground floor housed Alpha Control, running snipers, dogs, and patrols within the inner cordon, while a small SAS military support team and MI5 operated from the back. On the first floor was the "intelligence cell" set up by the Anti-terrorist Branch (C13), Special Branch, and the Technical Support Branch (C7), this last the police unit responsible for surveillance, eavesdropping, and "gathering intelligence by technical means" using gadgetry, technology, and science. Zulu Control took up residence on the third floor, and there was a small adjoining conference room where Dellow could sleep. Feeding facilities were provided in the basement. The negotiating team set up shop on the fourth floor. Luff had now been joined by five more hostage negotiators. These would operate in teams of three on twelve-hour shifts, along with Farsi and Arabic translators.

As a police headquarters, the place was not ideal. The tiny nursery chairs were far too small to accommodate police-size bottoms, and to use the miniature urinals accurately officers had to kneel. Technicians re-laid the cabling already installed next door and set up monitors in Alpha, Zulu, and the negotiation room. Adult chairs and desks were brought in through the back entrance, along with camp beds and mattresses. Number 24 was swiftly enveloped in a fresh fug of cigarette smoke.

Detective Sergeant Graham Collins of the Anti-terrorist Branch joined the throng of police filing out of the Royal School of Needlework and into the Montessori nursery school, past a "row of tiny coat pegs, each marked with a cardboard cut-out of an animal." C13's primary task was to use the "intel cell" to try to make sense of the situation inside the embassy.

"At first it was absolute chaos," said Collins. "We had no idea who the terrorists were, or the hostages."

To fill in the blanks, C13 brought in two typists, a bank of telephones, Rolodex devices (a rotating card-file index), blackboards, and pinboards. They then set about building a picture using the two central pillars of spycraft: human intelligence (humint) and signals intelligence (sigint), information gathering and eavesdropping.

Trevor Lock had been identified in the opening minutes, and the BBC soon reported that two of its journalists were missing, having gone to the Iranian Embassy to apply for visas. The Foreign Office furnished a list of diplomats accredited to the Iranian Embassy, and the medical officer, who escaped in the opening moments of the siege, was able to identify some of those inside. Next, an "all stations message" was sent by telex to every Metropolitan Police station, requesting reports of anyone who had gone to the embassy for any purpose in the previous twenty-four hours and had not returned. Once an individual hostage was positively identified, a policeman was sent to talk to relatives, obtain a recent photograph, and build up a profile: "Did the person have a medical condition, or psychiatric issues? How do they behave under stress?" Discreetly, police also sought to obtain a hairbrush, comb, or some other object carrying the missing person's DNA. In 1980, the science of genetic mapping was in its infancy, but, if the gunmen followed through with their threat to blow up the building, a few scraps of human tissue might be all that remained to identify the dead.

The pinboard collage of names and faces expanded steadily, but gaps remained. Some would never be filled. Gul was a tourist traveling alone, visiting the embassy on a whim: no one knew he was there. Several of the diplomats had arrived in the UK so recently that they did not appear on official lists. A few of those inside would not be reported missing for days. The numbers on the hostage list fluctuated as names were added and removed.

As the last of the morning mist cleared, John Dellow's picture grew clearer: at least six armed men were holding hostage a British policeman, several journalists, and more than a dozen Iranian diplomats and embassy staff, including at least five women. The intel cell could put names to most of them.

The gunmen were, as yet, mere ghosts.

Thousands of people from the Middle East entered and left Britain every day. This group might have been lying in wait for months or even years; they might be residents or British citizens. Police began making inquiries at hotels and nearby boardinghouses, and within London's Iranian and Arab communities. Taxi and minicab drivers were asked to contact police if they had dropped any Middle Eastern men near the embassy on Wednesday morning. MI5's informants in the Iranian exile community were squeezed for any rumors that might be circulating about the gunmen, their backgrounds, and their goals. As the news spread, unhelpful and sometimes racist members of the public began calling in with reports of swarthy men "acting suspiciously." Every lead was followed up.

Clifford Jacques, an Essex-based architect who refurbished the embassy building in 1978, provided Dellow with a complete floor plan. The construction and layout were almost identical to the Ethiopian Embassy next door. The intel cell next traced the company that had installed the new central heating, the district surveyor, and, finally, the embassy caretaker. He described in detail every inch of the interiors, from the stately reception rooms to broom cupboards, from skylights and bathrooms to doorways and windows, and even the position of larger items of furniture such as the conference table and the grand piano. He confirmed that the ground-floor and first-floor front windows had recently been replaced with armor-plated glass, and a secondary steel security door installed behind the front door. The ambassador's offices on the first floor had also been fitted with reinforced walls and steel doors to form a secure redoubt inside the building in case of attack. The Iranians had followed SAS security advice to the letter: the building was virtually impregnable from the ground. By chance, the Group of the Martyr was holed up inside one of the most defensible buildings in London, a cross between a warren and a fortress.

While the caretaker described the interior, dozens of unseen eyes watched the exterior of the embassy. Police photographers with telescopic lenses trained their cameras on the building, while the snipers kept watch through high-powered rifle sights. Every figure appearing at a window, however fleetingly, was greeted with a silent volley of camera shutters. The incident already had its own printed stationery, a questionnaire headed IRANIAN EMBASSY SIEGE SIGHTING REPORT. This form, "to be completed by any officer sighting an occupant of the embassy," asked for such details as "hostage or terrorist," "height," "build," "facial features," "complexion," "facial hair," and so on. "When completed, hand in to C13 control."

Within hours, the police technicians of C7 had set up closed-circuit television cameras with remote-controlled zoom and focus, covering the front and rear of the embassy, the park, and the adjacent buildings. Live images were fed to the screens inside the control center. Before dawn, an additional camera was installed behind a poster on the brick wall facing the embassy. High-powered aerials were spotted on the embassy roof, from which "it was assumed that radio communication existed with Tehran." The wires were cut, along with TV cables and "any other form of wiring associated with communication." Compared with the vast array of digital surveillance measures available today, the technology of 1980 appears basic, but by the standards of the time it was on the cutting edge. Some of it was useless. The newest gizmo was a laser-based listening device that could hear through glass windows. The gunmen had unintentionally nullified this in the first hours, simply by drawing the curtains.

Observing and recording outside the embassy was only half of C7's brief.

In theory, "sound stethoscopes" could be inserted into the party walls to eavesdrop on the gunmen and hostages. This first required drilling a hole three millimeters in diameter. When the tip of the drill was less than one centimeter from breaking through on the other side, a drill bit just one millimeter wide was used. The resulting hole was the size of a pinhead. Into this was inserted a tiny microphone, like a surgeon's endoscope, held in place with a dollop of glue to reduce ambient noise in the listeners' room. The probes could pick up some sounds even without fully penetrating a wall.

Dellow studied the plans and concluded that "the stronghold presented a very tough and complex target." The walls were twenty-two inches thick on one side and fifteen inches on the other, constructed of granite and dense Victorian brick. He knew that power tools were out of the question since the sound would be heard inside the embassy. The best place to insert an audio probe was behind a power socket, where it could not be seen, leaving only a few millimeters of plastic between the microphone on the tip of the probe and the room. But precisely locating a socket on the opposite side of a wall was partly guesswork, with the added danger that the drill could hit an electric wire. Drilling a tiny, straight hole through almost two feet of solid wall was a protracted, painstaking, nerve-shredding business, and, even done slowly and by hand, quite noisy.

Police technicians moved into the Ethiopian Embassy at Number 17 and began drilling exploratory holes using a hand-cranked, slow-revolution surgical drill with a muffled bit. On the second-floor landing, engineers started carefully chiseling out the bricks: a thinner wall would be easier to insert an audio probe into. Dellow needed to hear and, if possible, to see what was happening inside the Iranian Embassy but without alerting the gunmen to what was happening. The holes might be tiny, but so was Dellow's margin for error.

Although the police were proficient at eavesdropping, the spies were even better.

In his 1987 book, *Spycatcher,* the renegade MI5 officer Peter Wright revealed how the Security Service "bugged and burgled its way across London at the state's behest." MI5's "A" Branch was responsible for covert surveillance, telephone tapping, secret photography, and the illicit copying of documents; subsection "A1A" handled technical operations, such as covert entry, planting bugs, and audio and video surveillance; and "A2A" dealt with recording, transcription, and translation. MI5 routinely listened in on the conversations of communists, IRA terrorists, Islamic extremists, and other "subversives." The Security Service also targeted foreign embassies, to overhear what was being said by the state's enemies and, sometimes, its friends.

MI5 arrived at the Iranian Embassy discreetly but in force. Eventually some thirty-five officers were deployed by the Security Service to support the Metropolitan Police, along with another sixteen from other branches of the intelligence community. They appeared in plain clothes and unmarked cars, and quietly slipped into Number 24. The authorized history of MI5 records that it "played a vital part" in the siege by positioning "a variety of ingenious eavesdropping devices." Security Service technicians lowered microphones down the chimneys, positioned long-distance sound-interception apparatus, and began drilling a swarm of bugs into the walls on both sides.

Some MI5 bugs had been in place before the siege began: the shah was an ally but a fickle one; his Islamic successors were viewed with suspicion by the British authorities; MI5 had been listening in to embassy telephone conversations for years, most importantly through the spies' independent line in the telex room.

In 1970, MI5 employed just one Arabic linguist. A decade later, with the growth of Middle Eastern–sponsored terrorism and the influx of Arabic-speaking exiles, it could call on half a dozen Arabic translators, as well as several Farsi speakers. These were now placed on an around-the-clock rotation, with instructions to "take down every word" overheard in those languages. According to MI5's official history, "it was preferable for a small number of linguists to build up a detailed mental picture of the gunmen and their hostages, their attitudes and actions, rather than a large number of linguists being deployed with a resulting loss of continuity." Every word earwigged by MI5 would be recorded, translated if necessary, collated, typed up in an intelligence briefing, and then passed up the chain of command, all without any indication of its source.

Intelligence operates on a need-to-know basis. The SAS did not know that MI5 (or Box 500, as it was known, after its post office box number) had arrived on the scene; the police technicians of C7 were only dimly aware of what the spies were up to; the press knew nothing of this bugging operation; and the occupants of the building had no inkling that they might be overheard.

The only person with a need to know all of this was the chief of Zulu Control.

John Dellow, crisp in his uniform, sat in his office on the third floor of the Montessori nursery school with a soldier on one side and a civil servant on the other. Dellow of Scotland Yard, Lieutenant Colonel Michael Rose of the SAS, and Hayden Phillips, assistant secretary at the

Home Office, represented the operational core of the command center. "This was solely a police operation, supported by the Home Office and the army," said Rose. "John Dellow was the boss." Phillips's role was to pass on all pertinent information to the Home Secretary, and relay back decisions from the Cobra committee: a secure telephone and fax machine connected Zulu Control directly to the cabinet committee room for this purpose. Rose was on hand to prepare for the possibility that, if negotiations failed, the military would have to be sent in. The three men knew each other well, having rehearsed for precisely this situation during counterterrorism exercises. But none had ever faced a real situation of this magnitude.

THE COBRA COMMITTEE reassembled early to hear what the intelligence experts had gathered overnight, which was not much.

MI6 did not have a single officer stationed in Iran, or any clear idea of the situation in Khuzestan. Since the Islamic Revolution, its sources inside the country had virtually dried up, and the few that remained were focused on the American Embassy siege, not some obscure ethnic conflict in the southwest of the country. Nonetheless, both MI6 and the Foreign Office swiftly concluded that Saddam Hussein had to be behind the attack. Iraq openly supported the armed Arab liberation movement, and the Mukhabarat had a history of exporting violence to the UK. The weapons used to kill General Abdul Razzaq al-Naif in 1978 were smuggled into Britain by Iraqi intelligence agents under diplomatic cover. The same method, MI5 surmised, had probably been used to arm the gunmen inside the Iranian Embassy. "We assumed the Iraqis were behind it from the start," said David Tatham, assistant head of the Middle East Department at the Foreign Office, who attended the Cobra meetings. "We had a pretty scratchy relationship with the Iraqis. Their secret service operated in London, and they were an able bunch." The gunmen were Iranian Arabs, but the people behind the plot, with the money and motive to stage a terrorist spectacular on British soil, were Saddam Hussein's thugs and their Palestinian allies. War between Iran and Iraq was looming, and the opening battle was being fought inside 16 Princes Gate.

Mrs. Thatcher's position had been relayed by Willie Whitelaw to

David McNee, the Metropolitan Police commissioner, in the clearest possible terms: police could negotiate for as long as necessary to obtain a peaceful solution, but the gunmen would not be permitted to leave the country, even if they surrendered and released the hostages. "I could not have asked for a more clear-cut response," McNee wrote.

Thatcher raised two key questions: What action by the gunmen should be considered grounds for an immediate military assault on the building? And, in that eventuality, what were the chances of success? Dellow sent back a swift answer: "Should there be good evidence that two or more hostages have been murdered [those] circumstances would dictate military intervention. One death still leaves room for a relatively peaceful solution. Two, however, would suggest the commencement of a pattern." This red line was drawn and agreed on within twenty-four hours of the initial attack, and never shifted.

Phillips passed a message back from Cobra to Dellow:

If a need to commit military in immediate action, if there is time COBR would like to be informed, so that the Home Secretary can consider the matter. However, if no time to contact COBR and lives are being or about to be lost and the commitment of the military teams is likely to save some of the lives then the decision rests with the police officer commanding the operation and he may in those circumstances commit the military.

Whether such an assault would succeed was a different matter. Rose's assessment was grim: a 40 percent likelihood that the situation would end like the Munich standoff, with the deaths of most of the terrorists and every hostage. De la Billière passed on that sobering assessment, and Phillips immediately relayed the prime minister's response: "If things went horribly wrong, then she would take the blame, not the soldiers or policemen."

The second Cobra gathering was a more efficient and focused affair than the first but also more alarming. The officials left with the clear impression that an armed assault was becoming more likely, and with it would come the possibility of disaster.

After a night in the relative comfort of Regent's Park Barracks, Blue Team joined Red Team in the Doctors' House. Reinforced by other members of B Squadron and additional snipers from other squadrons, the assault team now numbered more than sixty men. If the hostage-takers killed once, they would all be placed on high alert; if the gunmen killed twice, Thatcher would unleash the SAS.

7

CRAMER'S GAMBIT

"We shall have some breakfast soon," Towfiq announced cheerily, at 08:30. "What would you like?"

Again, the BBC sound recordist Sim Harris was struck by this man's sudden mood swings, taking "orders for breakfast" with a machine gun in his hand.

Roya Kaghachi piped up: "I am happy to go out to the takeaway to fetch some fresh warm baguettes."

Towfiq grinned. "See what you can find downstairs." A few minutes later Roya returned with bread, jam, carrots, hard-boiled eggs, biscuits, and a handful of oranges. "This is all that is left." She broke off a very small piece of pita and handed it to the Iranian who had irritated Chris Cramer by hogging more than his share of food the previous evening. "Here you are, you can have this piece of bread only today."

Trevor Lock ate nothing. Ron Morris made tea and handed it around on a tray, in strict order of precedence: women first, then the chargé and other diplomats by seniority, then the British and other non-Iranians, and finally the staff, ending with the doorman Abbas Fallahi. Morris had taken off his tie to sleep, but now it was back on again. "There are plenty more biscuits and lots of tea," he said. "I always buy in bulk."

Harris was taking notes in a blue reporter's notebook. In a journalistic reflex, he needed to keep a record, though he might not survive the day. "I knew this was an important story and I wanted to remember the details." Wiry, wily, and resourceful, Harris had survived numerous foreign scrapes. At a street demonstration in Tehran the previous year, the man standing next to him had been shot dead. On assignment in the Congo, he had seen two French foreign legionnaires killed. Harris would never have described himself as brave, but he possessed an almost animal instinct for self-preservation. Like many experienced war reporters, he had developed a worldly, almost cynical carapace: the world was full of stupid and dangerous people; his job was to get in, record what was happening, and get home in one piece to his wife, Helen, and their two children. He intended to leave the embassy alive, and he would bring the story out with him.

Harris noted how differently the gunmen treated the diplomatic officials: "At each turn of guard duty, they shuffle the Iranian hostages around, just to be awkward and assert themselves."

At 08:45, young Fowzi took over as jailer. The injured Afrouz was lying under several layers of coats near the window. Shivering and groggy, he shuffled across the carpet toward the radiator, which had now come on.

Fowzi gestured with his gun, thinking he might be about to open the curtain. "Hey, you," he barked in Farsi. "Go back to your corner."

Afrouz did not move.

"Quickly! Quickly!" shouted Fowzi.

The chargé might be injured, but his dignity was intact. Who was this child to order him about?

"Why are you talking to me like that?" he snapped. "Show some respect."

"Go back to your place, I am telling you," Fowzi said, the color rising in his face.

"Why? If I don't listen to you, would you kill me?" Afrouz was shouting now. "If you want to kill me, here I am . . . kill me!" Afrouz tore open his shirt to bare his chest. "I am the senior official here, and everyone else is an innocent victim. Kill me and let all the hostages go!"

Fowzi raised his pistol and, in a gesture that struck Harris as "re-hearsed," fired a single shot into the ceiling.

Everyone recoiled, several of the women screamed, and Afrouz scrambled across the room, helped by two of the other Iranians. Flakes of paint floated down from the bullet hole in the ceiling. They were not firing blanks.

Towfiq dashed in, gun raised.

"Don't worry, this dog needed to be taught a lesson," said Fowzi doubtfully, taken aback by what he had done.

"*Khoush, khoush* . . . Okay, okay, everyone quieten down," said Towfiq. He turned to the Iranians, huddled in one corner. "Listen, we are not here to kill anybody, but if we have to, we will not hesitate. Listen to our orders and don't argue with my comrades. If you have something to say, talk to me. Is that clear? We Iranian Arabs have suffered enough at your hands back home and we will not accept that over here."

From where he lay on the floor, Cramer surreptitiously scooped up the empty shell casing, still warm, and put it in his pocket.

Pretending to be ill can make anyone feel very sick, and Cramer was now exhibiting symptoms of a major dysenteric attack. He was doubled up, groaning, his legs shooting out repeatedly as if in spasm, his face drenched in sweat.

"Get me a doctor," he begged. "I can't stand the pain."

Towfiq eyed him, indecisive. "I've asked them to send in a doctor, but they won't," he said. "What drugs do you need?"

With trembling hand, Cramer scrawled "Lomotil" on a scrap of paper, the brand name of a diarrhea medication, and handed it up to his captor.

Karkouti overheard three of the gunmen discussing Cramer in Arabic.

"Will he die?" asked Fowzi.

"No, I don't think so," Jassim replied. "He may be making this pain up."

Abbas chimed in: "I think it is genuine. He looks really bad."

When Towfiq returned a few minutes later, he was shaking with fury, holding up a large poster torn from the wall of the press office. An Iranian tourism advertisement, it consisted of rows of photographs, twenty-four in all, depicting the country's various ethnic groups in colorful costumes, including Persian, Baluchi, Kurdish, Azeri, Turkman, Qashqai, Assyrian, Armenian Circassian, Gilaki, Mazandarani, Luri, and Mandaean.

"Read it aloud," said Towfiq, shoving the poster into the hands of Abbas Lavasani, the young Revolutionary Guard deputy press attaché. "I want everyone to hear."

Lavasani read out the Farsi text: typical government propaganda extolling Iran's multiethnic harmony. Towfiq spat out a simultaneous English translation.

"There's one large group missing," he said furiously. "We are not even mentioned. The Iranian government manage to ignore four and a half million Arabs. Now do you realize why we are here?"

WHILE THE POLICE tried to assess what was happening within the embassy, the situation outside it was becoming volatile with the arrival, in growing numbers, of two distinct groups, both equally unpredictable and hard to control: protesters and the press.

The drama at Princes Gate was suddenly the most important news story in the world. The media began arriving at first light and continued to pour into the Pressville enclosure throughout the day. They came from every corner of the capital, the country, and the globe. The American news network ABC dispatched staff from New York, Frankfurt, Beirut, Cairo, and Johannesburg. Half of all BBC news reporters were deployed to cover the siege. The journalists brought deck chairs and sandwiches, radio cars, and television vans loaded with equipment. Above all they brought questions, most of which the authorities could not or would not answer. As the press horde swelled, so did the police force needed to corral them. Whenever a police spokesman appeared at the enclosure with some small tidbit of information, he was mobbed. In midafternoon, the police chief, David McNee, took the rare step of asking the media to muzzle itself: "The Commissioner seeks your cooperation in refraining from publishing or broadcasting details of the deployment of personnel in the immediate vicinity of the embassy or the use of specialist equipment. Such information can provide valuable intelligence to the hostage-takers and seriously jeopardize the safety of the hostages and the success of the operation."

The police demanded to be allowed to do their jobs unimpeded by the media, and vice versa. This tension between journalistic inquiry and police control was never resolved; in a democracy with a free press, it never is. The police feared the gunmen might be listening to the radio or watching television, and accurate reporting could reveal their tactics, the position of snipers, the strength of the cordon, and other useful information. The press believed, equally correctly, that the public had a right to know what was happening, and they were prepared to go to extraordinary lengths to find out. Donna Leigh, an enterprising twenty-one-year-old reporter with the *Evening Standard*, befriended an elderly woman in one of the flats overlooking the rear of the embassy, and moved in for the duration. Radio stations called up local residents and requested eyewitness reports. Concerned that vital information might get out, the police prepared to cut off every telephone in Kingston House. Rebecca West would not have stood for that.

The scene was now set for the subplot, a seesawing tussle between an inquisitive press pack and the paranoid police, in which as much energy was expended on keeping the journalists out as keeping the terrorists in.

The police spokesman, Director of Information Peter Neivens, revealed little, but there was still plenty to report as hundreds of protesters converged on the site in rival demonstrations that threatened to degenerate into a comic mass brawl.

By midmorning, some three hundred Khomeini supporters, mostly earnest-looking Iranian students carrying placards, had assembled and were funneled into an enclosure inside the park surrounded by metal police barriers. "Death to President Carter," they chanted. Like everyone else, they linked this embassy siege to the other one: "Hands off the U.S. Embassy." A woman demonstrator wore a smock emblazoned with the words WE GIVE OUR LAST DROP OF BLOOD FOR KHOMEINI.

A rival group composed of British students, holidaymakers, and others with time on their hands formed an ad hoc choir and sang "Land of Hope and Glory" and "God Save the Queen." A cheery drunk sidled up behind the Iranians and performed what he appeared to think was an Iranian dance. A group of music students wheeled in a piano and began an impromptu concert. A man in a blue suit with a megaphone shouted, "Hands off the embassy!"—though it was never clear which embassy he was referring to. Some American students, under the impression that their fellow countrymen were being held hostage in Princes Gate, formed a separate group and chanted, "Free the Americans!" One man held up a banner simply reading ARSENAL FOR THE CUP. An elderly local resident was arrested after she belabored an Iranian student over the head with her walking stick. Richard Douglas of Albert Hall Mansions, Labor MP for Dunfermline, complained about the noise and threatened to raise a "question in the House" if the police were not removed.

A troop of skinheads arrived, intent on goading the Iranians into a fight. "There were ten ayatollahs hanging on a wall," they sang, while pelting the Iranian crowd with cabbage leaves and soft-drink cans. "And if one ayatollah should accidentally fall . . ." Hostilities paused briefly as a group of saffron-robed Buddhist monks passed through the crowd, intoning prayers and beating drums. Then the skinheads resumed with a tuneless chant: "Iranians are barmy, send in the army . . ."

Matters turned uglier when a radio station erroneously reported that the British Embassy in Tehran had been overrun by fundamentalists. In fact, it had been surrounded by Revolutionary Guard troops to prevent its seizure, the Iranian government having concluded that a second embassy siege in Tehran would play into the hands of "the Iraqi Ba'athists and America." When this fake news reached the demonstration enclosure, the pro-Khomeini protesters sent up a loud cheer, and mocked the skinheads. Fights broke out. Police tried to intervene. PC Michael Perkin of Paddington was hurled to the ground in the fracas, fracturing his leg. At 09:21, an Iranian carrying a Molotov cocktail was arrested outside the Royal Albert Hall.

To try to reduce the numbers, anyone leaving the demonstration area was prevented from returning. Deprived of food, the protesters claimed they were being "starved by police." An hour and a half before the midday deadline, Dellow received a troubling MI5 warning "to the effect that fifty young Iranians were going to acquire lorries, drive through the police cordons, assault the embassy and release the hostages." Dellow assessed the danger as remote, but he ordered up two sets of caltrops, road spikes to puncture the tires of any oncoming vehicles. These were laid across Kensington Road at either end of Princes Gate.

Finally, the Iranian consul general was persuaded to appear at the scene and ask the Iranians to disperse. "We have been asked by our government to leave," a spokesman for the protesters said. "That is the only reason we have agreed to go, not because of police requests. We want our brothers in the embassy to be free."

By the end of the day, ten people had been arrested: three Iranians, five skinheads, a seventy-five-year-old woman charged with breach of the peace, and a hapless Japanese tourist who had come to see what all the shouting was about. Adrian Street from Beckenham was fined seventy-five pounds for chanting "If you hate the ayatollah clap your hands" and telling the Iranians to go home "in very broad language." He took the opportunity to make a point about comparative legal systems, telling *The Sun:* "In Iran we'd probably have our hands chopped off."

The international implications were coming into focus. Britain might be considering the imposition of sanctions on Iran in solidarity with the United States, but the siege called for a different tone. Immediately after the Cobra meeting, Thatcher sent a formal diplomatic cable to Iran's new president, Abolhassan Banisadr, stressing her "deep personal concern about the situation at the Iranian Embassy in London" and declaring that "this intrusion constitutes an act of terrorism and an infringement of the immunity of diplomatic staff which the British government is acting firmly to counter." Banisadr responded with some inflamed bombast, declaring as part of his May Day speech: "We are ready to accept the martyrdom of our children in England, but we will not give in to blackmail." Sadegh Ghotbzadeh announced that the Iranian hostages were eager to embrace martyrdom. "Anyone who dies for Islam believes he goes directly to heaven," said Iran's foreign minister. "I am sure our people prefer to die for the Revolution than see the Islamic government concede." Told that the terrorists were threatening to blow up the embassy, he offered a two-word response: "Let them."

Admiral Ahmad Madani, the governor of Khuzestan and the butcher of Black Wednesday, added his voice to the chorus: "There is no possibility of [Arabs] getting independence or autonomy. What they are trying to do is damage the Revolution and in this, they are encouraged from abroad by the enemies of Iran."

Back in Tehran, Afrouz's wife was quoted as saying she was "ready to accept her husband's martyrdom"—an act of wifely devotion he could probably have done without.

The secretary-general of the United Nations, Kurt Waldheim, condemned the occupation of the embassy and called for restraint, as usual in every conflict. Predictably enough, since this was an Iran–Iraq battle by proxy, the press in Iran and Iraq took diametrically opposed views of the siege. The Iranian media condemned the "mercenaries" of Iraq's "traitorous Ba'athist regime." The Iraqi press hailed the Arab heroes delivering a "knockout blow to the Persian racists."

From the point of view of Saddam Hussein and his spies, everything was going according to plan.

TODAY THE SAS is a household name in Britain, a brand, a byword for military prowess, a legend, and, in part, a myth. In 1980, it was still an obscure cog in the military machine that attracted attention only when it malfunctioned.

The regiment was born in the North African desert in 1941, when an eccentric young officer named David Stirling came up with a plan to parachute small, agile, highly trained units behind the battle lines to attack Axis airfields strung out along the coast of Libya. The regiment was designated the Special Air Service, even though it soon swapped parachutes for Jeeps adapted to cross hundreds of miles of sand. The unit racked up some spectacular successes, destroying hundreds of stationary enemy aircraft by infiltrating the airfields at night, planting time bombs on the wings, and then escaping back into the desert. The regiment adopted the motto: "Who dares, wins." The stakes were high, and life expectancy low. Men volunteering for this kind of warfare needed to be resourceful, tough, fit, and extremely brave. Many were touched by a kind of martial madness, a willingness to take risks others regarded as insane. Some were borderline psychotic. "The boy Stirling is mad, quite, quite mad," observed General Bernard Law Montgomery. "However, in a war there is often a place for mad people." The unit expanded rapidly and fought behind the lines in Italy, France, and elsewhere, sabotaging fuel dumps, bridges, and railways; ambushing convoys; identifying air targets; and coordinating local resistance. In 1945, it was disbanded, only to be re-formed two years later.

The role of the SAS in the postwar, postcolonial world was more complex, more controversial, and even more secretive. Recruited across the armed forces, SAS troops saw action quelling insurgencies in Malaya, Borneo, Oman, Aden, and Dhofar, a region of southern Oman. It provided bodyguard training for foreign heads of state friendly to Britain. The SAS became exceptionally good at fighting rebels but developed a parallel reputation for propping up unsavory, undemocratic regimes as the British Empire dissolved. In 1976, the government ordered an SAS squadron to deploy to Northern Ireland in order to combat IRA terrorism. Elite shock troops in a brutal undercover war, the SAS was depicted in Republican propaganda as a hit squad, unaccountable assassins trained to shoot first and ask questions afterward (if at all). British governments have consistently denied that the SAS pursued a shoot-to-kill policy against IRA terrorists, insisting "like everyone else, the security forces must obey the law."

SAS tactics in its many theaters of operation followed a broadly similar pattern: small units deployed to infiltrate an area under the control of insurgents, guerrillas, or terrorist groups; gather intelligence; liaise with resistance forces; conduct sabotage, assassination, and ambush operations; and then slip away, unidentified and unseen. SAS recruits were trained in surveillance, close-quarters combat, explosives, high-speed driving, marksmanship, and urban warfare. Selection was (and is) famously demanding. In the final test of physical stamina, potential recruits were expected to traverse forty miles of unfamiliar mountain terrain carrying a fifty-five-pound pack and a weapon. Two months before the siege, an SAS candidate died of exposure in the Welsh hills, the third to perish there in thirteen months.

Like Stirling's "originals," SAS troopers were often resilient and intelligent, but, according to a Royal Army Medical Corps analysis, they also tended to be more introverted than other soldiers, and occasionally

ill-disciplined, exhibiting "expediency, shyness, seriousness, forthright-
ness, self-sufficiency and high anxiety." The officers were known as "Ru-
perts," mostly a term of endearment, and usually addressed as "Boss."
David Stirling's was a unit "classless but not rankless," highly disciplined and strangely informal, intense in its camaraderie but volatile.

Deployed correctly, the SAS was a highly effective weapon; misused,
it could blow up in your face.

The history, training, and qualities of the SAS uniquely suited the
regiment to the job it took on in 1973 following the massacre at the
Munich Olympic Games, as it was the force specifically tasked with
rescuing hostages in terrorist situations: a capability code-named Operation Pagoda. Democratic governments are rightly wary of deploying soldiers in civilian circumstances, but the mounting terrorist threat
in mainland Britain called for special measures. Military Aid to the
Civil Power was defined as "the provision of military assistance to the
Civil Power (the government) in the maintenance of law, order and
public safety using specialist capabilities or equipment, in situations beyond the capability of the Civil Power. Such assistance may be armed,
if necessary." The SAS had a specific constitutional role, to intervene
with force if ordinary policing could not cope. Like most SAS activities,
this function was unpublicized, largely unknown to the general public,
and shrouded in secrecy.

For six months in every twenty-four, one of the four SAS squadrons
was designated the Special Projects team, on standby at Hereford in
case of a major terrorist incident. For seven years the SAS had trained
for every conceivable constellation of targets, people, obstacles, and circumstances, shooting cardboard enemies and saving dummy hostages.
They prepared to fight large groups and small, theoretical terrorists
armed with guns and explosives, in the Killing House but also in airports, government buildings, and nuclear sites, on trains, planes, and
buses. An SAS team was deployed to a hijacking at Stansted in 1975,
but the gunman surrendered before it was required. The regiment offered advice during a train hijacking in Holland in 1977 and hovered in
the wings during the Balcombe Street siege. But no government had
yet invoked Military Aid to the Civil Power in a hostage situation, and
every government hoped it would never have to.

When the skinheads chanted "Iranians are barmy, send in the army," they were invoking a genuine contingency under British law.

By 1980, the SAS had come to occupy an anomalous, and precarious, position in British life, admired and distrusted, notorious in some quarters but unknown in most. Within the army, the special forces formed an elite, the summit of ambition for many young soldiers. Regular soldiers envied the SAS and resented its swagger. Politicians increasingly turned to the regiment in the savage war against the IRA. But the media and critics were circling, accusing the SAS of fighting dirty in Northern Ireland, a shadowy and mysterious force veiled in secrecy, expensive and invisible. There were rumors that the regiment might be attached to, or absorbed by, one of the larger regiments, or even disbanded.

But the controversy that eddied around the regiment was not at the forefront of British life.

Most people had never heard of the SAS.

AT 11:00, an hour before the deadline, Fred Luff approached the embassy carrying a long pole with a tin box taped firmly to one end. He poked it up to the ground-floor window. A hand reached through the curtain and grabbed the contents: a packet of Lomotil in a brown envelope with "On Her Majesty's Service" stamped on it, and a green telephone.

Towfiq had agreed to accept a direct telephone link but only as a short-term measure while Luff supposedly worked on getting the embassy phone lines reconnected. The police, of course, had no intention of restoring the landlines: the green telephone was a tool of control.

A field telephone, often used by the military to establish direct contact between units, ran on batteries with a dedicated open line, operating independently of a switchboard. Instead of a rotary dial, it had two illuminated buttons on top: a red one, which sounded a buzzer inside the police negotiators' room, and a black one, which was pressed to speak and remained lit as long as the receiver was off the hook. A gray flex cable ran out of the waiting-room window, down the street, then up to the top floor of the Montessori nursery school at Number 24. It was also connected to a speaker in Zulu Control, on the desk of John Dellow. When the negotiators and hostage-takers spoke, the command center would be listening in.

Police now controlled the means of communication. If the gunmen wanted to contact the outside world (and, for this group, that was clearly a priority) they would henceforth have to go through the negotiators. But the field telephone was also an approximate measurement device. The gray telephone line was 172 feet long: at full stretch, police calculated, it would reach no farther than the main hallway. If a gunman was speaking on the phone, he had to be on the ground floor. This information could be vital in the event of a military assault.

Towfiq was suspicious. The telephone might be a ruse to lure them to the front of the building, where they could be shot. He placed it out of sight on top of the radiator in the waiting-room toilet and took the Lomotil upstairs.

Cramer was now writhing on the carpet, his face contorted, clawing at his stomach, unable to sit up. Harris pushed a couple of Lomotil tablets into his mouth and tried to get him to drink some water to wash them down. Cramer retched.

"We need a doctor," Harris said. "Let me try and talk to the police. I'm British and I can try and plead with them and explain the situation."

Dubiously, Towfiq agreed.

It was the first time Harris had left the hostage room in twenty-four hours. Curtains had been torn down and placed across the main doorway, and chairs and tables stacked against the windows. The gunmen were expecting an assault from the ground as well as the roof.

Towfiq, who had retrieved the field telephone, thrust it into Harris's hand and told him to press the red button.

A voice answered instantly. "Hello, Salim . . ."

Harris pressed the black button to activate the mouthpiece on the handset. "No, it's Sim Harris from the BBC. I want to talk to you about the condition of my colleague Chris Cramer."

"Yes, Mr. Harris. Salim has asked us to get a doctor and this has been referred upstairs; we will let you have an answer just as soon as we can."

The voice was "very quietly spoken and balanced sounding, and very controlled." It belonged to Ray Tucker, one of the police negotiators, a Special Branch officer with specialist knowledge of Arab affairs.

"Please don't worry," said Tucker. "Please be assured that the only thing we want is to get you all out of there. Is anyone else listening to this conversation?"

"Yes, there is."

Towfiq had leaned in to hear what was being said.

"Chris is very ill," said Harris. "He's having convulsions, terrible stomach pains. He may have a heart attack."

"What are the symptoms?"

"He is sweating, and his heart is beating very fast."

"Please be patient; it's being dealt with at the highest level—"

Towfiq replaced the handset. The black light on the telephone went out.

Cramer was lying still now, deathly pale. Shaye leaned over him, trying to pour a glass of milk into his mouth. It dribbled down his chin onto the floor. Karkouti, in tears, knelt beside him. "It's going to be okay," he repeated. "Hang on. Hang on."

Cramer opened his eyes.

"Don't worry, mate," Harris told him. "They're trying to get a doctor. I've spoken to the police and they're doing what they can."

"Fuck the police," groaned Cramer. "They better be quick."

Cramer's worsening condition prompted a debate within Zulu Control. Why not, someone suggested, tell the hostage-takers that Cramer's illness could be contagious? If they could introduce "something into food sent into the stronghold that would exacerbate the symptoms without serious risk to health," the gunmen might believe they were facing an infectious epidemic, and surrender. Dellow rejected this idea on the grounds that "panic might be generated within the stronghold, especially among the hostages, which terrorists would be obliged to deal with by violence." Secretly poisoning the hostages also conflicted with his sense of fair play.

But the layers of deception were accreting. Cramer was pretending to be violently ill, deceiving his fellow hostages as well as their captors. The police were pretending they might reconnect the telephones and giving the impression that they were genuinely searching for a willing doctor. Karkouti was pretending to help Towfiq, while hoping to manipulate him. The leading gunman might or might not be lying about the bombs he had threatened to detonate in a few minutes' time.

Even the police deliberately kept some of their colleagues in the dark. Under established protocol, the negotiating cell was cocooned from the rest of the operation, told only what they needed to know to mediate, and no more. This ensured that those in direct contact with the gunmen could not accidentally reveal information through a slip of the tongue, an unguarded reaction, or a tone of voice. If a negotiator accidently divulged that he knew what was being said inside the building, for instance, that would instantly alert the hostage-takers to the eavesdropping: at best they would clam up; at worst it could trigger disaster. The negotiators did not know that the building was being bugged, or that a heavily armed force had already assembled next door, ready to attack. Luff repeatedly reassured Towfiq that his demands were being considered, the authorities were listening, and no assault was planned. This was all untrue. But since Luff did not know it was false, he was not, technically speaking, lying.

Towfiq ordered Harris, Morris, and Karkouti to carry Cramer downstairs. If a doctor came to tend to him, he did not want this happening in the hostage room. Moving Cramer was a challenge. He weighed 196 pounds, and his body was convulsing violently. His glasses fell off and clattered down the stairwell. Finally, they managed to maneuver the bulky BBC man down the stairs and into the ground-floor library of the commercial section at the back of the building, where the gunmen had laid out a mattress and a blue blanket brought up from the caretaker's basement flat.

Harris placed the blanket over the groaning Cramer, whose shirt was soaked with sweat, saliva trickling from the corners of his mouth. Harris turned to Towfiq: "He doesn't need a doctor anymore," he said. "He needs an ambulance. Look, he's going to die, he's going to have a heart attack. Please let me speak to the police again—"

The same voice answered the green telephone. "Hello, Salim?"

"No, it's Sim Harris again. Chris is getting worse. Please get a doctor."

"It's very difficult," Tucker calmly stalled. "We have to find a doctor who is prepared to come in. The men in there are heavily armed. Mr. Cramer obviously needs hospital treatment. Can't you persuade them to let him go?"

Towfiq hissed: "They don't want to send in a doctor. They don't care if he dies . . . I think they are tricking us."

Tucker was soothing. "I can assure you, Mr. Harris, there will be no tricks. I will come in the ambulance myself. We will just come and get Mr. Cramer."

Back in the library, a strange tableau greeted them. Shaye was leaning over the prostrate Cramer, gently massaging his chest, tears running down his face. The gunman was speaking in Arabic: "I'm sorry, Mr. Chris, we didn't mean to hurt you." Shaye had found Cramer's glasses and returned them to him.

Towfiq and Jassim huddled in heated consultation. Then the leader turned to the others, his expression a mixture of confusion, irritation, and anxiety. "Okay, we release him."

"Bravo," said Karkouti in Arabic. "You are a wise man."

"Fab," said Ron Morris.

Towfiq continued: "Mr. Chris must promise not to tell the police anything. Get him to promise. You will be put in a separate room. If anything goes wrong, we will kill you."

Harris knelt by Cramer's head.

"Look, mate, you're not to tell the police anything. If you do, you'll put all our lives at risk."

Cramer seemed to understand.

"Okay, I promise," he moaned.

Jassim told Harris, Morris, and Lock to kneel in a row facing the curtained window of the general office, with hands on their heads. Behind him, Harris heard "the very distinct sound of a gun being cocked." Glancing to his left, he saw the sweat pouring down Lock's face.

Towfiq opened the front door and peered through the crack. "You walk straight ahead," he muttered to Cramer, who stood, swaying, against the doorway. "You turn right or left, I kill you."

At 11:22, Cramer staggered onto the pavement. Moments later, he was in the back of an ambulance, with Ray Tucker and two anti-terrorist police beside him. He batted away the oxygen mask proffered by the nurse.

"I'm not as ill as they think I am." And then, in a rush, "You mustn't storm the building. There are six gunmen in there with machine guns and hand grenades. PC Lock still has his gun."

On the second floor of the Iranian Embassy, Harris heard the front door slam and the sound of a vehicle pulling away. He let out a slow, quivering breath, and looked over to Ron, kneeling beside him. "Christ, that was the nearest I've come to kissing death in the face."

8

TWENTY-FIVE
HAMBURGERS

Chris Cramer lay on a bed in a private room of the isolation wing in St. Stephen's Hospital, Chelsea, as two police detectives peppered him with questions. The clock on the wall read 11:55. "Oh, God," he said, out loud. "Only five minutes to go."

The consultant's diagnosis was that there was nothing physically wrong with the released hostage, save exhaustion and shattered nerves. The nurse gave him a cigarette. Cramer burst into tears. "Let it out," the doctor said.

The police had no time for sympathy. How many gunmen? What weapons? Did you see explosives? Which rooms were you held in? Were you split into groups? Did the gunmen seem nervous? Describe each one, as accurately as possible. How many hostages can you put names to? How many women?

At first, recalling his promise not to reveal anything to the police, Cramer's replies were hesitant. He explained that the lead gunman was listening to the radio news. "If they find out I've spoken to you, they'll kill Sim and the others—"

The detective brushed that away. "You've got to tell us everything; otherwise the hostages might die anyway."

Cramer reached into his coat pocket and handed over the spent bullet casing.

"Where did you get this?"

"From the guy who fired it above our heads this morning. I picked it up from the carpet."

Smiling, the policeman placed the empty 9mm casing in a plastic bag, the first forensic evidence from the scene, and labeled it.

The questioning resumed.

How dangerous do the gunmen seem? What clothes are they wearing? Who is the leader? Will they go through with their threats?

"It's only a giant publicity stunt," said Cramer. "I don't believe they will ever kill anyone." But then he added: "Salim is the leader and you must be careful of him. He knows what he's doing."

Cramer badly needed a drink.

Are you sure they had hand grenades? Are you certain Trevor still has his gun?

"Take your time," they said, making notes in turn. "We want to get everything down." Occasionally, one left the room to make a telephone call. The situation back at Princes Gate, they told him, was "under control."

Cramer's sister and parents were allowed in for a few minutes—"a brief conversation, a few tears"—and then shooed out again.

After three hours, Cramer was becoming incoherent, drained beyond speech. The police stood up: "Get some sleep. We'll be back."

Cramer was told not to leave the room or make phone calls, and not to speak to the medical staff about the siege. "If you want anything, the policeman outside will get it." He was as trapped as he had been inside the embassy but now alone.

The nurse gave him some pills, but sleep would not come. His own questions piled up as he chain-smoked: "Have I been a coward in running out on my friend and colleague? Could I have done anything differently?" What did his father, the stern police veteran and former soldier, make of his behavior? "How would he have reacted? Probably a lot better than his son had."

He picked up the notepad left by the detectives and offered an odd tribute to the men who had held him hostage. "I really like them," he wrote. "I don't know why, but I do. They had no reason to release me, but they did, and I will always love them for that." He rang the bell at the bedside. A policeman appeared instantly.

"Please pass a message to the police at the embassy. Get them to tell everyone inside that I'm recovering. Thank them."

Cramer had emerged from the embassy unharmed, bringing with him a raft of vital intelligence, and a burden of guilt he would carry for the rest of his life.

AS THE AMBULANCE raced Chris Cramer to St. Stephen's, the hostages were herded up to the third floor and into the reference library, a room some twenty feet long and fifteen wide, lined with shelves of newspapers, magazines, and press clippings. Chairs and tables were piled against the curtained windows facing the front of the building.

"Listen, everybody," said Towfiq, speaking alternately in English and Farsi. "If the police try to storm the building, we have no choice but to kill all Iranian hostages."

Ron Morris glanced sideways at Karkouti. "How will they be able to tell which hostages are which once they begin shooting?"

"God help us. I am telling you, they are bloody mad and erratic."

"Mustapha, do you believe the end is getting nearer?"

"Can't tell . . ."

Fowzi shepherded the women into the corridor. "This is a safe place for you," he said. "In case the police decide to attack."

"Don't go near the windows," Jassim instructed. "There are bombs. Don't touch anything."

A circle of newspapers had been laid out in the middle of the room, and the Iranian hostages were told to sit inside it, a sinister move, in Trevor Lock's view: "It was as if they planned to machine-gun them in close proximity."

As midday approached, the gunmen braced for an assault. Towfiq pulled up his hood and put on dark glasses, something he did at moments of tension, as if seeking anonymity in what he was about to do. "If your police attack," he told Lock, "we will kill you."

"The police will not attack," Lock insisted. "You're in England. We don't do things like that. If you don't hurt us, the police won't hurt you. All they want is for this to end peacefully."

Fred Luff had made the same point, urgently and repeatedly, when he reappeared on the pavement at 11:47. He thanked Towfiq for releasing Cramer, assured him the police were trying to reconnect the telephones, and promised to ask his superiors to release a press statement from the gunmen to the world's media. From three hundred yards away, the telescopic lenses of the press photographers captured Luff nodding emphatically and raising a clenched fist in salute to the man at the window.

Utterly unpredictable, Towfiq had backed down from his threat. In the first hours of the siege, he had seemed so certain of his plans, and the timetable of events. He was starting to waver.

As midday came and went, the hostages breathed again, and Harris noted: "For some reason, I know not why, the 12:00 deadline has passed."

Towfiq took off his sunglasses and lowered his hood. "We are now negotiating with the police, and the police have explained these complicated matters take some time. We decided to extend the deadline."

Relief rippled around the room.

"*Alhamdulillah,*" some of the Iranians murmured, thanking God. "*Allahu Akbar.*"

"Brilliant," said Ron.

At 12:20, Towfiq called the negotiators on the field telephone: "We are giving the Iranian government until 2:00 P.M. today. This is not a sign of weakness but out of humanitarian duty. After 2:00 P.M. all responsibility falls upon the Iranian government. If the Iranian government will acknowledge that they are negotiating with the British government that will extend the time."

In the crowded reference library, a surreal listlessness descended. Some of the hostages plucked magazines from the racks to pass the time.

Ron Morris found a copy of Frederick Forsyth's bestseller *The Day of the Jackal* and settled down on the carpet to read. The story was grimly appropriate: an international terrorist plot. When police were hunting the Venezuelan terrorist Ilich Ramírez Sánchez after the OPEC siege of 1975, they found a paperback copy of the book on his shelves: he was henceforth known as Carlos the Jackal. The book in Morris's hands was indelibly associated with the terrorist whose actions had inspired the young Arabs holding him hostage.

Harris scribbled in his diary: "12:30: Discussion on Arabistan."

"Listen, everybody, quiet please," said Towfiq. "I want to tell you some information about us, Arabistan, and our future aim in the new Iran."

What followed was a seminar on the tangled politics of southwest Iran, conducted in English, Arabic, and Farsi, passionate, articulate, and incongruous. Towfiq described the oppression of Iran's Arabs, first by the shahs and then at the hands of the ayatollah. He described the horror of Black Wednesday, and the betrayal of his people by the revolutionary government. "The promises we had had from Khomeini himself," he said, "were just lies."

At this, Abbas Lavasani, the Revolutionary Guard member, leaped to his feet: "The imam does not lie," he shouted. Several other Iranians also protested, including the chargé d'affaires, now sufficiently recovered to take part. He in turn was shouted down by the more liberal Iranians.

"You don't understand, do you, Dr. Afrouz?" said the banker Ali Tabatabai. "This is not the place nor the time to argue who is right and who is wrong. You should recognize that the Arabs, as a minority in Iran, are deprived of their basic rights, and this is a fact and all Iranians know it, but unfortunately they don't talk about it."

Karkouti heard Abdul Ezzati, the press attaché, muttering under his breath: "The term Arabistan has long been forgotten, only some local inhabitants in the province still call it that . . . These people are members of the Iraqi intelligence service."

Towfiq plowed on. "We sacrificed hundreds of our people to overthrow the shah," he said, "and now we are ready to die again to win our freedom."

Jassim spoke up, from his position at the doorway. "We are continuously subjected to discrimination in almost every aspect of our life," he said, before adding grimly, "I don't mind getting killed."

Shaye joined in, describing how his father and brother had been executed by the Iranians. "I have nothing to live for," he said quietly, with Karkouti translating from Arabic to English and Farsi. "They killed my whole family."

For a moment, the horrific, cyclical violence of southwestern Iran was distilled into a single room in Kensington.

Ezzati stood up and interrupted. "What you are doing is wrong," he said, explaining that using violence for political ends was contrary to Islamic teaching.

Towfiq gave him a long, cold look. Lavasani was now studiously ignoring the conversation, buried in his copy of the Koran.

"He was being deliberately defiant," Lock noted.

Sim Harris found the multilingual discussion hard to follow. "Mustapha was talking to the gunmen in Arabic, and sometimes when they were talking in Farsi he would ask them to repeat what they were saying in Arabic, so there was Arabic and Farsi spoken, with interludes of telling us in English what was happening."

The 14:00 deadline came and went. Towfiq picked up the field telephone and announced he would extend the deadline to 16:30 if police reconnected the telephones. "If not," he added, "the responsibility will be with the police."

With one ear pressed to his portable radio, Towfiq heard the news coming in but could not get his own message out. The BBC was reporting the siege but not his demands for a prisoner release and autonomy for Arabistan.

"Why have the British police cut the phones off? What are they trying to do?" he demanded.

"Perhaps it's just a fault on the line," Harris offered weakly.

Towfiq knew better. "The police want to be the only people we talk to, and to control what the outside world knows of our demands."

A few minutes later, he was back on the field telephone.

"I need twenty-five hamburgers," he said. Then he added: "You have five minutes."

But for the implied death threat, he might have been ordering room service.

The mobile police canteens went into emergency culinary overdrive.

From the vantage point of Zulu Control, the situation was improving. The lead gunman was talking, and through a single, controlled channel of communication. Audio probes were beginning to pick up faint fragments of conversation inside the building. Two deadlines had passed without bloodshed, and two hostages were free. And now Salim had established another point of negotiation: he was hungry, and ready to be fed.

Keeping both gunmen and hostages properly nourished was essential, Gunn told police: "A peaceful outcome may well depend on rational discussions, and so it is vital that the terrorists stay in good mental and physical health."

For Dellow, Towfiq's food order presented a major opportunity, because if hamburgers could be sent into the building, so could eavesdropping equipment. "The sooner one or more devices could be sent through the front door," he said, "the better."

Fred Luff staggered to the front door with a large tray. On it lay the best meal the police could knock up at five minutes' notice: three dozen white rolls containing hamburgers, each wrapped in a white napkin, along with packets of crisps and a two-foot-square aluminum tray of steak pie, of which one corner had already been consumed by a peckish policeman.

"We are starving," said Nawabzada Gul, seizing a hamburger in each hand.

The scratch meal was wolfed down with the same relish that diplomatic dignitaries had once devoured caviar and champagne in the days of the shah, bringing with it a flush of optimism.

Sated, Gul offered up one of his Delphic aphorisms: "If you have mangoes to eat, then there must be trees." No one had a clue what this could possibly mean.

"How was your hamburger?" Roya asked Shirazeh.

"It was okay."

"Was it well done?" Roya continued, as if they were at a restaurant dinner party.

"No, I think medium well."

"Mine was rare," Nooshin laughed.

AT 16:45 THE field telephone rang in the negotiators' room.

Towfiq read out a new list of demands:

We want:

- An aircraft to fly my group and Iranian hostages to the Middle East—the British hostages will be released at the airport
- The ambassadors of Iraq, Algeria and Jordan to mediate and the Red Cross representative must be waiting for us at the airport
- The crew of the aircraft should comprise mainly females
- A coach with curtained windows to convey group and hostages to the airport

This is our final demand and if it is not met by 7:00 p.m. hostages will be killed.

Towfiq entered the reference library and repeated the new list of demands for the benefit of the hostages.

"They're never going to get safe passage out of the country," Harris whispered to Lock.

The policeman agreed. "That's how police work; it's a classic tactic," he said. "The police will carry on negotiating. The idea is to wear the gunmen down."

"This could go on forever," said Harris. The U.S. Embassy siege in Tehran had already continued for six months, with no end in sight.

"Blimey," said Morris. "They are silly, aren't they?"

Karkouti spoke for them all: "We are in deep shit."

The youngest gunman, Fowzi, wandered over to the non-Iranian group. "What are you talking about?" he asked in Arabic.

"We are discussing what might happen after the new deadline," said Karkouti.

"Do you think it is possible they'll accept our demands?"

"My dear friend Ali," said Karkouti, using Fowzi's nom de guerre.

"Do you want me to be honest with you? It is unlikely, but a compromise is always possible. But my opinion does not matter; you'd better discuss this with Salim."

Towfiq was confident. He was offering a solution, a way to allow all sides to retire with their honor, and lives, intact. Other Western governments had made similar concessions. The Iraqi intelligence officers had assured him the British government would quickly accede to their demands, and let them all go home. So had the Palestinian organizer who had ducked out of leading the operation at the last moment.

But the Group of the Martyr and their backers had not reckoned with one immovable obstacle: Margaret Thatcher.

THE EMERGENCY COBRA committee was now sitting in permanent session, with full meetings morning and afternoon chaired by William Whitelaw, backup staff on twenty-four-hour duty and a link to Hayden Phillips, the civil servant sitting beside John Dellow in Zulu Control. The revised set of demands changed the landscape but at the same time altered little.

Significantly, the terrorists had dropped their insistence on the release of the ninety-one prisoners in Iranian jails. Perhaps that demand had only ever been symbolic. The British government had no leverage to encourage Iran to release political prisoners anyway, and Tehran, far from bending, had responded to that idea with typical belligerence, and instant violence.

Reports from Iran indicated that some Arabs held in Iranian jails had already been executed in retaliation for the embassy occupation. The press in Tehran published a statement, supposedly signed by ten of the jailed Arab activists, stating that they did not want the government to agree to the hostage-takers' demands, and preferred to remain in prison: this had been either extracted under torture or simply invented by Tehran's indefatigable propagandists. Towfiq never again raised the issue of releasing the prisoners. They were left to their fate, a predictably bloody one: most were executed, in the swelling holocaust of the ayatollah's enemies. The message from Tehran was unchanged: the siege was Britain's problem; if the hostages were killed, they would be going straight to heaven.

Towfiq's demand for Middle Eastern ambassadors to act as mediators added a new twist to what Whitelaw described as "a diplomatic as well as a terrorist challenge." Thatcher was distinctly lukewarm on the idea. Arab diplomats might have their own agendas and offer concessions she was not prepared to countenance. A crime was being committed on British soil, and the police, she felt, were perfectly able to conduct negotiations without outside help.

The request to bring in Iraq's ambassador seemed particularly suspicious. MI6 was now receiving "reliable intelligence that the terrorists had been recruited and trained by Saddam Hussein in Iraq." MI5 reported that the gunmen's cause was being loudly "supported by the government-controlled Iraqi press." There was something smelly here, and Foreign Office noses were twitching. Had Saddam staged this terrorist charade in order to be invited to step in and resolve it? Were these Arab terrorists and Iraq's government, diplomats, and media all working in league?

On the other hand, the Arab ambassadors represented another potential bargaining chip, a way to string along negotiations, keep Salim on the line, play for time. So long as the gunmen were talking to or about ambassadors, they were not shooting hostages. Douglas Hurd, the Foreign Office minister in Cobra, agreed to put out feelers to the embassies of Algeria, Jordan, and Syria. This was not yet revealed to the press. If the media discovered Middle Eastern diplomats were involved, that could complicate an already fiendish problem. Hurd did not contact the Iraqi ambassador.

Mrs. Thatcher's position was unchanged. The gunmen would not be permitted to leave the country. They could negotiate over food, ambassadors, hostages, medicine, and media publicity for as long as necessary, weeks or months if required.

Dellow delivered a situation report to the Home Secretary: "It is my opinion that the terrorists are still prepared to talk and not anxious to act on the deadlines that are threatened. Although the terrorists have turned their attention to leaving the country under the supervision of Middle Eastern ambassadors, there still seems to be room for exploiting the terrorists' desire for publicity."

Whitelaw agreed, and Dellow briefed the negotiators. Delay, he told them. Give no promises about leaving the country or providing a plane and indicate that the government is "looking into the question of ambassadors." Above all, "bargain for release of hostages."

"Our policy was very simple," Hayden Phillips recalled. "To be prepared to give the terrorists patience, and nothing else."

But, while the patience of Mrs. Thatcher's officials might be endless, that of the gunmen was not.

THE SAS LANCE CORPORAL Tommy Palmer was a poacher turned gamekeeper. But he remained a poacher at heart. Wherever the regiment sent him—the Middle East, Northern Ireland, Southeast Asia—he had an uncanny ability to slip away unnoticed and return with game stolen from a rich man's land: pheasant, rabbit, salmon, gazelle. Once, while the other members of B Squadron were wading across a river in Brunei, Palmer tossed in a hand grenade: "Just doing a spot of fishing, lads," he said as his stunned comrades staggered to the banks and dying fish flopped to the surface. When the Fijian members of the regiment wanted to roast some meat in their traditional earth oven, a *lovo*, Palmer turned up with a sheep, stolen from a field beside the Wye.

Born in an Edinburgh tenement slum, Palmer suffered a childhood that was a grim litany of neglect and deprivation. He had never met his father, a Canadian GI, and never would. His alcoholic mother walked out when he was eight, leaving five children, each by a different man. For a week following her departure, Tommy lived rough on the streets, drinking milk stolen from doorsteps. His next seven years were spent in a children's home run by monks near Falkirk, a joyless, cold place of beatings and harsh religion. At fifteen, already a scrappy fighter, he went to live with an older cousin, who got him work delivering coal, and then a job in a brick factory. There he tried to win workers' compensation by cutting off a finger: he retained the digit but lost the job. Slightly built, agile as a feral cat, Palmer could not be said to be going off the rails, since he had never been on them. But at eighteen he joined the Royal Engineers, and by twenty-one had passed selection for the SAS. The regiment was the family he never had.

Tommy Palmer met Caroline at a nightclub when he was twenty-three. He had arrived with another woman, but he preferred Caroline, and poured a drink over his date so she had to go home. He told Caroline his parents had been killed in a car crash. She was pregnant when they married. Two weeks after the wedding, he was deployed to Oman. "I killed a scorpion and Dave has killed some big tarantulas," he wrote home. "I hope you got the hoover fixed okay." Palmer returned a few days before the child was born, and a week later he disappeared again, this time to Northern Ireland.

"You never knew where they had gone," said Caroline, who accepted the role of army wife.

Tommy "Poacher" Palmer retained his strong Scottish accent, and the sense of impermanence from a fractured childhood. "I'll never grow old," he told Caroline.

Palmer's close friend in the regiment was Trooper Mel Parry, a Welshman with a thick mustache, an aptitude for fighting, and a nose for trouble. If the SAS had not embraced him, Parry would have ended up in prison, or dead.

Parry had a bullet wound across his shoulder blades from Dhofar, and a long scar down his neck and chest where a drunken hooligan had punched him with a razor blade in his fist when Parry was working nights as a bouncer in an Abergavenny nightclub. He joined the Royal Horse Artillery and served in the Parachute Brigade, before passing selection for the SAS at the age of nineteen, one of the youngest recruits ever. But in 1978 he was thrown out, or returned to unit (RTU-ed) in SAS parlance, after a fight with another soldier in Hong Kong. The banishment lasted a year, before Parry passed selection for a second time, now the oldest to do so at the age of thirty-four. He started again from scratch, reduced to the rank of trooper but back in the only institution that could tame him. Although expelled from school at fifteen for thumping the headmaster, Parry liked books, particularly those about Roman Britain and the Norse gods. He carried a copy of *The Hobbit* with him at all times. He did not ingratiate himself with the officers: "He was not a Rupert-liker." Within the SAS, Parry followed orders; outside it, less so. He decorated the bar at the Hereford base with swords and axes, and called it Valhalla. Whether tabbing (marching in full combat gear) over the Welsh hills, wading through the Belize jungle, or hiding out for five days in County Armagh watching for an IRA suspect from a pigpen, he never wore socks.

"You've got to know what you're marrying," said his wife, Gail. "You can stay at home for six months and not know where they are."

Parry liked to say of himself that he "didn't tolerate bullies." What that often meant was selecting the toughest, meanest person in the bar and picking a fight with them. "When he was ready for a fight," Gail said, "Mel went blank behind the eyes." On one occasion, he insisted on testing some new body armor by having Palmer shoot him from ten feet away with a 9mm to see if it worked: luckily for both, it did.

Parry and Palmer were two of the regiment's premier practical jokers, deploying that cruel species of humor intended to make someone else appear foolish or fearful, and amuse the crowd. If a snake appeared in your hammock, or your tea was laced with a laxative, Parry and Palmer had probably put it there.

TOMMY PALMER HAD been at home in Hereford the day before, when his bleeper went off. "Got to go," he told Caroline, and headed out. Mel Parry was in barracks when he got the alert. He left no message for Gail. He just didn't go home.

Palmer, Parry, and the rest of B Squadron made themselves comfortable in the majestic surroundings of the Doctors' House. The walls of their new bivouac were lined with glass cases of surgical instruments and leatherbound books. "Some of the lads are looking about to see what they can pinch," noted one of the troopers.

Much of soldiering is waiting, whether in an Irish pigsty or a Victorian mansion. Parry took out his copy of *The Hobbit*, and settled down.

9

OPERATION
NIMROD

The Royal Geographical Society, founded in 1830 for the advancement of geographical knowledge, was one of the few institutions in Britain that did not need to be told where to find Khuzestan on a map. Located just three hundred yards from the Iranian Embassy on the corner of Exhibition Road, it had a large lecture theater, ideal for press conferences. At 18:15, with another deadline passed, Metropolitan Police Commissioner David McNee stood up and planted his flag on the breaking story. His statement was aimed at the hostage-takers as much as the media packed into the auditorium.

"The gunmen must know that it is not within our power to meet all of their demands, whatever our views on the rights and wrongs of their cause," McNee declared, hinting that he had thought deeply about the issue, which he had not. "I appeal to them to remain calm. Hasty action may cause even more suffering to their own people in Iran. We must show patience and perseverance. That is what we propose to do."

Towfiq summoned Karkouti. "Ustaz Mustapha, head of the police issued a statement. I think he stated that the police wanted to end the siege peacefully, and this is what we want. We want you to listen to it and help us fully understand what he means."

At the top of the hour, the press conference was broadcast by the

BBC. Karkouti told Towfiq the truth: "When McNee says 'ending the siege without loss of life and upholding the law,' he means only one thing: giving yourselves up and facing a fair trial."

"That means we go to prison," said Towfiq bleakly. "But this was not in our plan."

Trevor Lock was asked to give his opinion on a likely sentence. "The law in the UK is the fairest in the world," he told the gunmen. "So far, your action is political, not criminal. Therefore, you will be sentenced to a few months and later deported."

This was not what Towfiq hoped to hear. "We want to leave the country with a few hostages to guarantee our safe exit."

He was suddenly enraged again. McNee had referred to their "cause" without giving a hint as to what that cause might be. The allusion to further Arab suffering sounded like a threat. The pious call for patience was a delaying tactic.

Towfiq went to the ground floor, seized the green field telephone, and threw it out the window.

"The police are treating us like children," he raged. "They obviously don't care about saving your lives. They are liars. We've been listening to every radio news bulletin and none of our demands had been broadcast and nothing had been said about the ambassadors. I'm not talking to the police anymore. If they want to talk to me, they can reconnect the phones."

A panicky gloom redescended.

"Do you think Chris was faking it?" Sim Harris asked Lock, wondering what his colleague was doing now. "Or was he really ill?"

The policeman considered this for a moment. "It doesn't matter either way," he said. "At least the police will get all the details about conditions in here. That's got to be good news for us."

Lock had eaten none of the hamburgers or steak pie. He was extremely hungry. And he needed to urinate. He would try to hang on until nightfall, when the gunmen might be less attentive as he unbuttoned his coat. The gun at his waist felt heavy.

Ron Morris put down *The Day of the Jackal* and began reminiscing about the old days at the embassy before the shah was ousted. "I have seen Iranian royals come and go to London, and what kind of lifestyle they had," he said. "You wouldn't believe how lavish things were then. The ambassador would send me to Harrods to buy a cut-glass vase and fifty roses for whoever had entertained him the night before."

Overhearing Morris's nostalgia for the shah's extravagance, Abbas Lavasani scowled. The oddly dressed Revolutionary Guard member sat apart from the other Iranians, reading the Koran, rocking gently back and forth. He spoke only to Afrouz, in a conspiratorial whisper.

Karkouti tried to engage him in conversation. "I see that you are reading the Koran; your Arabic must be very good. Where did you learn it?"

"I studied the language at religious schools," Lavasani replied, shutting down the conversation and returning to the holy book.

Towfiq noticed Harris scribbling in a notebook. "What are you writing?" he demanded.

Harris felt a sharp stab of fear. He explained that he was keeping a record.

"You mean *muzakkirat,* a diary? This is good. This is very nice."

Towfiq insisted Harris read out what he had written.

So far from being suspicious, the hostage-takers "seemed happy and flattered," Karkouti noted. "It was quite obvious that Salim in particular liked the publicity."

Towfiq did indeed crave exposure, but he wanted much more. By 21:30, it was getting dark, and the BBC still had not reported his demands. The siege led the news but with no mention of Arabistan, the plane to fly them out, or the ambassadors to mediate their exit. He had made his statement to three different branches of the BBC, and it was still unreported.

"Why don't you let me speak to the police?" Lock suggested. "They might tell me more than they tell you."

Harris suggested that he too could speak to a BBC colleague, and "question him or her to get an impartial view of how things were going on the outside."

"This is a good idea," said Towfiq.

Lock and Harris were ushered at gunpoint to Roya's first-floor office at the front of the building. Towfiq pulled up the sash window.

The profound night silence was unnerving. The demonstrators had long since dispersed. The park was deserted. Harris shivered. "There was no one in sight, no traffic running past, an eerie feeling."

In hostage situations police attempt to establish a bubble of sensory deprivation in which the perpetrators feel utterly alone. If terrorists see policemen, firemen, and ambulances dashing around, they may feel validation; when they see and hear nothing at all, they shrink. John Dellow considered putting up high screens around the building to prevent anyone seeing in or out, but decided that might be interpreted by the gunmen as the prelude to an assault. To eliminate ambient noise, police cleared the park and started evacuating local residents from neighboring flats, warning of a possible explosion.

The veteran war correspondent Rebecca West flatly refused to leave. She remained glued to her ringside seat, having a "whale of a time," according to her biographer. The writer insisted that her "petrified" housekeeper stay with her. Dame Rebecca was "electrified" and not budging from her kitchen.

There is always noise in a big city, but that night several acres of Kensington fell uncannily silent: no radio played, no dogs barked, no car horns sounded, no traffic grumbled.

Lock donned his peaked cap, leaned out, and shouted into the hushed darkness. "This is PC Trevor Lock. Is there anyone there?"

Silence.

"Nobody is replying, you see," Towfiq muttered. "They don't want to help you. They abandoned us."

Lock called out again. "This is Trevor Lock of the DPG—is there anybody there?"

A voice floated up from behind the wall. "Yes, Trevor."

Two figures emerged from the gloom: Fred Luff and Ray Tucker.

"Sir, it's very difficult in here," said Lock. "There are major problems. The gunmen want to speak to a journalist—would you please request the BBC to send a journalist who is personally known to Sim Harris as soon as possible?"

Luff's walkie-talkie crackled as he relayed the message.

Harris joined Lock at the window and shouted down: "If they can't find a journalist at the press encampment, they should telephone our direct lines at TV News, which are 749 1156 or 1157, and that should produce a journalist. I'm well-known. That shouldn't be a problem." Harris reeled off the names of three senior BBC journalists, including his immediate boss, BBC managing director, Tony Crabb.

The police officer repeated back the names and numbers. Towfiq closed the window.

"An hour should be long enough, shouldn't it?" he asked.

From Zulu Control, Dellow sent a personal message to Doreen Lock: "Looks well; been seen; Commissioner is proud of him."

Back in the reference library, Harris whispered to Morris: "Things look a little more positive now."

Gul was already noisily asleep.

An hour later, Towfiq, Lock, and Harris were back at what they dubbed the "talking window," now with Mustapha Karkouti.

"Have you found a BBC man?" Lock shouted.

"We have asked, but he hasn't arrived yet."

Harris knew this had to be untrue, a prevarication. "Unbelievable," he thought. "There must be dozens of them outside who'd love to get involved." He turned to Towfiq, and lied. "It's getting very late. Everyone's gone home. Why not wait until the morning and do things sensibly? Any publicity made at this time of night isn't going to get much showing, and won't make the morning papers."

Towfiq seemed to accept this flimsy explanation.

"Do you mind if I talk to the police?" asked Karkouti. "You can trust me."

Towfiq nodded.

"This is Mustapha Karkouti," he called down.

"Yes, Mr. Karoufi," Luff said, immediately mangling his name. "Go ahead."

"You've got to understand a very essential point. You out there lack basic knowledge about the people inside here, and the group here lacks significant knowledge about you."

"Yes, Mr. Karfuki, we are listening."

"The group is no longer insisting on the release of the ninety-one prisoners in Iran, so you need to look at the situation afresh, please. They have two objectives now: to ensure their statement receives wide publicity, and to reach a deal with the British authorities that would enable them to leave the country. They believe this solution worked successfully for other hostage-takers in other countries. We hope you'll understand that."

"Thank you very much," shouted Luff. "We will pass the information to the authorities. We suggest that you all have a very relaxing night. Goodnight to all of you."

The women were moved into the corridor while young Fowzi, as usual, stood guard over them. Karkouti noticed that the good-looking young gunman "obviously enjoyed playing this role, and the girls, on their part, seemed to relax with him." Fowzi was different from the others, less taut and wary. He told jokes, grinning as he made the tea and offering small compliments to each woman as he served it. Lock noticed his vanity, the way his glance lingered on Shirazeh and Roya. "He thought he was the poor girl's Clark Gable, or Omar Sharif."

The hostages nicknamed Fowzi "the Ladies' Man."

The Muslims took turns washing in the small handbasin of the third-floor lavatory, and then prayed.

Harris was irritated by the sound and tried to "concentrate on something else." For a second night, he stretched out on the hard floor. The reference library was smaller and much more cramped than the general office. The hostages had to arrange themselves head to toe.

Roya found a pile of old cushions in a cupboard. "Here is one for you, Mr. Mustapha," she said, handing an ancient brown corduroy-and-satin cushion to Karkouti. "You need one tonight. Maybe it will help you have a comfortable sleep. We need your energy."

Gul lay spread-eagled next to him, and Karkouti found himself marveling at the volume, range, and variety of the man's thunderous snoring. "His snores dwarfed everyone else's. It was so loud I could not think straight." He noticed Harris was also being kept awake. "Gul would start snoring with a low sound, gradually rising in volume until it reached its highest pitch, before it gradually subsided again. His snores came in rhythms, sometimes interrupted by a cough or a hiccup."

"What do you think we should do?" Harris whispered. "Wake him up? Maybe adjust his head?"

Karkouti gently nudged Gul's foot. The racket stopped for a few seconds, and then started up again, "the loudest so far."

It felt good to chuckle in the darkness.

"Where do you think this will lead to?" Harris asked Karkouti.

"Difficult to tell with this erratic bunch of young, fucking ill-trained gunmen. They seriously believe that the British government will simply give in to their demands and let them leave the country unpunished. They are somehow fully convinced of this. It is worrying."

Back in Dagenham, Doreen Lock danced in her kitchen to "Geno" by Dexys Midnight Runners. Two of Trevor's police colleagues had materialized with a bottle of whiskey and some Chinese takeaway. "They came round to cheer me up, and brought some flowers," Doreen said. One was already quite drunk: "He kept asking me to dance." It was a way to take her mind off what was happening to her husband at Princes Gate, but for all their forced gaiety she sensed Trevor's friends were deeply worried. "They thought he wouldn't come out. They wanted me to know they were there for me."

The two policemen finally wheeled off into the night. "I'm so drunk I'm going to get pistol-whipped by the wife when I get home," slurred one.

Doreen couldn't bear to turn on the TV or radio, fearing some terrible newsflash. Instead, she sat in the dark, surrounded by takeaway cartons and the tang of whiskey, and wept.

Sleepless, Harris wondered why the police had not produced a journalist, why the gunmen's demands had not been met, and why a bus had not already been provided to ferry them to Heathrow, and safety. The more he reflected, the more reasonable Salim's demands seemed, and the more dangerous the police stalling tactics. What were they doing taking so long? This Salim might be an Arab radical, but he seemed straightforward; the police, on the other hand, were lying, dithering, playing a double game. In a final diary entry, Harris wondered: "Have the police really asked the Beeb?"

Karkouti was also anxious, exhausted, and fully awake. The fears crowded out sleep. He had accurately conveyed the gunmen's demands to the police, but a recurring thought nagged him: "I am afraid I sounded as if I was the gunmen's spokesman." Moreover, he sensed Towfiq's waning confidence. The young man seemed to be "edging toward panic." With one foot in Britain and the other still in the Arab world, Karkouti understood the dynamics at play. The gunmen did not know what they were dealing with. Thatcher would not agree to fly them out. The police would continue to delay. Sooner or later, there would be an explosion.

In the darkness, Ron Morris sensed the dread running through Karkouti, recumbent on the cushion alongside him. He propped himself up on his elbow and leaned over.

"What's wrong, Mustapha?"

"I am frightened, Ron, really scared. I don't know if Salim and his fellows will be able to carry through to the end without bloodshed."

"What makes you think that?"

"These idiots came to occupy the embassy with totally the wrong brief. These gunmen were sent here to die. I am certain Thatcher will never offer concessions. If you give in to terrorists' demands, you are inviting other terrorists to do the same."

"Blimey," said Morris. "I hadn't thought of that. This is too deep for me, Mustapha. Let's be optimistic and wait till the morning." With that, Ron Morris rolled over on his side, and fell instantly asleep.

ON THE OTHER side of the wall, in an office lined with Victorian medical textbooks, Major Hector Gullan of the SAS worked through the night, fashioning a series of contingency plans that he firmly expected never to have to implement.

At thirty-two years of age, the officer commanding of B Squadron was already a revered and somewhat daunting figure within the SAS, a veteran of foreign wars who would see action in three different colors of beret: maroon for the Parachute Regiment (his own), green for the Commando Brigade, and sand-colored for the SAS. He had won the Military Cross in Dhofar for gallantry under fire. A birthmark curled his upper lip, lending him a permanently sardonic expression. Gullan was competitive, almost superhumanly fit, exhaustingly intense, convivial in company, and wholly ruthless in action. Mel Parry nicknamed him Cool Hand Luke. Others called him Hector the Corrector. With a voice like a machine gun, he delivered his opinions in a series of staccato volleys. Whatever he approved of was "cracking," and whatever he disliked was "shit"; there was not much in between.

B Squadron had been back in the UK for just two months, following five months of live counterterrorism operations against the IRA in Northern Ireland during one of the deadliest periods of the Troubles. Louis Mountbatten, the Queen's cousin, had been assassinated in August in a boat off the Irish coast with a fifty-pound bomb of gelignite. On the same day, a roadside bomb at Warrenpoint in County Down killed eighteen soldiers of the Parachute Regiment, including a company commander, one of Gullan's close friends. Half of B Squadron were Paras. Dozens of operations were mounted against suspected terrorist targets. But special ops can be frustrating, with weeks or months of planning that never come to fruition. "We were repeatedly stood down."

The squadron included veterans like Gullan who had seen plenty of action but also a substantial group of rawer recruits. More than half had never fired a gun in combat. Some were wholly inexperienced. "In truth, I had never seen an angry man," one observed. "Let alone an angry 'Iranian terrorist.'"

Each SAS squadron has a distinct character. B Squadron, in the words of one officer, tended to be "cheerfully wild." Another described it as "the character squadron," full of "the ones that are just that bit different." One of Gullan's trickier tasks was to keep men like Palmer and Parry on a leash but not so tight that they rebelled or grew soft; to permit practical joking but not bullying; to tolerate the blowing off of steam, the joshing, and the odd fistfight. Palmer and Parry never teased Hector Gullan.

The squadron's two teams, Red and Blue, rotated in twelve-hour shifts: one team (located on the second floor of the Doctors' House) would be tooled up in full combat gear and ready to deploy if the immediate action plan were to be activated; while the other (on the third floor) rested, slept, ate, and waited, or returned to Regent's Park Barracks for training and briefing. An intelligence operations room was established on the ground floor, where the American ambassador had once hosted drinks parties, to collate and analyze incoming information. The forward holding area in the Royal College of General Practitioners was now a temporary battlefield camp.

On the first-floor landing, the signaler Simon McGregor, a solid figure known as Squashball, set up a simple radio network for Gullan to maintain contact with his team commanders if the balloon went up. A forward operations headquarters was established in a small office off the second floor, with Gullan, his operations officer, and a clerk, Lance Corporal Mark "Wingnut" Gilfoyle, a cheerful twenty-year-old typist with protruding ears.

Gullan drew up a preliminary set of hostage-rescue options, taking into account various factors: incoming intelligence, reconnaissance, equipment, the building layout, available troops and reserves, the presumed location of the hostages and their captors, weaponry of the gunmen, access points, sniper positions, surveillance information, and police and police dogs. The armored glass on the ground and first floors added a complicating element. "If you hit the front door with a sledgehammer, it would have ended up in Hyde Park," observed one trooper.

Secrecy was paramount. Nobody outside Zulu Control and Cobra knew of the new occupants in Number 15; if the press discovered an elite military assault team was on hand and alerted the gunmen, the outcome might be catastrophic. Gullan pored over the plans of the building, a labyrinth of rooms laid out in the shape of the letter *H*, with a section of flat roof forming the bar connecting the two sides. Separated balconies ran along the first floor at the front, and the second floor at the back. The center of the building was a void, with a well between the first and third floors, at the bottom of which was a four-sided pyramid of glass, a skylight illuminating the ground-floor hallway below.

Any plan needed to take into account facilities to treat casualties, fire hazards, and evacuation routes. The demand for a bus to take both hostages and gunmen to Heathrow added another variable. This could be ambushed on the way to the airport, but all civilian traffic would need to be cleared from the route.

It was like playing three-dimensional chess, with guns.

By nightfall, Gullan had drawn up a list of possible options, which Gilfoyle typed up and distributed to Lieutenant Colonel Rose, team leaders, and the police.

The first was a commando-style immediate action assault, a full-blown attack at all possible points if there was no time for anything more sophisticated. That had been attempted in Munich, catastrophically. The initial emergency plan was modified to include a thermal lance to cut through the steel-reinforced front door, and an explosive-laden truck to ram the front of the building. But, in essence, the IA plan remained simple, as described by one of the troopers: "Smash through the ground-floor windows and the front door, guns blazing. No warm-up, the Wild West show, go in hard and hit them like an express train." Sober heads gave that idea a 5 percent chance of success. "It would have been a disaster."

An alternative was the "deliberate stronghold assault": troops would attack simultaneously at the front, at the back, and down the middle of the building, by abseiling from the roof, while other teams sought to gain entry using explosives from the ground floor and balconies.

Any direct attack carried significant risks. This was not the Killing House, or even a planned attack on an IRA bomb factory. With an unknown number of heavily armed and unpredictable adversaries to contend with, anything could go wrong, and probably would. As Gullan put it: "Military operations never go according to plan, because the other side is making plans too."

AS NIGHT FELL, two SAS men climbed out of a skylight in Number 15, and onto the roof of the Iranian Embassy. About halfway along the slanted north-facing roof was a sealed skylight over a small attic bathroom. With a knife, one of the men pried up the leadwork around the lower edge of the frame. The entire window could now be lifted out in one piece. They tied abseiling ropes to the chimneys and retreated across the roof. But, as they did so, one trod on a roof tile, which cracked with a noise that "sounded like a pistol going off." Both froze. And then crawled on.

The skylight offered an alternative plan: the "silent option," at night. Men armed with silenced weapons would drop down into the fifth floor through the skylight in darkness, flashlights mounted on machine guns. They would deploy down the main staircase and then, on a radioed command, attack every floor simultaneously. The media would not witness the night assault unfolding; the gunmen might be less alert, and possibly asleep. Even so, attempting to free the hostages in the dark was a daunting prospect.

The SAS radio network was unencrypted, and easily intercepted by anyone with a shortwave receiver. The press, amateur radio hams, and even the terrorists themselves might be able to listen in.

Battlefield drill called for a series of secret call signs and code words.

Some of these followed convention: the front of the building was "white"; the rear "black"; right was "green" and left was "red"; the radio communications hub was "Sunray," invisible beams radiating out from a central point; "Seagull" was the second in command. A "Yankee" indicated a hostage, whereas "X-ray" denoted a gunman. Salim was "X-ray One." Lock was "Yankee One."

In theory, any code word or code name specific to an operation or individual should be selected from a list of random and meaningless words. But soldiers, spies, and politicians can seldom resist choosing a word that hints at a hidden significance.

To date, the SAS deployment had been temporarily dubbed "Operation Salim." The occasion called for something more formal.

Nimrod was an Old Testament ruler described as "a mighty hunter before the Lord." In both Jewish and Muslim traditions, Nimrod confronts Abraham in a cataclysmic battle between good and evil. Edward Elgar named the stirring ninth movement of his *Enigma Variations* "Nimrod" after the warlike hunter-king.

The SAS operation to hunt out the terrorists and free the hostages now had an official code name: "Operation Nimrod."

DAY THREE

FRIDAY

10

STOCKHOLM SYNDROME

"We are going to have to kill one of you," Towfiq announced in Farsi, addressing the Iranians, a new anger in his eyes. "You can choose who it will be."

It was 08:00 on a Friday, rush hour in central London, a bright spring morning under an empty crystal sky. Nothing moved in the street outside.

Overnight the gunmen had washed their underwear. Sim Harris noted the damp washing drying on the corridor radiators as he headed to the lavatory. It was an oddly reassuring domestic touch. Do mass murderers bother with clean underpants? But the gunmen had also spent the early hours moving more furniture, including a large refrigerator, to barricade the stairs leading to the upper stories.

The hostages lay sprawled on the floor. Some had been dozing when the lead gunman burst into the room. All were now wide awake.

Roya translated: "They'll start killing us one by one because the police are refusing their demands," she explained, turning to Karkouti. "Please talk to him."

Towfiq and Jassim were in the corridor, locked in urgent discussion.

"Yes, what do you want?" said Towfiq as Karkouti warily approached.

"Brother Salim," he said politely. "What's going on?"

"I want to teach the police a lesson," said Towfiq. "We're not children and I think the government is laughing at us. Today is the third day and, as you know, our intention was to end the siege after twenty-four hours."

"Brother, you have to play the game exactly like the police: be as patient as they are."

"What do you suggest we do, then?" Jassim demanded.

"Continue talking to the police. Engage some of the Iranian hostages in your negotiation."

Towfiq dismissed him with an irate wave of the hand. A moment later he could be heard shouting out the window: "Our peaceful attitude is diminishing. We are now going to kill the hostages. We have given you enough time since Wednesday and you didn't do anything."

Then, as an afterthought, he added: "We want food for thirty people, and some drinks in cans."

MI5's accelerometers, which tracked movement, recorded him returning back upstairs.

Again he addressed the room, now in both English and Farsi. "You have forty minutes to choose who dies. We are left with no option. We will start sending bodies to show them we mean business."

Overnight, something seemed to have snapped inside Towfiq. He clearly had not slept.

Trevor Lock was amazed by the transformation, and suddenly as frightened as he had been in the first minute of the siege. The man's mood swings were so abrupt and erratic. On the previous evening he had appeared emollient, receptive, almost tender; now he was raging, murderous.

Standing side by side at the talking window, trying to find a way out of this mess, Lock had felt strongly drawn to Towfiq. "He was obviously very well educated, and he had the ability to listen. He treated me as an equal. I respected him because I realized the harsh environment he came from." It was hard not to admire Towfiq's commitment to his cause, his command of his men, and his sympathy toward his captives. He inspired something more complex and deeper than mere fear.

Lock instinctively felt for the revolver at his side. If the moment of crisis came, would he be able to kill a man he had come to like?

SEVEN YEARS EARLIER, on the morning of August 23, 1973, a Swedish criminal wearing a wig, makeup, and dark glasses marched into a large bank in central Stockholm, fired a submachine gun into the ceiling, and shouted, "The party starts!"

Jan-Erik Olsson's attempted robbery went awry almost immediately, and he ended up taking hostage four employees, three women and one man, inside the bank vault. He then negotiated the release from prison of a fellow convict to assist him. Six days later, the police attacked with tear gas and Olsson and his accomplice surrendered.

During that siege, something unexpected happened. Far from loathing their captors, the hostages bonded with them. The longer the standoff continued, the more they came to see the police as a greater threat to their safety than the men holding them at gunpoint. In the artificial isolation of the siege, they got to know their kidnappers, to like them, to sympathize with them. According to some accounts, a woman hostage even developed romantic feelings toward one of the gunmen. When their ordeal was over, the hostages refused to testify in court against either man and instead began raising money for their defense.

"Is there something wrong with me?" twenty-one-year-old Elisabeth Oldgren asked a psychiatrist after her liberation. "Why don't I hate them?"

The strange but intense attachments that can form between hostages and their abductors thereafter became known as Stockholm syndrome, a term coined by the Swedish criminologist and psychiatrist Nils Bejerot. The syndrome follows distinct patterns: initial terror gradually evolving into compassion, even admiration, for the hostage-takers; a shared resentment at outside forces for acting too slowly, aggressively, or uncaringly; and, finally, a refusal to cooperate with the authorities. These relationships may be reinforced by small acts of kindness, and the intimacy of joint confinement. Some psychologists see the syndrome as an enforced return to earliest childhood, when the traumatized hostage, fearing imminent death, becomes wholly reliant on the captor, a parent figure, for sustenance and survival. The psychoanalyst Anna Freud identified similar behavior among prisoners in Nazi concentration camps and called it "identification with the aggressor."

Abusive and controlling domestic relationships involve similar traits, in which a victim becomes dependent on, and subservient to, their abuser, mistaking this for love.

The flipside of Stockholm syndrome is so-called Lima syndrome, in which abductors develop warm feelings for those they have captured and begin to question their own aims. In 1996, armed members of the Túpac Amaru Revolutionary Movement took hostage hundreds of guests attending a party at the Japanese ambassador's residence in Lima, Peru. They threatened to kill all the hostages but could not bring themselves to do so, and freed most of their captives after a few days.

The Iranian Embassy siege was barely two days old, and both hostages and gunmen were already exhibiting both syndromes, Stockholm and Lima: positive feelings from hostages to captors, negative feelings from hostages to police, and positive feelings from captors to hostages.

Mustapha Karkouti was a man of peace, but he had trained with the Democratic Front for the Liberation of Palestine and supported the Palestinian cause. He felt an instinctive affinity with the Arab gunmen. Towfiq's ability to manage this complex and fast-changing situation impressed him greatly: "Salim was tremendous, capable of doing five or six things at the same time, all really well. He could discuss politics with the hostages, supervise and keep a check on security, answer all the telephone calls, and listen to the news." Karkouti sensed that, although these men were willing to kill and die, they did not wish to do either. "I realized that like me they loved life," he reasoned, "and did not want to end it."

The gunmen wanted their captives to understand them, and to see their action as justified. They had entered the embassy armed and shooting but were already apologetic. "We are not criminals," Towfiq insisted. "We released a woman on the first day. We released a man who was in pain. We cannot stand the idea of anyone being in pain." They urgently wanted the hostages to understand that if the siege ended in violence, they would all be dying in a good cause. Towfiq was consulting his captives on tactics, timing, and when and how to make contact with the police. Karkouti, in particular, had become his intermediary with the world outside. Some of the hostages were already persuaded that the group had legitimate grievances and reasonable demands. But, more than that, captors and captives now shared a common cause: to get out alive. As Karkouti reflected, "We, hostages and gunmen, were all in the same boat, facing the same fate."

Even Jassim, the toughest of the group and the one who seemed most likely to shed blood, wanted the hostages to know he was not an unthinking brute. Lock was scared of the one they called Faisal, "the hardest bastard I ever met in my life." But when the policeman asked him, "What would you have done if I had been standing guard outside, instead of drinking coffee when you attacked the embassy?" Jassim's reply was strangely tender.

"Do not ask me that, Mr. Trevor. You are now my friend."

The five remaining women seemed to have developed a liking for their appointed jailer, Fowzi Nejad. Karkouti overheard the young man "exchanging laughs with one or two of the ladies late at night when other hostages were asleep." The Ladies' Man was easier to talk to than the other gunmen. "The women apparently trusted him and some of them talked to him about their private lives, back home as well as in London."

Professor John Gunn noted that both hostages and gunmen were falling into distinct and complementary behavior patterns. "Man is an intensely gregarious animal," the psychiatrist later observed. "Vulnerable when alone or isolated, [he] develops strong group bonds when under extreme threat. Bonding or identification with an aggressor may well reduce the aggressor's hostility and ability to destroy the victim." But Gunn's experience also told him that individuals react to the stress of hostage situations in contradictory ways: "All kinds of strong relationships, both positive and negative, can develop within any given stronghold, and the bigger the number of participants in the incident, the more complex the relationships that develop. In the highly charged atmosphere of a siege, bonds and antagonisms will always develop. Such things are part of normal social biology; they are inevitable."

In the space of just forty-eight hours, Trevor Lock had bonded with Towfiq. Yet he perceived something darker in the man, a capacity for unrestrained violence beneath his cultured, apparently gentle surface. In fifteen years of police work, Lock had encountered many damaged and dangerous people, and he recognized the broken soul inside

Towfiq, a desperation in his sudden flashes of fury and shifts of temper. In his short life, Towfiq had been imprisoned and beaten, ejected from his home, separated from his family, and harried into a fugitive existence by the secret police. He had seen his friends die under machine-gun fire, and his political cause all but destroyed. Just six months earlier his older brother, the person he loved most, had been betrayed, tortured, and murdered, his mauled body left in the desert. Towfiq had come to Britain to win a battle in his dead brother's name; but he also came because, in the ravaged landscape of his heart, he had nothing left to lose. The surest way to turn a man into a killer is to kill the thing he loves.

Towfiq was ready to kill, and Lock sensed it. "He could explode at any moment."

Like some nightmarish hothouse, the embassy siege was nurturing unlikely, fast-growing relationships: alliances, friendships, flirtations, and complex mutual dependencies. But it was also generating friction, a fissile and growing antipathy between the Arab gunmen and the Iranian diplomats. Towfiq intended to strike a blow against the treacherous government that had murdered his brother, a regime represented by Afrouz, Ezzati, Lavasani, and the other officials. In the monochrome thinking of all militants, these Iranians were Towfiq's enemies; the non-Iranians, the women, and the British policeman were all merely unlucky bystanders.

If he needed to destroy them all, he would.

"EZZATI, YOU COME with us," said Towfiq at 08:39, pointing to the urbane press attaché who had admonished him on Islamic principles the day before.

Abdul Ezzati was hauled to his feet by Jassim and Shaye. The color drained from his face, and his breath came in short bursts. Ezzati had a heart condition. Towfiq beckoned to Karkouti and Lock to follow.

At the talking window, Towfiq pressed the muzzle of his submachine gun, hard, into the side of Ezzati's bald head and turned to Lock: "Tell the police we have got a senior diplomat here and that we'll kill him and throw his body out unless a BBC man is here in ten minutes."

Lock did as instructed. An acknowledging shout came from the policeman behind the wall.

At this point Ezzati crumpled to the floor with a groan. "Take him back up," said Towfiq.

The man appeared to be having convulsions; he was foaming at the mouth and clutching his chest. The terror had triggered a minor heart attack. "They are going to kill me, they are going to kill me," Ezzati moaned as his eyes rolled back in his head. "I am going to die."

The others clustered around. Roya wiped his sweating forehead with a damp handkerchief. Remembering his first-aid lessons, Lock massaged his chest. "He looked like a dead man."

Professor Gunn had warned that during a siege "anyone who has a preexisting physical disorder, such as chronic heart failure, will soon run into problems as the stress may destabilize the illness."

Ezzati lay gasping on the carpet, sheet white. There was no faking a heart attack.

Morris turned to the gunmen: "This man needs a doctor, now!"

Jassim shook his head: "We will never release him. If the police care, they will send a doctor."

A few minutes later, Towfiq bustled back in. He barely glanced at the man lying on the floor. "Mr. Sim, Mr. Trevor, Mr. Mustapha, you must all come now. A man from the BBC is coming. You must talk to him. Afrouz, you come too. You must demand in front of him that police put back the telex and telephone."

THERE ARE AMBITIOUS reporters who want to be part of the story, to describe events from the front lines, amid the drama and debris. The young television reporter Kate Adie was one of these. So was Sim Harris. But there is another breed of journalist, just as important and much more numerous, that oversees the reporting of events, editing, synthesizing, analyzing, and organizing. This latter species has little desire to witness the news, let alone make it.

Tony Crabb, a BBC managing director of long experience and Harris's immediate boss, was one of these.

Crabb was on duty at the BBC news desk when the message arrived from Scotland Yard urgently requesting his presence at Princes Gate. There he was met by Fred Luff, who reeled off some confusing instructions: Do not make any promises. Play for time. Say you must refer all decisions to the police . . .

Inside the embassy, Harris received a simultaneous briefing from Towfiq, who instructed him not to reveal what was happening inside the building, the number of hostages, or the number of captors. "If you do," the gunman warned, "there will be trouble."

Harris felt a sweaty stab of terror. Towfiq clearly meant to kill him if he sensed a trick. But, at the same time, like Lock, he could not help admiring him and the men under his command. "They're not stupid. They're highly intelligent, university educated. The tension has built up too high. They are not common criminals and should not be treated like it."

Heading downstairs, accompanied by Lock, Karkouti, and the limping Afrouz, Harris clutched the banister. For the first time in his life, he felt his body go rigid, the symptoms of an acute panic attack. Then his hands began to tremble uncontrollably, and tears welled up. "Come on, come on," he told himself. "Let's get it over with."

Lock saw Harris stagger as his lips turned blue, and caught him before he fainted. "Look, Sim, you've been bloody great so far," Lock urged. "Just keep calm."

CRABB AND HARRIS had been colleagues for years. Just a few days earlier, the BBC manager had dispatched the sound recordist to interview the wrestling housewives of Acton. A stout figure in a crumpled blue suit, Crabb stood on the pavement with police negotiator Ray Tucker alongside.

"This is really good," Harris whispered to Towfiq, when he saw who was waiting. "This is my boss. He's a very important man at the BBC." Harris leaned out of the first-floor window, while Towfiq hid behind the curtains. The time was 09:47.

"Hello, Sim, how are you?" said Crabb.

"Not too bad, Tony, considering," said Harris, his voice still shaking.

Towfiq jabbed Harris with the gun through the velvet curtain. They were not here to make small talk.

"Ask him why the police aren't doing anything," he hissed.

"Why haven't you broadcast these people's demands?" asked Harris.

"What demands?" replied Crabb.

Sim Harris felt a sudden surge of irritation. Panic gave way to anger. Crabb was being evasive. He could not possibly be ignorant of the gunmen's latest demands. Towfiq was right: the police didn't care. "The bastards," Karkouti muttered under his breath.

Harris exploded. "What the hell are they playing at out there?" he demanded. "They've cut off the phones and telex so the Iranians can't communicate. There were two statements yesterday about mediation."

"The police are doing their best," Crabb mumbled vaguely.

Harris was enraged: the police were putting their lives in jeopardy by stalling, deliberately goading the gunmen, pretending to cooperate, and doing nothing.

"Tony, are you aware that the gunmen have made a statement that they want broadcast?"

"What do they want to say?" asked Crabb, though he knew the answer perfectly well.

Towfiq ran through the demands once more. Harris repeated them through the window. Crabb scribbled notes in an A4 pad, leaning on the hood of a parked Mercedes. "This is not a BBC exclusive," Harris insisted. "It should be reported as widely as possible. Tony, please give me an assurance that this will be the case."

Crabb said nothing.

The siege had reached a new phase, with a hostage not merely relaying the captors' demands but actively demanding their fulfillment.

"I honestly believe these people are sincere," Harris continued, now addressing Tucker. "We have formed very good relationships with our captors, but the police are determined to upset things. These men have a cause. You mustn't treat them like children. I don't believe they want to harm any of us, but you're messing them about." One of the Iranian hostages seemed to be having a heart attack, Harris warned, and might die. "Your tactics are creating the most terrible problems for all of us inside here. Please understand that. The tension is reaching a dangerous level."

Towfiq pushed Afrouz forward with the point of his gun. "Tell them to reconnect the telephones."

"Unfortunately, telephone and telex lines are disconnected," said Afrouz. "We are not able to talk to our officials in Tehran. If the lines can be restored, I can continue direct negotiation with my government over the siege. I must be able to get through to my government to put an end to this—"

Tucker spoke for the first time: "Please be patient. Everything will be okay. Please tell Salim we hope the gunmen will consider this conversation as a sign of goodwill on our part. It is our intention to end this siege peacefully."

"Do you want to respond?" Karkouti whispered to Towfiq.

The gunman shook his head and lowered his gun, smiling.

IT IS PERFECTLY possible for different people to listen to the same spoken words and yet hear entirely opposite meanings.

The negotiators and police in Zulu Control interpreted the latest exchange as part of a holding pattern, in which nothing had been conceded, nothing gained, and nothing promised. Towfiq and the hostages who had accompanied him to the window believed they had heard something else entirely: a climbdown by police, a pledge to restore the telephone lines, and a solemn promise to broadcast the group's demands and political message, word for word.

Elation flooded the hostage room on their return, like light pouring through an opened curtain. Towfiq was grinning, convinced that the plight of Iran's Arabs would soon be all over the news.

"Thank you for being so helpful," he said to Harris.

"Well, it's a pleasure," said Harris, after the single most stressful experience of his life.

Ezzati had recovered slightly and was sitting up, color returning. Fowzi brought him a cup of tea. The hostages were moved from the third-floor reference library back down to the second-floor general office. "A pattern seemed to be developing," Harris observed. "The upstairs room was used as the tension room, and the downstairs room was more relaxed."

Towfiq had an exaggerated respect for the power of the BBC. Believing Crabb had promised to broadcast his statement, he was visibly calmer. Harris noticed a marked change in the body language of the gunmen. "In the way they guarded us, they were not pointing guns directly at us." Faisal usually stood with his little finger hooked menacingly through the ring of a hand grenade. Now he slipped it into his pocket.

Another discussion took place through the talking window. Towfiq's tone was much more reasonable now. "All we want is to meet the ambassador, and settle this peacefully by letting the hostages free," he said, but then the menace returned. "Don't take any action against this embassy because we can kill the hostages no matter how quick you think you are. We have no intention of staying here for two or three months. We will decide to finish this one day . . ."

The police promised to temporarily reconnect the telex so that the diplomats could send another message to Tehran. In return, Towfiq agreed to accept the return of the field telephone.

The atmosphere brightened further with the arrival of lunch, left on the doorstep on two trays: steaks, chops, peas, fries, cans of Coke, bottled water, and cartons of milk. There were individual portions of cheese and biscuits on paper plates, wrapped in cellophane. The gunmen joined in, eating heartily.

Roya noticed that Lock was not eating.

"I can't," lied Lock, who was famished. "I have a bad stomach. But I'll take a glass of water and some biscuits. I'm too fat anyway; it won't hurt me to lose a few pounds."

The gunmen unwound. In an office drawer Shaye found a Kodak Instamatic camera with a built-in flash, and shyly asked if he might make some photos, as mementos. He took six snaps of the hostages sitting on the floor, eating steak, and one of Jassim with a wide smile, holding his gun aloft.

Under the new embassy rules, female staff were expected to wear a headscarf, or hijab, as an expression of Islamic feminine modesty. Only the rebellious Roya refused. But by now all the women had removed their scarves. Karkouti (ever alert to female beauty) noticed that "Nooshin took a couple of minutes to comb her silky black long hair and swiftly lifted it up to reveal an elegant and most beautiful neck seductively sitting on her model-like shoulders, which were covered with a claret neckless blouse."

"A picnic atmosphere developed," wrote Karkouti. "Lovely Ron bustled around in butler-fashion with paper napkins and cups of water" as if catering at a normal embassy function. He was particularly solicitous to the Iranian boss. "Are you comfortable, sir?" Morris asked Afrouz. "Do you have enough to eat? Can I get you anything else?"

Harris was struck by the way Morris seemed determined to maintain standards: "Ron was marvelous, the way he would fuss around people."

Muhammad Faruqi, the devout Pakistani journalist, decided the moment required a souvenir, "something to remember us with." He flattened out the white cardboard food cartons, produced a pen, and suggested that everyone sign their names and leave a message. "May Allah save us," Faruqi wrote by his own name, and passed this makeshift visitors' book to Sim Harris, who signed "All the best." "Best Wishes," wrote Lock. "A pleasure to have met you," Ron Morris scribbled. "This is the beginning of new friendship," Karkouti declared.

When the piece of cardboard reached Towfiq, the lead gunman signed his nom de guerre, Salim, with a flourish. Jassim saw an opportunity to make a political statement and wrote in Arabic: "We have a great hope that the World will understand our aim in this operation, which we consider as a kind of a struggle against tyranny and enslavement directed against our Arab people in Arabistan. Long Live the People's Struggle against Imperialism, Long Live the Revolution: signed, The Fighter, Faisal."

The Iranians each signed, followed by the women hostages. One left a lipstick kiss on top of her signature. The Westernized press assistant, Ali Samadzadeh, was optimistic: "Looking forward for better times."

Roya Kaghachi summed up the prevailing mood: "May we meet again in a happier future . . . Roya."

At first Abbas Lavasani refused to sign, but then he relented and penned what sounded like a religious admonishment to his more secular colleagues: "Thanks to Him Alone. God is Great."

As Morris cleared away the plates and made tea, the brittle humor returned. Lock amused Towfiq by rehearsing the Arabic swear words he had learned on National Service in Libya. "*Gahba*," said the police-man. "*Ilhas teezy.*" Bitch. Kiss my arse.

"Your accent is very bad, Mr. Trevor," said Towfiq, the former language student, grinning.

Bushy-bearded Nawabzada Gul continued to utter Delphic pro-nouncements, with a slight stammer, in a "priestlike" manner that was not intended to be funny but made everyone snigger. "If God has de-cided our fate, then there is nothing we can do about it," he intoned. This fatalism did not extend to his approaching flight to Pakistan, a subject he raised with infuriating insistence. Lacking a sense of humor, Gul was the sort of person it is almost impossible not to tease.

"You look like Fidel Castro," remarked Ron Morris.

"No," said Gul gravely. "Fidel Castro looks like me."

The only hostage untouched by the fragile levity and convivial ban-ter was Abbas Lavasani. The young press officer sat apart, withdrawn and pensive. The gunmen had earlier demanded that the hostages se-lect a victim from among them. Ezzati had narrowly escaped becoming the first victim. Somewhere in Lavasani's fanatical mind, an idea of self-sacrifice was forming.

Martyrdom is central to Shia Islam, shaped by the deaths of the early martyrs of the faith, Ali ibn Abi Talib and Husayn ibn Ali, and carried into the modern age. Khomeini repeatedly called for the ulti-mate sacrifice during the Revolution, and the shah's victims were re-vered as martyrs in the Islamic Republic. Lavasani was a gentle man, but he was also a fundamentalist and a member of the Revolutionary Guard, saturated with the ideological propaganda of the regime he served. His faith in the ayatollah was absolute and unquestioning. A few hours earlier, the Iranian foreign minister, Sadegh Ghotbzadeh, had declared that the Iranians should consider it a privilege to die as martyrs. This was not the case with all the Iranian hostages, but it was very possibly true of this one.

Soon after 12:00 the green field telephone was passed back in through the window, along with some heart medication for Ezzati. These were placebo tablets, medically valueless. "It was part of the tac-tic not to relieve totally the symptoms of the hostage," John Dellow noted, "causing the terrorists concern in the hopes that the negotiators could play on that concern and force the release of the hostage. The terrorists did not want a hostage to die on their hands." Dellow might play by the rules, but the rules were changing: he was prepared to manipulate the gunmen's emotions and allow hostages to suffer, if that could help bring about a peaceful end.

The field telephone was the same one Towfiq had tossed out the window earlier but now with an important modification: it had been adapted into an eavesdropping device. The line remained open, even when the receiver was in its cradle and the black button unlit. The gunmen could never ring off. Anyone speaking within ten feet of the device would be overheard, around the clock, their words recorded and, if necessary, translated. Towfiq placed the telephone on the reception desk in the entrance hallway. Police now had a permanent live wiretap in the very heart of the building.

At 12:23, Towfiq reentered the general office and motioned urgently to Lock and Harris, a look of consternation on his face: "Come, quick, the women have heard something . . ."

In the cipher room next door, strange noises were audible within the wall.

"We are afraid the police are going to set explosives and blow us all up," Kaghachi whispered to Harris in English. "We had to tell the boys." Through the warping prism of Stockholm syndrome, the women trusted the gunmen, "the boys," more than they trusted the police.

Towfiq pointed to the plug socket.

"Be careful, Mr. Trevor, if the noise is preparation to storm the building, there will be a massacre in here."

Harris and Lock kneeled to listen. From inside the wall came a squeaking noise, not loud but repetitive and intermittent. The BBC soundman knew at once what he was hearing: a twist drill, very slowly grinding through the brickwork.

Lock also recognized the noise. He put his ear to the socket and tapped softly, then harder. The noise stopped. He rolled back the carpet and inspected the bottom of the skirting board.

Then the policeman rocked back on his heels, folded his arms, and pronounced: "This building is more than a hundred years old. I think they've got mice."

11

ONE WOMAN
AND HER DOG

While the hostages ate their lunch, a media feeding frenzy was taking place outside, a ritual with distinct mealtimes and a set menu.

First, like some vast and voracious swarm, the press consumes and regurgitates every morsel of news in reach, most of it inaccurate. Then, when real information dries up, some journalists start to invent it. If imagination runs out, they describe things that have nothing to do with the story, such as the weather or the irrelevant opinions of passersby. Finally, they report on each other.

Inside the press enclosure, rival news organizations erected platforms to get a better view down Kensington Road toward Princes Gate. The giant American TV network CBS built a scaffolding tower twenty feet high and engaged a security guard to prevent anyone else from climbing it. Not to be outdone, the *Daily Express* photographer Harry Dempster (considered to be that most dubious of icons, a "Fleet Street legend") contacted a scaffolding firm in Kilburn and by daybreak had built a structure even higher than that of the Americans. The BBC and ITN, the main UK television news broadcasters, went even further, and hired two cherry pickers, mobile cranes mounted on trucks with a cradle at the top that could hoist a camera operator a hundred feet off the ground. The BBC alone deployed over forty staff to the scene, with editing and transmission vans, two mobile cameras, and radio reporters with handheld microphones. "If it goes on much longer, this could be the most expensive operation we have ever mounted," a BBC producer told *The Times*.

The news organizations jostled for advantage. The director of the Royal School of Needlework was offered a thousand pounds a day (over five thousand pounds in today's money) to permit filming from the roof. He declined. *The Sunday Times* rented the top floor of the Royal Geographical Society, with a commanding view of the area. Around midmorning, two gentlemen in business suits pulled up in a taxi at the police cordon, unloaded their heavy luggage, and explained that they were staying with a friend in one of the flats behind the embassy. The police waved them through, and an obliging bobby helped carry their suitcases to the front door. They took the elevator to the sixth floor, entered the flat, and began unpacking camera equipment. An enterprising producer had contacted one of the remaining residents, who, for a fat fee, agreed to let the cameramen film from his windows and live in his spare room. ITN now had an unimpeded vantage point overlooking the back of the embassy, a better view than the police. Rebecca West continued her vigil at her kitchen window.

To meet the demand for on-the-spot communications, the post office wheeled in a bank of coin-operated phones for the journalists to fight over. Dempster persuaded the *Express*'s managing editor to equip his car with an expensive radio telephone. Ray Rogers, crime reporter of the *Daily Mail,* turned up with a lidded briefcase containing a portable radio telephone, an astonishing piece of technology that cost over a thousand pounds. With this, Rogers bragged, he could contact his office from anywhere, without needing a landline. Most reporters had never seen a portable telephone before. Stewart Tendler of *The Times* immediately nullified the *Mail*'s advantage by buying a small VHF radio from a shop in Earl's Court, which he used to eavesdrop on every call Rogers made with his newfangled gizmo: an early triumph of phone hacking. American broadcasters also deployed the latest technology, beaming reports via satellite to the morning breakfast shows in the United States. Known as "going on the bird," this new method of reporting cost a $150 a minute.

The weather had improved, and the media congregation on the edge of Hyde Park began to resemble an enormous, raucous outdoor festival as they waited, watched, gossiped, complained, competed for news scraps, and racked up expenses. Kate Adie arrived for the third day in a row, to find "lazing newsmen playing a giant game of Lego as they waited in the sunshine." The team from NBC hired a fleet of yellow bicycles to cycle to and from the scene through the traffic jams. ITN brought in a mobile catering van, and rival reporters "stared moodily at the teams of chefs preparing delicious cold collations or curry for the finicky eaters of the television technicians' union." The nearby pubs did a roaring trade. When these closed between 15:00 and 17:00, as required under the 1914 licensing laws, the hardest-drinking hacks headed to the off-license. The photographers enjoyed a selection of fine wines in the spring sunshine, accompanied by "a superb collection of cheeses provided by other people's wives."

The Iranian Embassy siege saw the largest gathering of news reporters since the queen's coronation in 1953, but there was, as yet, little to report. This did not stop the press from reporting a great deal about not much. The Iranian demonstrators, obedient to their government, stayed away, save for a few stragglers. A lone Japanese monk prayed for peace, "to prevent a possible disaster," kneeling among the daffodils. One of the first rules of Old Fleet Street was to fill gaps in the news with the grout of pure whimsy. Many column inches were devoted to the well-being of Nibbles, the Montessori nursery school's pet gerbil. The *Express* devoted part of its front page to the wild duck's nest on the windowsill; a woman was spotted taking a foam mattress through the police cordon to make a soft landing on the pavement in case her eggs rolled off. *The Sun* reported that "nurses in frocks" had come to see what was happening: this allowed the enticing word "frocks" to be set in bold type.

The press began arriving at Warley Avenue in Dagenham soon after dawn. Peeking through the curtains of her front room, Doreen Lock saw the metal police barrier erected across the road, and fresh strands of police tape. A throng of press spilled off the pavement into her neighbors' flower beds. Two women police constables stood guard at her door. "Stay in the house, love," they said.

A lugubrious commander from the Dagenham police station appeared.

"Do you want the good news or the bad news?" he asked, a question beloved of sadists the world over. Doreen nicknamed him Doctor Death.

"No, get it over. Give me the bad news first," said Doreen.

"There's been another deadline . . ."

"And the good news?"

"They haven't shot him. Trevor's still alive."

DETECTIVE SERGEANT Graham Collins of the Anti-terrorist Branch was summoned to the basement of the Montessori nursery school to attend "a briefing with some colleagues from other agencies." Four men were waiting. Collins recognized one as Detective Sergeant Jeff Chippendale, from Special Branch. The other three nodded in greeting but did not introduce themselves. A man in dark civilian clothes beckoned the group to follow him to the rear of the building and instructed them not to speak. "What on earth is going on?" wondered the young policeman. In single file, the little troop slipped silently along the hidden walkway between the houses and the garden, past the back of the Iranian Embassy, and into the Royal College of General Practitioners at Number 15, where they were ushered into an enormous first-floor room.

Ranged around the walls were some of the toughest and strangest-looking men Collins had ever seen. "It was full of SAS troopers, wearing overalls, balaclavas rolled down their necks, gas masks slung from their waists and adorned with various weapons, sitting in easy chairs, slouching about, munching bacon and chip butties." B Squadron was having lunch. "They were the most ragtag and bobtail group, and had it not been for the weaponry you wouldn't have known they were military. But they had their kit on. They were ready to go."

Collins knew the SAS was on standby. He had no idea they were stationed next door to the embassy. "My jaw dropped."

The man in civilian clothes explained that this was a "two-way briefing session"; the intelligence officers would relay the latest information on the siege, and the waiting SAS men would quiz them.

Collins and Chippendale introduced themselves as members of the intelligence cell of the Anti-terrorist unit and Special Branch. The three other men revealed that they were from MI5, MI6, and the Army Intelligence Corps.

The soldiers immediately peppered them with questions. How many hostages? Where are they located? How many embassy staff? How many gunmen? Some scribbled notes.

"It was really, really weird," thought Collins. "Myself and the other visitors addressing this throng of black-clad individuals, all different shapes and sizes. That was the other extraordinary thing. I expected them all to be six foot tall, built like the proverbial brick shithouse. But they weren't."

Not only did the SAS team defy macho stereotypes, but their questions were astute. "These are very intelligent guys," Collins reflected. "These are not raw-meat eaters."

Henceforth, all intelligence gathered by the police and secret services—from long-distance surveillance, probes inserted into the building, and humint or sigint—would be pooled and fed every day to the SAS team, along with their lunch.

To prepare for a possible assault, the SAS needed to understand every inch of the interior. So they built a replica embassy, twice.

Armed with the architect Clifford Jacques's floor plans and the detailed knowledge of the caretaker, police carpenters from the Architects and Surveyors Department constructed a scale model of the embassy in plywood and cardboard, floor by floor, complete with furniture, windows, and doors. Toy plastic figures represented the people inside. The hostages were tiny farmworkers carrying sacks on their backs; when the sacks were removed, they had their hands up in surrender. The toy hostage-takers carried guns. The little figures were moved around from room to room, and from floor to floor, as intelligence was updated on the suspected whereabouts of the hostages and their captors. The model was placed on a large table in the SAS intel room, for troopers on standby to study and absorb, memorizing the layout and the latest

positions of those inside. Here was a dolls' house for soldiers, a miniature Killing House in which the SAS could visualize what was taking
place in the building next door.

Meanwhile, members of the Irish Guards Assault Pioneer Platoon
were brought in to construct a far larger replica, two-thirds of the embassy's actual size, in the gym at Regent's Park Barracks. The structure,
representing the ground, first, and second floors, was built in just
twenty-four hours from burlap sacking and timber, and hammered into
the wooden floor with six-inch nails (much to the dismay of the police
training instructor). The windows and doors were the correct shape
and size, and each opened in the right direction.

Red Team and Blue Team alternated in twelve-hour shifts. Troops
not on standby for immediate action trained, slept, or studied incoming
intelligence. Tommy Palmer and three others were taken to an abandoned police building with a large internal courtyard, where they attached ropes to the railings and abseiled down a hundred feet. Others
rehearsed by storming the burlap-and-timber replica, rescuing hostages, and neutralizing their captors. Sometimes the soldiers were
blindfolded, feeling their way around the corridors and corners in darkness. Others practiced on the indoor shooting range at Regent's Park
Barracks.

Unnoticed by the press or anyone inside the building, at 13:20 a
white transit van drove into Hyde Park and parked 150 yards from the
front of the embassy, beside a tennis court. It looked a little like an ice-
cream van without windows. Inside were two snipers with Tikka Fin-
lander 5.56mm rifles mounted with high-powered scopes and loaded
with high-velocity rounds. A series of small holes had been drilled into
the side of the van, which enabled the snipers to watch the embassy
without being seen, and to report any movements. If the immediate
action plan was activated, they would emerge from the back doors and
take aim with different arcs of fire, one from the front of the vehicle
and one from behind.

All photographs, diagrams, maps, notes, and other pertinent information were transferred to a large board in the intel room on the
ground floor. Each soldier was ordered to memorize the names, faces,
clothes, and other features of those inside, as well as the clothes and

footwear of the gunmen. Police artists, using sighting reports and Chris Cramer's testimony, produced colored sketches of the hostage-takers. With their mustaches and new jackets, the figures in the sketches looked like a 1970s rock band. After each negotiation with the hostage-takers, police brought over a cassette recording, to be played to the assembled men. A precise description of each weapon carried by the gunmen was pinned up on a separate board: "Soviet anti-personnel RGD-5 egg-shaped fragmentation grenades used in hijacking of a Sabena airliner"; "Polish 9mm Model 63 Machine Pistols . . . a high rate of fire machine pistol best suited as a personal defense weapon."

Distinguishing friend from foe was hard enough inside the Killing House. In a real hostage situation it would depend on split-second timing, instant recognition, and copious amounts of luck.

Most of the SAS team thought all this frenetic activity was probably pointless: the gunmen would surrender, and the contingency planning and exercises would come to nothing. This had so often been the pattern in Northern Ireland: train, prepare, deploy, and then stop; tool up, and then stand down. But, as B Squadron waited in London, its sister, G Squadron, was locked in a bloody battle on the streets of Belfast that would have a direct impact on events at Princes Gate.

MOST MORNINGS, a young woman took her Dobermann for a walk down Lower Antrim Road in North Belfast. She was twenty years old, slim and attractive, but, in her own words, "not so pretty as to draw attention." In one ear, invisible beneath her long hair, she wore an earpiece, attached to a concealed radio. On her hip, under nylon workers' overalls, was a leather holster carrying a 9mm Browning semi-automatic pistol, which she knew how to use. This part of the city was a Republican stronghold, notorious for paramilitary activity. No one paid any attention to the woman with the dog.

The daughter of a schoolmaster in a military family, Janet Dillon joined the Women's Royal Army Corps at the age of seventeen, and was attached to the Intelligence Corps. Within a year she was in Northern Ireland, where she was approached by the staff officer responsible for intelligence gathering in the battle against the IRA. "Are you bored?" he asked. "I think I've got just the thing for you." After training and assessment she was selected for 14 Intelligence Company, later to become the Special Reconnaissance Regiment, conducting covert operations against Republican and Loyalist paramilitary targets in support of the Royal Ulster Constabulary and SAS. Women had not been employed in secret operations of this sort since the Second World War, when Winston Churchill's Special Operations Executive deployed female agents into Nazi-occupied Europe. Dillon was ideal for the task of spying on the IRA: highly intelligent, young, innocent-looking, preternaturally brave, and, on the busy streets of Belfast, almost invisible.

For months, Dillon and her colleagues had been monitoring the movements of Unit B2 of the Provisional IRA, a four-man active-service team of the Belfast Brigade known as the M60 Gang after the weapon they used during hit-and-run attacks: an American-made, heavy-caliber, rapid-firing M60 machine gun, capable of penetrating armor. The gun had been stolen from an American National Guard depot in Massachusetts in 1976 and sold to the IRA. In April, the M60 gang lured an RUC patrol into an ambush and opened fire, killing one constable and injuring three others. What the gang did not know, however, was that a tracking device had since been inserted into its prized gun. This practice was known as "jarking": removing a weapon from a terrorist arms dump with the help of informers, and then returning it without the gunmen realizing it has been tampered with. But 14 Intelligence Company knew where the gun was, and, on May 2, 1980, the third day of the Iranian Embassy siege, the M60 gang was inside a Victorian terraced house on Antrim Road.

Janet Dillon and her partner completed their morning-surveillance routine as usual, discreetly observing the IRA house. They were returning to headquarters by car when the radios crackled into life: "Contact! Contact!"

Acting on an RUC tip that the gang were about to stage an attack on a soft-skinned police Land Rover as it drove past, SAS G Squadron took preemptive action. One car carrying three SAS troopers in plain clothes, armed with automatic rifles, machine guns, and pistols, parked at the back of the building, while a second car with a five-man team drew up in front. The IRA machine-gunners spotted them. The soldiers were emerging from the car when the M60 opened fire from an upper room. Captain Richard Westmacott was hit in the head and killed instantly. The rest of his team took cover behind parked cars and returned fire. Additional forces were summoned. One of the IRA gunmen scrambled down the back stairs and was starting up the unit's escape van when he was captured. After a prolonged battle, the remaining three gunmen surrendered.

Westmacott was the highest-ranking SAS soldier to die in the Troubles. He had been a popular officer, just twenty-eight years old, and news of his death swiftly reached B Squadron in London. Soldiers sign up to fight and die, yet a shocked anger often spreads through the ranks when they do. The killing of Richard Westmacott lent Operation Nimrod a new, sharper edge. "Sad news in an already tense situation," wrote one trooper in B Squadron. "It appears we are hitting the news, although there is no mention of our presence in London, so far." For Michael Rose, the commanding officer of 22 SAS, the death of another man under his command was a "terrible blow," at a critical juncture. "My mind was immediately and simultaneously running on Northern Ireland," he said.

Back in Belfast, after debriefing, Janet Dillon and her colleagues retired to the bar to commiserate. At around midnight, a senior officer spotted the diminutive young woman among the burly, boozy, and increasingly belligerent troopers, and gently suggested "it would be a good time for Janet to retire to bed."

This was good advice, because, a few hours later, Janet Dillon would be in a helicopter, on her way to Princes Gate.

12

THIS IS NOT
A DRILL

Towfiq was no expert on Georgian architecture, but he was highly skeptical that "dozens of mice in the skirting boards" could be squeaking in concert, as Trevor Lock had suggested. He instructed the policeman to find out from the negotiators where the suspicious sounds were coming from.

Lock waved his peaked cap from the first-floor window, and then stuck it back on his head as a policeman emerged from behind the wall.

"Are you making the noises I can hear next door?" he said. "Are you planning an attack?"

"This is wild thinking," the officer outside insisted. "You must reassure Salim that we have no such plans at all." He was not lying. The negotiators were still unaware of the bugging operation.

Lock continued: "You must understand that everyone is frightfully tense inside the embassy and the continuous noises from behind the wall are making them dangerously nervous."

"We understand your situation, but can you assure Salim and everybody else that we are not considering any storming or attack of any sort."

"Sir, I've already explained to the gunmen that the building is so old, the noises were most likely made by mice."

"That is most probably the noises' source."

"Okay, thank you very much."

Lock was about to shut the window when the officer asked if he wished to convey a message to his wife. Lock thought for a moment and then replied: "Tell her to keep her chin up."

Lock had already explained to his fellow hostages that the noise was almost certainly being made by his colleagues in the technical unit, installing bugs. "The police have all kinds of electronic equipment," he said, opining on a subject he knew exactly nothing about. The English-speaking hostages found themselves enunciating more clearly for invisible microphones. "The thought that the police were listening or perhaps even watching us on cameras through the walls was weird but comforting," said Karkouti.

John Dellow ordered a halt to the drilling, and informed Cobra. "The suspicions of the terrorists aroused by the drilling seem to be associated by them with an attack on the stronghold by police rather than with intelligence gathering," he said. Both MI5 and the police were drilling holes, independently, into the embassy. MI5 claimed the "offending" noises were being made by the police. The police technicians blamed MI5. It was a pointless technical turf war and "an irritating management problem" for Dellow.

In a film or fiction, surveillance devices would produce a clear video feed and an audible soundtrack of events inside the building. The reality was different. Repeated attempts to insert a tiny video camera on a fiber-optic cable (another new science) came to nothing.

After three days, the technicians had yet to drill completely through any wall. "Some of the drills were deep enough to provide slightly better audio facility," Dellow noted, and the "accelerometers performed well especially in determining movement and occupancy." MI5's radar system had "no great effect." By far the most useful eavesdropping device was the field telephone. But the coverage was still patchy at best, often just single words or snatches of conversations in multiple languages, the sounds coming and going as people moved around the rooms, coughed, or spoke over one another. Deciphering full sentences, let alone complete conversations, was difficult, painstaking work.

Meanwhile, the drilling was ratcheting up the tension inside, and could trigger an explosion. Dellow was increasingly concerned about

Salim's psychological stability. The criminal psychiatrist John Gunn was warning that he might crack under the stress: "Any terrorist who goes into an operation of this kind must have an enormous personal investment which overrides his own safety. At all stages therefore he feels the strain of potential failure. A further strain is the diminishing control which the terrorist has over the siege and his own fate. One of the severest strains is isolation." Sooner or later, Gunn predicted, the lead gunman's "coping mechanism" would fail, and the sounds of drilling could be the last straw. Dellow was no gambler, but he decided to take a chance.

"It is obviously essential to recommence the technical attack on the stronghold as soon as possible to complete the work of providing listening and viewing probes," Dellow told Whitelaw, the Home Secretary. "The need for intelligence dictates that some risks be taken."

The only certain way to disguise a small noise is to make a much bigger one, and to solve this unexpected quandary the government turned to an unlikely ally: the British Gas Corporation. The office of the home secretary contacted the energy secretary, who contacted the gas corporation, which contacted the gas board's emergency control center at Staines. An hour later a van towing a large compressor set off for Princes Gate with two heavy pneumatic drills on board.

Unobtrusively, the government put out diplomatic feelers to the embassies of the Middle East. "We felt bound to follow up on the terrorists' request to see a group of Arab ambassadors," Douglas Hurd observed, with a palpable lack of enthusiasm. The Foreign Office first contacted the ambassadors of Jordan, Syria, and Algeria, explaining there was a "possibility" they could help by negotiating directly with the gunmen. A little later, similar calls went out to the embassies of Lebanon, Kuwait, and Qatar. Syria's canny ambassador, Adnan Omran, immediately asked: "What do you want us to *do*? What *sort* of intervention do you mean?" Here the Foreign Office was vague, because the British government really did not want the ambassadors to do anything, except help to keep the negotiation process going.

Margaret Thatcher certainly did not want foreigners wading in. "We were extremely doubtful about this," she wrote. "There was a risk that the objectives of such an intermediary might be different from our own." The Arab envoys should on no account agree to the gunmen's demand for safe passage out of the country, with or without the hostages. This, Thatcher insisted, should be "ruled out from the start." That gave the ambassadors little to bargain with. Omran quickly surmised that he and his fellow ambassadors were being "used as simply one more way of stalling the gunmen and wearing them down."

The Arab ambassadors agreed to contact their respective governments and report back. And there the matter was left to dangle, unresolved: a most satisfactory piece of diplomacy, in which all sides appeared to be doing something, while achieving nothing at all. Only the Iraqi ambassador offered to intervene and speak directly to the gunmen. His offer was respectfully but firmly declined.

AT 16:00, a small delegation gathered on the first-floor landing, consisting of Lock, Harris, Karkouti, and the Pakistani journalist, Muhammad Faruqi. The meeting was Karkouti's idea: "We decided to take advantage of the new atmosphere to start a conversation with Salim and impress upon him that patience was vital for the successful conclusion of their operation." The hostages arranged themselves in a semicircle, on office chairs. Opposite, on the stairs, sat Towfiq, with Jassim immediately behind him, both holding submachine guns. The discussion was conducted in English and Arabic, with Karkouti translating.

The Syrian journalist described the surreal scene. "We looked like two delegations meeting to discuss their mutual relations: hostages on one hand, and gunmen on the other." But what might look like a diplomatic mini-summit was really a plea for mercy: if it went wrong, one side might kill the other.

"British diplomacy is the best in the world," pronounced Harris. "But it takes time. You can't just dash round to an embassy and grab an ambassador. There are diplomatic channels."

Towfiq nodded.

Harris continued: "It's all a question of meetings, consultations, and more meetings. You can't rush these things."

Karkouti took over. "Always remember, my dear Salim, to keep calm when you talk to the police. You should make them feel that you are fully in control. You may think the police are playing games with you, but they are not. They negotiate with calm and persistence." He turned to Lock. "What do you think, Trevor?"

Lock was in a tricky position. The other two could advise the gunmen on tactics, but he represented Her Majesty's constabulary, as demonstrated by the police cap clamped on his head.

"Our final target in situations like this," Lock declared solemnly, "is to reach a peaceful end, no matter how long it takes."

The conversation shifted to the logistics of getting to the airport and flying out of it.

"Where would you be going from here?" Karkouti asked.

"My dear Mustapha," Towfiq replied with a dry smile, "it is too early to reveal that now. You'll all know at the right time."

Faruqi spoke up. "You have achieved most of your aims," he said. "If this continues as a peaceful demonstration, you would have made your point, right? Then you need to realize that if there is any violence you would have lost everything you have gained so far."

Towfiq's eyes narrowed. In Arabic, he muttered to Jassim: "What does he think he is doing, *gawad*"—that pimp—"trying to be clever?"

He turned back to Faruqi. "Please let us change the subject," he said, with a glint of menace.

Lock sensed the mood turning sour.

"Do you trust me?" asked the policeman, looking Towfiq in the eye.

Towfiq nodded slowly.

"Well, if you do, why not let me drive you and your comrades to a police station until all this is sorted out? I guarantee your safety if all of us get out unharmed. Just like the safe passage given to Leila Khaled in 1970."

This was a calculated gamble. A decade earlier, a twenty-six-year-old Palestinian woman named Leila Khaled hijacked an El Al flight traveling from Amsterdam to New York City. Two Israeli sky marshals on board killed her accomplice and overpowered Khaled. The plane was diverted to Heathrow, where the world's first female hijacker was arrested. Within a month, she was released in exchange for civilian hostages seized in another terrorist hijacking. Leila Khaled was the poster girl of Palestinian militancy. Lock guessed that Towfiq would know her story, and he was right. The Khaled incident had demonstrated British willingness to trade hostages for hijackers; that was partly why London was chosen for this operation. Towfiq was now paying attention.

"I can assure you that you won't be shot down as you leave the building," Lock insisted. "That's not the British way of doing things. They'll treat you with decency. Do the honorable thing now."

Towfiq did not reply immediately. When he finally spoke, his voice was resigned. "No. That would be the same as surrender."

The meeting lasted almost two hours. "The discussion we had was positive," Karkouti told the rest of the hostages, who clustered around when the delegation returned.

Harris agreed: "Everything is going to be okay. But it might take a bit of time. I don't think you'll be out in under a week."

The hostages dispersed around the room, and tranquility descended.

Ron Morris sat on his cushion, engrossed in *The Day of the Jackal*. He had just reached the part when the killers are seeking a mastermind to organize a spectacular terrorist operation in Europe. *In order to get the level of skill and of nerve necessary for this kind of operation, we need to engage a true professional. And such a man would only work for money. A lot of money.*

"I'll pass it on once I finish," Morris assured the others.

The toilet on the second floor was choked, emitting a vile smell. Harris volunteered to unblock it and cheerfully set to work: a nasty job but a brief reminder of normality.

The police sent in two cartons of cigarettes, Rothmans and John Player Specials.

Towfiq immediately called on the field telephone. "I wanted to thank you for the cigarettes."

"Salim, that's my pleasure," said Ray Tucker. "We sent two hundred tipped and two hundred plain. We didn't know what else to do. Is that all right?"

"Thank you very much."

The box on the end of the pole had been replaced by a "smooth, clean container." By "tilting the box at the time the cigarettes were being taken," Tucker ensured that Towfiq left a clear set of fingerprints.

Towfiq's next request was odder: a pair of trousers with a forty-two-inch waist.

Gholam-Ali Afrouz had ripped his suit trousers jumping off the balcony, but finding a suitable replacement pair at short notice was a challenge. The only person in the vicinity with sufficient girth was the head cook in the mobile food van, who gallantly agreed to surrender his spare pair of blue-checked chef's trousers. The garment was passed up to the window, and the press were delighted with the pictures that resulted. Iran's most senior diplomat now looked like a caterer.

"Dr. Afrouz," said Towfiq, beckoning to the Iranian diplomat. "The police have finally approved your request to get in touch with Tehran." The telex line had been restored. Afrouz got to his feet with as much dignity as a diplomat can muster while wearing blue-checked chef's trousers. For three hours, his first secretary, Issa Naghizadeh, had been working on a message to send to Tehran, a tricky balancing act, since this had to "please both the terrorists and the other hostages," without displeasing Iran's foreign minister. The note took a swipe at "world imperialism, meaning the US and all its supporters," but stressed that the demands being made by "our Iranian/Arab brothers attached to the Group of the Martyr Muhyiddin Al Nasser" were "reasonable and definitely worthy of investigation." It ended by calling on Iran's Revolutionary Council and minister of foreign affairs to provide "speedy cooperation and assistance" and then "announce a positive result": in other words, to negotiate with the gunmen and get them out alive. Towfiq looked over the Farsi text and nodded his approval.

MI5 was monitoring the telex line, ready to cut it off if necessary. The message undoubtedly reached the Iranian Foreign Ministry. Just as certainly, it was completely ignored.

Karkouti was not enjoying the role of middleman, "playing the dangerous role of 'aiding' or 'guiding' the gunmen in running the scene inside and outside the embassy." He feared that the other hostages might think he was somehow close to the gunmen or even collaborating with them. The others seemed to believe he possessed insider knowledge of the group's intentions. "When will they let us go?" they asked. If he managed to survive the siege, the British authorities would take a close interest in him. At home in Ealing, Karkouti had a forged passport, which he had used to travel undetected in his days as a militant. Would the police find it? Would he be thrown out of the country?

The British hostages trusted Karkouti completely. Lock, in particular, saw him as a vital ally, someone who might steer them all to safety.
But some of the Iranians were openly distrustful of this pro-Palestinian
Arab, who seemed to be getting on suspiciously well with the hostage-
takers. "It's too much of a coincidence that he was here when the gunmen stormed the building," Afrouz told Harris. "We don't trust him,
and you shouldn't either." Even the gunmen were initially suspicious of
the Syrian: "We were not expecting to find non-Iranian people inside
the embassy," Jassim told him. "Let alone an Arab."

Karkouti sat alone with his thoughts. Gunmen and hostages had
entered what he called "a period of deep silence and relaxation." For
almost an hour, no one spoke. "How long before Salim snaps?" wondered Karkouti. "How long before the police lose patience?"

Then, without warning, the calm was shattered by a cry from the
corner of the room. Abbas Lavasani leaped to his feet, gesticulating
wildly. "I am willing to be the martyr," he shouted in Farsi. "The next
time they want to kill someone, I will volunteer."

Jassim, standing guard, was as stunned by this statement as everyone
else. Lavasani was now speaking fast, the words tumbling out, as if re-
hearsed: "For the last four years, I have lived as a dead man. SAVAK
arrested a very close friend of mine, tortured him until he died. Since
then, I have been willing to embrace martyrdom."

Karkouti placed a calming hand on his shoulder. "Please do not
speak about martyrdom now . . ."

Lavasani's odd flare-up subsided as quickly as it had ignited. The
young man in the yellow cardigan returned quietly to his corner and
opened the Koran once more. The silence resumed, now suffused with
tension.

Ali Samadzadeh, Lavasani's Westernized colleague in the press department, shuffled over to Karkouti. "Watch out, Mustapha," he whispered, glancing at Lavasani. "He is trouble, we don't trust him."

Karkouti liked Samadzadeh, "a sensible, reasonable, honorable
man, neat in his three-piece suit." He might serve the ayatollah, but he
wore his religion lightly.

"What do you mean, you don't trust him?" asked Karkouti.

"Lavasani works for the revolutionary intelligence service. People here in the embassy are scared of him and avoid talking politics in his presence. He is trouble," Samadzadeh repeated.

Faruqi began a hushed conversation with Ron Morris. The Pakistani journalist was the eldest of the hostages, a "frail-looking, tiny man in his fifties with glasses and a straggly beard." Trained as an entomologist, with a PhD from Imperial College, London, Faruqi had worked for the Plant Protection Department in Pakistan and then in East Africa, controlling locusts. In 1970, he switched to journalism and founded *Impact International,* a magazine focused on Islamic affairs: he interviewed Khomeini shortly before his return from exile. A devout Muslim, Faruqi exuded an inner calm, which made his next suggestion so bizarre.

"These gunmen are now relaxed and nonbelligerent. Why don't we try to overpower them?"

Morris stared at the little man in astonishment. Here was someone "who had never held a gun in his life" suggesting they take on six heavily armed and well-trained guerrillas.

But Faruqi was serious. "What if we get hold of some of their guns and ammunition? We could barricade ourselves in a room and the police might be able to come in and get us safely out."

Lock, overhearing the conversation, intervened: "That is a very bad idea."

Faruqi dropped it, but his suggestion had been just as shocking, in its way, as Lavasani's outburst.

Like cracks in thinning ice, tension was spreading—among the hostages, between the police and gunmen, and inside every individual.

AS DARKNESS FELL and the streetlights came on along Kensington Road, Towfiq separated men and women for the third night running. Fowzi placed a chair strategically in the doorway between the general office and the cipher room to monitor both groups. When Towfiq switched off the overhead light, Fowzi abandoned the chair and settled on the floor "with the top half of his body slightly inside the women's room." From his sleeping position on the floor, Karkouti listened in to his conversation with green-eyed Shirazeh Boroumand.

"What do you do in the embassy?" Fowzi asked.

THIS IS NOT A DRILL 179

"I am a secretary," she said. "I've been living in London for about seven years and I found a job at the embassy four years ago."

"Are you married? Do you have a family?"

"Yes, married to an Englishman but no children yet."

"But you are too young to be married."

Shirazeh laughed. "It is very nice of you to think I am young. Thank you very much."

"I am sure you are not more than twenty."

"I am twenty-seven years old and I came here to experience living in London, something I always dreamed of doing."

"But how come you are working for the embassy of this horrible regime in Tehran?"

"This was not my choice. I was working for the embassy of the old regime, the shah's regime, and when the Revolution took place I was already in my job."

"You look much nicer without a scarf," Fowzi cooed.

"I use it to cover my hair only during working hours, and we female staff usually take the scarves off when we leave the embassy after work."

Nooshin Hashemenian, lying a few feet away, could take no more of this flirtation. "Stop talking, please, I am trying to sleep," she said with mock severity.

Fowzi and Shirazeh giggled. "Sorry," they said.

Roya was laughing in the background.

The rooms fell silent.

Then the pneumatic drills started up, the sudden explosive percussion of metal pounding into asphalt.

"What the hell is that?" said Harris, bolting upright. The racket was deafening, reverberating through the foundations.

Fowzi leaped to his feet, gun in hand.

"What the fuck? Drilling at midnight?" said Karkouti. "They are digging up the bloody road at this time of night!"

"No, they're not," whispered Lock. "This is a part of police tactics."

"Do you mean keeping the gunmen awake or in preparation to storm the building?"

Towfiq unslung his machine gun and rushed to the first-floor window to look for the source of the noise, and what it might mean.

Away to his right, under lights, two men in the workers' overalls of the British Gas Corporation were digging a large and entirely unnecessary hole in Kensington Road. The thunderous drilling was audible at the press enclosure, prompting one journalist to call the gas board press office: "It's some kind of emergency, a gas leak, all quite routine," he was told. Meanwhile, the police and MI5 technicians resumed their own drilling, the sound now masked by the cacophony from the street. Only Gul did not stir in his slumbers. Inside the embassy, Karkouti noted, "you could hardly hear yourself speak." The same was true for the SAS on standby in Number 15, and the police in the Montessori nursery school. Complaints flooded in from the neighbors.

During a pause in the noise, one of the probes picked up a disturbing snatch of Arabic conversation between the gunman Faisal and the hostage Karkouti.

"Salim is worried and believes the drilling is part of a police plan to storm the building. If this is the case, there will be a massacre in here, you must know that."

Karkouti tried to reassure him that there must be an emergency gas leak, "otherwise nobody would drill at this time of night."

"Let us hope this is true."

AFTER AN HOUR and a half, Dellow called off the gas board drillers, fearful that the noise could trigger bloodshed by causing "irritation to the terrorists and doubtless the hostages too."

Karkouti was beginning to feel an acute pain in his stomach. He could not get comfortable. He was finally drifting off after midnight, when he was gently shaken awake by Jassim. "Salim wants you . . ."

For a terrible moment, Karkouti wondered if this was it, the summons to execution.

The lead gunman was in the small room off the corridor. He politely motioned for Karkouti to sit. Jassim stood behind him.

"Ustaz Mustapha, we would like to have a political discussion with you about the Middle East, do you mind? Since we have met you, we have been thinking of benefiting from your experience as a journalist in this country, and hearing your views on several issues."

The Towfiq of that morning had been ready to kill. This one was a completely different man, inquisitive, well-mannered, and mellow.

"Where do you want me to start?" said Karkouti, rubbing his eyes.

"Tell us about yourself. How did you become a journalist?"

Karkouti described his childhood in Syria, his arrest by the secret police, his support for the Palestinian cause, his years in Beirut, and his decision to settle in London.

"Why do you not live in Earl's Court?" Towfiq asked with a grin. "I love that area, and I would love living there if I ever had the opportunity. So many nationalities, so colorful and cosmopolitan. You can even buy Arabic newspapers and *shawarma* sandwiches—"

"And there are attractive women too," Karkouti added, who felt himself drawn to this capricious man, with his gentle curiosity and hunger for knowledge. They plainly shared common political ground, including opposition to the Israeli occupation of Arab territories. Two of the other gunmen, Makki and Shaye, joined them and squatted on the floor at Karkouti's feet.

"Listen, guys," said Karkouti. "Maybe your cause is as just as the Palestinians' cause, but don't spoil it with any foolish move—"

"No, Brother Mustapha," Jassim interrupted. "It is about time we show these dogs in Tehran our real mettle." Towfiq's hard-faced deputy was not interested in discussing the quality of the food in Earl's Court.

The talk ebbed and flowed into the small hours, as the conversation widened into a general discussion of Middle Eastern politics, the growing tensions between Iran and Iraq, Saddam Hussein's rise to power, and the role of the PLO leader Yasser Arafat. In a huge London town house, surrounded and outgunned, they debated and discussed, around and around, as if casually chatting in an Arab café.

"The gunmen seemed fully relaxed," Karkouti noted. The front door must now be unguarded. They had just launched into a discussion on the difference between the shah and the queen, when Towfiq glanced at his new designer watch.

"Oh, my God, it is two-thirty in the morning," he said. "Sorry we've kept you awake until now, you should join your friends. We are very grateful for this important information and analysis."

The other gunmen drifted back to their posts, leaving Towfiq and Karkouti alone.

"Please accept our apology for the discomforts we have caused you," Towfiq said gently. "I hope we will meet again in better circumstances, maybe in Beirut, *inshallah*." God willing. "Hopefully we will end this operation tomorrow—I mean later today—and you can return in peace and good health to your home, your wife, and your little baby girl."

Karkouti was about to leave the room, when Towfiq gestured that he should stay.

The lead gunman had a secret he wanted to share. He described being recruited for the operation after his brother's murder, his training near Baghdad, and the role played by a Mukhabarat officer nicknamed the Fox.

But there was another overall organizer behind the plot, Towfiq continued, the brains behind the operation, a fighter with "much more experience of guerrilla war" than himself who had been expected to lead the group but then dropped out. Only Towfiq knew the operation had been hatched, organized, and armed by this shadowy figure. He had met this person only once, in Baghdad, with the Iraqis. "None of the other gunmen involved had any knowledge that he was the mastermind, acting on behalf of Saddam Hussein."

When Karkouti heard the name, he gasped. The man was a legend among Palestinian militants, a mercenary psychopath whose reputation for brutal killing eclipsed even that of Carlos the Jackal.

The mastermind behind the Iranian Embassy siege was the world's most notorious terrorist: Abu Nidal.

DAY FOUR

SATURDAY

13

ONE THOUSAND
AND ONE NIGHTS

Abu Nidal led a group of fanatics described by the U.S. Defense Department as "the most dangerous terrorist organization in existence." Starting in the early 1970s, his militant Palestinian faction killed over three hundred people in twenty countries in an orgy of shootings, bombings, and hijackings. His targets included Arab and Western diplomats, PLO officials, Jews, Israelis, synagogues, offices, and, above all, embassies. Born Sabri al-Banna, he was the son of a prosperous citrus farmer from Jaffa. Ejected from his home by Israeli forces in 1948, impoverished, enraged, alcoholic, paranoid, and possibly psychotic, he emerged as the most extreme radical inside the PLO, adopting the nom de guerre Abu Nidal, meaning "Father of Struggle." Ruthless and uncompromising, he was determined to destroy the state of Israel by violence, rejected compromise, and was prepared to kill any moderate Palestinian leaders who sought peace. Following a vicious split with the PLO leadership in 1973, he settled in Baghdad and began building an independent power base with the help of the Iraqi intelligence services. Under the protection of Saddam Hussein's Mukhabarat, Abu Nidal was hired as a freelance terrorist adviser and mercenary assassin, provided with a lump sum of between three and five million dollars, and supplied with fifteen million dollars' worth of Chinese-made weapons.

Abu Nidal had a method. In his first terrorist operation, in 1973, five Palestinian gunmen entered the Saudi Embassy in Paris, took eleven hostages, and threatened to blow up the building unless a Palestinian terrorist held in Jordan was released. The attackers apologized to the French government for the inconvenience and demanded that the Iraqi ambassador be brought in to mediate. By nightfall, the gunmen had reduced their demands to safe passage by air to an Arab country accompanied by some of the hostages. Sure enough, France provided a plane, and the gunmen flew to Kuwait, where they released the remaining hostages. A month later, Abu Nidal's gunmen were freed and left for Syria. The operation, mounted at the behest of the Iraqis to destabilize Saudi Arabia, was a foretaste of atrocities to come.

The 1960s had seen a rash of plane hijackings and political kidnappings, but by the 1970s the most fashionable form of terrorism was storming diplomatic buildings. Between 1971 and 1980, terrorists attacked embassies around the world on forty-eight separate occasions. "Taking hostages at embassies appears to be contagious," a 1981 RAND report into the phenomenon noted. "One event inspires another." The gunmen's demands—most commonly the release of political prisoners—were directed to the host country, the government of the seized embassy, or both. Not all these attacks on diplomats and diplomatic premises were the work of Abu Nidal, but a large proportion were, including an attack on the Syrian Embassy in Pakistan, the Jordanian Embassy in Athens, and the British Embassy in Jordan.

Abu Nidal treated terrorism as a business, and the balance sheet for embassy attacks was cost-effective. In one-third of the seizures, demands were fully or partially met; and, in roughly half of all cases, the gunmen were flown to another country, or simply walked away unscathed and unpunished. For the terrorist mastermind, this was an acceptable return on investment, although half his men ended up arrested, captured, or killed. The UK was seen as a soft target. In 1978, Abu Nidal's men had killed the moderate PLO representative in London, Said Hammami.

By 1980, Abu Nidal had settled in Baghdad, enjoying every comfort an international terrorist might desire: training camps in Hit and Ramadi, offices, passports, a farm, a newspaper, a radio station, and a stipend of around $150,000 a month. In return for shelter and largesse, he did Iraq's dirty work, hand in glove with the Mukhabarat: mounting operations against Saddam's Syrian rivals, his enemies in the PLO, diplomats around the world, and Iraq's communists. Abu Nidal's young militants were recruited in Palestinian refugee camps and Lebanon; targets were selected by his Committee for Special Projects.

This, according to Towfiq, was the hidden hand behind the attack on the Iranian Embassy, an operation with Abu Nidal's bloody fingerprints all over it. The siege was not some isolated incident, but part of an international terrorist conspiracy, an offshoot of Middle Eastern political violence erupting, suddenly, in the heart of London.

NAWABZADA GUL WAS still snoring at 08:00.

"It's not a laughing matter anymore," complained Mustapha Karkouti, who had lain awake for hours, his stomach aching, as the large Pakistani thundered and roared in his sleep.

"Do you think he's married?" wondered Sim Harris.

"I don't think so," said Trevor Lock. "No wife would ever stand for that."

Gul opened one eye. "You are wrong, my friends—my wife has never complained," he said. "And I don't snore."

Ron Morris bustled around making tea for everyone and distributing biscuits. The mess offended his ingrained sense of order. "Time for a good tidy-up," he announced. "We look like a bunch of squatters. It's a pigsty."

In the basement Morris found two garbage bags, into which he emptied the wastepaper baskets, ashtrays, empty drink cans, plastic cutlery, paper plates, and other refuse strewn around the rooms. He plumped up the cushions and straightened the furniture. Then he cleaned the bathroom basin with Domestos.

"He's a bit of a Jeeves," noted Harris, admiringly. "He makes everything almost civilized. The sort of man you couldn't possibly dislike."

"Can I do some hoovering?" Morris asked Towfiq.

The lead gunman, perplexed by the unfamiliar word, shook his head.

The toilet was choked again. With a grin, Harris volunteered to unblock it once more.

"There's a job for life for you there," said Lock.

Harris's offer was a characteristic mixture of charity and calculation: no one shoots the man who unclogs the toilet. It took twenty minutes of vigorous plunging to clear the waste pipe. Harris took the opportunity for what he called "a leisurely strip wash" before returning. He urged Lock to do the same.

"Do I smell?" Lock asked.

"No worse than the rest of us," Harris assured him.

This was not true. For three days, the policeman had been wearing an undershirt, a shirt, the two pullovers Doreen had insisted on to keep out the chill, a jacket, and his gabardine coat. The weather had turned warm. He was sweltering under his uniform and starting to itch. Lock knew he "stank like a goat." The gunmen politely asked if he wanted to take off his jacket.

"No, thanks," he said. "I'm still on duty."

The banker Ali Tabatabai amused the others by setting numerical riddles and pretending to be a cashier.

Harris demanded that "Ali the Bank" cash him a check for fifty pounds as payment for clearing the lavatory.

"What did you do with the hundred pounds I gave you yesterday?" said Tabatabai, in his best bank managerial voice.

"Oh, I spent the lot," said Harris. "I nipped out last night when you were all asleep and had a slap-up dinner at the Savoy."

Abbas Lavasani was dozing, Koran clutched to his chest. Abdul Ezzati remained deathly pale. "He is still quite ill," noted Harris, unaware that the pills he was feeding him were merely placebos. "Heart trouble almost hourly."

Karkouti was also visibly ailing. "He is beginning to show quite a bit of strain, suffering stomach pains and diarrhea," thought Harris. "Mustapha is really taking the brunt of the negotiations with the gunmen, talking Arabic, constantly trying to keep the tension down." But Harris was feeling the tension too. The fear came in waves of nausea, and sudden dizzy spells. Writing in his notebook helped.

The women sat apart. Several were menstruating heavily, another side effect of stress.

Consciously or unconsciously echoing the greatest storyteller in Middle Eastern folklore, Roya encouraged them to tell "secretive stories about their own private lives."

In the collection of medieval tales known as *One Thousand and One Nights*, the mighty King Shahryar, on discovering that his wife has been unfaithful, resolves to marry a new virgin every night and then behead her in the morning before she can dishonor him. When he runs out of virgins of noble blood, the beautiful Scheherazade, daughter of the king's vizier, volunteers to marry him. On their wedding night she tells him a story but stops before daybreak, leaving the tale unfinished. The monarch, enthralled by the tale, postpones her execution so that she can finish it the next day. This she does, and then starts another story, again without revealing the ending, and then another . . . for a thousand and one nights. Finally, Scheherazade has no more stories and prepares to bid farewell to the three sons she has given the king during three years of storytelling. But by now Shahryar has fallen in love: he spares Scheherazade's life and makes her his queen. *One Thousand and One Nights* (also known as *Arabian Nights*) is the fruit of multiple ancient cultures—Arabic, Persian, Sanskrit, and Mesopotamian—a tale of death averted, and an enduring testament to the power of the cliffhanger.

Roya told her life story first: the move to Britain as a teenager, the sumptuous embassy parties under the shah, the cosmopolitan Iranian crowd in London. Then Nooshin spoke, describing how her husband, Michael Hashemenian, a British citizen of Iranian origin, had spotted her photograph in an Iranian newspaper, taken during a street protest against the shah in 1978. Instantly besotted, he flew to Tehran, tracked her down, proposed, married her, and brought her back to London. The story told by Shirazeh Boroumand described her move to England in search of adventure, her marriage to an Englishman named Houghton, and her life in the London suburbs. English people called her Sherry.

Since the gunmen had released Frieda, thinking she was pregnant, Roya suggested that Hiyech Sanai Kanji, who really was pregnant, try groaning loudly, to see if they would let her go too. Hiyech laughed, saying she didn't know how to fake groaning. Roya offered to whimper on her behalf, a thought so absurd it provoked another fit of giggling.

Lavasani woke up and stared daggers at the women "laughing loudly and freely."

Roya returned his glare with interest and remarked loudly: "Life is short, isn't it?"

As the women took turns relating their life stories, Fowzi listened from the doorway, rapt.

The youngest gunman seemed to be having doubts. He did not want to kill anyone, let alone these attractive women. The operation was meant to be over in twenty-four hours. Towfiq and Jassim were bossy toward him, and sometimes threatening. Abbas Maytham was clearly unstable.

At the opposite end of the room, Ali the Bank, so cheerful a moment earlier, suddenly burst into tears and lay with his head on the carpet.

No one was as tense as Towfiq: glued to the radio, uncertain of his next move, he was baffled and exhausted. Where were the ambassadors? Why were the police not sending buses to take them to Heathrow? Above all, why had Tony Crabb, that supposedly powerful BBC magnate, failed to broadcast his statement as promised? The press was reporting Lock's stiff-upper-lip message to Doreen—KEEP YOUR CHIN UP, LOVE ran the headlines—but almost nothing about Arabistan.

John Dellow was firm: "The statement had not been broadcast because no certain agreement could be arrived at with regard to the release of hostages and for such a major concession this was essential."

At 11:30, Towfiq burst into the hostage room, furious. "Why are your media not broadcasting our statement?" he shouted at Harris. "What is going wrong? Why the media in England is not transmitting our demands?" He waved his submachine gun. "Someone will have to die."

Lock was marched downstairs to the first-floor window. (Towfiq used the field telephone on the ground floor for ordering food, cigarettes, and trousers; the talking window on the first floor was for face-to-face confrontations, usually conducted via one of the hostages.) He was told to relay a simple message: Crabb must return immediately and ensure that the message was aired on the BBC. If he did not appear within the hour, a hostage would be killed.

Moments later, Towfiq was back on the field telephone.

"No, we do not want breakfast," he snapped, switching to Arabic, in answer to Luff's first question. "We have got to see Tony Crabb and could you get him now?"

"Is he prepared to release a hostage after seeing Tony Crabb?" Luff asked the harassed translator Mrs. Shadloi, who was still wearing her bulletproof vest and fur coat.

"No, we are not prepared to free any of the hostages," Towfiq replied to the translated question. "But if you want to see a dead body of any of the hostages, you may see it in a few minutes."

"Will you say to Salim: I did not report back that threat before because it will destroy our argument?" Luff asked Mrs. Shadloi. "And I wish to keep this threat, at the moment, between ourselves. Because it will not help." Luff was pleading.

"I refuse to listen," said Towfiq. "Please don't do something which would cause us to kill the hostages, because we don't really wish to do so."

Luff agreed to bring Crabb to the window and thus, inadvertently, broke one of the key rules of negotiation, by making a promise he could not fulfill.

Because Tony Crabb did not answer the telephone at his home in Sunbury-on-Thames, Surrey, thirteen miles from Central London: he was out shopping with his wife.

THE POLICE AND MI5 could overhear some of what was being said inside the embassy but not enough. "In different locations, you'd be picking up different snippets of information," said Graham Collins of C13. MI5 and the Police Technical Unit wanted to insert more probes into the walls. Dellow feared the noise might tip the gunmen into violence. The pneumatic drills had only made matters worse. But if the sound could not be masked at ground level, perhaps it might be camouflaged from the sky down.

Dellow contacted the Civil Aviation Authority with a formal request that planes landing at Heathrow be rerouted to fly at low altitude over Kensington. The air traffic controllers complied, and by midmorning commercial jets were sporadically rumbling over the area, flying so low that the passengers aboard could clearly make out the area cordoned off around the embassy below them. Airliners were louder in 1980 than they are today, and, flying at 1,500 feet, 2,000 feet lower than usual, they produced an earsplitting noise. Whenever the technicians heard the rumble of an approaching plane, they resumed drilling and dismantling the brickwork in the Ethiopian Embassy wall. As the sound of the aircraft faded, they stopped. The task of bugging the embassy continued, albeit intermittently, supplemented by a fresh set of gizmos, brought in by the scientist-spies.

At the back of the embassy, to determine where the hostages were being held, MI5 set up an untested radar system and a thermal-imaging camera able to detect body heat. The technicians also detected movement with the accelerometers, and harnessed the emerging science of interferometry, a method of measurement using the phenomenon of interference of sound, radio, or light waves. In theory, when two or more microphones were inserted in a single room, MI5 would have been able to pinpoint where the hostages and gunmen were located. Since people moved constantly inside the rooms, between them, and from floor to floor, it was decided not to pass on this intelligence as a live feed. "That would have been too much information," one SAS officer observed. "We'd have had brain freeze."

From where John Dellow sat in Zulu Control, the situation was broadly running according to plan. No hostages had been harmed since the initial attack. The lead gunman was angry and volatile but talking, sometimes politely, and accepting food, cigarettes, medicines, and repeated delays. His deadlines came and went, a sure sign of indecision. Knowing that the gunmen were closely following the news, Dellow had the police spokesman issue a statement intended to mollify. "I have no reason to think that these people are doing anything other than trying to make a point," said the police spokesman Peter Neivens, carefully referring to the group as "hostage-takers," not terrorists.

With every passing hour, the police intelligence cell added detail to the rogues' gallery of gunmen, with Photofit (facial composite) sketches and descriptions gleaned from Chris Cramer, the bugging operation, and visual surveillance. Salim was designated "Suspect 4: leader," and described as "5'7", 25–6 years, slim build, oval face, neck-length black hair, parted on right, thick black mustache and eyebrows, big dark eyes, wearing fine brown check sports jacket, blue vest fairly low at the front, black trousers and belt, black metal-framed sunglasses (most of time), red/whi scarf around mouth. V polite, calm, v good Persian and Arabic, passable English. Right-handed. *Weapon:* Machine Gun." Distinguishing features were picked out: the "sense of humor" exhibited by Makki; Shaye's habit of walking barefoot, and his "boney [*sic*], gaunt features." The "nervous, excitable" gunman labeled "Suspect 5" (probably Abbas Maytham) had a "bit of a gut" and wore a "casual jersey with three buttons at the neck." Faisal gave most cause for concern: "Speaks loudly, right-handed, nervous, made threats to kill . . . *Weapon*: Machine gun with collapsible stock." The group's visa applications, located by the British consulate in Baghdad, arrived in London. The names were false, but the small black-and-white passport headshots gave police their first clear images of the gunmen's faces.

THE HOSTAGE BOARD now included photos of the embassy staff, the journalists, and at least some of the unlucky visitors.

Each SAS trooper was issued with an annotated floor plan of the embassy, covered in sticky-back plastic so that the soldiers could amend it in felt-tip. On the second floor, it showed the hostages represented by crosses, men in the general office, women in the cipher room, Iranians along one wall, non-Iranians along the other. A small stick figure lying on the floor was identified as IRANIAN CHARGÉ D'AFFAIR [*sic*] WITH FRACTURED JAW; another, in the center of the room, was labeled POLICEMAN ON CHAIR.

Officially, all hostages were equal in the eyes of the law. However, some were more equal than others. Graham Collins described the order of precedence: "The number one priority was the recovery of Trevor Lock, alive and uninjured, safely and quickly. Priority number two was the other British hostages. Priority three was all non-Brits. Then, if any terrorists were left alive, their detention." As Collins observed, "Yankee One"—Trevor Lock—"was one of ours."

Even within those categories, distinctions were emerging. Just as he feared, Mustapha Karkouti was immediately identified by MI5 as a "subject of interest." An Arab nationalist with links to Palestinian militants, the Syrian journalist had met Carlos the Jackal in Britain in 1973, shortly before the terrorist attempted to assassinate Joseph Edward "Teddy" Sieff, a prominent Zionist and the chairman of Marks & Spencer. (The Jackal shot Sieff in his bath in St. John's Wood, but the bullet was deflected by his teeth, and he survived.) There was no indication in MI5's files that Karkouti had a role in that or any other terrorist action, but he had trained in the camps run by the Democratic Front for the Liberation of Palestine, and had some unsavory contacts in the Palestinian underworld. Could it really be a coincidence that he had wandered into the embassy moments before it was taken over by fellow Arabs? At times Karkouti also seemed to be speaking on behalf of the gunmen, insisting that the government accede to their demands. That morning, speaking to police out the window, he had stated: "We are seeking the humanity of the British because it seems it is the only way out."

That made the intel cell sit up: "Karkouti's use of the pronoun 'we' was . . . striking."

Sim Harris was also a focus of police suspicion, equally unfairly, but for different reasons. With Cramer released, Harris was the only other person in the embassy who knew Lock still had his gun. According to Graham Collins, by confiding in others, Lock had made "a big mistake," since Harris might, in extremis, reveal this valuable piece of information to their captors to save his own skin. "Human nature is human nature," Collins explained, "and if it gets to a point where you're so desperate, you believe that your only way out alive is to trade that piece of information [you do so] . . . It was a big worry. If the terrorists knew Lock had his gun, they would have executed him." The audio probes had also picked up some worrying conversations between Harris and the gunmen, in which he seemed to be "telling others what is likely to happen."

"I'm interested in your cause, and I would like to know a bit more about it," Harris told Towfiq. "I think you have a cause. I think you can come out of [this] smelling of roses if you release us."

In another exchange, Harris "compared the Arabs in Iran to black slaves in the American South and asked [Towfiq] if he had seen the program *Roots*," the popular television drama based on Alex Haley's novel about an African sold into American slavery.

In his own mind, Harris had merely struck up conversation with the lead gunman "to humor him, also to pass the time, and out of genuine interest."

The police heard something else: a hostage trying to curry favor, advising the gunmen on what would happen next. "He was trying to ingratiate himself with the terrorists," Collins concluded. "We felt that he was a loose cannon, a dangerous, dangerous individual."

At the morning briefing, Collins relayed instructions from Dellow: if the military option was implemented by the SAS, all those involved should assemble afterward behind the embassy, where their details would be taken and their weapons removed for forensic examination.

This announcement was met with silence by the assembled men.

When Hector Gullan spoke, he was polite, Collins recalled, "but steely cold."

"If there is a military operation," said the officer commanding of B Squadron, "the troopers will *not* remain at the embassy: they will do their job, and then they will be exfiltrated, very quickly." They would do whatever was required, and then get out fast, leaving no names, no testimony, and no guns.

"It ain't going to happen, governor," Collins reported back to Dellow. "I've met these people; there is no way they're going to stop for anybody. If a police officer tries to stop anybody coming out of that building carrying a firearm, take their details and seize their firearm, this could lead to a serious situation. It is a recipe for disaster."

Dellow liked to play strictly by the police rulebook, but if the special forces went in, this would be a military, not a police, operation; they would not be hanging around to be interviewed by the police or the press.

"We were feeling our way," Collins reflected. "There was no game-book for this. This sort of operation had never happened before on British soil."

John Gunn, a slight, bespectacled, academic figure, sat at the back of the negotiators' room, taking notes. The psychiatrist could sense the stress inside the embassy, but he was witnessing the impact on the police at first hand. Some, he said, were already showing symptoms of "anxiety, irritability and excessive smoking." A prolonged standoff could provoke insomnia and heavy drinking (an occupational hazard among police at the time), and in extreme cases "affective disturbance, depression, or hypomania."

After each negotiating session, the police mediator manning the field telephone would "collapse into a chair," exhausted by keeping up the charade of being the gunmen's ally. "We were the good guys, not politicos," said one of the negotiators. "We didn't have to pretend to grasp the situation. When they wanted something we were there to ask for it on their behalf." But it was a nerve-grinding process: "I knew that if I made one mistake, said one silly thing, they would all die."

Gunn urged the six negotiators to cut down their shifts from twelve hours to eight, and to work in pairs. He advised bringing in women negotiators, to provide a different tone and perspective. The police rejected both suggestions. "It was crazy that women were not used," thought Gunn. "We all have mothers. Women often take a softer, gentler approach; there is no macho competition."

Even the phlegmatic Dellow was showing the strain. Gunn had seen the signs before: huge pressure to make instant decisions, compounded by "the glare of publicity and the watchful eye of senior politicians." The psychiatrist found himself counseling the police, commanding officers, and negotiators, encouraging them to talk, relax, and express their feelings. He dispensed reassurance and advice on sleeping, making off-duty arrangements, and drinking sensibly.

Fred Luff's behavior was particularly troubling. Plainly exhausted, he was chain-smoking and increasingly petulant. He snapped at Mrs. Shadloi, the Arabic interpreter. For three nights he had barely slept. His tone toward the man he knew as Salim veered between wheedling and demanding. At times of high tension, he bowed his head in prayer. He was starting to make mistakes. It was Luff who told Tony Crabb he did not need to remain on standby.

"Siege negotiation creates a strange, artificial world," said Gunn, and Luff seemed to be disappearing into it. The psychiatrist worried that Salim was near the breaking point. But Fred Luff might crack first.

The Iranian Revolution of 1979 shocked the world, bringing public demonstrations to the streets of London (*bottom*). A portrait of the new leader, Ayatollah Ruhollah Khomeini, is hung on the wall of the Iranian Embassy at 16 Princes Gate (*center right*). An Iranian protester outside the U.S. Embassy in London (*top left*). A propaganda poster in English and Arabic appeals to Western journalists to report honestly on the new regime (*top right*).

Ron Morris,
embassy majordomo.

Mustapha Karkouti, Syrian journalist.

LONDON EMBASSY SEIZED

Policeman held with Iranians

By KENNETH CLARKE, ROBIN GEDYE and
T. A. SANDROCK

THREE gunmen were holding about 20 hostages, including a policeman and two members of the staff of the B B C, in the Iranian Embassy in London early today.

As armed police surrounded the embassy in Princes Gate, Kensington, the gunmen threatened to blow up the building and kill the hostages if their demands are not met by noon today.

Describing themselves as members of the Mahealdin Al Nasser Martyr group they prison

TE
TH
DI

Daily
A TE
ins
Embass
the gu
It wa
Cramer,
news or
Simeon
recordist,
Both me
visas to
gunmen
said:

The hostages included embassy employees, casual visitors, journalists, and the policeman on guard as the gunmen burst in. On the back of a BBC assignment form, Cramer scribbled a hasty note to his parents (*right*), to be discovered in the event of his death.

PC Trevor Lock of the
Diplomatic Protection Group.

Abbas Fallahi,
doorman.

Chris Cramer, BBC producer.

Sim Harris,
BBC sound recordist.

Roya Kaghachi,
senior secretary.

Dr. Gholam-
Ali Afrouz,
Iranian chargé
d'affaires.

Princes Gate:
aerial view
(*opposite*) and
rear of nos.
14–16 (*below*).

Hiyech Sanai Kanji, secretary.

Nooshin Hashemenian,
secretary.

Shirazeh
Boroumand,
switchboard
operator
and secretary.

No. 16 Iranian Embassy

No. 17 Ethiopian Embassy

No. 24 Montessori Nursery School

No. 25 Royal School of Needlework

Nawabzada Ghazanfar Ali Gul, Pakistani landowner and tourist.

Seyyed Abbas Lavasani, deputy press attaché and Revolutionary Guard.

Ali Tabatabai, banker.

Abdul Ezzati, press attaché.

Police list of hostages (*right*).

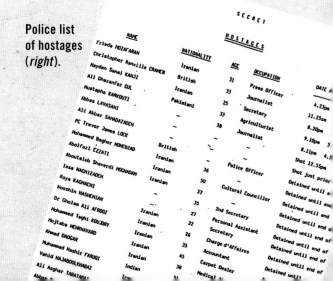

SECRET

HOSTAGES

NAME	NATIONALITY	AGE	OCCUPATION	DATE A
Frieda MOZAFARAN	Iranian	31	Press Officer	
Christopher Ranville CRAMER	British	33	Journalist	4.23pm
Hayden Sanai KAHJI	Iranian	25	Secretary	11.25am
Ali Ghazanfer GUL	Pakistani	33	Agriculturist	8.20pm
Mustapha KARKOUTI		38	Journalist	9.10pm J
Abbas LAVASANI				8.11pm 4.5
Ali Akbar SAHADAZADEH				Shot 12.55pm
PC Trevor James LOCK	British		Police Officer	Shot just prior
Mohammed Bagher MOHEBZAD	Iranian			Detained until e
Abolfazl EZZATI	Iranian	36		Detained until end
Aboutaleb Shaverdi MOCHADAH	Iranian	50	Cultural Councillor	Detained until end
Issa NAGHIZADEH		37		Detained until end o
Roya KAGHACHI		35		Detained until end of
Nooshin HASHEMIAN	Iranian	27	2nd Secretary	Detained until end o
Dr Gholam Ali AFROOZ	Iranian	22	Personal Assistant	Detained until end of
Mohammed Taghi KOUJORY	Iranian	26	Secretary	Detained until end of
Hojtaba MEHRNAVARD	Iranian	35	Charge d'Affaires	Detained until end of
Ahmad DADGAR	Iranian	45	Accountant	Detained until end of
Muhammad Hashir FARUQI	Indian	38	Carpet Dealer	Detained until end
Vahid HAJABDOLKHABAZ	Ira	51	Medical	Detained until
Ali Asghar TABATABA				
Abbas				

Iran in turmoil. The Shah of Iran, King of Kings, Monarch of the Peacock Throne (*left*) is ousted in November 1979; two years earlier, he enjoys the hospitality of U.S. President Jimmy Carter (*center*).

December 1978. Rioters burn a portrait of the Shah in protest against his regime (*bottom*).

Members of SAVAK, the Shah's hated secret police, are rounded up (*top*); February 1, 1979: the Ayatollah Khomeini is greeted with rapture on his return from exile (*center*); December 2, 1979: armed Iranian protesters occupy the U.S. Embassy in Tehran (*bottom*).

Students occupying the
U.S. Embassy (*top right*).
The hostage crisis reported
in the Iranian press (*top
left*). American hostages
are paraded (*center*). After
months of negotiations failed
to free them, President Carter
launched Operation Eagle
Claw on April 24, 1980,
an ambitious rescue attempt
that ended in abject failure
with the loss of three
helicopters and nine deaths.

The leader, Towfiq Ibrahim al-Rashidi (alias "Salim").

The six gunmen are Arab Iranians from the Iranian province of Khuzestan; they formed the Group of the Martyr, seeking political rights in Iran.

(*Clockwise from top left*) **Makki Hanoun; Abbas Maytham; Jassim Alwan al-Nasiri (alias "Faisal"); Shaye Hamid al-Sahar (alias "Hassan"). Towfiq spent several days composing his statement in fractured English (*right*).**

Fowzi Badavi Nejad (alias "Ali").

A statement

Al Nasir .

DOCU
No.

Dear Britishs,

May you excuse us for the armed ope
that we committed on yours land after the racial
of Iran and closed the legitimate ways for obtaining
the simplest right .

The Iranian peoples were pleased after
overthrow of the Shah's agent regime as a result to hu
sacrifices rendered by all the Iranians . The new Ira
rulers pretended an adherence to Islam and its great
principles , that called for peace , right and equi
like the other holy messages which aim
humanity from   otecting
                                                          ritude
and the fac   covered
to be plotti   seemed
as well as ex   les ,
themselves th   r
                                                cri
blood bath wit   to
followers to pur   th
lar and
saved   f:
erthrowi

hoping to obtain t
national rights , their freedom and their
rous life .
                    " I "   DOCUMENT
                                     PAGE No.
e also warn against any action aiming   at
tion without carrying out its goals
uld kill the hostages and explode the
group   as well .
ope that you would co-operate with as
gure the human ends of the operation .
and eternity for A'rabstan martyrs
s an Arab free region .

Flat 3, 105 Lexham
Gardens, Earls
Court,
West London

A SERVICE flat offering complete
anonymity. Staff described the
occupants as "typical Arab tourists"

Towfiq pictured at a student party in Tehran shortly before
the fall of the Shah (*top left*). The flat where the gunmen
gathered (*top center*). The only known photograph of Iraqi
intelligence officer "Sami Muhammad Ali," known as "The
Fox" (*center right*). The Group of the Martyr, posing with guns
on April 30, before setting out for Princes Gate (*clockwise
from top left*): Shaye, Towfiq, Fowzi, Makki, Jassim, Abbas.

"Black Wednesday," May 30, 1979 (*top and bottom*): Arab demonstrators in Al-Muhammara are attacked by the security forces and masked militia loyal to the ayatollah, a confrontation that leaves hundreds dead. Iraq's Saddam Hussein (*center right*) viewed Arab unrest as an opportunity to destabilize the Iranian regime, and ordered the Iraqi intelligence services to bankroll and train the Arab militants.

SAS soldiers: Tommy "the Poacher" Palmer (*top left*); Tom MacDonald (*top right*); Fijian-born Tom Morell, on active service in the Middle East (*bottom left*); Mel Parry in Dhofar (*bottom right*).

The officers (*clockwise from top left*): Major Hector Gullan, officer commanding, B Squadron, emerging from a dugout in Dhofar; Brigadier Peter de la Billière, director of special forces; Lieutenant Colonel Michael Rose, commanding officer of 22 SAS. The SAS practice assault techniques at Bradbury Lines, the SAS headquarters in Hereford (*bottom*).

British demonstrators gather in a cordoned off area in Hyde Park (*top left*) demanding the release of the hostages. Two Iranian women run from the building within minutes of the assault (*top right*). John Dellow (*center right*), the deputy assistant commissioner, commander of police operations throughout the siege.

Fred Luff, police negotiator, approaches the building and opens talks with the gunmen, accompanied by the translator Mrs. Shadloi in a fur coat and bulletproof vest (*right*).

ILFORD HP5 PLUS

1   3   5   4

ILFORD HP5 PLUS

21   21A   22   22A   23

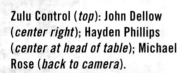

Zulu Control (*top*): John Dellow
(*center right*); Hayden Phillips
(*center at head of table*); Michael
Rose (*back to camera*).

The gunmen's threat to kill all the
hostages and blow up the building
makes front-page news (*center*).
Veteran writer and journalist Rebecca
West (*top right*) witnessed events
unfolding from her kitchen window
overlooking the embassy gardens.
Police seal off side roads (*bottom*)
and establish inner and outer cordons,
manned by hundreds of officers.

EMBASSY OF THE
ISLAMIC REPUBLIC OF IRAN
London

Date: 30.4.1980

Note Verbale
MOST URGENT

... the Islamic Republic of Iran
...nts to His Excellency the Foreign
honor to draw His Excellency's
...ence at this Embassy today in
...odd Diplomats and staff includin
...everal women is under constant

...that His Excellency the Foreign
...te the severity of the threat
...urity forces to take all possible
...safeguard their lives.

...mbassy of the Islamic Republic of Iran
...f of this opportunity to renew to His
...he Foreign Secretary the assurance of its
...ideration.

...d Commonwealth Office,

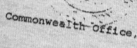

Margaret Thatcher (*top*) was conducting
an interview with Radio 2 DJ Jimmy Young
at the BBC when the news broke. The
Iranian government issues a sternly worded
communiqué (*center right*) to Britain,
calling for the hostages to be liberated
without delay. Home Secretary William
Whitelaw, chairman of the emergency
Cobra committee, took over political
control (*center left*). Iranian Foreign
Minister Sadegh Ghotbzadeh (*bottom left*).

14

THE NINE O'CLOCK NEWS

t was 14:20 before Tony Crabb and his wife returned home with the weekly groceries, to find an agitated policeman waiting on their doorstep in Sunbury, and an unmarked car in the street with the motor running.

By 15:10, Crabb was back on the pavement outside Number 16, with Fred Luff and Ray Tucker behind him. All three wore concealed radio microphones. "Anything we do for these gunmen must be reciprocated by an act of goodwill from them," Luff instructed him. Crabb was a journalist; but, like it or not, he was now also a negotiator.

Sim Harris appeared at the window.

"Where the fuck have you been, Tony?" he shouted. Karkouti, pale and sweating, stood alongside him. Towfiq lurked behind the curtain. Harris could not help noticing that Crabb was wearing casual clothing, "as though he had come from home" or a trip to the supermarket. This was infuriating.

"Why hasn't the statement been broadcast? Don't you realize lives have been put at risk by the delay?"

Crabb prevaricated. "I didn't know it was supposed to be broadcast. I thought it was just a statement of demands."

This was untrue, and Harris knew it. His colleague was deliberately feigning ignorance, no doubt under police instructions. "Tony is just a pawn," Harris wrote in his diary.

"But you're powerful enough to do *something*," Harris remonstrated. "You must put out the right statement—otherwise everyone could be killed."

Tucker stepped forward. "Well, look, if you want to make a statement, fair enough. We are all here. Let's get the statement dictated, and let's get it right."

"We're going in circles," Gunn observed, listening in from the negotiators' room. But the suggestion seemed to defuse the situation.

Towfiq dictated in Arabic, Karkouti translated into English, and Crabb leaned once more on the hood of the parked Mercedes and took it all down: the promise that the hostages would be unharmed so long as the police did not attack; a threat to kill everyone in the building if they did; the demand for the Algerian, Jordanian, and Iraqi ambassadors (to be substituted for the Libyan, Syrian, or Kuwaiti ambassadors if these were unavailable) to mediate their exit.

For the first time, Towfiq added a demand for the "Red Cross to start their jobs in negotiating between us and the British government to secure the safety of the hostages as well as the group's members and to terminate the whole operation peacefully." He ended with a swipe at the Iranian government for "the oppression in Arabistan" and an apology to Britain for any "inconvenience." Towfiq's grim expression suggested this was his final, definitive statement. He would not be making another.

Tony Crabb read the statement back. "Are you happy with it?"

Towfiq nodded to Harris from behind the curtain.

"Just promise me that it will be broadcast," said Harris.

"I don't control what the BBC broadcast, Sim. You know that. But I'll do my best."

Crabb turned to leave but then swung around. "If the statement is broadcast, would the group show some sign of goodwill?"

"Do they mean release a hostage?" Towfiq asked Harris.

"Yes."

Towfiq nodded.

"Let's talk about this on the telephone," suggested Tucker.

Harris was suddenly shivering.

"Are you okay, mate?" asked Crabb.

"Bloody marvelous," shouted Harris. "It's really great in here having a gun pointed at your head."

On the way back up the stairs Harris staggered and almost fell. Makki sat him down, and returned a moment later with a glass of milk and a biscuit.

In the general office, the mood lifted. "Perhaps they'll release more than one hostage," said Ron Morris. "They should let all the women go."

Nawabzada Gul pointed out that he had a plane to catch. "I have a very important meeting to attend next week . . ."

Everyone groaned.

Towfiq was still agitated. "The police are playing games with us," he told Karkouti. "They want us to release a hostage in return for broadcasting our statement."

"What do you expect, Brother Salim? This is how police negotiate."

"But we've given them already two hostages . . . ," said Towfiq.

SURE ENOUGH, the police wanted to haggle.

"How many hostages will you free in return for the broadcast?" asked Luff, when Towfiq called on the field telephone.

"One."

"We need more."

"Two."

"Very well. Two."

THE SAS ASSEMBLED its arsenal.

Most of the men carried a compact Heckler & Koch MP5 submachine gun, the regiment's weapon of choice: light, accurate, capable of firing thirteen rounds a second, and reliably lethal. Some had the silenced or the shorter version. Each man had four magazines with thirty rounds of full-metal-jacketed 9 × 19mm parabellum bullets (whose name derived from the Latin saying *Si vis pacem, para bellum,* "If you seek peace, prepare for war"). The low-muzzle velocity of the MP5 meant that, instead of passing through a body, the rounds tended to explode inside it, inflicting greater damage. It also made the bullets less likely to fly through walls, furniture, or human targets and hit hostages, or "friendlies." In addition, each carried a holstered Browning semi-automatic 9mm pistol, the standard weapon for close assaults, with a magazine capacity of thirteen rounds (though the SAS used only twelve, to avoid wearing down the spring or causing a jam). A single-action pistol, it had to be cocked before firing the first round; the SAS tended to carry the weapon already cocked with the safety catch on, for swifter draw and fire.

If an assault was ordered, and before firing a single bullet, the soldiers would deploy tear gas, nerve agents, and stun grenades, a wave of thunder, lightning, and poison to blind, deafen, and disorient the gunmen.

The G60 flash-bang, or stun grenade, was developed by Royal Ordnance Enfield to a specification provided by the SAS after the formation of the Counter Revolutionary Warfare wing, in 1973. Composed of mercury and magnesium powder, on detonation the grenade creates a blinding flash of 300,000 candlepower, an explosion of light so bright that it temporarily activates all the photoreceptor cells in the eyes, causing a few seconds of total blindness followed by blurred or double vision for several minutes. The volume of the detonation, at 160 decibels, also induces temporary deafness and disturbs the fluid in the inner ear, causing loss of balance. Whereas the police had stun grenades, emitting a single explosion, the SAS version both flashed and banged, repeatedly.

Through training, the SAS troopers were partially inured to the flash-bang's effects, but to anyone within range, unprotected and unprepared, the effect was instant and dramatic: temporary loss of hearing and sight, along with dizziness, disorientation, and nausea. Standing beside a flash-bang when it goes off is like dying for about five seconds. The main disadvantage of a stun grenade is the intense heat of the explosion: the G60 stun grenade is an incapacitating bomb but also an incendiary device.

CS gas, better known as tear gas, was developed in secret at Porton Down, the Ministry of Defense Science and Technology laboratory, in the 1950s. Its defining component is a cyanocarbon that causes burning eyes; weeping; irritation of the nose, mouth, and throat membranes; nasal mucus discharge; sneezing; coughing; vomiting; and restricted breathing. The effects usually wear off after a few hours, but sometimes persist for months. CR gas, nicknamed "firegas," is similar but far more potent. A report from Porton Down described the effects as "like being thrown blindfolded into a bed of stinging nettles." Developed in the 1960s, it caused coughing, temporary blindness, panic, and acute skin irritation. CR gas can also kill a person in poorly ventilated spaces, through asphyxiation and pulmonary edema.

B Squadron, the designated Special Projects team, had three varieties of handheld flash-bangs, manufactured in small quantities at Porton Down: a "normal" flash-bang, with twelve flashes and twelve bangs; a flash-bang CS, with tear gas added; and a flash-bang CR, which emitted the even more toxic nerve gas. The last, a stun device and gas bomb rolled into one, is known as an L29; each is roughly the size of a can of beans, with a half-second fuse. In addition, the regiment had specially adapted flash-bang CRs, canisters fired from a Polecat launcher that could be shot through a closed window at a distance of two hundred feet, filling the building with gas in a matter of seconds.

Every soldier would carry an S6 respirator, a gas mask worn in conjunction with a black rubber NBC (nuclear, biological, chemical) hood, attached to black polyester overalls worn by tank crews. Over this was a Kevlar vest, into which ceramic plates could be inserted as additional body armor. Most wore standard-issue army boots, "good for running in and kicking down doors." A knife was sheathed in the vest at the shoulder. The respirator protected the face, eyes, lungs, and throat of the wearer from gas and smoke, with an air seal inside the mask. Some also wore balaclavas, more for anonymity than for military purposes. One man in each team had a sledgehammer clipped to his belt. The outfit was completed by a pair of thin green leather aviator gloves, which fit over the hands like an extra layer of skin.

The assault kit was the best the British Army had, but it was far from perfect. "Looked good, fucking useless," was one verdict. The leather holster was too loose for the Browning, and the pistol tended to drop out; some troopers used black masking tape to keep the weapon in place, which made it harder to draw. Mel Parry had replaced the standard-issue holster with one of his own design. With the shorter model of the MP5, the MP5K, a finger might stray over the muzzle. Most of the machine guns were without flashlights attached. The rubber hood and boot soles melted quickly in high temperatures, and the overalls and gloves were not fireproof. The gas masks leaked easily, and the glass "whited out" in extreme heat and smoke, or misted up, giving the wearer what one trooper described as "that detached, underwater feeling." The vest might hold off a 9mm round fired from a distance but not at point-blank range. The men often rejected the bulky ceramic body armor, since it impeded swift movement. "Better to be fast and wounded than slow and dead," said one.

THE MILITARY PLANS were revised with each additional morsel of intelligence. Hector Gullan's diary gives a taste of the frenetic pace of modification: "Options, recces, discussion, info, rehearsals—continually." Some considered the best option to be a "deliberate stronghold assault": the gunmen were contained inside, and the SAS had an increasingly clear picture of where they and their hostages were located, as well as the building's topography. Much of the cement pointing around the bricks on the interior wall of the Ethiopian Embassy had by now been removed using a silent abrasive machine. With an air cannon, or "kinetic impact system," the wall could be collapsed, enabling a "non-explosive entry." But attacking a fifty-six-room building would be hard. The hostage-takers had already erected barricades and probably laid booby traps; they would be braced for an attack.

Alternatively, the SAS could provide the bus requested by the gunmen, and then ambush it. This could take place as gunmen and hostages were climbing aboard in Princes Gate, somewhere on the way to an airport, or airside on the tarmac. The SAS had trained in all three types of assault. A team set off to reconnoiter various potential ambush sites on the way to, and inside, London's airports.

Two thirty-three-seater police buses were delivered to Regent's Park Barracks. Driven by an armed solider in police uniform, these buses could stop wherever and whenever the SAS wanted. Everyone inside would be incapacitated using flash-bangs with CR gas, and the forces lying in wait at the ambush site could move in. The police also lent the SAS two cars, a pair of Triumph 2000s: these would pose as a police escort to the bus, traveling behind and in front, with armed troopers inside wearing police uniforms. When the bus halted, they would join the ambush. If the assault took place immediately outside the embassy, two trucks would simultaneously ram the bus from either end of the side road, jamming it in place. The SAS forces from Number 15 would then move in. The thermal lance would be on hand to cut hostages out of the vehicle.

The gunmen had specifically demanded a mainly female crew to fly the plane they wanted. A woman bus driver would be less threatening and more inconspicuous than a man. Back in Northern Ireland, Gullan had worked closely with the tiny handful of women in 14 Intelligence Company, and he knew what Janet Dillon was capable of.

"Cracking brave as hell" was Gullan's assessment of Dillon. "Cracking good-looking girl, she could shoot as well as any of us. I wouldn't like to be in a fight with her."

Dillon and two female colleagues were woken at dawn, and told they were going to London. At Regent's Park Barracks, they were issued with police uniforms and led to the waiting buses. Dillon had never driven a bus before. For hours, she hauled the big blue vehicle around a maze of traffic cones erected on the parade ground, stopping, starting, suddenly braking, and accelerating. That afternoon she climbed aboard an army truck, along with several members of B Squadron: on the bench opposite, she saw "a petite female colleague dwarfed between faceless SAS soldiers dressed in black assault kit." In the Doctors' House the women were shown into the intelligence operations room and given "an idea of the scale of the task and the challenges that lay ahead." The briefing officer then handed Dillon a pair of black tights "as worn by women police constables" in his words, and instructed her to put them on and await further orders.

The bus ambush outside the embassy was the most popular option. As one soldier put it: "You gas them, and everyone collapses. There's nowhere they can go, and they're disabled immediately."

If that moment came, Dillon would drive an empty bus to Princes Gate and come to a halt immediately in front of the Iranian Embassy. The gunmen and hostages would climb aboard. She would close the door. Then the bus would be rammed from either end, the SAS would attack, and everyone inside would be gassed, along with Dillon.

IN ZULU CONTROL and Cobra, an intense debate was under way over whether to broadcast Towfiq's statement. Dellow was determined that this should be granted only in return for "the clearest concession." Another consideration, he knew, was "the risk of reaction by the Iranian government or people against British citizens in Iran if the impression was conveyed that HM Government was in any way compromising with the terrorists." But if the statement was suppressed, or broadcast only in part, "we run the risk of their carrying out their often repeated threats to kill somebody."

WHILE THE POLICE and politicians wrestled with the problem, Towfiq spent the afternoon listening to three different radios, becoming steadily angrier. On a small green portable transistor, he switched between local stations, searching in vain for evidence that Crabb had put out the statement. The large gray-and-black radio was tuned to the BBC World Service. In the ambassador's office he found yet another radio already tuned to Tehran Radio, the mouthpiece of the Iranian regime. What he heard made him even more incensed.

At 19:20, Towfiq burst into the general office and addressed the Iranians in Farsi. "Radio Tehran claims in its news bulletin that you've sent a signed letter to your government declaring your allegiance to the Islamic Revolution and your readiness to die." The ayatollah had earmarked them for martyrdom.

The Iranians reacted furiously, jumping to their feet and protesting loudly.

"Fucking liars," spat Ali "the Bank" Tabatabai.

"They are trying to get us all killed," shouted another Iranian hostage.

Even Gholam-Ali Afrouz, loyal servant of the regime, was outraged. "Bastards," he shouted. "Don't believe them—this is a lie."

But Towfiq had more. Tehran was reporting that Arab diplomats had been asked to mediate, but "the Iranian government had rejected any role for the Iraqi ambassador because it considers the siege is a plot organized by Iraq, the U.S., and CIA." The radio announcer claimed British police were awaiting permission from Tehran before storming the building.

This was, of course, pure propaganda. No such letter had been sent; the British government had rejected the Iraqi offer to mediate; the CIA had no involvement; and if Thatcher opted to use force, the last thing she needed was the ayatollah's approval.

"That's not how things are done here," said Trevor Lock.

Sim Harris agreed: "You can't see the British police doing a raid with a nod from a foreign power—"

"Tehran government radio tells lies. Why do you believe them now?" Mustapha Karkouti asked Towfiq.

In response, the gunman grabbed Karkouti by the arm and hauled him down to the field telephone in the ground-floor hallway. Jassim followed with Lock, at gunpoint.

Picking up the receiver and stabbing the button, Towfiq shouted: "Why the statement has not been broadcast? We are very angry and losing our temper. We were expecting to put an end to this operation in twenty-four hours and now we are at the end of Day Four."

Fred Luff was on the line. "We will put out the statement when you release two hostages."

"I will release one before the broadcast, and one afterward," said Towfiq.

Luff insisted on the release of two hostages first.

Towfiq exploded. "What sort of game are you playing with us? Do you want me to begin sending you bodies? I will send you a body, I will kill a hostage right now, and will repeat this every hour."

The threat was immediately relayed to the SAS in Number 15, and the Blue Team was placed on high alert.

Towfiq thrust the telephone into Karkouti's hand, cursing in Arabic.

"Try to calm Salim down, please, will you?" said Luff, trying to sound calm himself. "The last thing we want to see is bodies."

The telephone passed back and forth as they bargained over lives. Luff was intransigent, Towfiq livid, Karkouti increasingly terrified. Lock looked on, pale and wordless.

Karkouti could sense Towfiq reaching the end of his tether, girding himself for violence. The Syrian journalist's knees sagged. "My mouth and throat went completely dry . . . I felt totally helpless and very weak, physically and mentally."

For ten minutes Luff and Towfiq bartered, voices rising, the air crackling with hostility. Adrenaline surging, Lock found himself staring fixedly at the submachine gun in Towfiq's hand, wondering how many bullets it could fire in a single second.

Finally, Towfiq seemed to snap.

"Right, that's it," he screamed. "You obviously don't care. You don't mind if we start shooting people. I am going back upstairs to kill a hostage." He slammed the phone down.

Karkouti sank to his knees and wrapped his arms around Towfiq's legs, sobbing. "You gain nothing by killing . . ." he pleaded.

Towfiq shook him off. "What can we do? We treat you well, we like you, we agree with what you say, but the police do not keep their word . . . You say I should not kill a hostage. What should I do?"

"Show a goodwill gesture," Karkouti sobbed. "Release a hostage . . ."

This desperate exchange could be heard on the open line in the police negotiators' room and Zulu Control.

Back upstairs, Lock slumped back into his chair with a groan, his face in his hands. "It's all going bloody wrong, mate," he told Harris. "It's all screwed up." For the first time, the policeman seemed truly frightened.

"He looked dreadful, absolutely awful," Harris noted. Karkouti was in a worse state, "completely broken down," tears streaming down his face.

Towfiq and Jassim marched over to the women's group and beckoned Hiyech Kanji, the pregnant secretary, to follow them. She rose to her feet unsteadily.

"Christ," whispered Lock. "They're going to kill her."

The time was 20:15.

Moments later, the front door opened, and Hiyech was thrust into the street, where she was bundled into a waiting ambulance. The secretary had brought a simple, stark message from the gunmen, which she passed on to Dellow: the statement must be broadcast and, they'd told her, "if it's not done by nine o'clock we're going to kill all of your friends."

Dellow was astonished. The talking seemed to be going nowhere, but now a hostage had suddenly been released. "Although Salim seemed resolute, the police negotiations must have had more effect on him than we realized." Hiyech was "almost hysterical," reckoned Dellow, but "there was no doubt in her mind that the threats were real."

At 20:27, Dellow instructed the negotiators to inform Salim that the police had formally asked the BBC to issue the statement.

Towfiq refused to believe it. The hostages were told to put their hands up and shepherded back upstairs to the reference library on the third floor, the "tension room," as Harris called it. Towfiq put on his dark glasses and raised his hood. The gunmen were shouting.

An experienced journalist, Harris knew how hard it would be to coordinate a radio broadcast of this sort. In Iran, there was one government-run radio station. Britain's media was more diffuse, less obedient, and more liable to make mistakes. Fearing "there would be a cock-up," Harris suggested he call the police to find out which radio station the statement would be broadcast on. Towfiq agreed.

At 20:39, the field telephone rang in the negotiators' room. "Hello, Salim, what is the problem?" said Max Vernon, the latest addition to the team.

"No, it's Sim Harris of the BBC."

"Hello, Sim, what's the problem?"

"About the broadcast."

"Yes, we are hoping that the BBC will make the broadcast at nine o'clock."

"Can you find out please what frequency it is going on? Because it's all going wrong in here. They're going to shoot a hostage if it doesn't go out at nine o'clock. I want to be absolutely sure that the leader listens to the right frequency."

Vernon asked Harris to hold the line while he made a call. The negotiator noticed his hands trembling: "It was the first time I had spoken to a man with a gun."

"You're winning," Harris told Towfiq. "Just stay calm, the broadcast is going to be made, you're getting there."

The policeman was back: "Radio 1, Radio 2, and the BBC World Service."

Vernon fervently hoped this was true. Through his head ran a terrible thought: "If we do it, we'll have a hostage. If we don't, we'll have a dead one."

B Squadron braced themselves once more. The immediate action group was assembled at the door.

Towfiq sat on a blanket in the room with the women, a radio on either side. At 20:53, he began twiddling the knobs. The fizz of static filled the air. Jassim, Abbas, and Shaye were ranged around the walls, faces set.

"The tension was unbearable," noted Harris. "I felt my heart thumping and sweat trickling down my face."

Lock stared at the ceiling, clenching and unclenching his fists. Two of the women wept silently.

An announcer declared: "We are breaking into our program to go over to the scene at the Iranian Embassy siege, where there has been a dramatic development . . ."

Then came the voice of the police spokesman Peter Neivens, measured and precise. A low-flying plane drowned out his voice. Towfiq turned up the volume.

"We swear to God and the British government . . ."

The room erupted. Karkouti burst into tears of relief.

Harris found himself hugging Towfiq. "You've won, you've won. It's being broadcast word for word, it's fantastic . . ."

All were on their feet, whooping, laughing, crying, and embracing, hostages and hostage-takers alike. Several of the gunmen were in tears. Even Jassim stood sobbing, Karkouti noted, "his submachine gun dangling at his side."

"There were scenes of fantastic emotion," Harris recorded. "Everybody was kissing everybody else."

Karkouti clasped Towfiq. "It's history," he declared tearfully. "Never before has this happened. It's incredible." The jubilation could be clearly heard on the audio probes. In the negotiators' room, Max Vernon let out a long, slow breath. Luff sat dazed, smoking one cigarette after another. The SAS stood down.

"Everybody felt that we had won," wrote Harris, unconsciously using the collective pronoun. "It seemed at that point that it was everybody inside against everybody outside. We hadn't won the war, but we had won a battle."

Towfiq smiled but seemed otherwise unmoved, even a little embarrassed at his comrades' emotional elation. "He spoke sharply to them in Arabic and they quickly pulled themselves together." There was, thought Harris, "a look of near-pity in his eyes."

"I am going to release another hostage," he said, looking around. Harris assumed Towfiq would select another woman. Instead, he beckoned to Gul, the portly Pakistani with the bushy beard. "Come," he said.

Gul promptly burst into tears, and then rushed around the room shaking hands and kissing both gunmen and hostages: "You are all my friends. Everybody in here is my brother."

At 21:14, Gul left the room.

Harris turned to Morris and grinned. "He'll catch his bloody plane after all. And perhaps we'll get some sleep." Nobody objected to Gul's unexpected release.

Gul was a charmingly eccentric man, but an exceptionally annoying and demanding hostage. His aphorisms were ponderous and baffling. His insistence that he be set free to catch a plane was bizarre, and infuriating. But the main reason for his release was more banal: Gul had snored his way to liberty.

At 22:00, everyone gathered around the radio for the evening news on Radio 4. Almost the entire program was dedicated to the siege, the statement, and the release of Hiyech and Gul. They were still listening when Towfiq announced that the police were offering to send in "a celebratory meal."

"What do you want?" asked Towfiq. "Do you want Persian food? Who wants English food?"

Pars was one of the best Persian restaurants in London, a favored hangout of Iranian expatriates. That night, its chef produced a banquet: kebabs, stew with herbs and kidney beans, flatbreads, rice with saffron and sultanas, and Shirazi salad. "Send the bill to the Metropolitan Police," the restaurant was told. The next day the chef would cook it all again, for the benefit of the press.

The food was brought to the doorstep shortly before midnight in two large plastic orange crates. One of these was carried by an SAS intelligence officer, who took the opportunity, Dellow reported, "to inspect covertly the door and lower windows of the stronghold." The crates contained aluminum cartons with Farsi writing from Pars, and a huge shepherd's pie courtesy of the police caterers. Additional tubs held steak, carrots, French beans, and fries. There was even the vegetarian meal requested by the devout Muslim Faruqi. In the second crate were cans of Pepsi and Tango, cheese, butter and biscuits, apples, and bunches of grapes and bananas. The police also supplied two large insulated electric catering urns, one containing tea and the other coffee, along with a large green thermos.

Ron Morris turned over the crates to make a table and laid out the food, drink, paper plates and cups, plastic cutlery, and green napkins.

Embedded inside one of the crates was a radio-controlled listening device operated by MI5.

The women arrived from the cipher room, "all with elegant makeup," Karkouti noted.

"Very, very elated," noted Harris, who demolished three helpings of pie but avoided the foreign food.

Lock chewed a couple of fries.

Karkouti could not stomach solid food. He was beginning to feel extremely unwell and sweating profusely. He longed for soup.

As an honorary Iranian, Morris ate only the Persian food and pronounced it a "damned good meal." As they sat around afterward, there was talk of "having a reunion one day."

"You'll never catch me here again," muttered Lock.

"Oh, you'll be on duty here next week," Morris told him.

"Like hell I will . . ."

For dessert they ate Bandit biscuits.

A milk-chocolate wafer produced by the biscuit manufacturer William Macdonald, the Bandit was a popular snack in 1980. Its advertisements played on the name, showing a group of brigands stealing the bars and then getting caught: "Now capture the rich taste of Bandit."

Morris decided the choice of biscuit must be an intentional pun. "Trust the police," he said. "We're being held up by bandits, and they send in Bandit biscuits."

Everyone laughed.

"Someone has a fucking terrible sense of humor," said Harris.

After the meal, the group was moved down to the ambassador's suite of offices to sleep. "Be very quiet when you walk downstairs, and do not speak," instructed Towfiq, aware that the police must be tracking movements inside the building.

Carrying their cushions, they trooped into the suite on the first floor, facing Princes Gate. These quarters were more ornate, with thick Persian carpets, a large overhead chandelier, and antiques in place of the worn carpet and office furniture in the general office and cipher room. Trevor Lock moved the grandest chair to the middle of the room and sat in it.

Towfiq switched off the lights. "Please keep quiet," he said.

Harris immediately collapsed into a deep slumber, compounded in equal parts of exhaustion, good food, and profound relief.

Tomorrow, surely, they would all be going home.

DAY FIVE

SUNDAY

15

SNOOKER

"Everyone is demob happy," wrote Sim Harris, comparing the group to soldiers being demobilized. Even Mustapha Karkouti had slept for a few hours, despite his grinding innards.

"I slept like a baby," Ron Morris said, grinning. "Thanks to this cushion."

Morris made tea in the new urns, and then bustled around distributing it, along with biscuits from his inexhaustible supply of Rich Tea and Garibaldi.

A strange atmosphere gripped the place, relieved and expectant. Towfiq was calm, rested, and extremely fragrant. "He had his face washed and probably his hair as well after snatching a few hours' sleep somewhere in the embassy," observed Karkouti. Using a razor blade from the medical room, Towfiq shaved his cheeks and upper lip, accentuating his goatee. He also discovered a bottle of Old Spice aftershave ("Fresh, clean, masculine, sensual," proclaimed the 1980 television advertisement) and liberally soaked himself with it.

"Look at his face, very fresh," Karkouti whispered.

"It's a positive sign," Lock replied. "When he's relaxed, everyone's relaxed."

Lock himself was cleaner, and a lot more comfortable.

During the night, the gunmen had repeatedly asked him if he wished to take a bath. He "politely refused," but feared his disinclination to wash was now becoming suspicious. At around 03:00 Lock asked Jassim to escort him to the bathroom next door. Once inside, he asked to close the door, explaining that he "suffered from excessive wind and wanted some privacy." After nearly four days of heroic self-induced constipation, Lock's relief was indescribable and, thankfully, never described. Hastily pulling up his trousers and refastening belt and gun holster, he rebuttoned his coat. Lock was tempted to risk a bath, but settled for what he called a "sluice down" at the sink, washing the dried blood from his face with warm water and rinsing his hair.

In an expansive mood, Towfiq announced that the hostages could take turns bathing, women first. They returned, Karkouti noted, "looking refreshed with clean hair." Roya Kaghachi found a small supply of toothpaste; they smeared it on their teeth with their fingers and then rubbed vigorously. The other gunmen also drenched themselves in Old Spice. After four days of confinement everyone wanted to look (and smell) their best. After all, the siege might end in front of the television cameras.

"You could hold a press conference inside the embassy," Karkouti suggested to Towfiq. "News agencies, cameramen, and reporters. They talk to you, and they talk to representatives of the hostages. After half an hour, or an hour, they leave the embassy. They broadcast this press conference. Immediately afterward, you release the hostages. Trevor Lock will stay behind to collect your guns in a box and come out with you."

This suggestion was well-meaning but completely unworkable. The authorities would never insert civilians into a hostage situation, or stage a press conference with armed men.

"It's time to move back upstairs to the room where you were on the second floor," Fowzi announced. "Please collect all your coats, jackets, and cushions." Towfiq intended to keep them on the move.

Ron Morris gathered up the remains of the meal from the previous evening. "Just enough for breakfast," he said happily.

Back in the general office, they listened to the radio news: ambassadors from the Middle East had "expressed a willingness to mediate," and the Red Cross was standing by to help if required.

"If the BBC are saying that, it's because the government have agreed for them to say it," Harris explained. "It means that things are moving."

Towfiq launched into yet another trilingual lecture on the grievances of Iranian Arabs. Some of the Iranians politely took notes, "attentively listening to what had become a little boring," as Karkouti put it. Harris passed the time doodling caricatures of the gunmen in his notebook.

Once again, Abbas Lavasani pointedly ignored the political sermon and read his Koran.

Intrigued by this "dignified young man" who had earlier volunteered to die, Harris shuffled over. "We think you were very brave for doing that," he said. "But you know, we can all get out without any need for anyone to die."

Lavasani put down the holy book, and a strange, distant expression came over his face. "No one will miss me if I die," he said.

AN HOUR LATER, Towfiq called the police on the field telephone.

"Hello, Salim. No news from the Arab ambassadors; they haven't arrived yet."

Dellow had instructed the negotiators to focus on the health of the hostages and "the propaganda value of a peaceful exit in front of the world's media." On the issue of the ambassadors, they were told to procrastinate.

"We'll wait for them," said Towfiq. Then, as an afterthought, he "congratulated the chef on the quality of his cooking."

In the general office, he took Lock and Karkouti aside, out of earshot of the other gunmen. What crimes could he and his men be prosecuted for? How long might they have to spend in prison?

"Two, three, maybe four years," said Lock (who really had no idea). "With good conduct that would be reduced."

"You'll be out by the time you are thirty," Karkouti added. "You'll still have at least thirty or forty years ahead of you for the struggle."

Towfiq wandered off down the corridor, deep in thought.

AT THE CRUCIBLE THEATRE in Sheffield, Cliff "the Grinder" Thorburn and Alex "Hurricane" Higgins chalked their cues for the World

Snooker Championship final. The best of thirty-five frames, the match would take place over two days, culminating on the evening of May 5, the Monday bank holiday.

Snooker is an odd spectator sport that involves staring at a table for up to fourteen hours while two men slowly knock colored balls around it with great precision. But this match had seized the public imagination like no other. Thorburn was a tall Canadian with an unhappy mustache and a slow, methodical style, in contrast to the volatile Higgins, a sharp-faced, unpredictable Northern Irishman with a nervous tic and a drinking problem. Both epitomized the style of the era, with their tight satin vests, bow ties, and constant smoking. Sponsored by Embassy, the cigarette manufacturer, the contest was the Embassy World Championship. A phlegmatic Canadian versus an extrovert Brit, the two rivals detested each other. "Snooker was bollocks before I came along," said Higgins, who had already won the world title in 1972. "Aggravation just seemed to follow him around," said Thorburn, who was said to have floored Higgins with a single punch during a bar brawl. Millions of snooker fans across the world, as well as many who did not particularly like or understand the game, were preparing to watch this much-hyped two-day grudge match. These included the SAS.

A large television was installed in the reception room of 15 Princes Gate, and several dozen heavily armed members of B Squadron settled down to watch the snooker.

AT THE FOREIGN OFFICE, a polite diplomatic fistfight was under way. Seven Arab ambassadors had been contacted by telephone, and four agreed to come to discuss the delicate situation with Douglas Hurd and his advisers. The first to arrive, at 9:00, were the Kuwaiti ambassador and the Jordanian chargé d'affaires (his ambassador was away). These were followed by the Algerian and Syrian ambassadors. Hurd approached them crabwise: Were they willing to talk to the hostage-takers? "It might be useful," he said, with studied vagueness.

Over the previous twenty-four hours, the Arab diplomats had agreed on a joint position, with three salient elements.

First, any negotiation must involve at least three ambassadors: "We don't want to be in a position where we have been singled out," they declared. Hurd nodded. Second, there must be no use of force by the British government while talks with the gunmen were ongoing. But, Hurd asked, what if the terrorists started killing hostages "while you were engaged on your mission"?

"That would create a new situation," said the Jordanian, Kasim Ghazzawi. "We would of course withdraw our mission immediately." That seemed sensible enough. Accidentally shooting an ambassador was not on Britain's agenda.

The Arab diplomats now reached the sticking point: "We will not be going in there for social pleasantries. They will ask us for something. And we think we should be able to offer them safe conduct."

Hurd's refusal was adamant. "The decision has been made at the highest level that there is no question whatsoever of a safe conduct out of this country for these men."

The Jordanian tried to argue. "You say your decision has been made at the highest level. Well, presumably it can be reversed at the highest level."

Everyone in the room knew who they were talking about.

Hurd shook his head. This was nonnegotiable.

Sir John Graham, Britain's ambassador to Iran (recalled due to the hostage crisis in Tehran), now chimed in. "Permit me to point out," he said (a grave insult in diplomatese), "your position is inconsistent. You are saying that your governments do not condone terrorism, do not want to negotiate with terrorists, want nothing to do with terrorists. Yet you want safe passage for these particular terrorists."

Ghazzawi permitted himself to point out, in turn, that the British position was inconsistent. The ambassadors were being asked to negotiate between the British authorities and the gunmen. "If we intervene," the Jordanian chargé d'affaires explained, "we cannot act on behalf of *one* of the parties. We cannot act as messengers. If you want a pigeon, anyone can do that. We cannot go in there and say: 'I am Ambassador of so-and-so and I say surrender.'"

But this was *exactly* what the British government wanted the Arab ambassadors to do, and everyone knew it.

Hurd agreed to relay their views to the prime minister. The ambassadors said they would speak to their governments. The meeting broke up with many warm handshakes and mutual expressions of goodwill, and in stubborn deadlock.

INTO THIS HIGHLY inflammable situation, Iran's foreign minister lobbed an incendiary device, overnight, in the form of a press release containing a public message addressed to the Iranian hostages:

> You, the revolutionary members of the Iranian Embassy in London. We admire your steadfastness and forbearance against the criminal actions of Ba'athist Iraq as well as those of the agents of imperialism and international Zionism. The nation and government of Iran are intimately standing beside you. Since it is a fact that the whole of the Iranian nation is prepared for martyrdom for continuity of our glorious Revolution, and will under no circumstances yield to any kind of force and pressure exerted by imperialism and international Zionism, we feel certain that you are also ready for martyrdom alongside your nation and do not expect the Iranian nation to pay ransom to the agents of world imperialism.

Then Ghotbzadeh added a threat, directed squarely at Britain:

> You must rest assured that we shall spare no effort for your release and should you so wish, and if needs be, tens of thousands of Iranians are now ready to enter the premises of the embassy not with weapons but with cries of Allahu Akbar and bring punishment upon those mercenaries of the Ba'athist Iraq in a manner they deserve . . . If the British government fails to solve the situation, we shall take matters into our own hands.

Ghotbzadeh's bald menace was relayed, via the Foreign Office, to John Dellow in Zulu Control.

"If this is a real threat, we shall have sufficient people to deal with it," Dellow declared. That morning he had polished his shoes to their habitual Sunday sheen, but his air of unruffled calm was becoming harder to maintain. The besieged U.S. Embassy in Tehran was proof of the ayatollah's capacity to mobilize an angry mob of supporters. If thousands of furious Iranians descended on Princes Gate, it would take more than one SAS squadron to hold them back.

At 09:10, the Montessori nursery school experienced a complete power cut, bringing Zulu Control to a temporary standstill, without lights or electricity. "No money in the meter," Dellow noted, battling to control his irritation as a constable hurried to the basement with a bag of fifty-pence pieces.

Then came intrusion from another quarter, in the shape of His Royal Highness Prince Andrew.

At 11:41, a message arrived at Zulu Control from Inspector Peter Prentice, of the Royalty Protection unit. The queen's second son, and second in line to the throne, had been watching television coverage of the siege and wished "to be allowed to visit the scene." In fact, Prentice explained, the prince would like to "visit for lunch."

Prince Andrew was then a twenty-year-old trainee helicopter pilot in the Royal Navy.

The last thing Dellow needed, at this delicate moment, was a princeling and his entourage in the building standing around asking questions and eating sandwiches. The royal request was denied "on the grounds of safety." Instead, deftly passing the buck upward, Dellow "suggested that HRH might like to attend New Scotland Yard to be briefed by the commissioner." But Prince Andrew did not want to see David McNee. The young royal wished to be where the action was. He wanted to see the drama unfolding. And he was used to getting what he wanted.

Dellow was besieged on all sides, and to make matters worse he now faced another crisis, inside his own camp.

Fred Luff seemed to be going mad.

The police negotiator had been behaving increasingly oddly since the shouting match with Towfiq the previous day. Dellow noticed that he seemed "very frustrated, and occasionally insolent, directing his annoyance upward toward the police commander." He had even complained that he was being treated like "the meat in the sandwich": receiving pressure from the terrorists on the one hand and being obstructed by Dellow on the other.

Much of the time Luff simply sat silent, head bowed in prayer.

Suddenly he jumped to his feet and announced that he had a plan that would end the siege: "We should bring in the Salvation Army."

The other policemen stared. Was this a joke?

The Salvation Army is a Christian charity dedicated to meeting the physical and spiritual needs of the poor and destitute. Music is central to the ministry, and the brass bands of the "Sally Army," complete with bonneted women playing beribboned tambourines, were a familiar sight on the streets of London. Despite its uniforms and ranks, the Salvation Army is wholly unmilitary, an organization as different from the SAS, poised next door, as could be imagined.

But Luff was deadly serious. "They can play music and sing hymns outside the embassy. It will make the gunmen think about God."

This bizarre suggestion was met with bemused silence by the other negotiators and, when Luff returned to his prayers, looks of consternation.

John Gunn went to find Dellow in Zulu Control. "You'll have to take him off," said the psychiatrist. "He's got to go."

Fred Luff was told to return home for some well-deserved rest, and stay there. He never fully recovered from the psychological strain of the siege.

The policeman now heading the negotiating team was David Veness, a thirty-two-year-old Cambridge graduate with a shock of prematurely white hair. Veness had worked in the Criminal Investigation Department combating organized crime and fraud. In 1980, he was setting out on a career fighting terrorism. He had attended the negotiation course, but this was his first live hostage situation. Gunn was confident Veness could handle it, and they shared a scientific approach. "Your terms of reference are built upon the beginning of the incident," said Veness. "You need to recognize that a whole series of dynamics, tensions, emotions, and interchanges will be occurring within the cauldron of the event, which will be fundamentally changing the nature of the judgments you have to form in order to optimize the chance of saving the hostages."

Veness was as calm and pragmatic as Luff was brittle and inflexible.

Prince Andrew had not given up. An hour after his request for a visit was denied, the persistent prince sent another message to Dellow: "It was suggested on his behalf that he could attend incognito." The idea that this highly recognizable royal might wander around the site in disguise was absurd, an unnecessary and pointless distraction. Dellow lost his temper and sent what amounted to a two-fingered salute to Buckingham Palace: "HRH would be informed as soon as the operation was complete so that he could attend if he so wished . . . one hour after its conclusion."

BOREDOM IS AN important and misunderstood trigger in human affairs. Because boredom occurs when nothing much is happening, it is often overlooked by historians. But when people have little to do, particularly in taxing circumstances, they can act in the most unpredictable ways.

In the eyes of the world's media, the siege had gone quiet. On a warm Sunday afternoon, with little to report, members of the press played soccer in the park, gossiped, and lounged in the sunshine. Negotiations with the gunmen were described as "affable," a word that might have been calculated to induce lassitude. The Cobra committee was told that the situation was stabilizing. Willie Whitelaw returned to Dorneywood, the home secretary's country residence outside London, leaving instructions that he should be informed immediately of any significant developments.

To maintain flagging police momentum, Dellow had ordered the publication of a daily "bulletin of events indicating the progress of the siege for circulation among those doing duty." Mostly it stated what every policeman already knew: "Negotiations are proceeding in a calm manner." Sometimes it was gently admonishing: "Who were the officers who allowed a gentleman with a Marks and Spencer carrier bag to enjoy a peaceful stroll through the closed-off area of Hyde Park? You are posted to prevent unauthorized persons passing through, not to stand amiably by whilst they wander past." But, as the siege entered its fifth day, the police bulletin-writers, like the reporters, were running out of new material: "A Mallard duck nesting on the window ledge of Number 24 next to the Iranian Embassy appears undisturbed by proceedings, and is due to hatch her eggs at any time." Dellow was insistent that such nuggets "assisted in keeping up morale, especially of those officers posted to the more remote parts of the cordon."

Ron Morris finished his novel ("*the day of the Jackal was over*") and closed it with a satisfied sigh. "Bloody excellent," he declared, passing it to Ali Tabatabai. Sim Harris idly flipped through some official correspondence found in a drawer: the most interesting item was an order for British tanks from the days of the shah. Mustapha Karkouti was increasingly pale, sweating copiously. Morris served tea and biscuits promptly at 13:30, and then again at 16:15.

Morris was already thinking about the big tidy-up he would have when this was all over. "Sim, we will never get this place sorted out again," he sighed. "Look at the way they have piled all the furniture up the stairs to my office."

Guard duty is tedious work, and the gunmen set out to explore the embassy. On the fourth floor, Abbas discovered Morris's collection of replica guns but not his savings. He helped himself to the air pistol and stuck it in his belt like a cowboy.

AFTER FIVE DAYS of repeated alarms, lethargy gripped the SAS team: the siege seemed to be winding down to a whimper; they would soon be heading back to barracks. "Even the television people are sounding less excited now," one of the waiting troopers noted. "We get bored. We don't believe we'll be called in next door to do the business." One soldier found he could not pick up his boots: while he was napping, someone had nailed them to the floor. Another poured himself some hot tea and found it all over his overalls, as a hole had been drilled into the bottom of the mug. The morning intelligence briefing produced little new information. The man from Box 500 proudly announced that the thermal-imaging camera at the rear had detected a pattern of movement. Every morning, he reported, at exactly 08:00, the hostages gathered in the commercial section on the ground floor. An SAS officer tartly pointed out the central heating was timed to go on every morning at that hour: the "hostages" detected by MI5's machine were radiators warming up.

To stay alert, one trooper inscribed a message to himself on a small card: "Move forward with silence, then act with extreme violence. Observe absolutely everything, yet assume nothing." He kept the aide-mémoire in his pocket. "Between the many 'stand-tos' and 'stand-downs,' I'd pull the card out, and it helped to clear my clogged memory and reset. A bit like an old-time boxer sniffing smelling salts." Another soldier stared out the top-floor window onto Hyde Park, glorious in the afternoon sunshine. "I'd love to be wandering around the park right now," he reflected. In the distance, the Royal Parks gardeners were planting out the beds. "That's what I need to be doing back in my garden."

Mel Parry was bored. Even *The Hobbit* could not hold his attention. When inactive, Parry became volatile. He decided to pick on someone. Casting his eye around the room, he spotted Mark "Wingnut" Gilfoyle. The young clerk was reclining on an embroidered throne and looking, to Parry's mind, altogether too comfortable. A practical joke was called for.

Parry and Tommy Palmer marched up to him. "Gilfoyle, we're one man short. You're going to have to join the fun. You'll be abseiling. Get ready. You're on the immediate action team." The young soldier was handed black overalls, a hood, a respirator, body armor, a rope, and a machine gun (minus firing pin). "We didn't give him a 9mm because he might have shot himself."

Gilfoyle had been in uniform for less than two years. He could type and take dictation but had received no training on how to fire a gun, let alone how to abseil into the middle of a violent hostage situation armed to the teeth. Having typed up the immediate action plan, he knew exactly how perilous the assault would be. As Parry intended, he was wholly terrified. But Gilfoyle did as ordered: he changed into the assault kit he had never worn before and took his place, visibly shaking, among the other troops on standby. These had all been let in on the joke and could barely contain their sniggers. Gilfoyle was far too frightened to notice.

Every animal that hunts in a pack sometimes behaves this way, picking on the weakest member to solidify the cohesion of the rest. B Squadron was bonded by an esprit de corps that was strong, even by SAS standards. They ribbed one another mercilessly and fought among themselves from time to time, but they would also have died for one another, and fiercely protected their own. If anyone from another squadron or regiment had tried to bully Gilfoyle, the pack would have turned on them instantly.

Not every member of B Squadron was made of the same abrasive material as Parry and Palmer. One who seemed to stand a little apart was Tom MacDonald, with a streak of gray in his hair that earned him the nickname "Badger." The son of a butcher, MacDonald did not mix socially with the others, in part because he had been in the Territorial Reserves before joining the Paras, a distinction that put him on a slightly lower plane in SAS eyes. His friends were mostly outside the regiment. While Parry, Palmer, and the others drank at The Grapes in Hereford, starting on Friday night and sometimes not returning home until Sunday morning, MacDonald preferred to tend his vegetable patch or spend the weekend sawing wood. On the third day of the siege, he called his wife, Cherry, from a phone booth. He did not say where he was or what he was doing, but he did not have to: Cherry had been watching the news. "When I married him," she said, "I knew exactly what I was getting myself into. I signed up for this." None of the other troopers called their partners. That was not what you did. A man on the squadron periphery, Badger MacDonald was a slightly different animal, and never fully trusted; none of the other troopers could have explained why.

Another outlier, for very different reasons, was Staff Sergeant Tom Morell, a paratrooper who had seen service in Cyprus, Borneo, Libya, Malta, and the Middle East before joining the SAS in 1969. At thirty-nine, Morell was the oldest and most experienced soldier in the squadron. He was also one of only two nonwhite men on the assault team.

Morell was born in Suva, Fiji, in 1940, one of many soldiers from that South Pacific Island nation to fight for Britain. When Captain Cook first arrived in Tonga in 1773, he heard reports of the "famed warriors" and intermittent cannibals of "Feegee." Fiji was one of the few places in the world to request British colonization, and, as a demonstration of allegiance, King Cakobau of Fiji sent Queen Victoria his best warclub. The British Empire immediately began recruiting these warlike men. Fijians saw action against Japan during the Second World

War, where they gained a reputation as fierce jungle troops, and later in Malaya, Borneo, Oman, and Iraq.

One of Morell's grandfathers was a Methodist pastor from Fiji, the other a white pioneer from New Zealand named Morell. At sixteen, he left school and joined the post office, becoming a district postmaster at nineteen, communicating with the 333 islands in the Fiji archipelago by telex or Morse code, and frequently delivering mail by canoe. Morell had seen a film about the Parachute Regiment as a schoolboy, and when the British Army arrived on a recruiting drive in 1961, he was among the first in line: from a thousand Fijian volunteers, the army selected two hundred for training in Britain. With his expertise in Morse code, Morell joined the Royal Signals and served with the Parachute Signals Squadron, part of the Parachute Brigade, much to his Fijian mother's dismay. "What's this I hear about you jumping out of aircrafts?" she scolded him. "Can you please wait until the aircraft lands like a proper human being?" In 1969 he passed selection for the SAS. More than a decade later, he had become an almost avuncular figure to many of the men. When Tommy Palmer was kicked out of D Squadron for bad behavior, Sergeant Morell stepped in: "They wanted to get rid of him. And I said: 'I'll have the Scotsman in my troop.' He turned out to be a good lad. He just needed to be looked after." In Northern Ireland, Morell served as Hector Gullan's operations officer; the two men saw eye to eye.

Tom Morell never experienced racism in the ranks of the SAS. No one would have dared to mock his accent or the color of his skin. Morell did not fight, swear, or drink. There was something almost chivalric about him: the rest of the squadron called him "Sir Thomas." He was deliberate, calm, a good man to go into the jungle with and as hard as Fijian mahogany.

FOR LUNCH, the police produced a rich, creamy, garlicky pork dish, which was not popular with the troops. The SAS soldiers demanded "something English," and ten pizzas duly appeared, courtesy of Carlo's, a nearby Italian restaurant. The Red Team remained on alert a floor below, prepared for the immediate action plan that few believed would be implemented. Among them sat Gilfoyle, a look of white terror on his face, still in black combat gear. The clerk had recently quit smoking. The other soldiers noticed he was now smoking "two at a time."

The Blue Team settled down with their pizzas in front of the snooker.

Cliff Thorburn took the first frame at the Crucible Theatre, but Hurricane Higgins won the next five. Thorburn then won the seventh to make the score 5–2. Higgins complained that Thorburn was standing in his line of sight. By the end of the first session, he was leading 6–3. *The Times* contrasted "the shrewd cumulative processes of Thorburn against the explosive break-building of Higgins." Thorburn accused Higgins of distracting him by loudly dropping a piece of ice into his glass as he was about to take a shot. By the end of the second session, they were level, at nine frames apiece. Confident of victory, Lynn Higgins baked a cake proclaiming her husband the victor. Most of the SAS contingent were rooting for Higgins: something about this twitchy, tough, turbulent character chimed with the spirit of B Squadron.

The Embassy World Snooker Championship final would be won and lost the next day.

"After a long game of cat-and-mouse," *The Times* reported, "an exciting finish is in prospect."

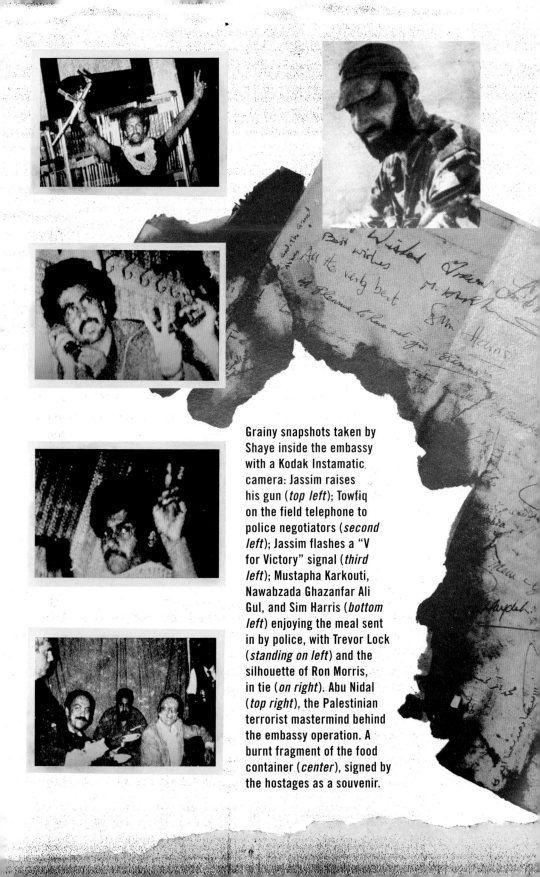

Grainy snapshots taken by Shaye inside the embassy with a Kodak Instamatic camera: Jassim raises his gun (*top left*); Towfiq on the field telephone to police negotiators (*second left*); Jassim flashes a "V for Victory" signal (*third left*); Mustapha Karkouti, Nawabzada Ghazanfar Ali Gul, and Sim Harris (*bottom left*) enjoying the meal sent in by police, with Trevor Lock (*standing on left*) and the silhouette of Ron Morris, in tie (*on right*). Abu Nidal (*top right*), the Palestinian terrorist mastermind behind the embassy operation. A burnt fragment of the food container (*center*), signed by the hostages as a souvenir.

Violence mounts outside the embassy, as Iranian demonstrators clash with British protesters. Trying to keep the two sides apart, PC Michael Perkin is hurled to the ground in the fracas (*bottom right*), fracturing his leg. Iranians hold massed prayers on the road leading to Princes Gate (*bottom left*).

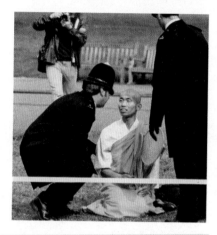

Iranian protesters march outside the Royal Albert Hall (*top*); Faten Karkouti (*center left*) anxiously awaits news of her husband, Mustapha. A lone Tibetan monk prays at the barricades (*center right*). The growing crowd of media mills around "Pressville" (*bottom*), the enclosure constructed by police on the corner of Princes Gate and Exhibition Road.

MI5 technicians lower a miniature microphone down the chimney (*top left*), while others drill listening devices into the walls on either side of the embassy.

The first image of Karkouti obtained by police (*top right*) in his days as an activist for the Palestinian cause.

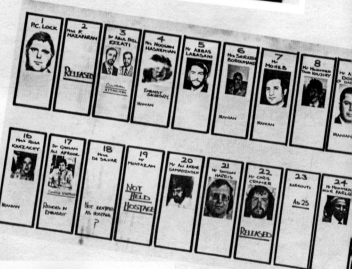

Towfiq (wearing keffiyeh) receives a message and medicine from a shoebox attached to a pole (*bottom left*).

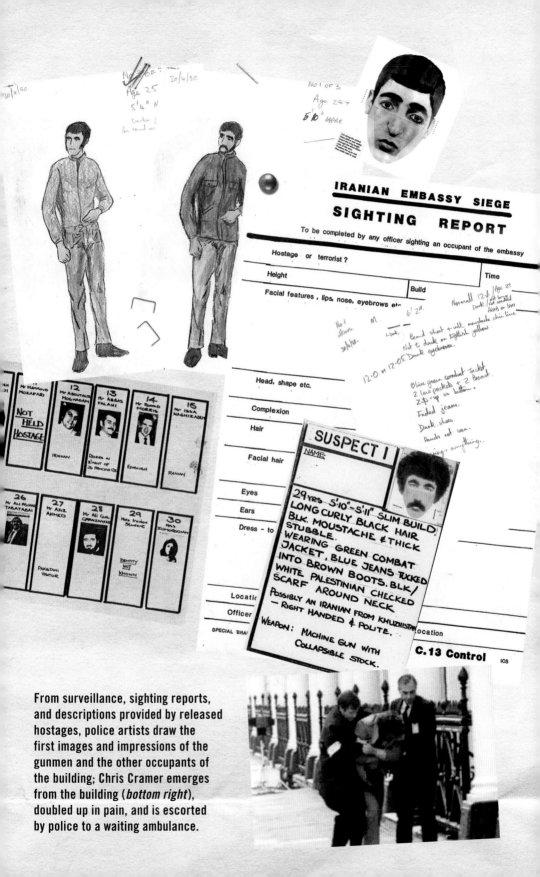

No 2 of 3
30/4/80
Age 25
5'4" N
Darker
[illegible]

No 1 of 3
Age 29+
5'10" APPROX

IRANIAN EMBASSY SIEGE
SIGHTING REPORT

To be completed by any officer sighting an occupant of the embassy

Hostage or terrorist?

Height | Time

Facial features, lips, nose, eyebrows etc.

Build

No 1 released. M. | 6' 2". | 30/4/80 | L-Dark. | Normall 12 ot / Age 29 Dark / not curled ARAB on lent

Beard short + silk moustache chin line
Not to dark on tightish yellow

12·0 - 12·05 Dark eyebrows.

Olive green combat jacket
2 low pockets + 2 breast.
Zip-up on bottom.
Faded jeans.
Dark shoes.
Hands not seen.
[illegible] anything.

Head, shape etc.

Complexion

Hair

Facial hair

Eyes

Ears

Dress - to

Location

Officer

SPECIAL BRANCH

SUSPECT I
NAME

29 YRS 5'10"-5'11" SLIM BUILD.
LONG CURLY BLACK HAIR
BLK. MOUSTACHE & THICK
STUBBLE.
WEARING GREEN COMBAT
JACKET, BLUE JEANS TUCKED
INTO BROWN BOOTS. BLK/
WHITE PALESTINIAN CHECKED
SCARF AROUND NECK
POSSIBLY AN IRANIAN FROM KHUZHISTAN
— RIGHT HANDED & POLITE.
WEAPON: MACHINE GUN WITH
COLLAPSIBLE STOCK.

C.13 Control | ICS

Mr Mahmoud Mozafari
12 Mr Abdulah Moghadam
13 Mr Abbas Falahi
14 Mr Ronald Morris
15 Mr Issa Naghizadeh
NOT HELD HOSTAGE
IRANIAN
RESIDENT IN [illegible]
ENGLISH
IRANIAN

26 Mr Ali [illegible] Tabatabai
27 Mr Aziz Ahmed
28 Mr Ali Gul Ghanzanfar
29 Male Iranian Student
30 Mrs [illegible]
PAKISTANI VISITOR
IDENTITY NOT KNOWN

From surveillance, sighting reports, and descriptions provided by released hostages, police artists draw the first images and impressions of the gunmen and the other occupants of the building; Chris Cramer emerges from the building (*bottom right*), doubled up in pain, and is escorted by police to a waiting ambulance.

The SAS prepare to go in. A briefing in the intelligence room (*top*) in front of boards showing the gunmen and their weapons. The frame charge to be used for blowing out the armored front windows of the embassy (*center*). The waiting soldiers study the wooden replica of the embassy, the floor plans, and the photographs of the hostages (*bottom*). Inside the replica, toy plastic figures are used to represent each hostage (a farm worker with the sack removed so hands are raised in surrender) and each gunman (a farmer with a shotgun).

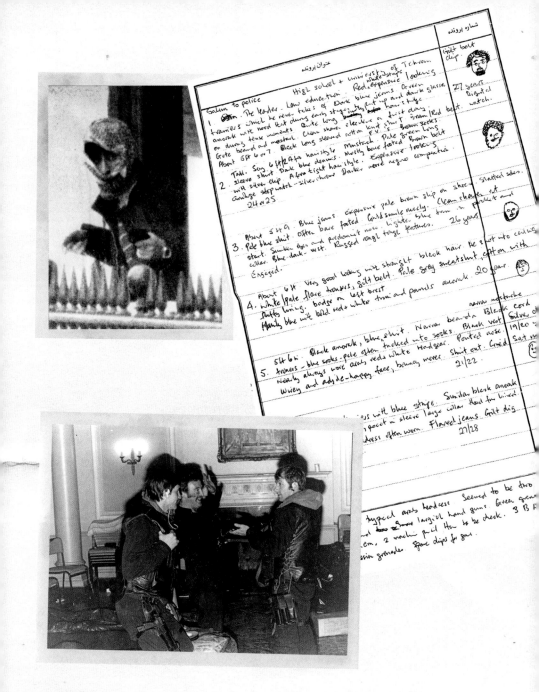

The veteran BBC reporter Sim Harris drew up detailed descriptions of each of the gunmen (*top right*) and included their clothing and hairstyles, along with sketches. One of the gunmen, probably Makki, appears at the front door (*top left*), pistol in left hand, to collect food containers. Horsing around (*bottom*), one of the troopers points a submachine gun into the chest of another.

Bulletin No. 3

A number of armed men
the Iranian Embassy,
11.30 am last Wednesda

Since yesterday a furt
Mustapha KARKOUTI, has
brings the total number
a further approximate 1
LOCK, of DPG. He has now been seen on a number of occasions. Each time he has
appeared calm and collected and is behaving as one would expect an officer of
this Force to do.

to five, and we believe
held. Amongst those still held is PC Trevor

A Mallard duck nesting on the window ledge of No. 18, next to the Iranian Embassy
appears undisturbed by the proceedings, and is due to hatch her eggs at any
time.

Who were the officers who allowed a gentleman with a Marks and Spencers carrier
bag to enjoy a peaceful stroll through a closed-off area of Hyde Park yesterday
afternoon? Please don't forget you are posted to cordons and barriers specificall
to prevent unauthorised persons passing through, not to stand amiably by whilst
they wander past.

Reporters and other Press people
Force as from 6 pm on Monday 5.5.80.
ll Road and Imperial Institute Road.
s well as both sides. After parking,
e west footway of Exhibition Road
sington Gore.

ssures and problems arising for us all
ponse from everybody is as efficient
I will soon be able to say the matter
turn to normal, but in the meantime

DAC 'A' (OPS)

To keep up morale, John Dellow issues
a daily bulletin (*background*), updating
police on developments, ranging from the
release of hostages to the nesting duck
on the window ledge of a neighboring
building (*bottom*). Among the waiting
media, a "picnic atmosphere" develops
(*top*), while police enjoy a cup of tea
provided by catering vans (*center*).

High tension as Higgins edges ahead

Alex Higgins, seeking to regain the title he won at his first attempt in 1972, ended at 9-9 with Cliff Thorburn, the Canadian champion, in their 35 cable table manners, one could see no justification for the Irishman's complaint, an echo, incidentally, of an allegation he made against Terry Griffiths following frame when the Irishman's 54 break was superceded by the 53 clearance which gave Thorburn a black ball success.

The nation is gripped by the World Snooker final taking place in Sheffield. Alex "Hurricane" Higgins prepares to take a shot (*center*). The gunmen daub anti-Khomeini graffiti on the embassy walls (*bottom*): "The nation of the Arabs shall not die. . . . We will continue the struggle for the complete freedom of Arabistan." On the metal food canister (with concealed listening device) is written: "Long Live Arabestan [*sic*]."

Tense negotiations at the "Talking Window" (*from top to bottom*): Sim Harris and Trevor Lock; Lock, his face still bloodied by the effects of flying glass, calls down to the police negotiators alongside Mustapha Karkouti; Karkouti and Lock with Towfiq (in keffiyeh); Karkouti, Afrouz, and Towfiq with hood up. A negotiator calls up to the window (*top right*). Doreen Lock leaves the family home in Barking (*right*), just a few hours after a message is relayed from her husband inside the embassy: "Tell her to keep her chin up."

A dead body is carried from the front steps (*top*) with an arm, clad in a distinctive yellow cardigan, trailing over the side of the stretcher. The handwritten note (*bottom left*), scrawled by John Dellow on a piece of paper torn from a notebook, transferring authority from the police to the SAS. Waiting for the assault: police scramble to their positions (*bottom right*).

24 PRINCES GATE
LONDON SW7.

AT 19.07. ON 5ª MAY 1980
I , JOHN D DELLOW , DAC 'A',
PASSED CONTROL OF IRANIAN
EMBASSY INCIDENT TO LT CO...
HM ROSE .

Dellow
5 MAY 1980

HM ROSE

J D DELLOW

"HYDE PARK": The four men in the first wave of Alpha One in position to abseil down the rear of the building to the second-floor balcony (*top*). Police race to the "reception area" at the back of the embassy and up the steps to the terrace (*center*). The sniper's view from the sixth floor of Kingston House, Flat 53 (*bottom*): Hector Gullan's operational HQ for Operation Nimrod.

Tommy Palmer abseils safely down to the balcony (*top*), but the rope of team leader Tom Morell jams and he is left suspended above the central window of the general office. Palmer has thrown a flash-bang and the room is ablaze (*center right*), but Morell is stuck fast, with flames lapping at his legs. Palmer has torn off his burning hood and gas mask (*bottom left*) and re-enters the room accompanied by Paul Sanford. Morell, his trousers on fire, dangles above the flames (*bottom right*).

Bravo Four assault the front of the embassy in full view of the television cameras. Mel Parry and John McAleese clamber from the balcony of Number 15 on to the embassy balcony (*top left*); the office ablaze, Sim Harris climbs through the rubble and out on to the balcony (*top right*); with flames leaping from the windows, Harris clambers on to the balustrade (*center right*) and prepares to jump across to the balcony outside Roya's office. Harris runs past a police dog and handler along the back walkway (*bottom right*). SUNRAY (*bottom left*): Hector Gullan (speaking on handset) maintains contact with the various teams via a portable wireless communications station carried by "Squashball" McGregor.

Two masked SAS snipers with Polecat launchers fire a volley of CR-gas canisters through the windows of the telex room on the second floor (*top left*). The doorman Abbas Fallahi waves a white pillowcase from the window of the telex room (*top right*). The wreckage of the telex room (*bottom right*). The remains of Roya Kaghachi's office, minutes after the final struggle between Lock and Towfiq (*bottom left*).

Aftermath: the view from the hall to the front door after the shooting has stopped (*top*). The hostages are made to lie on the back lawn, while their hands are secured with plasticuffs (*left*), with the last gunman (*in red jacket at right*), as an SAS soldier stands over him. The final gunman is identified by the SAS and handed over to the police (*right*), who haul him away as firemen douse the burning building.

16

WRITING ON
THE WALL

A rabic culture has a long history of drawing defiant public statements in public places. The eighth-century Arab and Persian poet Yazid al-Himyari daubed walls in southern Iran with messages condemning the ruling Umayyad caliphate. The walls of Khuzestan were liberally spattered with graffiti attacking first the shah, and later the ayatollah.

In the stationery cupboard next to the bathroom, Jassim found a stock of Magic Markers. With nothing better to do, he decided to try his hand at some graffiti himself.

On the second-floor landing, in large letters, Jassim wrote "Death to Khomeini" in Farsi across the wall. Towfiq joined him and added his own message: "Down with the Turbaned Shah." Returning from the bathroom, Harris saw what they were doing and offered a suggestion: "After this is all over, British television crews will come and film the inside of this place. It makes sense to write in English."

Towfiq considered this an excellent idea.

"Is it correct English to write: 'We demand fundamental changes'?" he asked.

Sim Harris said it was.

Towfiq started writing, and then paused. "How do you spell 'funda-mental'?"

Harris spelled out the word. "He just seemed to be passing the time by doing this writing."

Then Jassim wrote out another message, this time in Arabic: "Death to Khomeini. Long live the Arabistan people."

At 17:15, the two gunmen stepped back to admire their handiwork.

The injured diplomat Gholam-Ali Afrouz had been watching from the doorway to the general office, with a look of rising indignation. These Arabs had barged into his embassy and now they were covering the place with their godless slogans. The reference to the "Turbaned Shah," suggesting the ayatollah was merely an Islamic version of the detested king, was particularly offensive. Unable to restrain himself, the diplomat in checked chef's trousers shouted at them to desist.

Jassim yelled back a stream of insults in Farsi and pushed him back-ward into the room.

Abbas Lavasani leaped up and joined in, jabbing a finger at the gun-man. "Do not dishonor the name of the ayatollah," he screamed.

Suddenly everyone was on their feet and shouting.

Shaye produced a hand grenade and took a step toward the Irani-ans. "Shut up!" he yelled.

Muhammad Faruqi tried to calm Afrouz. "Khomeini is not going to die because someone writes a slogan on a wall," he pleaded.

But Afrouz was enraged. "No, no, we can't take this any more, we have to fight these people."

Terrified, Roya hauled Karkouti to his feet. "Come and help, please—it's a very dangerous situation."

Karkouti also tried to reason with Jassim. "You're just upset, Faisal. You don't really mean 'Death to Khomeini'—"

"Yes, we do," snarled Jassim.

Roya turned to Towfiq. "Please, Salim, tell them not to do that," she said, gesturing toward the graffiti-covered walls.

From just a few feet away, his face bright red, Lavasani harangued the gunmen at volume with a torrent of expletives, the worst insults he could think of in both Arabic and Farsi. The shouting was so loud, Jas-sim could not make out Lavasani's precise words.

"What's that son of a bitch saying?" he demanded.

"Nothing important," stammered Karkouti. The air thrummed with imminent violence. In a matter of moments, the atmosphere had shifted from near serenity to ferocious confrontation.

Harris watched aghast. "Come on, let's keep calm. Everybody just stay quiet," he implored.

Lavasani seemed "completely out of control," in the grip of righteous fury, taunting, sneering, goading the Arabs to react. Suddenly he lurched across the room, "screaming in Farsi and beating his chest with his right arm," lunging toward the tallest gunman. Jassim took a pace back and cocked his machine gun, then seized Lavasani by the throat and hurled him onto the floor, followed by "a stabbing motion with his gun as if he was about to shoot." Roya screamed.

"Are you mad, you idiot?" Karkouti shouted at Lavasani, stepping between the gunman and the man on the ground. At the same moment, two of the Iranian hostages fell on Lavasani, pinning him down. The doorman Abbas Fallahi rushed forward and kicked him.

Trevor Lock had been sitting speechless through the wild confrontation. Now he rose from his chair, strode across the room, and bent over Lavasani. "Okay, that's enough. You just cool it," he growled. "Bloody cool it. Just shut up and keep still."

To Harris, he sounded like "a typical copper gone to control an incident between a group of blokes, putting a bit of authority into his voice."

Karkouti joined the little knot standing over Lavasani.

Lock by now held Lavasani in a neck lock. "If you don't stop jeopardizing everybody's safety because of your own principles, then I'm going to hurt you."

Lavasani continued to writhe and bellow.

"Mustapha, somebody must smash him in the face," Lock said, as if delegating an unwelcome but necessary duty.

Instead, Karkouti crouched beside the struggling man on the floor and stared into his eyes. "Listen to me, you. If you want to hit someone, hit me in the face, release your rage, I don't mind."

Lavasani stopped struggling and stared back, wide-eyed, and then burst into tears. "I swear to Allah, Mr. Trevor, I will never argue with these men again."

The bizarre scene ended with Lavasani and Karkouti rocking "back and forth on the floor in each other's arms, like mother and child."

The fight went out of Lavasani as quickly as it had erupted. He lay on the floor now, utterly meek. Harris's heart pounded in his chest. *"Christ, we were doing so well . . ."*

Jassim stalked out, still furious. From the corridor came the sound of Arab voices raised in loud argument.

The tall gunman reentered the general office and hurled another volley of curses at Lavasani and the other Iranians.

"Awlad al-qahba"—you sons of bitches—"we'll teach you a lesson," he roared.

Karkouti followed him into the corridor uttering soothing words in Arabic, but Jassim shrugged him away.

"I am going to write now on the walls inside the room where everybody is, and I will shoot anyone who protests," Jassim hissed furiously. "We must teach them a lesson."

Karkouti dashed back into the general office.

"In a minute, the gunmen are going to come in and write on the wall," he told the prostrate Lavasani. "You've got to keep calm and you mustn't be roused by it, or you will put everyone's life in danger." Addressing the other Iranians, he continued: "For God's sake, talk to Lavasani, and make sure he doesn't do anything."

Having ignited the conflict, a chastened Afrouz knelt by Lavasani and spoke softly in Farsi.

Jassim appeared at the doorway, a marker in one hand and a submachine gun in the other. "I want you to carefully look at that wall and understand," he shouted. Behind him stood Shaye holding a hand grenade, his finger through the pull ring.

Slowly, deliberately, Jassim wrote on the wall, turning occasionally, daring anyone to challenge him. All eyes were fixed on the young Revolutionary Guard member: if he spoke a word, he would be shot. First in Arabic, then in Farsi, Jassim scrawled across the wall in large, sloping letters: "Death to Khomeini, the Turbaned Shah."

No one moved.

The Arab gunman then strode over to where Lavasani lay and addressed him in Farsi, spitting out each word.

"What the hell is going on?" Harris whispered to Karkouti.

"Faisal's offering Lavasani a choice. He's saying: 'If you want to die, we'll kill you right now.' "

Jassim Alwan al-Nasiri, the Arab Iranian rebel, and Abbas Lavasani, the Persian Iranian revolutionary, were both believers in martyrdom, a willingness to die for righteousness. They just believed, with equal violence, in very different things.

Jassim returned to the corridor, and the angry debate continued among the Arab gunmen.

"What are they saying, Mustapha?" Lock asked.

"One or two of them are suggesting to kill him. They're all bloody jumpy."

Suddenly Jassim broke off from the disagreement and began chanting the revolutionary anthem of Arabistan. Shaye joined in. Towfiq did not.

The police and MI5 listened in on the audio probes, trying to make sense of the noises. In his diary, John Dellow recorded the sudden flare-up of tension but struggled to identify the cause: "sounds of furious argument, a woman crying, the sound of patriotic songs." Something had broken, suddenly and irretrievably.

A few slogans idly scrawled on a wall with markers had unleashed something new, unpredictable, and ugly. In the hostage room, no one uttered a word. "Tension terrible, really dreadful," wrote Harris.

The gunmen stalked around, glowering, barely speaking to one another. The disagreement over what to do with Lavasani was, Harris reflected, "the first major breakdown of discipline" among the hostage-takers, putting everyone in even greater danger.

Karkouti agreed: the gunmen were "beginning to crack up."

The probes in the walls picked up the tremors of a looming eruption, confirmation that the group was losing its coherence and, perhaps, its purpose.

Jassim and Shaye were ready to kill Lavasani; the Iranian cur had demanded martyrdom, so why not grant his wish? Abbas pointed out that this was supposed to be a bloodless operation. Fowzi also argued against killing anyone. That had not been part of the plan.

Jassim shot him a nasty look. "Anyone who objects to this will be killed."

Fowzi and Abbas fell silent.

Towfiq sat apart, oddly detached.

Karkouti was struck by his changed demeanor: "He looked pale and somehow seemed mentally switched off, as he sat by himself at the end of the passage, the radio playing softly." Hitherto his authority had been undisputed. Now his "grim look and hazy eyes" indicated to Harris that the leader no longer "had complete control over his men," and increasingly did not care.

The power balance was shifting, Karkouti noted, with Jassim emerging as "the hard-liner."

DOWNSTAIRS ON THE field telephone, Towfiq angrily rejected the offer of more food, and demanded to know where the ambassadors were.

"We have told the government what you want, and they will tell us the minute they have some definite answers," said David Veness.

Lock, Harris, Morris, and Karkouti huddled in a group. "Time was ticking so slow with overwhelming uncertainty and total fear."

"What's going to happen, Mustapha?" Harris asked.

There was a long pause. Karkouti was "deathly pale, with bloodshot eyes." His stomach cramps were now one continual, searing pain. He spoke, in a gasp: "I think I am going to die in here."

Soon after 19:00, Towfiq appeared at the doorway and beckoned to Karkouti. "Come with me, please."

The Syrian journalist rose unsteadily and followed him out.

When Karkouti had not returned after half an hour, Harris began to wonder whether the gunmen had found him "a comfortable bed to sleep in or offered him a bath." After an hour, the other hostages became alarmed. Had he collapsed? After two hours, the truth dawned: Karkouti was not coming back.

KUWAIT'S AMBASSADOR, Sheikh Saud Nasser al-Saud al-Sabah, convened a gathering of his Arab counterparts at the grand Kuwaiti residence in Belgrave Square. To avoid putting Saddam's nose out of joint, the group included Iraq's ambassador. In theory, the meeting would explore how to help mediate the crisis; in reality, it was called to find a way not to, without losing face. An hour earlier, Syria's Adnan Omran had visited Douglas Hurd at the Foreign Office and suggested that, instead of using an Arab ambassador, a better negotiator would be Nabil Ramlawi, the PLO representative in London, who did not speak for a state and might be able to "engineer a peaceful climbdown" by the gunmen. That idea was flatly rejected (as Omran knew it would be). The PLO had just one aim and would undoubtedly try to use any mediation role for political advantage.

From a diplomatic perspective, the situation was fraught with peril. The embassy siege was a proxy battle between Iran and Iraq, and none of the Arab countries wanted to get embroiled. The Foreign Office had ruled out giving the gunmen safe passage out of Britain—which gave the ambassadors, as they saw it, no room to maneuver. If these armed men sensed they were being manipulated and stalled by fellow Arabs, they could make matters worse. Kasim Ghazzawi, the Jordanian, put it bluntly: "The situation in there is very tense, very dangerous, and very volatile. These are dangerous people. They are extremely uncompromising. Any single miscalculation in dealing with them could result in a human tragedy. In our view, to go in there and *not* to be able to offer safe conduct would not, we think, lead to a peaceful solution."

The meeting at the Kuwaiti residence ended on a note of unanimous agreement: the ambassadors would not get involved.

Had they been fully apprised of the psychological situation inside the embassy, they might have chosen differently. Towfiq was no longer demanding the release of prisoners or more publicity for his cause. He had released four hostages already. He had even started talking about surrender, and how long he and his men might have to spend in a British prison if they did so. And he was losing control. But he still demanded to be taken seriously. Towfiq wanted an Arab ambassador to talk to him, to listen, and to treat him as the legitimate representative of the unacknowledged state of Arabistan.

The psychiatrist John Gunn was increasingly convinced that if just one diplomat went to the embassy and spoke to the lead gunman on the field telephone, the standoff could resolve itself without a shot being fired.

Dellow agreed. The gunmen appeared to be fixated on "the ambassador issue" and were "becoming dangerously frustrated." The longer this was denied them, the more he feared the situation could spin out of control.

In this volatile environment, anything might trigger an explosion; including, bizarrely, Tchaikovsky's *1812 Overture.*

The great overture in E-flat major, composed in 1880, was being performed that night as the finale to a Tchaikovsky evening in the Royal Albert Hall. The concert featured the New Symphony Orchestra and the Band of the Scots Guards, conducted by the Czech maestro Vilém Tauský.

Only at 19:30, with the concert under way, did someone in Zulu Control remember that the *1812 Overture* ends, famously, with a climactic volley of cannon fire. This would be clearly audible in the Iranian Embassy, Dellow noted, and "might be misinterpreted by the terrorists." Tchaikovsky's musical gunfire could be mistaken for an attack on the embassy, and trigger a bloodbath.

A surreal discussion ensued. Would it be possible to intercept the conductor in the interval and ask him to drop the overture? Could the *1812 Overture* be performed without its signature cannonade? Could the explosions be made quieter?

Dellow ruled that the show must go on: "It was decided after due consideration not to interfere with the program."

TOWFIQ LED KARKOUTI down to the entrance hall, sat him on the lowest stair, and offered him a glass of water.

"We have decided to let you go. We are sorry for all the troubles we have caused you," he said gently.

Surprised, Karkouti protested. Should they not release one of the women?

Towfiq shook his head. "No. It is you or no one."

"Now?"

"Now."

The chief gunman offered no explanation for the decision to release the Syrian. Perhaps he had simply come to like the older man, whose political views echoed his own. Karkouti was plainly suffering, doubled up in pain.

"I must tell you," Towfiq said sadly. "I am afraid that we don't know what to do without you." He seemed so young.

Karkouti felt a surge of guilt, and a flash of anger. In distant Baghdad, the terrorist mastermind Abu Nidal, the Mukhabarat spy Fowzi al-Naimi, Sami the Fox, and their boss Saddam Hussein would care nothing for the fate of Towfiq and his crew, "helpless kids sent by vicious people on an operation to cause havoc and die."

Towfiq shook Karkouti's hand and smiled wanly as he opened the door. "Tell the police that we want a way out, and we don't want to hurt anyone."

With his hands raised, Karkouti stepped onto the pavement to the distant melody of Tchaikovsky's Piano Concerto No. 1 in B-flat minor.

Moments later, the fifth hostage to be released was being questioned in Number 24.

"Get one of the Arab ambassadors soon," he said. "Or something bad will happen."

The cramps had ceased the moment Karkouti walked out. Dellow put his condition down to stress, but ordered that he be carried on a stretcher to a waiting ambulance to demonstrate to anyone watching from the embassy that the police were taking his health seriously.

News of Karkouti's release was greeted by the twenty-one remaining hostages with relief, envy, and apprehension. The multilingual Syrian had acted as a mediator: among the hostages, between the hostages and the gunmen, between the gunmen and the police.

"With Mustapha out," Harris reflected glumly, "it will be hard to control the situation. Our great friend had left, the man that had controlled so many electric situations had gone."

Lock agreed: "If some sort of mediator is not produced, they might soon go over the top."

Beyond that lay another dread, unexpressed but urgent: Had the gunmen released the only Arab hostage because they intended to kill everyone else?

THEIR MEAL THAT night was as plain as the previous night's feast had been lavish: stale leftover white rolls and black tea.

Sounds were coming from the walls again: the high-pitched squeaking was now joined by a low rumble, and the occasional thump. Towfiq summoned Lock to listen.

"Mice come out at night," the policeman offered. Realizing how feeble that sounded, he changed tack. "Old buildings warm up during the day and then cool down at night, and they creak as the wood moves . . . or perhaps it's the heating system."

Towfiq knew he was lying. Lock knew that Towfiq knew he was lying. Trust was dwindling.

"These noises are being made by the police," the gunman said blankly.

AT THE SAME MOMENT, MI5 delivered a report to Zulu Control that "drilling was almost through on the second floor," and in a few more hours the technicians would have "complete penetration" through the fifteen inches of brick between the embassy and the Doctors' House. Audio coverage was improving by the hour. Dellow ordered the technical attack to continue but warned: "Should tension heighten, all drilling would have to cease."

Karkouti's unexpected release presented the police with an intelligence bonanza. In a flood, the journalist described everyone and everything in the building: hostages and gunmen, their names and personalities, the layout of the various rooms and much more. "He reported having seen grenades but no explosives, and he was able to tell us where the field telephone was at the time of his release," noted Dellow. Some of what he revealed was deeply disquieting: the extremists on both sides, Arab and Iranian, were in open conflict; the gunmen were fighting among themselves; Salim, so courteous and calm when the siege began, was beginning "to lose control."

The negotiators called the field telephone, to thank Towfiq for releasing Karkouti. At first Towfiq did not pick up. When he did, he sounded depressed. He refused food, demanded the ambassadors once again, and then rang off, Dellow noted, "with a degree of petulance and hostility."

The situation had entered a new and highly unstable phase.

This sobering assessment was passed on to the SAS intelligence operations room at Number 15 and the Cobra committee in Whitehall. Michael Rose, the commanding officer of 22 SAS, and Peter de la Billière, the director of special forces, retired to the latter's flat in Philbeach Gardens for a supper of spaghetti Bolognese. When the plates were cleared away, they laid out a plan of the embassy on the floor. Rose remained "irrepressibly optimistic," observed de la Billière.

The senior officer was less so: "I felt certain the siege would end in bloodshed."

Dellow handed over to the night shift at 21:00 with a sense of impending calamity, noting in his diary: "The parlous state of negotiating ploys and the diminishing hopes of providing an ambassador meant the following day would be most difficult and fraught with risk."

Hector Gullan, officer commanding, B Squadron, had been working on contingency plans for five days, revising and refining, expanding and tweaking. One of the traditions unique to the SAS is what the regiment calls the "Chinese parliament," in which all voices, of whatever rank, will be heard (though not necessarily followed) at the planning stage. "Anyone, at any time, is encouraged to give an idea. But the boss decides." Gullan consulted his seniors, the two troop commanders, and old hands like Tom Morell. But the final plan was his alone, and by Sunday evening the military options had boiled down to a choice between the bus and the building, an ambush, or a stronghold assault. Like the politicians, the soldiers were acutely conscious of the continuing siege of the U.S. Embassy in Tehran, and the failed hostage rescue ten days earlier by soldiers of America's Delta Force, some of whom had been trained by the SAS. Operation Eagle Claw had been carefully planned, and wholly disastrous. Operation Nimrod might meet the same fate.

Gullan had not closed his eyes since Wednesday. In his diary he wrote: "Very tired. Immense pressure. Living on one's nerves. Clear sitn [situation] becoming more tense as times goes on."

"Hey, boss, you've got to get some sleep," said one of the troopers. "There's a bed upstairs—we've prepared it for you."

Fully clothed, Gullan climbed into a four-poster in one of Number 15's sumptuous guest rooms, and immediately passed out.

A "MISERABLE, TENSE SILENCE" settled on the general office and the adjoining cipher room. There were no prayers that night, no banter between Fowzi and the women. No one noticed the remote thunder of Tchaikovsky's cannons as the concert came to an end. The hostages shared the seat cushions, and spread out to sleep for the fifth night in succession. The gunmen avoided eye contact with the hostages, and with one another. The cigarettes had run out. Everyone was hungry. For the first time, Lock abandoned his chair and lay on the floor, wrapping his coat tightly around him. Harris was again struck by the strange sense of community among them, people from different worlds, cultures, and religions, with almost nothing in common save a shared humanity. "There was no back-biting. The predominant thing was the cooperation between the hostages."

At 04:00, in the pitch darkness, Lock felt Towfiq's hand on his shoulder, shaking him awake. "We think there is a stranger inside. Go and see, Mr. Trevor."

Makki thought he had heard noises coming from the basement.

With a sigh, Lock got to his feet and donned his peaked cap. Four of the gunmen were gathered in a tense huddle on the landing, guns pointing down the stairs.

No one thought to point out the absurdity of hostage-takers asking a British policeman to check if there was an intruder. Lima syndrome was entering new realms of irrationality.

"This is PC Trevor Lock," he called out, gingerly heading down the stairs. "Is there anybody there?"

Harris was now wide awake, sitting upright. He could hear Lock's voice echoing in the stairwell below. The audio probes also picked up the policeman shouting into the darkness.

"This is PC Lock . . . Is anyone there?"

In the entrance hall, Lock found himself alone in the spot where, five days earlier, he had been captured, with blood streaming down his face. He might simply have opened the front door and walked out. But he did not. Indeed, the thought never crossed his mind.

Minutes later he was back, shaking his head. "There is no one down there."

From the second floor, however, came the distinct scratch of drills: to Towfiq's half-addled mind, the sound of an imminent assault.

Towfiq pulled Lock down to the field telephone and shouted into it: "If you want the incident to end peacefully it must stop now!"

He handed the telephone to Lock.

"They don't like the noise at all and they asked me to say that, however fast you are, they will be faster, and all hostages will be killed."

After a few moments, the drilling stopped.

GULLAN AWOKE WITH a start and looked at his watch. It was 04:30. Returning to the operations room, he noted in his diary, "Much clearer idea of how to crack the problem," and reached for a set of colored crayons. Going through his notebook, page by page, he underlined the elements that were, in his estimation, "cracking" and ignored those that were "shit."

By dawn, the final battle plan was complete.

Gullan had spotted that food and other items delivered to the embassy remained on the front doorstep for up to half an hour before being collected. That must mean the terrorists were monitoring the exterior of the building only intermittently. This supposition substantially raised the odds in favor of a daytime rescue operation, since daylight would, he reasoned, "ensure quicker movement through the various rooms of the embassy, easier identification of own troops, hostages and terrorists, and additional surprise."

Operation Nimrod would be a concerted stronghold assault, attacking all floors simultaneously with guns, gas, and explosives, the largest peacetime military engagement ever attempted on the British mainland.

Red Team would clear and hold the second, third, fourth, and fifth floors; Blue Team would attack the basement and ground floors.

The operation, Gullan advised, should ideally take place in late afternoon or early evening, "at the end of a long day, when both terrorists and hostages would be beginning to think of another night and day to come," and during a period of negotiations when Salim would be speaking on the field telephone in the ground-floor hallway. It would begin with the detonation of a large bomb over the skylight in the central void running down the middle of the building. The cascading glass and ironwork should land directly on top of the leading gunman in the hall, giving him, in Gullan's words, "a close haircut."

The explosion would be the signal for five separate SAS teams to go into action:

- Six men (call sign: Sierra One) would enter from the roof through the bathroom skylight, clear any gunmen from the upper floors, and proceed downstairs.
- Four men (Alpha Three) would enter the third floor by scaling down the inside shaft on rigid steel caving ladders and climbing in through the windows facing inward. These would have been blown out by two men engineering a second, simultaneous explosion inside the shaft. Having cleared that floor, they too would head down.
- Four men (Bravo Four), including Mel Parry and Tom MacDonald, would clear the first floor from the front: they would climb onto the embassy balcony from the adjoining balcony on Number 15, attach explosives to the armored windows, and blow them in, before climbing inside. This floor was expected to be empty, and thus relatively easy to clear.
- A team of ten men (Bravo One) would go in through the rear ground floor after blowing off the doors to the commercial section. A first group of six would pass through the library and into the hall, aiming to intercept Salim, or what was left of him after the explosion. The remaining four would clear the basement.
- The most difficult target was the second floor. In Gullan's words, the plan had to be such "that no damage would be caused to the hostages, who were known to be held in the back rooms of the second floor," the general office, and cipher room. The first wave of four men (Alpha One), led by Tom Morell and including Tommy Palmer, would abseil from the roof onto the second-floor balcony at the rear. Then they would smash their way into the general office,

neutralize any gunmen inside, and liberate the male hostages, followed by the women in the cipher room. A second wave of four abseilers would follow the first onto the rear balcony.

To limit the danger of shooting one another, "blue-on-blue casualties," each team would stick to one floor—the "limit of exploitation," an invisible threshold that should not be crossed. The hostages would then be passed down the main staircase as fast as possible and out through the rear.

During the assault a pair of snipers would fire the more potent CR-gas canisters through the four windows of the second floor using Pole-cat launchers, and saturate the area where the hostages were being held with disabling fumes.

Four more SAS men, armed with 9mm revolvers, would receive the hostages at the rear terrace and pass them down the stone steps to another eight-man team waiting in the gardens. In case any gunmen tried to hide among the hostages, every civilian would be made to lie face down on the grass, and handcuffed until formally identified. Having passed the hostages and any surviving gunmen to the police, the SAS would depart swiftly in unmarked vans, taking their weapons with them, and then rendezvous at Regent's Park Barracks.

A total of fifty men would take part in the assault: thirty-four inside the building and sixteen in the reception area and on sniper detail. Gullan estimated the abseil team would need twenty seconds to reach the rear balcony from the roof. Simultaneous preparations to blow the armored windows at the front and the basement door at the rear should take around thirty seconds.

The successive stages of the operation would be activated by call signs on the radio network:

- BANK ROBBERY: Ready to go.
- ROAD ACCIDENT: Move into position.
- HYDE PARK: Groups in position; explosives primed; abseilers hitched and ready.
- LONDON BRIDGE: Begin abseiling.

- STAND BY, STAND BY, GO: Abseilers on the balcony, and second wave ready to descend.

The bombs in the central shaft, the explosives attached to the armored front windows, and the frame charge on the back door would all go off simultaneously, at the same moment as Tom Morell and Tommy Palmer would burst into the hostage room from the balcony.

In theory, no more than half a minute would elapse between HYDE PARK and GO.

If at any moment the assault was compromised, all teams would "go noisy" and launch into the planned assault immediately, on the call sign GO, GO, GO.

Gullan left no one in any doubt what that word meant: "In now, and I mean NOW. No messing."

The SAS had trained for this moment for seven years. Operation Nimrod would last no more than a few minutes, and the success or failure of the assault would depend on timing, discipline, and luck. The plan was also based on the assumption that the hostages and gunmen would remain where they were.

Which they did not.

DAY SIX

MONDAY

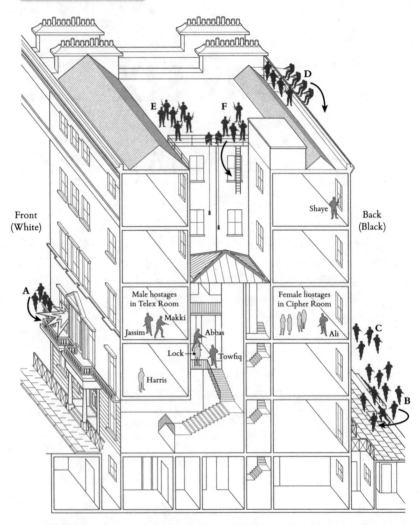

Operation Nimrod

Front (White)

Back (Black)

Shaye

Male hostages in Telex Room

Female hostages in Cipher Room

Makki

Jassim

Abbas

Ali

Lock

Towfiq

Harris

A   Four men of Bravo Four, Blue Team, to assault first-floor front after blowing out windows: Mel Parry, Tom MacDonald, John McAleese, Denis Pringle.

B   Ten men of Bravo One, Blue Team, led by Rob Timson, to enter rear ground floor after blowing off the doors to the commercial section. Six to hallway. Four to basement.

C   Four men to receive the hostages at the rear terrace and pass them down the stone steps to the gardens.

D   Four men of Alpha One, Red Team, to abseil from the roof on to the second-floor balcony at the rear and enter General Office: Tom Morell, Tommy Palmer, Paul Sanford, Peter Garmon. Followed by second wave of four abseilers.

E   Six men of Sierra One, Red Team, enter from the roof through the bathroom skylight to clear top floors.

F   Four men of Alpha Three, Red Team, scale down the inside shaft on rigid steel caving ladders to third floor and climb in through windows facing inwards. Two men lower bombs on detonator cords down the central shaft.

17

YELLOW-CARD RULE

Chronic sleep deprivation affects the human mind and body in multiple and unpredictable ways: irritability, inattention, hyper-anxiety, hallucinations, and mood swings, as well as drowsiness and lethargy. For centuries, sleep denial has been used as a form of torture, to extract confessions. Suspects held after the 9/11 attacks were kept awake for up to ninety-six hours as part of the CIA's "enhanced interrogation" techniques. One of the first signs of sleep deprivation is difficulty concentrating, followed by slurred speech, lower body temperature, and increased appetite. If deprivation continues, effects include disorientation, visual misperception, apathy, social withdrawal, and, above all, deteriorating judgment. Without sufficient sleep, people make poor and risky decisions.

By the sixth day, the siege was entering a jittery miasma of extreme sleeplessness: the press, the politicians, and the police were weary. The SAS knew all about uncomfortable camping, but even they longed for a few hours in a warm bed. After five nights on the floor, the hostages were aching and drained, but the gunmen were even more depleted. They were told to sleep in shifts, but remained awake most of the time, alert and nerve-strung.

Most exhausted of all was Towfiq al-Rashidi. The lead gunman had slept for a total of about 5 hours, on the fourth night, during 120 hours of unremitting stress. His skin was sallow and his eyes sunken. He spoke in monosyllables. Harris could tell, from his twitchy body language, that the man was close to the edge. "He is getting very jumpy."

"Fatigue is one of the most pernicious stress factors which all participants in the stronghold have to face," warned John Gunn. The professor feared that Salim could break at any time, "considering the small amount of sleep he must have been able to obtain." Every hour without rest would be making him more unstable, Gunn believed. "Loss of sleep may determine when the siege will end."

Abdul Ezzati, the press attaché, complained that his legs were growing numb. The heart medication did not seem to be working.

No one spoke.

AT 09:00, John Dellow made his way to the negotiators' room, where the night shift was handing over to the day shift: David Veness, Max Vernon, and Ray Tucker. His briefing was somber. Negotiations would only become harder, Dellow warned, "as there was very little room to maneuver." Salim would doubtless continue to insist that the government provide ambassadors and safe passage out of the country. The possibility of either eventuality was "remote in the extreme." For once, Dellow did not really say what he meant: the situation was on the brink of catastrophe.

Vernon called the field telephone at 09:47. "Salim sounded more dejected than he had at any other time," Dellow noted. "Obviously frustrated and in a vastly different mood." He bleakly repeated the demand for an ambassador, and rang off.

Fred Luff had treated the negotiation with Towfiq as a struggle of wills, a collision of rival beliefs. Vernon and Veness were made of more subtle material. Over the last forty-eight hours they felt they had come to know the man they were dealing with, and the impossible situation he was in. They could not openly sympathize with him—the rules of engagement forbade that—but they had tried to understand him, and now they could hear his desperation rising with every exchange. In a standoff, the negotiator seeks to grow gradually closer to the hostage-takers. At first, Towfiq had seemed approachable, even accommodating. Vernon, in particular, felt he had established a human connection. But now Towfiq was pulling away; the gulf was widening. The negotiators were deeply uneasy.

Dellow asked Gunn to assess the mood of the terrorists. The psychiatrist's response was ominous: Salim was under "extreme pressure," exacerbated by discord between the gunmen, some of whom clearly believed he "was not being firm enough and was therefore failing to achieve their objective." Prepare for the unexpected, Professor Gunn advised Dellow: "The actions of both Salim and the other terrorists could become progressively unpredictable."

TOWFIQ LED TREVOR LOCK and Sim Harris to the second-floor landing and pointed to the wall adjoining the Ethiopian Embassy, where he and Jassim had daubed anti-Khomeini graffiti the previous day. The plaster was cracking, and in places the wall bulged alarmingly inward.

"The police are going to attack," said Towfiq. It was not a question. "The wall was flat when I wrote on it yesterday. They are going to come in through the walls."

"Nonsense," said Harris.

"Of course not," said Lock.

They knew how unconvincing they sounded.

Towfiq instructed Makki to stand guard on the landing.

"Things are starting to look grim," Harris scribbled in his diary. "I really do think they mean business this time. I have to do something."

At 11:10, the seventeen male hostages were hustled out of the general office and herded along the second-floor corridor to the telex room, facing Hyde Park. The hostages had never been corralled into this room before. Desks and chairs were stacked against the windows, along with the two telex machines. The women remained in the cipher room, at the back of the building, with Fowzi guarding them. The gunmen wound their keffiyehs around their heads. Towfiq had his dark glasses back on, and his hood up.

Ron Morris mobilized his remarkable gift for understating the obvious: "They were fed up."

At 11:12, Towfiq picked up the field telephone and said: "We will shoot a hostage in thirty minutes if there is no news about an Arab ambassador."

GULLAN FINE-TUNED Operation Nimrod.

The bombs lowered into the central shaft would need to be big enough to destroy the glass roof below and distract the gunmen, but not so powerful as to bring down the whole building. Much of the brickwork in the wall of the Ethiopian Embassy was now gone. Too much explosive, and it would crumble.

"I want that roof to be blown straight down," Gullan told his demolitions and sabotage specialist. "I want those terrorists to have a real haircut, and I want it blocked so it's damn difficult for Salim to get back up the stairs to the hostages quickly because there's glass and shit all over the place."

Two explosive experts from the Inter Services Research Group were brought in to advise on the optimal size of the charge. They recommended two devices made from military-standard plastic explosive (PE4) with a detonation velocity of twenty-six thousand feet per second: one with 1 pound of explosive to blow out the internal windows, and a larger bomb weighing 1.5 pounds directly over the glass roof to the atrium. These would be lowered into the internal shaft on detonator cord attached to two firing devices known as "clackers," a handheld electric detonator adapted from an American Claymore antipersonnel mine. The SAS got the impression that the experts were using guesswork and had walked away "with their fingers crossed."

The moment the bombs went off, the team on the roof would toss down smoke and gas grenades (CS rather than the more toxic CR type) into the void where the glass roof had been, to form a cloud of gas that would start in the hallway on the ground floor and billow up through the building.

"We'll increase the blockage," said Gullan. "So you have a false wall spreading as well." Without a gas mask it would be virtually impassable.

Immediately after the first explosion, the back door and armored front windows would both be demolished using "shape charges," plastic explosive encased in lead and bent around wooden squares resembling empty picture frames that fit snugly into the windows and doors. Wedged in place, these would then be triggered by a clacker. The triangular strips of explosive, roughly the shape of a Toblerone, would be ridged on the inside: in theory this would send most of the blast inward.

Plastic explosive was simply known as PE. As one soldier observed, the bombs for Operation Nimrod were assembled "using the intricate explosive formula: 'P for plenty.'"

The yeoman of signals (the squadron communications technical specialist), Colin Clapton, known as "Clutchplate," erected a magnetic aerial on the bin store beside the embassy, to form a simple radio network, in effect a simple walkie-talkie system. Each soldier would have a Pye Pocketfone radio with a range of around one kilometer, connected to Gullan (Sunray) via a portable wireless communications station carried by Squashball McGregor in a backpack. The troop commanders, team leaders, and snipers all wore throat microphones to communicate with Gullan during the action. The others had "fist mics": these consisted of a pressel switch connected by a wire to a single earpiece; the switch was attached to the vest with masking tape, and the earpiece to the ear with Sellotape or surgical tape.

Clutchplate Clapton erected a second, taller aerial on the roof, to communicate with Regent's Park Barracks, where a high-frequency station was connected to SAS headquarters in Hereford via an encrypted, secure teleprinter. This link would be used, if necessary, to summon reinforcements. "If everything goes tits up," Clapton observed, "Hereford's the focal point."

Two teams of SAS snipers in pairs would maintain surveillance and report all movements to Sunray via a separate radio network. If, for example, a gunman was spotted in the third window from the right on the first floor at the front of the embassy, the sniper would radio: "White, one, three." Two would watch from the van parked at the front of the building, and two from the balcony of flat number 53 on the fourth floor of Kingston House. When Nimrod was under way, Gullan instructed, the snipers would emerge from their hiding place and "provide covering fire on an opportunity basis," picking off the gunmen if presented with a clear headshot. Each sniper had "an area of responsibility" to monitor: "If a target appears, you act accordingly," they were told. Police snipers would remain in position also looking for targets of opportunity.

The police made a final effort to remove the remaining inhabitants of Kingston House. After several hours of cajoling, the writer Dame Rebecca West was finally persuaded to move out of her flat, much to her irritation. Complaining that she did "not want to leave the scene of the crime," she reluctantly packed a small suitcase, wondering if her home might soon be destroyed in a terrorist blast. "To go meant desolation," she wrote. "I looked round me and saw every vestige of my life I had cared to keep, and I knew I might never see again."

The neighboring flat on the sixth floor of Kingston House offered an unrestricted view of the back of the building: this would serve as operational HQ for Gullan and his communications hub. Clapton fetched a crowbar to lever up the window, and placed another antenna on the ledge. He had also purchased some net curtains to keep out prying eyes. Once the operation was in progress, Gullan and his communications team would descend to the ground floor and reassemble at the back of the embassy, armed with pistols.

On the "Go" command, three smoke generators would be activated simultaneously at the back and sides of the building, to form a dense screen of white, blue, red, and green smoke, and prevent any lurking press from observing what was happening. A powerful lighting gantry had been erected by the media to the west of the building, to illuminate the scene if anything occurred in the hours of darkness. This would need to be disabled, using explosives if necessary. "If we blew up the press as well, too bad," said the officer in command of this aspect of the operation.

A specialist medical team was mustered to treat the wounded on-site, with additional dressings for gunshot wounds and burns. The reception team at the rear would also carry "shell dressings/plastic for lung injuries." A police stretcher party would be on hand, for use "only [in] extremely serious cases." Wounded civilians would be taken to hospital by ambulance, but B Squadron's battlefield casualties would be treated by a separate SAS triage medical team in a horse trailer drawn up in Princes Gate.

There would be no stopping to treat the injured until the operation was complete. "If you get hurt, you're down," in Gullan's words. "Pick him up later." The squadron sergeant major would "stay with any wounded man, accompanying him to hospital and securing all his items of equipment, including guns." The medical teams and firefighters would remain at Knightsbridge barracks until the last moment: if the gunmen saw ambulances and fire engines approaching, the element of surprise would be lost. The buses equipped would remain on hand in case of a last-minute change of plan. Janet Dillon stood ready in her policewoman's tights.

Five police dog handlers with "hard dogs," trained to attack on command, would be held in the basement of Number 15 until the "Go" signal, and then deployed around the perimeter to bring down anyone attempting to break out of the cordon. The SAS troops did not scare easily, but they were wary of the Alsatians, which were trained to bite hard, with all their teeth, and repeatedly. "These dogs didn't sniff, they chewed."

The bomb squad was placed on high alert, but otherwise the plan took no account of the gunmen's threat to blow up the building. This was assumed to be a bluff. If it was not, and the embassy was demolished with everyone inside it, no amount of planning would make any difference.

TWO MEN FROM Red Team climbed onto the roof and attached five abseiling ropes to the chimneys, leaving them neatly coiled on the rear parapet: one for each man in the two teams of four, plus a spare, longer rope that could reach all the way to the ground. If for any reason they could not enter the second floor, they could clip on to this additional rope, abseil down, and join the team on the ground.

Hawser-laid rope consists of three strands twisted together in a left-handed direction, which are then twisted in a right-handed direction to make the rope. The more modern kernmantle rope is made with an inner core protected by a woven exterior sheath, giving additional tensile strength and reducing the danger of kinking as the rope runs through the belay device. The abseil ropes used by the SAS were the older, hawser-laid, snag-prone type.

Three wide ladders, or "trellises," were constructed and positioned out of sight. If the main staircase was blocked by fire, smoke, or bomb damage, these would be used to evacuate the hostages through the second-floor windows. Gullan's requirements were specific: "Must be custom-built. Not improvised, bulky, and awkward."

Freed hostages would be detained on the grass lawn behind Number 15; any surviving gunmen would be separated and removed to the space behind the Ethiopian Embassy at Number 17, before being handed over to the police anti-terrorist unit. This was a new task for the SAS. "We'd always kill the terrorists in training," observed one officer. "We never had any live ones. And here we might have live ones." But on active service in Northern Ireland, SAS soldiers carried plastic handcuffs attached to their flak jackets, in case a suspect needed to be restrained. Gullan asked the police liaison officer to provide a stock of these "plasticuffs," and a policeman duly appeared with a large cardboard box. "I don't know what you want these for," he muttered. Inside were two thousand plastic cups.

Every soldier was told to replace the batteries in his radio, memorize call signs, and learn two words in Farsi by heart: *Beeya paeen!* Get down!

The objective of Operation Nimrod was clearly laid out. "Mission: To Rescue Hostages." The plan did not say whether the gunmen would be killed, stating only that the soldiers should use the "minimum force necessary to achieve aim of releasing hostages unharmed." In practice, any "X-ray" who resisted or appeared to pose a threat would be met with lethal force. He would not be given a warning or the benefit of the doubt. In Northern Ireland, soldiers were issued with yellow cards containing the standing instructions on when they could open fire. As the veteran SAS noncommissioned officer Tom Morell put it, the assault would follow "the 'Yellow-Card Rule': anyone can fire so long as your life is threatened; there is no need to wait for a command."

Hector Gullan expressed the terms of engagement in his own inimitable way: "If you're a terrorist and you surrender, the police have got you. But if you look at me and you're aggressive . . . I've got three children, a wife at home: I'm going home, you're dying. It's as simple as that. Don't fuck with me. I'll kill you and I mean it."

SOMETHING "SEEMED TO SNAP" inside Towfiq, noted Sim Harris, who observed his expression closely: the lead gunman appeared almost detached from what was happening, a spectator in his own drama. The BBC soundman had been scared for five days. Now he was terrified.

"We're on your side in trying to resolve this situation," he begged. "Please let me and Mr. Trevor convince the police that you are serious . . ."

Towfiq shrugged wearily, and led them downstairs to the talking window. It was 11:45, three minutes past the deadline.

Lock shouted down to the police: "It is absolutely critical. We must talk to the negotiators and find out what is going on. They are threatening to shoot a hostage in a few minutes' time."

"Can you please ask the Foreign Office to speed things up?" pleaded Harris. "They are going to shoot one of us . . ."

Negotiators David Veness and Max Vernon were on the pavement now.

"These things take time. It's not in our hands. Try and keep calm . . ."

Towfiq was not listening.

Veness changed tack: "If you listen to the World Service at twelve o'clock, there will be confirmation that people are meeting at the Foreign Office. Douglas Hurd is meeting ambassadors."

This was true, although Hurd's consultations with what he called "the useless ambassadors" were achieving precisely nothing. The Jordanian ambassador had returned, and Hurd "tried unsuccessfully to get him into action . . . but he refused to budge." The British position did not shift either, though Hurd was happy to pretend the diplomacy was moving forward: "Because it was important to keep the terrorists in play, we persuaded the BBC to broadcast news of my meeting with the Jordanians at noon. It was the dullest news item they had ever led with."

"Talks are taking place," the BBC newsreader declared at 12:00. "All is quiet at the embassy."

Towfiq was unimpressed. "This is nothing," he said, and switched off the portable radio.

Lock made another, desperate appeal to him: "Is getting an ambassador the only way out of this? There are other alternatives. Honorable alternatives. You could honorably surrender to a police station and give yourselves up. If you start shooting hostages, that makes you into common criminals, it changes the whole game, you have lost the peaceful nature of your cause, you will lose the sympathy of the British public, you will lose the sympathy of the world public, you would have lost everything after gaining so much . . . Why not end it all now without violence? Show that you mean peace. Walk out like a man, in any order you choose, but show that you mean peace."

A man of few words, Lock had probably never made a longer speech in his life.

Towfiq shook his head, a man drained. "No. They are messing me about, they have taken so many hours, this operation was only meant to last twenty-four hours, and we have gone for a hundred and twenty-eight and are still nowhere. The British police just want it to go on forever, they are plotting to invade, they don't care about you, they don't care if you die, they don't care if you are here for weeks on end, they wish to wear us down and make us tired, they make noises in the night to keep us awake, so that we can't sleep. They have had their chance, I have been fair with them, and they have not been fair with us. They do not care."

This was partly bravado, and partly surrender, not to the police but to forces he could not control. Towfiq was no longer fully in command.

"I have had enough," he said quietly.

The Group of the Martyr was crumbling. Fowzi and Abbas were ready to give up.

"The sooner we surrender the better, as I'm dying for sleep," said Fowzi. "At least I could sleep in prison."

Jassim ordered him to shut up.

Abbas was also losing heart, his pockmarked face a mask of misery, his eyes twitching uncontrollably. Clearly Abbas had "some psychological problem." Jassim told Abbas to pull himself together. Shaye had wept over Chris Cramer on the second day, thinking he was dying; now he was ready to kill. Makki gave little away.

Jassim was taking over. Lock noticed the alteration in his body language: "Number Two had more influence than before. He was the force that kept it going. He was willing to die for the cause. The others were making out they were willing, but Number Two was the danger man, the power behind the aggression of it all."

At 12:06, Abbas Lavasani raised his hand, asking to go to the lavatory. Fowzi beckoned him out of the room.

From below, the hostages heard the sounds of an argument in Arabic. After twenty minutes, Lavasani had not returned.

18

SIX DAYS

At 12:26, Towfiq escorted Lock and Harris to the ground floor. In the entrance hall stood Lavasani in his yellow cardigan. Harris thought he looked "a bit distraught but in control of himself." The young Iranian had taken off his peculiar slippers. Shaye stood beside him, gun drawn.

The field telephone was on the reception desk in the hallway. Towfiq gestured to it.

"Mr. Trevor, tell the police we have brought a hostage downstairs and we will shoot him in five minutes unless we get what we want."

Lock pressed the button with trembling fingers. Max Vernon picked up.

"Please, sir, will you understand, they intend to shoot a hostage. They have brought one downstairs and he's standing right next to us."

In the stationery cupboard, Jassim had found a ball of parcel twine. Lock and Harris stared in horror as he knotted Lavasani's hands behind his back and bound his legs together. Then he pushed the young Iranian into a sitting position by the bottom step, and began lashing him to the iron spindles at the foot of the stairs. Jassim's movements were slow and deliberate. Harris could not watch.

Lock gave an appalled running commentary, while Vernon listened, dread rising.

". . . They have one of the hostages. They have some brown string, and they're tying the hostage to the banisters of the stairs, his hands behind his back."

"Trevor, tell them this won't get them anywhere." Vernon's voice was beseeching. "Try and calm them down."

"Sir, I implore you. They are trussing him up like a chicken. I believe they're going to kill a hostage."

"Don't let them kill him, Trev." Vernon was becoming hysterical.

"He is panic-ridden," thought Lock. "You can feel it coming through the phone."

Towfiq seized the receiver. "You've had enough time. If you really cared someone would be here already . . . We are going to shoot one."

Towfiq gestured at Harris and Lock to go back upstairs.

As the policeman passed Lavasani, the tethered Iranian looked up at him. His expression was terrified, but his voice was calm.

"Please don't worry, Mr. Trevor, I'm not afraid to die . . ."

Jassim stepped forward and tied a strip of cloth over Lavasani's eyes.

"Oh, God, do you think they're going to shoot him?" whispered Harris as they made their way upstairs.

"It looks pretty convincing to me," said Lock, aghast.

Harris and Lock were on the first-floor landing when Towfiq held up the telephone receiver to Lavasani's mouth.

"My name is Abbas Lavasani. I am tied up and they are going to kill me. Please help me . . ."

"You shouldn't have told them your name!" said Towfiq, snatching the telephone away again. "This is the final word. Sorry." Towfiq put the phone down.

The line remained open and, according to Dellow, "picked up sounds of an argument." Dellow was convinced "Salim was being put under pressure by the other terrorists . . . He did not wish to be as 'hawkish' as the others."

Back in the telex room, Harris felt a sudden, irrational surge of hope. "A deal is being done," he told himself. "An ambassador will come at three o'clock. That's it. Saved again."

AT 12:55, Jassim Alwan al-Nasiri walked up behind Abbas Lavasani and fired three bullets at point-blank range into the back of his head.

Harris buried his face in his hands at the sound of the shots. Fowzi and Abbas, standing guard, exchanged horrified looks. In the cipher room, the women also heard the gunfire; several began to weep inconsolably.

Towfiq entered the telex room, flushed.

"Have you really shot him?" asked Ron Morris.

"Yes, we have—do you want to see the body?"

It was a "straight cold-blooded answer," Harris noted. "I couldn't even look at him: I blocked out his bearded face as he stood in the doorway." For the first time, Harris felt a spasm of hatred.

Towfiq continued: "We have told them we will shoot one of you every forty-five minutes until they give an answer about the ambassadors. It is in their hands. They don't care about you."

"Look, you've shot one man, don't shoot any more," said Morris. "You won't achieve anything: one man or twenty men, it doesn't matter now. If you've killed one hostage, you might as well kill us all. You won't get from this place alive."

"It doesn't matter," said Towfiq, echoing his words. "We are prepared to die."

THE PREPRANDIAL GIN and tonics were being quaffed in the drawing room at Dorneywood, the Home Secretary's country retreat, when the call came through from the police: shots had been heard inside the embassy. Willie Whitelaw apologized to his luncheon guests and summoned the ministerial car and chauffeur, Jack Liddiard. Preceded by a motorcycle escort, the 4.2-liter Jaguar shot out of the gates of Dorneywood, through Slough, and onto the M4. Liddiard hit the Hammersmith flyover at over 120 mph, drove the wrong way up Constitution Hill between Hyde Park Corner and Buckingham Palace, and screeched to a halt outside the Cabinet Office. The thirty-mile journey into central London had taken eighteen minutes, in what Whitelaw described as an "exhibition of superb fast driving."

In the Cobra meeting room, Whitelaw was met by Metropolitan Police Commissioner David McNee and Brigadier Peter de la Billière. The director of special forces reported that both Rose and Dellow believed that the sounds, recorded from the field telephone, indicated someone had been shot. A bullet entering the human body makes a distinctive noise. But as yet there was no proof. "Was it a bluff?" wondered de la Billière. Whitelaw would not authorize the assault unless he was certain. Until then, negotiations should continue. This message was relayed to Hayden Phillips in Zulu Control, and on to the negotiators.

Dellow played the tape of the gunfire over and over, trying to work out what had happened. "There appeared to be a shocked silence throughout the stronghold. But there was insufficient evidence to establish that a killing had taken place."

The SAS was on standby with a complete battle plan in place, de la Billière told Whitelaw. But, he added, there was no guarantee it would work: "If things go well, we must expect 40 percent of the people in the building to become casualties. Anything less than that will be a good outcome. The decision to go in must be a political one, even though it leads to the use of military force."

Whitelaw was firm: "Peter, I want you to understand two things. The first is that if and when the operation is launched, I will not interfere in any way; the second is that if it goes wrong, I will take the responsibility afterward."

IT WAS, SAID WHITELAW, an "odious period of waiting." Cobra was coiled and ready to strike, with nothing to do.

De la Billière stared at the far wall of the briefing room, transfixed by "a digital clock with small flaps, one of which tumbled down with a snap every time a minute ticked by."

INSIDE THE EMBASSY, the hostages were gripped by what Harris called a "numbed tension," a listless, expectant terror. "Everyone is lying around in a state of shock," he thought. "What else can possibly happen?"

A "DEATHLY SILENCE" pervaded Zulu Control. "Poor Dellow was seriously shaken," said Rose.

IN THE DOCTORS' HOUSE, the men smeared black camouflage cream on faces and necks, checked weapons, loaded fresh batteries, and waited. One of the team took a toy frog out of his pocket, a gift for his infant son, and pulled the string that made its legs extend to either side and emit a croaking noise. The silliness cracked the tension for a moment.

Mark Gilfoyle was told to stand down and discovered the whole performance had been a joke at his expense. He immediately quit smoking again. To his credit, Gilfoyle had never once objected to being handed a gun, a bulletproof vest, and an abseil rope he did not know how to use. There is courage too in the willingness to risk your life, without that bravery ever being tested.

In midafternoon, de la Billière and Rose arrived to inspect the troops. The senior officer noticed that, although the men knew they were facing a heavily armed enemy and a building that could be wired with explosives, there was no sense of anxiety or overexcitement. The men exuded "quiet confidence," wrote de la Billière. But a new expectancy had taken hold.

"This time we're going in, aren't we?" said Gullan's operations officer.

"I'm not saying 'yes,'" Gullan replied, recalling the repeated standdowns in Northern Ireland. "Every time I do we end up not going in. Let's wait and see."

Once the senior officers had departed, some of the men gathered around the television to watch the buildup to the snooker final on BBC2. Others were pensive. One of the team preparing to attack from the roof retired to a well-appointed bathroom in the Doctors' House. "I sat on the toilet, and I said a little prayer, though I am not a religious man." He feared a bloodbath. "Because you're attacking a defensive position, there're going to be booby traps, they're going to be able to open up on you coming down the stairs. Anything can happen. We're going to take casualties."

DOUGLAS HURD HELD a long conversation in French with the Algerian ambassador, knowing there was nothing to be gained by it. The discussions were, Hurd explained, "simply so the BBC could calm the terrorists by reporting that a diplomatic effort was continuing."

DOREEN LOCK SWITCHED off the news, tied a scarf over her head, opened the back door, and then clambered over the garden fence into the alleyway behind Warley Avenue. Unseen by the press pack, she headed down Whalebone Lane to the Holy Family Catholic Church. Trevor Lock considered himself a "ten-a-penny agnostic," but Doreen was a firm believer. She lit a candle and said a prayer for her captive husband. Then she walked slowly home, climbed back over the fence, and resumed her vigil in the lounge. "That was all I could do."

AT THE SAME MOMENT, Trevor Lock was being escorted back down to the embassy entrance hall. There was no sign of a body. Instead, a strip of carpet was now lying over the floor where Lavasani had been tied up. The marble floor was wet, as if someone had sluiced a bucket of water over it.

Towfiq handed him the telephone. "Make sure they know we mean it. One hostage every forty-five minutes."

Lock did as instructed, and handed the phone back.

"I don't want to hear you again until I've heard from the ambassadors," Towfiq told Max Vernon on the other end of the line, and rang off.

But did Towfiq mean it? Lock saw a man swept along by events, unwilling to complete his own threats, running out of time, and will. Half an hour later, Towfiq abruptly declared that the deadline for killing another hostage had been extended to 17:00. He gave no explanation. For the first time some of the hostages suspected the gunmen were now stalling the police, as they had been stalled, waiting for the other side to make a move. Had the scene in the hallway been "a horrible bluff," Harris wondered, to try to force the police into action? Was

Lavasani being held somewhere in the basement, in an elaborate and cruel charade?

"Do you reckon they did it?" asked Harris, when Lock reentered the room.

"I don't know," said Lock. "He's not there any longer. I couldn't see any blood. It's all dark down there."

The policeman was deeply troubled. Why had he not intervened, with Lavasani blindfolded and tied to the banisters, pleading for his life? He had a gun. He could have taken out two, perhaps three of the gunmen. Lock played and replayed the ghastly scene in the hall. "I did nothing. I kept on walking."

The gunmen seemed, Harris thought, to have entered a "trance-like" state, all their swagger gone. Fowzi and Abbas appeared "on the verge of tears." They had run out of cigarettes and cadged, apologetically, from the hostages' dwindling stock. Only Jassim seemed fully wired up. He had just killed, and the set of his jaw suggested he was ready to do so again. He was now the leader. He did not expect to go home. Perhaps he never had. Towfiq sat in a corner, taping together two magazines for his submachine gun, as they had been taught in Iraq; when he emptied one, he could just turn it around and insert the other.

"What will your police do now?" he asked Harris.

"I don't know. I really don't know—"

"Will they attack?"

The question hung there.

At 16:00, the police spokesman Peter Neivens held a press conference in the Royal Geographical Society. "What sounded like two or three shots were heard from the direction of the Iranian Embassy," he said.

The media sat up. The sounds of gunfire had not been heard in the press enclosure.

"The significance of these noises is being investigated," said Neivens.

THE AMBASSADORS MET at the Arab League in Mayfair to draft a press statement. The statement stressed their "overriding concern to save lives," and the more subtle but equal determination not to get involved.

AT 16:36, a letter arrived at the embassy, addressed to Dr. Afrouz from the Iranian Foreign Ministry. It informed the chargé d'affaires that President Tito of Yugoslavia had died, and he should fly the embassy flag at half-mast. Someone in the protocol department was not keeping up with events.

"The atmosphere in the room is unbearable," Harris scrawled in his diary. "We have all sunk into despair. People weep. For the first time, no one is comforting each other. Every one of us is preoccupied with his own destiny. Every avenue has been explored. I can't think of anything else I can do."

Ron Morris thought of something he could do. He did what Englishmen have always done in moments of utter hopelessness: he made everyone a nice cup of tea.

EIGHT DOORS AWAY, Dellow and the negotiators also debated what to do, as the minutes ticked down. What possible avenue remained unexplored? One of the hostages had probably been shot, but, until they knew for sure, their orders were to continue talking to the gunmen. The ambassadors were not coming. There would be no bus, no plane to the Middle East. They had even refused food. What was left to talk about?

The psychiatrist John Gunn came up with an idea: Why not have the police commissioner write a personal letter to the gunmen, explaining the situation and appealing for calm?

Dellow agreed: "The terrorists seemed to have some regard for the published statement, using it themselves in the early part of the siege. Such a document might impress them."

At the same time, an officer in the anti-terrorist squad suggested contacting a senior figure in the Islamic community who might speak to the hostage-takers. Perhaps they would listen to a co-religionist, someone with moral authority who could persuade them to surrender? One policeman rushed off to find David McNee; another went in search of Dr. Sayed Mutawalli ad-Darsh, the senior imam at London Central Mosque.

These were straws, and the police were clutching at them.

———

THE LETTER, in a plain brown envelope, landed on the doormat of Number 16, between the outer door and interior steel door, at exactly 17:15. David Veness had called on the field telephone to say that Britain's top policeman had written to the Group of the Martyr. Towfiq was initially unwilling to receive the letter, suspecting an ambush.

"Please at least read it," urged Lock.

Towfiq shrugged and sent Harris down to collect it. "If you try to escape," he said, almost as an afterthought, "Mr. Trevor will be shot."

David McNee, commissioner of the Metropolitan Police, was pleased with his own letter, which was mostly about David McNee.

The envelope contained two sheets. Harris read the one in English and handed the other, in Farsi, to Towfiq:

> I think it is right that I should explain to you clearly and in writing the way in which my police officers are dealing with the taking of hostages at the Iranian Embassy. I am responsible for preserving the peace and enforcing the law in London and do this independently of politicians and government. I and my officers deeply wish to work toward a peaceful solution of what has occurred. We fully understand how both the hostages and those who hold them feel threatened and frightened. You are cut off from your families and friends, but you need not be frightened or threatened by the police. It is not our way in Britain to resort to violence against those who are peaceful. You have nothing to fear from my officers provided you do not harm those in your care. I firmly hope that we can bring this incident to a close, peacefully and calmly.

"What does it say?" asked Trevor Lock, anxious to know what the boss had written.

"Bugger all," said Harris.

McNee's letter was solid police boilerplate, an invitation to unconditional surrender with not a word about Arabistan, the ambassadors, or anything Towfiq cared about.

He looked up with an expression of contempt. "This doesn't mean anything."

Jassim scanned the letter and threw it aside. Ron Morris read, and then accurately summarized the contents: "Something about the police being reasonable and hoping everyone would keep calm."

McNee's letter was intended to pour oil on troubled waters. Instead, it lit another flame.

Morris's slow but steady mind had been churning through the possibilities. If Abbas Lavasani *had* been killed, it was only a matter of time before the police ended the siege by force; any assault on the building would probably take place in darkness; and, if that happened, they would need to make a run for it. He whispered to Lock and Harris: "I think we should all keep our shoes and socks on tonight."

Morris was not alone in making contingency plans.

As for the youngest gunman, Fowzi had not come to London seeking revenge, or blood. He and Abbas were not heartless, ruthless killers. The main point was for publicity to let the world know what was going on in Iran. Surely that had been achieved. They had been promised they would all be going home after twenty-four hours. What was it the Iraqi intelligence officer had told them before the operation? "You must do your best to ensure nobody gets shot, especially British people." Now Lavasani was dead. Fowzi approached Towfiq in the corridor. "We must stop this," he stammered. "Come on, at least release the women: release them. Abbas and I think you should end it."

Towfiq had passed the point of no return. One man had been killed. Others would have to die, including himself, including his comrades, to finish this thing. His response to Fowzi's plea was bleak, simple, and terrifying: "If you go against me, I will kill you both."

Fowzi relayed the threat to Abbas. Minutes later, the pockmarked gunman Abbas sidled up to Vahid Khabaz, the student journalist; whispered in his ear; and pressed a scrap of paper into his hand. Khabaz had played little active part in the drama so far, which may be why Abbas had picked him out. He also understood enough Arabic to read what Abbas had written. Khabaz swallowed hard and crossed the room to sit beside Lock.

"Ugly says his name is Abbas and he wants to escape," he explained.

"He wants you to write a note saying he had nothing to do with the shooting. He says it's all going wrong, and he wants to run away."

"What does it say, exactly?" asked Lock.

Khabaz translated Abbas's semi-literate scrawl, partly a cry for help, partly a suicide note: "I promised nothing would happen to you. I have fights with my friends. I beg you to look after me. I leave you for Allah. Do not forget I did save your life. Pray for me."

Lock was stunned. He had failed to save Lavasani from the gunmen; now one of those same gunmen was asking to be rescued.

"Please tell him I can't write notes for him," he said to Khabaz. "Tell him to escape if he wants to. I can't give him safe custody. I just don't have the power to do that."

AT 17:30, Rose informed Dellow that B Squadron was "at ten minutes' readiness for a full assault."

Within five minutes, Dellow recorded, "three separate snippets of conversation were picked up in close proximity to each other" by the bug inside the field telephone. These were translated from the Arabic, and then rushed over to Zulu Control:

"We do something before sunset . . ."

". . . kill two or three or four . . ."

". . . kill all by ten o'clock."

19

ONE HOUR

D r. Sayed Mutawalli ad-Darsh, the Egyptian-born imam at London Central Mosque, had no idea how to negotiate with armed hostage-takers, and no desire to try. His knowledge of what was happening at the Iranian Embassy extended no further than what he had heard on the news. But the policeman who arrived outside his mosque in a squad car with siren wailing told him the situation at Princes Gate was desperate. Darsh was a gentle, devout, self-effacing *alim* (scholar) and a former missionary who preached a brand of Islam based on tolerance and compassion. By the age of twelve, he had memorized the entire Koran. He offered advice, through a column in a Muslim magazine, on issues such as contraception, usury, and whether women should wear the veil. Reluctantly, Darsh picked up his Koran and climbed into the back seat of the police car.

Rushed to the Montessori nursery school, the imam was instructed to promise nothing, to try to defuse the situation by reassuring the gunmen they would not be harmed if they surrendered. He should emphasize the blasphemous nature of what they were doing. Darsh took this to mean he was there to provide spiritual guidance and give a sermon on Islamic ethics. Were these Arabs Sunni or Shia? No one seemed to know the answer, or what the question meant.

At 18:22, David Veness handed the field telephone to the imam. Towfiq was on the line. Darsh introduced himself in Arabic, and then launched into a homily about the Koran's prohibition on killing innocents and the sanctity of human life. "If anyone slays a human being it shall be as though he had slain all mankind . . ."

If sending David McNee's letter had been a mistake, recruiting the holy man was a calamity.

Towfiq had demanded an ambassador, a person of substance, to act as an interlocutor and end the siege. Instead, to his fury, they had produced some village mufti to recite chunks of the Koran at him. In Towfiq's mind the Group of the Martyr was not a jihadi cell but the representative of a significant international protest, on an operation designed to secure specific aims. This was not about religion but about the politics of freedom. He wanted action, not a moral lecture. The police were misjudging who they were dealing with.

"We are not interested in such talk . . . ," he said.

Darsh did not hear the menace in his voice and plowed on. "Killing is against our law—"

Towfiq interrupted him, furious: "I will extend the deadline to thirty minutes, then we will kill not one but two hostages."

"HE IS BAWLING, really shouting," Harris noted as Towfiq's voice echoed up the stairwell. "That's not like him."

IN THE BACKGROUND Darsh could hear someone else bellowing in Arabic: "*Aademhoon colohom* . . . I'll execute them all." It was Jassim.

Towfiq rang off, but then immediately called back, now barely coherent. "I have changed my mind. If they don't tell me something in two minutes, a hostage will be killed."

"Please, wait," pleaded Darsh. "I'll see what I can do." But the line was dead.

He turned to the policemen in the room with a look of desperation. No one spoke.

At 18:41, the field telephone rang again. Sayed Darsh picked up the receiver.

"Hello . . . Salim?"

Instead of a voice on the other end, he heard a click, and then three shots in deliberate succession, one after the other.

Veness grabbed the phone. "That's no answer. It's not going to help anyone . . ." But Towfiq was gone.

THE GUNFIRE WAS heard by the police negotiators, by Zulu Control, and by the SAS waiting next door, but, to John Dellow's frustration, the audio probes could not pinpoint precisely where inside the building the gun had been fired.

THE SHOTS WERE audible upstairs in the telex room, where the hostages stared in bewilderment. No hostages had left the room since Lock's return, so were the gunmen now shooting each other? "Had one shot three of them?" Harris wondered.

Ron Morris heard what sounded like furniture being dragged across the hallway.

The front door opened, a corpse wrapped in an orange blanket was pushed out onto the front steps, and the door closed again.

Suspecting the police might attempt a shot when the door opened, Towfiq had already moved the field telephone to the first-floor landing, threading the cord up through the banisters. He was no longer standing at the reception desk directly beneath the glass roof of the atrium. "There's a body on the doorstep," he said bleakly. "You can come and collect it. Another one in half hour. All hostages will die."

TWO PLAINCLOTHES ANTI-TERRORIST officers rushed forward with a stretcher. As they carried the body away, one arm, clad in a yellow cardigan, flopped over the side.

The dead man was identified as Abbas Lavasani, whose frightened voice had been heard on the telephone. The blood on the back of his head had dried, the body was cold, and rigor mortis had set in. A report was sent to Dellow immediately: "It was not freshly killed and was at least one hour dead."

If Lavasani had been killed at 12:55, the second volley of shots, played down the telephone to the shocked imam, suggested another murder had taken place.

But there was no second body. Towfiq was bluffing. He was ready to kill again, but perhaps he would not have to.

Dellow moved to the logical (and wrong) conclusion: "There was a very strong likelihood that further deaths had resulted from the shots heard later, that at least two hostages had been killed, and that the terrorists were embarked on a course of systematically killing the hostages."

Michael Rose was not so sure. "That sounds like a fake," he said. "They're winding you up. To heighten the tension."

"I cannot take that risk," said Dellow.

Two deaths were the threshold for a handover to the military, for which the police needed the highest political authorization.

There was silence in Zulu Control as Dellow prepared to make the most momentous decision of his life. In the next few minutes, because of the orders he was about to issue, people would die: perhaps many people, possibly everyone—hostages, gunmen, soldiers. For the first time in his life, the gentle, restrained, rule-abiding, watercolor-painting policeman prepared to unleash chaos.

Barely disguising the shake in his hand and the tremor in his voice, Dellow picked up the direct phone to Scotland Yard and advised the commissioner of police that, in his opinion, "the circumstances that dictated a military assault now obtained."

David McNee informed the home secretary in the Cobra meeting room. William Whitelaw put a call through to the prime minister.

MARGARET THATCHER WAS in her car returning from Chequers, the prime minister's country residence, and at that moment driving through a valley in the Chilterns. The first call to her radio car-phone did not go through. Whitelaw waited, a long, tense minute, and tried again.

At 19:01, Mrs. Thatcher picked up but could barely hear what her home secretary was saying due to interference on the line. She instructed the driver to pull over.

"The hostages' lives are now at risk," Whitelaw told her. "I want your permission to send in the SAS."

"Yes, go in," said the prime minister.

Operation Nimrod was triggered from a pull-off area north of High Wycombe.

Her decision was immediately relayed to Zulu Control: "The timing of the assault is a matter for the police commander in consultation with the military commander."

"Well, I'm not going to do this until I have written authority," said Rose. "I need a signature."

Dellow pulled a page from his lined notebook and wrote in capital letters:

AT 19:07 ON 5TH MAY 1980 I, JOHN A DELLOW, DAC "A," PASSED CONTROL OF IRANIAN EMBASSY INCIDENT TO LT COL HM ROSE

He signed the paper and handed it over, with a look of infinite sadness. In John Dellow's mind he had failed. Rose countersigned.

For the first time since its inception seven years earlier, Military Aid to the Civil Power went into force. The soldiers took over.

"Hector, get your guys ready," Rose told the commander of B Squadron. "As soon as you're prepared to go, we'll go."

AT 19:08, St. Stephen's Hospital was alerted to clear an entire casualty ward and bring in additional medical staff.

From his hospital bed, Mustapha Karkouti watched the television footage of the body being removed from the front step of the embassy: "I immediately knew whose body that was because of the bright yellow color of his cardigan." Faten clung to him.

IN THE CRUCIBLE THEATRE, the snooker final was on a knife edge. Hurricane Higgins was hanging in grimly and leveled the match three times. The contest was tense and fractious, with both players showing signs of what *The Times* called "mental weariness." Cliff Thorburn moved ahead, but then Higgins fought back, and the scores drew level again at sixteen frames apiece. In the thirty-third frame, Thorburn cleared the table with a break of 119, in "a masterly display of concentration, accuracy and staying power." With a maximum of two frames left to play, the game "moved toward its tremulous climax."

DOUGLAS HURD WAS eating a slice of pizza at his desk in the Foreign Office when he was summoned, as he put it, "back to the bunker," the Cobra meeting room.

TOWFIQ INSTRUCTED MAKKI and Fowzi to blockade all doors and windows on the lower floors; gather whatever furniture, bundles of paper from the press room, and other combustible material they could find; and soak the lot in flammable liquid. In the embassy basement were several jerricans of paraffin, white spirit, and gasoline for the generator, as well as a stock of highly flammable duplicator fluid for the photocopiers and telex machines. As usual, Ron Morris had bought in quantity. If the police attacked, Towfiq instructed, they should lock every internal door and ignite the barricades; the last act of the Group of the Martyr would be to set fire to this hated symbol of the Iranian government and burn it to the ground.

COMMAND WAS PASSED to Hector Gullan, in a message from Rose: "You have control."

THE FIRST FOUR abseilers, led by Tom Morell, pulled their ropes through the figure-eight descenders, with one large and one small end, and hitched these to their belts with carabiners. The rear-assault team moved to the basement of the Doctors' House. The five police hard dogs, straining at their leashes by the back door, suddenly sent up a ferocious barking. "The dogs must have picked up the tension because they went absolutely mad," one officer noted.

One lunged forward to bite a passing trooper and was yanked back by his handler. Mel Parry's team gathered at the first-floor window of Number 15, ready to climb onto the balcony.

Gullan and his communications team took up position in the flat on the sixth floor of Kingston House. The men knew their instructions. Now, inside his own head, Gullan issued orders to himself: "Whatever you do, ice cold. In your voice, dead cold, dead calm. Ruthless. You've got to get the hostages out, that means ruthlessly. Cost what it will." But even Gullan was feeling the pressure. "The tension was terrific," he recalled. Beyond the lives and careers at stake, the future of the regiment might depend on the outcome. The squadron was ready, he told himself: "The team was well-oiled, well-rehearsed. We'd done lots of this sort of thing in Northern Ireland from small to big operations and working together. This was a cracking good bunch of blokes."

In a few minutes' time, he would order them to take a greater risk with their lives than ever before.

The anti-terrorist police team eerily sensed the military were going in, before being told. Inside the intelligence cell, Graham Collins felt "an electric tingling in the air." Minutes later, the team members were instructed to put on gas masks and get under the desks. "Do not leave the building," they were told.

HELEN REDDY, "the Queen of Housewife Rock," was preparing to give a concert a few hundred yards away at the Royal Albert Hall. The Australian American star, known also as "the Singing Nun" for her role in the film *Airport 1975,* had a string of number one hits in the 1970s, and she still enjoyed a huge following in the UK. A few concertgoers stood at the police barricades in the early-evening sunshine, or watched the press milling about inside their enclosure.

POLICE IN THE Montessori nursery school were also issued with gas masks, but told to keep the windows open, lest closing them gave the game away.

"BANK ROBBERY," said Hector Gullan into the radio handset, at 19:10.

The SAS abseiling team climbed onto the roof of Number 15, and made their way silently across to the rear parapet of Number 16. Tommy Palmer tapped his partner, Paul Sanford, on the shoulder and pointed to a window in one of the flats in the building opposite: "An old lady casually looking out of her window, washing dishes. Little did she know that in about two minutes' time, the whole place was going to explode in fucking fire."

To the disappointment of some in the SAS team, the media lighting gantry had not yet been illuminated since it was still light, and would not therefore need to be blown up.

MARGARET THATCHER "tried to visualize what was happening" as she made her way back to Downing Street.

IN THE COMMUNICATIONS room alongside the Cobra meeting room, Peter de la Billière listened in through headphones to the radio network. "I could hear Hector Gullan giving his orders," he recalled, "and the men talking to each other as they moved into position." He relayed each step to the rapt committee from the open doorway of the communications room:

"They're on the roof."

"They're laying out their ropes."

"They're getting the charges down the lightwell."

"They're ready."

De la Billière sensed the tension rising steadily inside the room: "The talk died away until no sound remained except that of the digital clock on the end wall. *Snap!* went the little flap as it fell, marking the passage of every minute. *Snap* . . ."

WILLIE WHITELAW ROCKED back in his committee room chair and stared at the ceiling. "I felt very lonely and yet strangely calm," he recalled. "I knew that there was really no alternative."

THE STENCH OF gasoline and duplicator fluid wafted through the Iranian Embassy.

At 19:12, the field telephone rang on the first-floor landing.

HITHERTO, THE JOB of the police negotiators had been to act as honest brokers, establishing a level of trust with the gunmen. Now their role was to lie, and to keep Salim on the telephone for as long as possible, in the expectation that several tons of glass and steel would fall on top of him in the ground-floor hallway.

John Dellow briefed David Veness: "Contact Salim and inform him that, having seen the body, the government now realized the serious-ness of his intent and had conceded an airplane to take the group from the country. Then spend as much time as possible arranging details of the move by terrorists and hostages to the airport."

Veness took a deep breath and picked up the field telephone. "Hello, Salim," he said. "Let's talk . . ."

FOR SIX DAYS, Towfiq had been stonewalled, sidetracked, and stalled. Now, it seemed, the police were prepared to discuss, in detail, his de-mands for an ambassador, a bus, and a plane to safety. He was intensely suspicious.

"They are going to invade," he said, summoning Lock and Harris downstairs.

Lock took the phone once again. "He's insisted I come down and speak to you and tell you directly that if anything is done re attack, all hostages will be killed," Lock told Veness.

"Trevor, what we're doing . . . We're trying to make arrangements for the Iraqi ambassador and the airport. You know this is what we've got to accept now, Trevor."

"Yes, sir, but it's got to be done urgently."

"We're doing it now."

"They're worried about the fact that you're going to attack the em-bassy in the meantime."

"Trevor, what I'm trying to do is get him on the phone to agree to arrangements."

THIS WAS NOT going as Veness intended. He needed Lock out of the way, back upstairs with the other hostages, and Salim on the line stand-ing where he was supposed to be, under the glass skylight.

Veness pressed on: "Look, I want to speak to him about the airport, Trevor, that's all."

LOCK HANDED THE phone to Towfiq.

"Hello."

"Now look, Salim, it's between eight-fifteen and eight-thirty that the aircraft will leave. Now the coach, we hope, will be there in about twenty minutes . . . I'm going to go back upstairs to say that you agreed to the Iraqi ambassador coming."

Harris exchanged a smile of relief with Lock. "It really looked as if things were beginning to get better."

Lock was astonished. "The bastards are giving in."

"And the driver will be Mr. Trevor?" asked Towfiq.

"Well, let me discuss these things, because it's important we get these right, Salim."

"Mr. Trevor, he will lead the bus to the airport."

"What kind of bus do you want?" asked Veness. "How many seats? Twenty-five?"

"Yes," said Towfiq, and then corrected himself, realizing he had inadvertently confirmed the number of people in the building. "No, make it thirty-seven."

"If we have one coach, is that going to be enough, as Mr. Trevor is only going to be able to drive one coach, won't he?"

"One will be enough."

"It will have curtains, but we will leave the curtains open until you tell us to close them. Where do you want it parked? Do you want it parked outside?"

"I want to search it first."

"Okay."

"Now whereabouts shall we put that coach first?"

"Opposite of the door."

"Well, opposite the door is a very vague phrase. If you're looking out of the window."

"After you get it, you will put it outside the door."

"Let's talk about that, then. Opposite the front door, you're looking straight over the park . . ."

DE LA BILLIÈRE was impressed by the negotiator's "masterly prevarication" as he gabbed on about bus curtains and parking.

Veness continued: ". . . Can you listen to me and we'll just talk about the first movement of the coach up to the front door. If you look out of the window directly ahead of you, there is a park. To the right, there is the end of the wall, and that is where those gas men were working on the generators, where they were working on that gas leak . . ."

TOWFIQ WAS LOSING TRACK. "Talk to Mr. Trevor," he said, handing the telephone back to Lock and leaning in to listen.

Their faces were so close, Lock could smell his sweat and aftershave.

"Sir, the group are very concerned that you are going to invade. Can you give me any kind of assurances that this is not going to happen, and everything is being done as you said to Salim?"

"Now come on, Trevor, the most important thing right now is to get this sorted out. We've got to get this coach and plane sorted out as soon as possible. All we're trying to organize, Trevor, is the coach and the aircraft, and the movement of the Iraqi ambassador. Now, in order to do that, I want to do that as calmly, as safely, as possible. I need to speak to Salim. Can you give me back to Salim?"

"ROAD ACCIDENT," said Gullan, at 19:14.

The SAS moved into the assault positions.

As he began lowering the larger of the two bombs into the light well, the soldier on the roof thought, "Detonator cord explodes at twenty-six thousand feet per second. If my mate with the clacker goes early, in the heat of the moment, this is going to blow my arms off."

SHAYE WAS ON the fourth floor, preparing for a possible attack from above. Fowzi stood guard over the women in the cipher room, at the back of the second floor. On the same floor, at the front of the building, Jassim and Makki guarded the male hostages in the telex room.

Four men were now standing on the first-floor landing: Towfiq and Lock with the telephone between them, cord pulled tight, outside Roya's office door; Harris stood a few feet away, at the door to the chargé d'affaires' office; Abbas loitered farther down the corridor, nearer to the ambassador's office door, with his gun drawn and Ron Morris's air pistol in his belt. None of them was directly beneath the skylight. But had they looked up, they might have seen, through the obscured glass, the shadow of a large bomb being lowered into the light well.

Lock handed the telephone back to Towfiq, who transferred the submachine gun into the crook of his left arm and held the receiver with his right.

"Are the Iranian hostages prepared to go along with this idea of going on a plane?" asked Veness.

"Yes, oh, yes," said Towfiq. "They are all happy about that."

"WE'VE GOT ABOUT a minute now," Gullan told Rose by radio. "And then we're going."

At 19:15, the accelerometers "identified the location of four of the terrorists" on the second floor: three in the telex room (code-named Victoria) and one in the cipher room (Charlie) with the women.

Dellow was on the telephone. At 19:20, he turned to Rose. "Stop it. We've got some new intelligence come in."

The bugs had "picked up what appeared to be discussions about releasing British and female hostages," Dellow noted, "but the real purport was unclear." The translators warned "the message was so muddled that no sense could be made of it."

"I need a nine-minute delay," said Dellow.

Rose shook his head. "You can't stop it, John. They're there. We're going. It's too late to stop now. The guys are on the ropes."

Dellow fell silent. "Okay. We'll have to go."

A face appeared at a window on the fourth floor. Shaye was looking out.

"HOLD," Gullan said, and sent a message to Zulu Control. "The SAS required one more minute of negotiations."

Veness would have to keep Towfiq talking until the coast cleared.

The face disappeared again. "GO ON . . ."

At 19:22, the order "HYDE PARK" crackled through the SAS earpieces: "Groups in position; explosives primed; abseilers hitched and ready."

The leader of each team indicated readiness—to the men on the roof, the troopers holding the clackers attached to the detonating cord, the abseilers, the soldiers poised in the garden and inside the balcony window—with a double-click on the pressel button of his radio.

Another flap turned over on the clock in the Cobra meeting room: *Snap* . . .

"LONDON BRIDGE," barked Gullan.

TOM MORELL AND Tommy Palmer pushed off the rear parapet and began to descend, the abseil ropes fizzing softly through the figure-eight devices. Paul Sanford and his partner, Peter "Ginge" Garmon, followed.

The first pair reached the second floor. Then Palmer's foot went through a window.

TOWFIQ LOOKED AROUND sharply at the clatter of breaking glass.

"Okay, I phone you after a few minutes. I think there's something wrong."

"No, no—" said Veness.

"Just three minutes I go. I come back."

"Salim . . ."

From the top of the building, Shaye shouted down a warning in Arabic to the other gunmen: "They are coming!"

Towfiq still held the telephone. "We are listening to some suspicious movements—"

"There're no suspicious movements."

"Okay."

"Salim—"

"Just a minute I come back in a minute. I go to check."

"Salim, there're no suspicious movements . . . Salim there is no suspicious movement . . . Salim?"

AT 19:23, the building was rocked by an enormous explosion.

20

ELEVEN MINUTES

The following events, a series of cascading and overlapping moments, occurred in roughly the time it takes to cook a hard-boiled egg.

19:23

Tommy Palmer abseiled down thirty feet and landed softly on the rear-second-floor balcony, a second ahead of his Alpha One teammates Paul Sanford and Ginge Garmon. They looked up. Suspended, ten feet overhead, was their team leader, the burly Fijian Tom Morell.

Some blamed the older hawser-laid abseil rope for snarling. Some said the kink was caused by excess rope pooled on the balcony below. Morell thought the hem of his Kevlar vest had snagged in the figure-eight device. Whatever the cause, the rope was jammed fast, with Morell hanging off it.

FROM THE SIXTH floor of Kingston House, Hector Gullan heard the glass smash as Palmer's boot went through the window, and now he saw Morell, dangling in midair just above the window to the general office, struggling with his harness.

"GO, GO, GO!" Gullan shouted.

THE TWO SOLDIERS crouching behind the lip of the central shaft squeezed their clackers simultaneously. Some twenty feet below, two and a half pounds of plastic explosive detonated in the void, blasting out the internal windows and sending more than a ton of glass, iron, wood, plaster, and brickwork cascading into the entrance hall.

A MURDER OF startled crows rose from the trees in Hyde Park in a cawing cloud. The explosion was audible inside the Royal Albert Hall.

THE SIX MEN of Sierra One scrambled down through the skylight into the attic bathroom. The Alpha Three roof team hurled CS-gas grenades and flash-bangs into the acrid cloud of dust and smoke belching from the central shaft. Then they lowered the caving ladders, hooked them over the roof railings, and clambered down. "You couldn't see anything," said one of the team, "it was just a black pit full of smoke."

On the first-floor landing, Towfiq dropped the field telephone and staggered back as the debris crashed past him into the hallway below. Sim Harris stumbled through a doorway and into the chargé d'affaires' office. Abbas was nowhere to be seen. For a split second Trevor Lock and Towfiq stared at each other in shock. For six days Lock had pleaded with this man, helped him negotiate, listened to his political lectures, and almost liked him. Now the policeman lowered his right shoulder and charged into Towfiq's left hip, sending him crashing into the half-open door of Roya Kaghachi's office. The momentum carried Lock through the doorway, and he landed heavily on top of the sprawled gunman. Towfiq's submachine gun flew out of his hand and skidded across the carpet under Roya's desk.

IN THE TELEX room, Jassim felt the building lurch and buckle with the explosion, followed by the ragged detonations of the flash-bangs. The Iranians were crouched against the far wall, Gholam-Ali Afrouz in the middle, the others around him. Ron Morris and Muhammad Faruqi stood just inside the doorway to the right.

Jassim took a step forward and screamed at the senior diplomat:

"Now I have a chance to get you, Afrouz." Then he opened fire with his Skorpion, spraying the group indiscriminately, firing in short bursts, back and forth. Makki joined in with his Browning.

The hostages scrambled for cover under desks, under chairs, and behind the upended telex machines. "The shots were fired at random, like a madman almost," thought Abbas Fallahi. The doorman felt a thump of pain in his upper thigh and twisted into a heap.

In the same second, the marksmen behind the wall at street level fired two CR-gas rounds with Polecat launchers into what they thought was an empty second-floor room. The canisters smashed through the windows, spun on the floor, hissed evilly, and detonated. The walls rocked.

Six bullets thudded into the medical orderly Ahmad Dadgar: one each in his chest, back, arm, and leg, and two in his side. Afrouz ducked as a round clipped his nose and a second embedded in his leg.

Ali Tabatabai saw the smaller gunman turn toward him. "He raised his pistol and fired," the banker recalled. "I heard and felt nothing, but within seconds my clothing was covered with blood. I clutched at my jacket in a pitiful attempt to shield myself. He aimed a second and a third shot directly at me."

"God, is there anything I can do?" Ron Morris asked himself as the room erupted in a welter of blood, gas, and bullets. "No," he answered himself.

"Surely, I must die," thought Tabatabai.

FOWZI LEFT THE four women, screaming, in the cipher room and ran down the corridor to the telex room as smoke billowed up from below. He was met with a scene of carnage.

Dadgar was gasping in a pool of blood. Beside him lay the body of a young man in a blue three-piece suit.

Ali Akbar Samadzadeh, the Westernized press assistant with the Irish girlfriend, had turned his back as the gunmen opened fire and was crawling on his knees, trying to hide beneath the desk, shielding his head with his hands. The first bullet went into his buttocks; the second traveled the length of his body, hip to skull, killing him instantly.

The room filled with choking gas. Eyes streaming, Ron Morris clamped a cushion over his face as he coughed in great, gouting spasms.

"These are the last minutes of my life," thought Afrouz as blood poured down into his mouth. He placed his handkerchief over his face. "I am going to die."

MEL PARRY CROSSED over to the first-floor balcony at the front, followed by John McAleese, a hefty Scot with a handlebar mustache, carrying the frame charge. Tom MacDonald, clacker in hand, crouched on the balcony of the Doctors' House with his partner, Denis Pringle, alongside. McAleese placed the square charge in the window and wedged it firmly in place with a baton of wood, cut to length.

Then the curtains opened, and Bravo Four saw a thin, pale, bespectacled figure peering out.

THE CHARGÉ D'AFFAIRES' office had been dark when Sim Harris half ran, half fell into it, but a chink in the curtains threw a strip of sunlight across the carpet. Harris felt his way toward the light and opened the curtains and shutters. There, on the balcony, stood a frogman, wearing goggles and a peculiar black wetsuit, pointing a machine gun at him. The frogman was gesticulating and shouting something. Through the armored glass and the mask, still partially deafened by the blast, Harris could not make out the words.

"GET DOWN," screamed Parry, recognizing Harris from his photograph. This floor of the building was supposedly empty. What was the BBC man doing here? He gestured frantically at him to back away from the window, and to the right. "Get DOWN!"

Harris ducked out of sight. Parry and McAleese clambered back over the balustrade to Number 15. Parry signaled to MacDonald, who squeezed the clacker.

"The frame charge we used was a new thing to the regiment," reflected Pringle. "We didn't know what it would do, so we went for the biggest charge."

The huge explosion blew a hole in the wall six feet wide. Half the balcony vanished, sending rubble crashing into the street below. The sledgehammer they had with them to knock out the remains of the window was redundant: the frame was gone, along with the surrounding brickwork. Harris had disappeared.

TOM MORELL DANGLED on the rope. The more he twisted and pulled at the figure-eight, the tighter it jammed. "Cut the rope," he shouted up to the second wave of abseilers poised on the roof edge. "CUT IT!"

Immediately below him, Paul Sanford smashed the right-hand window into the general office with a sledgehammer and hurled in two L29s, combining CR gas with a stun grenade. He followed them in, Palmer and Garmon immediately behind him. Two dozen magnesium flares fizzed and popped around the floor as the walls reverberated. The floor plan had depicted the hostages arranged neatly around the wall, but the room was empty. The Queen Anne chair stood in the middle of the floor, but without the policeman in it. The door into the adjoining cipher room was locked and barricaded from the inside with filing cabinets. They could hear the voices of terrified women on the other side. Palmer tried to open the door into the corridor; that too was locked. He stepped back and fired an extended twelve-round machine-gun burst into the lock, and shoulder-rammed it. The solid mahogany door did not budge. The room was now alight, not with the gradual ignition of a normal fire but with a great rush of flame as the flash-bangs found the paraffin-soaked paper and duplicator fluid. The three men climbed back out the window as the curtains ignited.

TWO FLOORS ABOVE, Shaye leaned out the window and fired his pistol at the figures on the balcony below. Sergeant Geoffrey Gogdell, a police sniper observing from Kingston House, saw the muzzle flash from the fourth floor through his telescopic sight. The shot appeared to be directed at the man suspended in midair and the soldiers below. "One ducked and looked up. They were under fire." Gogdell could not get a clear shot. The window was half-open, the glass reflecting the evening sun. He "aimed toward the end of the flash" and squeezed the trigger.

THROUGH THE HAZE from the smoke generators, Gullan could see Morell twisting on the rope. He watched the rest of the abseil team re-emerge from the general office, and the spout of flame that followed them out. Garmon climbed onto the window ledge to try to release his trapped team leader, but Morell was stuck fast, his weight pulling down on the carabiner, making it impossible to release. The rope was inextricably knotted into the metal loops of the abseiling device. The curtains of the general office were now fully alight, the flames licking up toward Morell's legs. He pushed himself away from the wall, trying to escape the heat, but on each inward swing he swayed back into the spitting blaze, which gathered fury by the second.

But most worrying of all was what was happening, or not happening, on the rear ground floor. The ten men of Bravo One were standing around the French windows into the commercial section, not entering, looking up at Morell struggling above them.

"Get in," commanded Gullan.

The explosion in the central shaft was supposed to direct the attention of the gunmen inward, giving the assault teams valuable moments to lay the entry explosives, front and back. Every second of delay allowed the gunmen more time to recover from the initial explosion and prepare for the coming storm. The frame charge at the front had exploded thirty seconds later than planned; the one at the back had not been detonated at all, and for a simple reason: Tom Morell was suspended directly above where the charge would explode, and the upward blast might kill him. On his own initiative (for which he was substantially berated afterward), the soldier holding the clacker pulled the detonating wire out of the plastic explosive on the frame. He was not going to kill the man on the rope.

"GET IN!" yelled Gullan.

19:24

Rob Timson, leader of Bravo One, the ground-floor assault team, saw Tom Morell twisting in the flames directly above them. "It's all going wrong and we haven't even started yet," he thought. "The guys should be in by now. Improvise, adapt, overcome . . . Get the sledgehammer."

A fifteen-pound hammer had been brought along to wedge the shape charge in place, its shaft wrapped with additional explosive to add force to the blast. A trooper named Ben Canon raised it over his head and swung at the window to the left of the doors. The glass, metal, and wood gave way with a crash. A second blow removed the rest, and the men poured through: six headed straight into the entrance hallway, where they expected to find Salim lying under the wreckage of the glass roof. The remaining four made for the basement. They were now over a minute behind schedule. As he ran into the hall, Timson fired a machine-gun burst into the wall. "There was no time to set off the flash-bangs." The first thing he noticed was the gray telephone wire, snaking up through the banisters of the staircase. The air in the hallway was thick with gas, smoke, and dust, and of the leading gunman there was not a sign.

TREVOR LOCK AND Towfiq al-Rashidi grappled furiously on the carpet of Roya's office, punching and kicking, as the window-frame charge exploded into the room next door.

"You caused this, you bastard," shouted Lock, unleashing the fury he had kept buttoned beneath his uniform for six days. "I fucking begged you to surrender, and you wouldn't . . . This is all your fucking fault."

The Arab was younger and fitter, but Lock was bigger, and more experienced in hand-to-hand combat. During twenty years of policing, he had subdued many drunk soccer fans. "Like a squirming rabbit," Towfiq struggled to free himself and reach the gun, but he was pinned to the floor by 217 pounds of prime Barking policeman.

Lock had his left arm tight around Towfiq's neck, and one knee on his chest. "I had him. He wasn't going anywhere."

The door had been kicked shut in the struggle, and from around the building came a muffled cacophony of explosions and gunfire.

Lock's "Dagenham-isms," as he described them, poured out of him: "You've fucking caused this. I gave you an alternative, but you wouldn't take it, you bastard."

At this moment, Lock remembered his gun. Reaching down with his right hand, he pulled the .38 from the holster and jammed it into Towfiq's temple.

The astonishment written on the gunman's face was even more pronounced than the fear. "His eyes near popped out." The policeman had succeeded in keeping the weapon hidden since the first day.

Only now did Towfiq understand that Lock could have shot him at any time.

"You didn't have to do this," Lock continued to shout. "I told you what would happen if you surrendered peacefully."

"It wasn't me," Towfiq said bleakly as the fight went out of him. "It was the others."

Who did Towfiq mean by "the others"? Jassim and the other hardliners among the gunmen? Or someone else? Someone back in Iraq? Fowzi al-Naimi? Sami Muhammad Ali, the spy known as the Fox? The Palestinian mastermind, Abu Nidal?

For almost a week, Towfiq and his group had repeatedly threatened to kill Lock and the other hostages. In the space of a minute the tables had turned, and the executioner's choice now lay in the hands of Trevor Lock.

He moved the muzzle of the revolver from Towfiq's temple to beneath his jaw. There were five bullets in the gun. Just one would blow this man's head off. "I'm going to kill the bastard," he thought. But then he hesitated.

If the other gunmen were still at large, Towfiq might be more use alive than dead, "something to barter with": a hostage. Lock knew he was thinking like a typical cop as he debated whether to pull the trigger. "Soldiers don't think like that."

"Don't hurt me, Mr. Trevor," pleaded Towfiq.

"Do I kill him?" pondered Lock. "Do I *need* to kill him?"

THE BASEMENT STAIRS were barred by three maintenance ladders that had been pulled up from the storeroom and jammed into the space. "Improvised explosive device," thought Rob Timson. "That's a booby trap on a pull switch, so when you trip it, the whole lot goes up." Gingerly, he reached down into the spaces between rungs, probing each one in turn. "Clear!"

Two men hauled the ladders onto the landing, while the next two headed down. Operating in pairs, they began working through the nine

basement rooms. Some were locked and had to be shot open with machine guns.

"Drill the lock, kick the door in, throw in flash-bangs . . . Room
clear!"

One soldier spotted a dark shape crouched menacingly at the end
of the corridor and emptied his magazine into what turned out to be a
trash can.

The same clearing process was under way in the eleven attic rooms
of the fifth floor, by the men of Sierra One spreading out from the top
bathroom. The Alpha Three team scrambled in through the shattered
interior windows and began sweeping through the third-floor rooms,
one by one, starting with the press room. The building shuddered with
each stun grenade explosion, and the choking gas-fog grew thicker.

In the ground-floor hallway, the soldiers stepped over the carpet
strip covering Lavasani's dried bloodstains and searched the waiting
room, the anteroom where Abbas Fallahi made the coffee, and the
commercial section's library. "Room clear!" All were empty.

Timson stood at the bottom of the stairs and looked upward, beyond his formal "limit of exploitation": All he could hear was "shooting, flash-bangs, and screams."

The battle for Princes Gate was raging on the first and second floors.

"RON, PLEASE GET me to hospital," gulped the medical orderly Ahmad
Dadgar as Morris tried to stanch his wounds with a cushion. "My lips
are dry. Please, get me an ambulance."

"Don't worry, sir," said Morris. "The police will be here in a minute."

It dawned on Ali Tabatabai, covered in the blood of the dead Ali
Samadzadeh, that he was unwounded. A bullet had mysteriously
twisted into his clothing. Another round had struck the fifty-pence piece
in Abbas Fallahi's pocket and ricocheted into the ceiling.

"I'm bleeding," groaned Gholam-Ali Afrouz. "I've been shot."
Blood poured from the wound to his right thigh.

The gunmen ceased firing.

"They stopped as suddenly as they had begun," Morris observed.

Jassim seemed stunned by what he had done. The hand grenade fell from Makki's hand, rolled across the floor, and stopped, rocking gently. Fowzi stood bewildered, waiting for an order.

A second volley of gas canisters clattered through the window.

In seconds, the atmosphere in the telex room went from murderous, to indecisive, to fearful.

Muhammad Faruqi saw the change in the gunmen's faces and realized they were starting to panic.

"Don't kill us," said Tabatabai, quite quietly. "It's no use. Everybody is finished."

"Tasleem!" someone shouted, Arabic for "Surrender!" Others picked up the cry. *"Tasleem! Tasleem!"*

"Surrender! Surrender!" shouted Morris, and then watched, astounded: "They just put down their guns."

Makki dropped his automatic pistol. One of the gunmen threw a grenade out the window. This was followed by the Astra .38, which clattered into the street.

ONE OF THE SAS snipers in Hyde Park had his rifle trained on the second-floor telex room. Suddenly he glimpsed the shape of a man with a gun at the window. He fired and missed, hitting the stone lintel. The target "was seen to drop his weapon and withdraw into the telex room."

PARRY, MCALEESE, MACDONALD, and Pringle moved along what remained of the front first-floor balcony toward the smoking hole in the facade of the embassy. A grenade landed beside them with a heavy clunk. This was followed, in seconds, by the spent bullet fired by the park sniper.

"Fuck," thought McAleese. They were under attack. "That's it. I'm done."

The grenade failed to explode.

"The window just disappeared," said Pringle. "There was shit everywhere. Smoke, dust, rubble."

Parry and McAleese flung two stun grenades through the opening, jumped aside to avoid the explosion that followed, and dived into the office. Through the miasma, they could see a pair of legs sticking out of the debris. Pringle hauled Harris to his feet.

The BBC recordist was covered in dust, but, apart from a few facial cuts and bruises, miraculously unhurt. His first thought was "I still have my glasses on."

Shards of black rubber from the exploded grenades littered the floor. The curtains were burning, and smaller fires erupted on the carpet. The sofa was on fire. The room was shattered, and filling with smoke. The large tapestry to their left was alight.

"Don't panic, stay down," Parry shouted to Harris, who could not hear a word.

Pringle grabbed him and forced him back onto the floor. "Stay where you are, don't move . . ."

MacDonald and Pringle moved forward, opened the door on Mac-Donald's signal, and tossed two more stun grenades onto the landing. Parry and McAleese turned left down the corridor, and MacDonald and Pringle turned right, toward Roya's office.

As the four black-clad frogmen disappeared, in the burning, gas-soaked room, flat on his face, deafened and choking, Harris felt a surge of elation. "Go on, lads, get the bastards!" he shouted.

Badger MacDonald paused at the closed door. Despite the gunfire and explosions from all parts of the building, he could hear shouts and the sounds of a struggle coming from inside the room.

19:25

In the communications annex adjoining the Cobra meeting room, Peter de la Billière listened through earphones to Hector Gullan's command channel. What he heard was a disaster unfolding. The special forces chief had expected one almighty explosion. Instead, the first detonation had been followed, after a delay, by a second, smaller one, and then a confusing mass of shouting, screaming, shots, and further blasts.

"I knew at once that something had gone wrong," de la Billière reported. "The explosions should have been synchronized. Had the whole building gone up?"

De la Billière put his head round the door into the Cobra meeting room, where the committee was assembled, and addressed the seated grandees. "I'm afraid there have been two explosions," he said gravely. "It may be that our people have failed to coordinate, or the terrorists may have blown up the embassy, and our soldiers with it."

The news was met with gasps. William Whitelaw went pale. "I tried to appear outwardly calm in front of my team, but in the end we all abandoned such pretense. The tension was hard to bear."

De la Billière continued: "We should expect casualties."

TOM MORELL DANGLED, his legs dancing over the spouts of flame that gusted from the window.

Clutchplate Clapton leaned out of the Kingston House flat and shouted to the reserves on the ground: "Shoot the fucking rope. Get him down."

"Shut up, for fuck's sake," shouted Gullan. Shooting through a swinging rope half an inch thick from a hundred yards away was virtually impossible, and the bullet would more likely kill Morell than save him. "Cut him down!" he commanded through the microphone to the men on the roof above.

That was easier ordered than done. If the rope was severed on the outward arc of his swing, Morell could miss the balcony and crash sixty feet onto the stone terrace below; if it was cut as he swung inward, he might tumble into the flames.

The abseilers who were supposed to form the second team paused. They would have to rope down through a raging fire. One jumped anyway. In his effort to avoid the blaze, he bounced too hard off the wall, upended on the rope, and hit the balcony headfirst. Dazed but conscious, he staggered to his feet.

The fire was no longer leaping from the window in ragged bursts but surging in a thick, roaring wave of flame. The right trouser leg of Morell's overalls ignited. Above, one of the soldiers stood poised over the rope with a knife.

Sir Thomas was being burned alive.

KATE ADIE CROUCHED behind a parked car, the embassy windows belching smoke behind her, reporting breathlessly, live and unscripted, with the sounds of barking dogs, shrieks, and explosions in the background.

The press broke out of its enclosure and swarmed toward the building on the first explosion. From their cherry pickers, the cameramen had a clear view of the front balconies and recorded every second: the black-clad figures blowing up the window, then clambering across, throwing in stun grenades, and jumping inside, flames erupting from the room.

The ITN producer monitoring the live feed from the secret camera in Kingston House witnessed the abseilers sliding down the back, the explosion of the flash-bangs, and then the lone man struggling on the rope, fire lapping at his feet.

"Put me to air, put me to air!" he shouted at the producers back at ITN headquarters, only to be told, sternly, that *Coronation Street* had not finished yet.

"It can't be interrupted," the producers insisted. As soon as the theme tune started, they would go live.

The BBC did not wait. On BBC1, the John Wayne film *Rio Lobo* was replaced by Kate Adie outside the burning embassy.

With two frames left to play in the Embassy World Snooker Championship in Sheffield, BBC2 cut away with an inspired, impromptu segue. "And now from one Embassy to another . . . ," said the husky-voiced commentator, "Whispering Ted" Lowe, not quite believing his own words.

Some fourteen million people were tuned in to the snooker championship. Millions more gathered around screens across the country to witness the longest news flash in British television history, described by *The Observer* as "the most haunting live pictures since Jack Ruby murdered Lee Harvey Oswald in Dallas, Texas."

David Stirling, founder of the SAS, was enjoying the snooker final in White's Club, whiskey in hand, when BBC2 cut away to Princes Gate. Initially furious at the interruption, he was gripped by the spectacle of "the old firm," as he called it, going into action on live television.

Rebecca West witnessed the unfolding drama from her temporary billet at the Lansdowne Club, still seething at having been denied her ringside seat.

The novelist John le Carré reached for his pen. "It had all the ingredients. More than all. In showbiz terms it was over the top." Everyone at home for the bank holiday was gripped by "the first live political siege to be televised on British soil . . . A hit-team of black uniformed frogmen roping down the side of the Iranian Embassy, Action-Man personified, a bunch of 007s on a tight rein *live on screen* at peak viewing time."

John Dellow gave instructions that "no information was to be given to the press without reference to him," a pointless command, since, as the Zulu Control chief admitted, "the news media had almost more material than it could handle."

Bizarrely, some of the few people *not* watching the unfolding drama were gathered in the Cobra meeting room.

"Had we realized that television camera crews were about to cover the assault live," observed Peter de la Billière, "we could have switched on our sets and watched one of the most astonishing spectacles ever seen on the small screen." There were three television screens in the Cobra meeting room. "Somehow this idea never occurred to us." So, while the rest of the country watched the live images, the most powerful officials in the UK listened to a "running commentary" from de la Billière, via his earphones, head craned around the door.

PARRY AND MCALEESE moved along the dark corridor on the first floor toward the small office at the far end. It was locked. Each man fired a burst into the lock, with no effect. They moved left to the door of the ambassador's office. This swung open, and each threw in a stun grenade. Parry glimpsed a figure in a combat jacket and a keffiyeh a second before he "disappeared into the smoke caused by the grenade." He fired a burst from the doorway. "I know I hit him, as he dropped a magazine and I heard him yell and groan."

Parry tossed in two more stun grenades, and then followed on his hands and knees. The room was pitch dark. As he crawled inside, he felt blood on the floor. Something moved in the far corner.

"What is your name? What is your country?" he shouted in Arabic, remembered from his time in Dhofar.

"Police . . . police," came Abbas Maytham's faint cry from the back of the room. Or perhaps he was saying "Please."

Parry's machine gun was one of those without a flashlight attached. He could see nothing through the murk. "X-ray, white, ambassador's office," Parry shouted into his throat mic, backing out of the room.

Sunray could not hear him.

GAS GRENADES RAINED down into the stairwell. John McAleese was coughing and retching violently. His respirator had not sealed properly, and CR gas was seeping under it. The SAS called this "getting a whiff." He suddenly threw up violently inside the face mask, the vomit spattering into his eyes.

They needed a flashlight, and reinforcements.

At the other end of the corridor, Badger MacDonald turned the handle on the door to Roya's office. It opened a few inches and then slammed shut again, as two struggling bodies rammed against it from within.

Denis Pringle positioned himself immediately behind MacDonald and tapped him on the shoulder, the signal that he was ready to attack the room. MacDonald unclipped two more stun grenades.

THE SOLDIER ON the roof severed the rope, a single slash with the knife from his vest, as the Fijian staff sergeant swung back toward the flames. Tom Morell fell ten feet onto the balcony, landing hard on his shoulder. He stood up immediately. His leg was blistered and blackened up to the knee with third-degree burns, the boot partially melted into his foot. Morell felt no pain. Adrenaline is a powerful anesthetic. Resuming command, he beckoned to Tommy Palmer and Ginge Garmon, and plunged in through the burning window, determined to find a way out of it. The general office was now fully ablaze, the flaming curtains billowing out with the heat. All three men fired into the lock this time, to no avail. Women were screaming on the other side of the locked connecting door to the cipher room. The troopers climbed back out. As Palmer emerged for a second time, a strip of burning curtain detached and landed on his back, setting fire to his hood. Palmer tore off the hood, along with his mask, his neck badly scorched.

With all the movement outside the window, the longer rope, for abseiling down to the ground, if necessary, had become entangled. To

Sanford, it looked "like a ball of spaghetti." That contingency plan was out. The four men of Alpha One were trapped on the balcony.

Studying photographs of the embassy the previous night, Morell had spotted a narrow ledge, housing for a redundant sink pipe, running along part of the wall toward the left-hand window, that of the accountant's office; from there, a door led out onto the second-floor landing. This had briefly been considered as another entry point but then rejected as too dangerous: the gap between balcony and window was at least six yards; the tiny ledge might not be firm enough to bear a man's weight; the drop to the ground was at least fifty feet.

"Tommy, window!" yelled Morell, pointing to the left. Slinging his gun over his shoulder, Palmer climbed over the stone balustrade and began inching along the ledge. Reaching the windowsill, he looked in through the window. The curtains were not drawn. At the far end of the room, perhaps fifteen feet away, was a crouched man. Shaye had failed to shoot anyone on the balcony, and narrowly escaped being shot by a police sniper himself. He had rushed down two floors, and was now trying to start a fire, some sort of flaming brand in his hand. Palmer smashed the window with his gun butt, tossed in a stun grenade, fired a single burst, and vaulted in through the shattered glass and splintered wood. Tom Morell rolled in after him, followed by the others. Maskless, Palmer set off through the gas and smoke in pursuit of the retreating figure. On the landing, Shaye turned and fired a single, wild shot. Palmer aimed his gun and pressed the trigger. Nothing. The MP5 was jammed, or perhaps the magazine was empty. He pulled the trigger again. Only the sound of a firing pin hitting space.

Soldiers call this the "dead man's click."

19:26

In the telex room, Jassim emptied his jacket pockets of bullets, which rattled and bounced on the floor. Then he threw his machine gun at the window, but missed. The Skorpion bounced off a desk and landed by the wall. Vahid Khabaz picked it up and flung it out the window.

Despite a severely bruised leg where the bullet had hit the fifty-pence piece in his pocket, Abbas Fallahi climbed onto a desk and began waving a white pillowcase out the window. A tear-gas canister struck the doorman full in the chest, and he somersaulted back into the room. Fowzi dropped his Browning, threw himself to the floor, and crawled over to where the Iranians were huddled, removing the keffiyeh from around his neck and concealing it under his body. Morris noticed him "wriggling in among the hostages." Fowzi had a basic survival plan.

Makki stood immobile in the middle of the room, oblivious, it seemed, to the shouting, the explosions, and the gas.

Muhammad Faruqi sensed that the gunmen had intended to kill everyone in the room. "They didn't spare us for any moral reason, but for the simple reason that they felt cornered and confused. It was not lack of will, it was lack of morale." Merciless killers one second, in the next they lost heart.

Choking and gasping, eyes pouring, Ron Morris opened the door of the telex room as wide as it would go. If help was on the way, he wanted to welcome it. Inconspicuously, he picked up Makki's hand grenade from the floor and put it in the fireplace.

SIM HARRIS WAS ALONE, in a burning room.

The flaming curtains crackled and whirled in the heat. The hanging tapestry dividing the chargé's office from that of the ambassador (the SAS had believed, wrongly, that it was a solid wall) was ablaze. Suddenly part of the heavy curtain gave way and crashed to the floor in a cloud of sparks and acrid black smoke. Somewhere in the darkness on the other side, amid the ambassador's elegant mahogany furniture, crouched Abbas.

"I need to get out of this room and onto the balcony," thought Harris.

Flames crawled up the window frame, burning paint peeling off in strips, as he clambered out into the surreal evening sunshine and peered over the stone balustrade.

A policeman sheltering behind the front wall shouted: "Get down, get down, stay flat!"

Then another voice: "That's Harris, that's Harris. Don't move."

Harris dropped to his knees. The burning curtain billowed over his head as particles of scorching debris rained down, singeing his hair. "I am going to burn to death," he shouted. "I am burning to death."

"Stay flat. Stay where you are."

To his left, Harris could see the balcony outside Roya's office. It was just a few feet away, the embassy flagpole sticking out at an angle between the two balconies. He could jump that easily and get in through the next office, which, importantly, was not on fire.

"Can I go on to this other balcony?" he shouted.

"Just stay flat!"

Harris sensed that if he stood up and tried to jump, someone would shoot him.

A FEW FEET AWAY, in Roya's office, Lock had Towfiq pinned to the carpet, police revolver jammed under his chin, wondering whether to shoot him.

It would have been easy to do. Few could have blamed him. Some would have found credit in such a killing. But Lock's courage was not the violent variety. He was holding a gun, but he did not believe policemen should have them. He had never wanted this one.

"If I kill him," he thought, "I'd be doing it out of anger and hatred, and that's not the way I've been trained."

At that moment the door opened a few inches, and two objects clattered into the room. To Lock's eye, they looked like "two green lemons." Lock's first thought was these must be hand grenades rolled in by the gunmen. Then the L29s exploded with a blinding flash, sending CR gas spuming into the small room.

The force and noise of the blast bucked Lock sideways, and he relaxed his grip on Towfiq's neck. Suddenly he could not breathe. His eyes were "screaming in pain." But through the excruciating mist he could see Towfiq trying to crawl away, hand outstretched toward his submachine gun under the desk. Both were coughing and retching. Lock lunged forward and grabbed Towfiq's wrist, pulling it away from the gun.

The door burst open behind him, just as Towfiq tore his hand free.

"Trevor, move away!" yelled Tom MacDonald. "GET AWAY!"

Lock rolled to the right. Towfiq was upright now, submachine gun in his right hand, stretching out his left arm, as if to ward off the gunfire.

The first bullet entered Towfiq's right eye and the last, running in a diagonal line across his chest, struck him below the heart. Denis Pringle, standing behind MacDonald to his right, fired an almost simultaneous spray of five rounds into his head. Towfiq toppled into the fireplace. Pringle fired another burst.

Towfiq al-Rashidi, alias Salim, alias Oan, died from the impact of fifteen high-velocity parabellum bullets, fired from a distance of about three feet.

"There was no blood," Lock noticed. "Just holes."

THE MOMENT FOWZI left the women unguarded in the cipher room, Roya Kaghachi slammed the door to the corridor and locked it, just as she had done on the first day when she fled upstairs in terror. She pulled open the small window into the central shaft. A great gust of black smoke and dust billowed in, and she closed it quickly. Then she switched off the light.

The four women clutched each other, screaming, too terrified to move. They heard the windows smash next door in the general office, the blasts of the stun grenades, and then repeated bursts of machine-gun fire as the SAS tried, and failed, to blow out the door locks. Then came the ominous, swishing roar of a fire. Gas seeped in under the connecting door to the general office. One of the women suddenly rushed for the locked door. Roya held her back and gently coaxed her to rejoin the group. Another flash-bang exploded, very near this time. "In total darkness the women huddled, sobbing, in one corner." Nooshin Hashemenian buried her head in her hands.

Then came the sound of footsteps running in the corridor. The door handle turned and the door rattled against the lock, followed by a loud hammering, metal on wood.

"We are women in here," shouted Roya in English, and then in Farsi.

The others joined in: "Women. We are women!"

A heavy boot kicked open the door and a sharp light shone into their faces, a black figure framed in the doorway.

"Beeya paeen," he shouted. "Stay where you are."

Then the man was gone, closing the door behind him.

19:27

Hector Gullan had lost radio contact with the men on the first and second floors. He watched Tom Morell fall to the balcony and get back to his feet, and saw the men clamber across the ledge and in through the left-hand window of the second floor. Fire was pouring out of the general office. This was a deliberate conflagration, swifter and more intense than any fire started by a flash-bang. "It went up like an inferno," said an eyewitness. Gullan ordered his communications team to follow him downstairs to take up their secondary position immediately behind the embassy. If needed, they would go in with handguns.

Tear gas wafted through the open windows of the police intelligence cell at Number 24, bringing fits of choking and coughing. The police gas masks were brand new. No one had explained that the cardboard inner casing needed to be removed before strapping them on.

In Zulu Control, the sounds of battle resounded through the feed from the field telephone, abandoned by Towfiq on the first-floor landing and still live: explosions, gunfire, shouting, the soundtrack to the live footage of the assault and fire. Sim Harris could be seen on the front balcony, occasionally popping his head above the balustrade.

THE EXPLOSIONS AND gunfire had unsettled the pet gerbil in the basement of the Montessori nursery school; the animal, an officer noted, was now "in the middle of his play wheel, tearing round and round with a clatter."

DAVID MCNEE, the Metropolitan Police commissioner, standing immediately behind John Dellow in the forward control room, was also agitated. His mind turned to his own prospects: "The flames that burst from the windows made me think that my career might also be going up in smoke."

Michael Rose did not like what he was seeing and hearing, and, to make matters worse, he had no radio contact with Gullan. "It did not look good," he thought. "Smoke, fire, bangs, screams, barking dogs, shootings. It looked like chaos."

He glanced across at the man who had handed over control to the SAS. Dellow had fallen completely silent. The policeman stared down at his polished shoes. He seemed to be praying.

Ian Crooke, Rose's second operations officer, piped up. "Well, it may not look good, but I can tell you, our soldiers are well-trained, and they know what they're doing. And this thing will be a success." Crooke's proclamation was based on pure, unadulterated (and uninformed) optimism, and it did nothing to lift Dellow's spirits.

McNee saw the "sadness and disappointment" etched into Dellow's face. People were dying inside that building. His job had been to prevent bloodshed, rescue the hostages, and arrest the gunmen. To Dellow, the images and sounds emerging from Princes Gate were proof of failure.

TREVOR LOCK GASPED for air, his throat and lungs choked by the sudden inhalation of cyanocarbon. The firegas seemed to be boiling every inch of exposed skin. He could barely speak. "Six gunmen . . . ," he croaked.

Tom MacDonald hauled him over to the window. "Breathe!" he shouted.

Lock reached to open what had once been dubbed the talking window, and, as he touched it, the window suddenly vanished: "It just disintegrated. One moment it was there and the next it was gone, wood, glass, the lot." The blast from the stun grenades had loosened the frame, and the glass clattered into the street. Lock leaned out and gulped "the biggest lungful of fresh air" that he could get. Somehow, he had found his police cap and put it on.

The cameras were rolling. "He appeared with his regulation police-issue Smith & Wesson .38 revolver in his hand. He wiped his brow, adjusted his cap and then disappeared inside again," recorded *The Sunday Times*, calling this "the most dramatic television appearance of the decade."

MacDonald hauled the policeman back into the gas-filled room and bundled him onto the landing. "Room clear! PC confirms six gunmen!" he yelled, shoving Lock toward the stairs.

The first of the ground-floor team was nearing the first floor, when he saw a figure emerging from the smoke with a gun in his hand. He raised his MP5 and turned on his mounted flashlight. About to squeeze the trigger, he spotted the blue of Lock's uniform and lowered his gun.

MacDonald put out his hand for Lock's revolver and then escorted him downstairs.

"Mag check!" yelled Mel Parry, seconds before he too headed downstairs, calling for a flashlight.

DENIS PRINGLE CHECKED his weapon, changed magazines, and knelt by the door. For three or four seconds he was alone in the corridor and able to "take a breather." Then he remembered Sim Harris, and plunged back into the chargé's office. The room was on fire, thick with smoke. There was no sign of Harris. "I've killed him," thought Pringle. As he moved forward, the last of the burning tapestry collapsed. Something moved in the darkness beyond it, catching Pringle's eye. "Bloody hell," he thought. "Where do you come from?" This was supposed to be a solid wall, but a shape was moving in the swirling gloom, coming toward him. It was Abbas with his Browning in hand, possibly already wounded. "He was suffering from the gas," Pringle realized, and may not have seen the figure in black until too late. Pringle opened fire, a long, sustained burst. He was sure he had hit him. Abbas dropped the pistol and fell backward into the darkness. Pringle picked up the gun, put it in his pocket, and backed out. He did not spot Harris, still crouched on the balcony.

FOR THE FIRST time in history, breaking news was beaming live to the public from all three television stations simultaneously. What viewers witnessed looked like a catastrophe unfolding. Black-suited men had attacked from front and rear, but none had since emerged. The building was on fire, with no firefighters in sight. A terrified man squatted on the front balcony, flames billowing above him. A policeman had appeared at the next window, only to be pulled roughly back inside.

Something had been hurled from an upper window into the street, and a man in plain clothes had dashed forward to retrieve it.

"A minute ago on the second floor, there was a signal with a white handkerchief being waved," Kate Adie reported. Now that too had vanished.

Some reporters, inevitably, were tempted into speculation. John le Carré heard the ITN commentator risking "a disaster theory, a theory of total and ignominious failure":

> The "police," or whoever they were, had mounted an attack,
> the terrorists had rumbled it and blown themselves and their
> hostages to kingdom come. The sight of flames pouring from
> the building, the atmosphere of total confusion, the meaningless
> fumbling on the balcony, the bitty soundtrack with its screams
> and moans, its recriminations, its untraceable *putt-putting* and
> eerie jagged silences . . . all these fed our worst apprehensions
> that we were watching a debacle of tragic dimensions.

The country was agog.

TREVOR LOCK WAS flying downstairs. The SAS men lining the stairs and forming a chain to the back door did not so much pass him as hurl him down and out. "They picked me up, elbows and armpits, and carried me, two men to two men." Hefty Trevor Lock had never felt so light, or so lightheaded.

"Thank you," he said to each soldier who hoisted him on. "Thank you. Thank you!"

Suddenly he was standing on the back lawn of the embassy.

HECTOR GULLAN SAW him emerge, blinking, onto the terrace. Lock had been held hostage for nearly a week, survived a death struggle with a terrorist, and then been comprehensively gassed by one of the nastiest substances devised by man. To Gullan's immense surprise, he seemed "fit and composed." MacDonald handed over Lock's gun.

"PC Lock is alive and well," said Gullan into the radio. "He is a great credit to the Metropolitan Police."

———

WHEN DE LA BILLIÈRE repeated those words, a collective sigh of relief ran round the Cobra meeting room. Applause broke out.

THE ORDERS WERE to restrain every civilian emerging from the embassy ("gazelles," in police parlance) until formally identified. An exception was made for Lock, who was led away to a waiting van of the police Special Patrol Group.

Lock knew all about the SPG, "our heavy mob," as he put it, and he assumed that the men in black who had just rescued him must be members of that elite, heavy-handed, and highly controversial unit.

"That operation was absolutely fantastic," he congratulated the driver. "If anyone ever says anything derogatory about the SPG to me again, I'm going to put them right."

Lock might be a hero, but he was still just a copper.

The van driver glanced at him sourly. "That wasn't us, you wanker," he said. "That was the SAS."

19:28

Shaye burst into the telex room, Tommy Palmer a few paces behind him. Obedient to the last, he called out to Jassim in Arabic: "*Hamleh kardand!*" They attacked!

Palmer stood maskless in the doorway, his melted hood and balaclava removed. This was the only SAS face any hostage or gunman ever saw clearly. Palmer had dropped the jammed MP5 and now had his 9mm pistol in his hand. The man he had chased down the corridor was standing in the center of the room, his head half turned away as he shouted to Jassim. Shaye was holding something in his hand—Palmer thought it was a grenade and he was "moving as if to detonate it." Palmer fired a single round, from about three yards. The bullet entered Shaye's skull beneath the left ear, and emerged from the right temple. Palmer leaned over to check he was dead, and then took in the scene around him.

"Don't move! Don't move!" he shouted.

One man lay dead under the desk. Another was badly wounded, his jersey soaked with blood, though still alive. Everyone was screaming. Abbas Fallahi had climbed back onto the desk and was waving a strip of telex paper out of the window.

"Are there any terrorists in here?" yelled Palmer. "Which are the terrorists?"

"British! British! British!" shouted Ron Morris. "I am British."

Palmer pushed him down onto the floor.

Gholam-Ali Afrouz, terrified he might be mistaken for a gunman, had taken out his diplomatic pass and was waving it in the air. "Diplomat! Diplomat!"

Palmer pointed his gun at Afrouz. "Which are the terrorists?" he shouted again.

Afrouz pointed to Jassim and Makki, backed up against the wall by the door.

"Students! Students!" they shouted.

THE POLICE ON the street below had by now gathered four weapons: Jassim's submachine gun, two Browning pistols, and the .38 Astra revolver. A second submachine gun was lying by Towfiq's body on the first floor, along with his hand grenade. Abbas's Browning was now in Denis Pringle's pocket. Of the other grenades, one was in the grate where Ron Morris had hidden it, one was lying on the front balcony below, one was behind the door of the telex room, and one was under the desk, beside Shaye's body.

The only weapon still in the hands of the gunmen was the last remaining hand grenade, in Jassim's pocket.

FOR SIM HARRIS, in his own words, "things were getting pretty dodgy."

The window frame above him was burning fiercely, with fragments of flaming wood dropping onto the balcony where he squatted. Sparks scorched the back of his neck. The heat was intense, but worse was the noise, a great sucking rush of oxygen into the chargé's office. Black smoke curled out over his head. His jacket was smoldering, the diary stowed in the inside pocket. Harris could feel the sweat running down his forehead.

JOHN MCALEESE CLEARED the vomit from inside his mask and re-attached his respirator. Leaning out of Roya's office, through the smears he saw Sim Harris cowering on the neighboring balcony.

"Come over here, mate!" shouted McAleese, beckoning with a gloved hand.

Harris put one foot up on the balustrade, pushed himself off, and leaped over the embassy flagpole like a hurdler. McAleese caught him on the other side and dragged him in through the remains of the talking window. Harris scrambled over Roya's steel desk and typewriter, and bolted out onto the first-floor landing.

He did not notice the dead body, wearing red-and-white sneakers, sprawled in the fireplace.

TOM MORELL REACHED the telex room one minute behind Tommy Palmer and Ginge Garmon.

"They were like Martians," recalled Abbas Fallahi, of the men in black bursting in. "They frightened the life out of us."

Morell had stopped to attend to the women, and then cleared away a barricade of chairs and paper outside the general office. He was breathing hard and starting to feel lightheaded. His badly burned leg was still not painful exactly, but the adrenaline was wearing off.

Morell could see Garmon in one corner, attempting to revive Ali Samadzadeh with mouth-to-mouth resuscitation. Palmer was pressing a field dressing to the wound in Ahmad Dadgar's chest. The other Iranians huddled in the middle of the room, Shaye's body sprawled alongside them. Everyone was shouting. A stout man in blue-checkered trousers crawled toward Morell, waving some sort of card, blood running down the lower part of his face.

"British!" shouted the dark-haired man by the door, wearing a tie.

Morell pushed Ron Morris out into the corridor, just as Paul Sanford entered.

Two men huddled together against the left-hand wall, almost hidden behind the door.

"Who are you?" barked Morell, in English.

"Students!" they said in unison, getting unsteadily to their feet.

Morell did not believe them.

Seizing the taller man by the collar of his green combat jacket, Morell threw him out of the door. "Terrorist!" Morell shouted. In the noise and confusion, no one heard him.

At the same time, Sanford tackled Makki. "We were toe-to-toe," Sanford said, "and too close for me to bring my MP5 to bear and too close to pull my secondary weapon, a 9mm strapped to my leg holster." Instead, Sanford "grabbed him by both arms and wrestled him to the ground."

"Search him," ordered Morell.

The radio network was up again. Alpha One radioed Sunray: "Room cleared, Yankee down, Yankee injured, one X-ray dead."

19:29

The men clearing the upper rooms reached the second floor and formed a line down the stairs and along the landings to pass the hostages out. The women, some barefoot, faces shocked and eyes streaming, were led from the cipher room. Smoke and gas billowed up from below in a thick fog. Organized confusion reigned as hostages streamed onto the landing and into the arms of the soldiers, who began tossing them downstairs, as one put it, "like rugby balls," the women first.

Sim Harris had just emerged from Roya's office when the first of the freed hostages reached the first-floor landing. He was immediately pulled into the human chain. "They literally threw us down the stairs, just threw us from one man to the next, shouting 'Keep moving, get out, get out!'" Even the walking wounded, like Abbas Fallahi, were unceremoniously bundled down. Everyone retched and coughed, tripping and stumbling in the half darkness. As the hostages passed, some of the gas-masked soldiers clamped hands over their faces to try to limit the inhalation of CR fumes.

Harris saw the switchboard operator, Shirazeh Boroumand, "wrenched from one soldier to another, screaming with pain as her neck was pulled out of joint."

Harris was among the first into the daylight, liberated but not yet free. "We were thrown out of the building onto a patio at the back and then down some steps and onto a lawn, where we were thrown face-first onto the floor and really roughly tied up with plastic tie straps." The women found themselves expertly tipped over and placed face down. The men doing the tipping were wearing plain clothes, and most were members of the Feltham Police Wrestling Team, brought in for the purpose of flipping people onto their faces.

Harris found Nooshin Hashemenian hog-tied beside him, cheek to the grass. "That was fantastic," she said, through tears. "That was marvelous."

Harris was crying too. "I think you have just been rescued by one of the finest anti-terrorist squads in the world."

A man with a clipboard appeared, wearing scruffy jeans and a Levi's sweatshirt, accompanied by a Farsi interpreter.

"Are there any terrorists among this group?" he asked Roya.

At that moment Fowzi Nejad emerged onto the lawn and lay face down next to the four women.

"No," said Roya.

THE NEWS COMING into Whitehall from Zulu Control changed, in seconds, from calamitous to almost hopeful. Peter de la Billière had re-layed each development, for better or worse, in a single staccato bullet point:

"The assault is going ahead."

"At least one hostage is dead."

"The majority are alive."

"The terrorists don't seem to be doing too well."

"The building is on fire."

"Hostages are on the lawn . . ."

The situation remained confusing. Even after the hostages began to appear at the back, it was not clear how many had survived. Some were injured. It was hard to decipher what de la Billière called the "cacophony of shouting and shots" still coming through on the live microphone. Michael Rose clattered down the stairs of the Montessori nursery school and out the back door, to see for himself what was happening on the embassy lawn.

———

THE SYRIAN AMBASSADOR, who was plainly not watching the television, chose this moment to call the Foreign Office with another suggestion for resolving the situation. He was put through to David Tatham of the Foreign Office in the Cobra meeting room.

"Ambassador, it's too late," said Tatham. "The army has gone in. Listen!" He held the mouthpiece to the speaker. "Shots and screams. The conversation was over."

DELLOW WAS STILL deeply worried.

Only two gunmen had been reported killed. Which meant that four must still be inside.

AS THE LIBERATED hostages streamed down the staircase, Mel Parry ran back up it, now accompanied by two men from the Bravo One ground-floor unit with flashlights mounted on machine guns: Ben Canon, the sledgehammer wielder, and his team leader, Rob Timson.

Denis Pringle knelt outside the door to the ambassador's office. "There's a shot terrorist in there," he said, pointing into the darkness. "I'm not going in alone. These lads have got grenades."

The four men formed up on the landing, checked weapons, and then, on Parry's signal, burst into the office and fanned out: Parry in the center with Pringle on his left, and the flashlight men, Canon and Timson, to his right. The room swirled with smoke and gas. Fires from the flash-bangs dotted the rug. They inched forward, flashlight beams scanning the room between floor and eye level. Even with lights, they could barely see six feet in front of themselves.

Timson heard a gentle rattle to the right and swung his flashlight toward the sound. Canon's light followed instantly. The beams crossed to find Abbas on his back on a chaise longue, "half lying, half sitting." He might almost have been resting, or asleep. Bullets were tumbling from a box in his jacket pocket with a metallic clatter, one by one, onto the floor. His left arm lay across his chest. His right arm was raised, clutching a pistol. Parry saw "some movement with his hand."

All four men fired simultaneously, controlled bursts at a range of around three yards. The postmortem found twenty-one bullets in Abbas, including two direct to the heart.

Parry tore down the curtains and pulled open the shutters, flooding the room with evening sunlight.

The body of the gunman lay quite still on the ambassador's velvet sofa. Bullets still dripped from his pocket onto the floor. His weapon lay where he dropped it on the Persian rug. Police investigators later found it was a Diana .177 air pistol, for shooting rats.

"This man had an air pistol in his hand," the coroner concluded. "A toy that looks very much like a Browning."

Abbas Maytham, the pockmarked youth nicknamed Ugly, died brandishing one of Ron Morris's harmless toys.

19:30

Fire gripped the building from both sides. The television coverage was now intercutting dramatic scenes of the initial assault with live reporting from the street.

Word of Trevor Lock's escape reached the press, and the reporting took on a new tone. "The tragedy became triumph," wrote John le Carré.

A police car was dispatched to Warley Avenue to collect Doreen Lock and bring her to Scotland Yard.

BACK IN HEREFORD, the SAS wives watched with excitement, recognition, and apprehension.

"So that's where the bugger is," thought Gail Parry.

"That's Dad!" squealed the Parrys' toddler daughter as the figures in black blasted their way into the embassy front window.

"How do you know?" asked her mother.

"He's not wearing any socks."

THE ONLY HOSTAGES left in the telex room were the two most seriously injured, Ahmad Dadgar and Gholam-Ali Afrouz. Ali Samadzadeh was beyond help. Ginge Garmon reattached his gas mask, his mouth now smeared with the dead man's blood, and turned his attention to Dadgar. The medical assistant had lost a lot of blood and was now only half-conscious. Tommy Palmer and Garmon tried to chair-lift him, by placing linked hands under his backside and hauling him out, but this was proving "too much hassle." Time was running out, Palmer realized. "The place was on fire."

Paul Sanford set about frisking the remaining gunman, while Tom Morell stood over him, machine gun leveled.

"Are you a terrorist?" shouted Morell in Arabic.

Makki did not answer. He was, Morell recalled, "not quite face down, but on his left, twisted round, looking over his right shoulder."

Sanford knelt by his head and repeated the question, this time in English. Makki stared up at him, "left cheek to the floor, looking up out of his right eye."

"Lie still," shouted Sanford, placing him in the letter T position, with arms outstretched. He began to pat him down, starting at his neck. "Don't move!"

Sanford then parted Makki's legs, checking for a concealed weapon.

Morell immediately spotted, just below Makki's crotch, what he took to be the yellow holster of an automatic pistol. Sanford glimpsed the same object, which he identified as "a magazine for an automatic pistol and a light-colored magazine holster."

At the same moment, Makki "pulled his arms in toward his body as if to reach for something underneath his stomach."

Sanford's first thought was "Grenade!" and he lurched backward.

Morell also saw Makki move "his hand up beneath his body" and came to the same instantaneous conclusion: "I thought he was going for a weapon."

Morell emptied his machine gun, a burst of five rounds, into the small of Makki's back. "Changing mag!" he shouted as the wounded gunman rolled onto his right side.

The bullets had passed so near Sanford's arm that he could feel the pressure waves. "Fucking hell, that was close," he said.

Makki's hand was still moving when Sanford fired a second burst into his chest.

No gun or grenade was found near Makki's body, and nothing resembling a holster. None of the gunmen had possessed such a thing. An empty magazine lay nearby, probably discarded by Jassim.

Investigators did, however, find a crushed yellow packet of biscuits.

Amid the swirling smoke and gas, the soldiers "might have mistaken those biscuits for some sort of holster," the coroner decided.

Afrouz limped painfully to the staircase, where the human chain was waiting to throw him down it. Palmer and Sanford hoisted the unconscious Dadgar and "carried him bodily between them," stepping over the bodies.

Tom Morell was the last person to leave the blood-spattered telex room. He reloaded his machine gun and checked that Makki was dead.

Suddenly he began seeing double. His leg buckled.

Morell staggered forward and clutched the doorframe for support.

19:31

"Hostages out on black!" Gullan shouted into the radio.

The once-elegant entranceway to the embassy was a gloomy, reeking mess of smoking debris, spent gas canisters, and rubble. A huge chandelier lay, smashed, in the center of the vestibule, the crystal droplets catching the light of the flashlight beams. Miraculously, a gold Persian urn in a glass case stood untouched. A single high-heeled woman's boot lay at the foot of the stairs. The fleeing hostages "fell from one set of arms to another, tumbling down the stairs through the black smoke" and then on, crunching through broken glass, to the back door.

"Run, run, run!" the SAS shouted. "Go, go. Out. Get out."

In the rough manhandling, one woman's blouse had been torn, provoking lewd remarks from some of the rescuers.

Each new arrival on the lawn was flattened by a member of the Feltham Police Wrestling Team.

The SAS evacuation process was so swift and sudden, many could not even remember their flight from the second floor to the outside.

"I came to on the lawns," said Abbas Fallahi. "Lying down, with a policeman standing over me telling me to breathe into the lawn."

Ron Morris did not even see his assailant coming before he was up-ended. "My hands were grabbed, pulled behind me, and then a plastic strap was placed around my wrists and pulled tight."

He lay with his face in the grass, inhaling the warm scent of the earth—but not for long.

Someone grabbed his hair and yanked up his head.

"Oh, you're Morris," said a voice from behind a gas mask.

"How the hell do you know that?"

"We know everybody in here," said the voice. "We've been studying your photographs for a week. Inside out, back to front. We know who you are. You feeling all right, Ron?"

"Yes, thanks very much," said Morris.

His face was dropped back into the sweet-smelling grass.

"Well," he thought. "So that's the end of that."

AMONG THE LAST group of hostages making their way down the stairs was a tall man with an Afro hairstyle and cowboy boots. Jassim had put up the collar of his green combat jacket to cover the lower part of his face. He avoided eye contact with every soldier who grabbed him and passed him along to the next. In the chaos, he had lingered on the sec-ond floor, and then joined near the end of the evacuation line, stooping low. He leaned over the banister of the half landing and looked down into the hall, where half a dozen SAS troopers stood waiting amid the debris.

It is very hard not to stand out when trying to be unobtrusive.

Several soldiers simultaneously spotted the gunman known as Faisal.

Tom MacDonald caught a glimpse of the distinctive drooping mus-tache from the first-floor landing. "I knew that I had seen him. And, for a second or so, I couldn't remember where I had seen him from." Then he recalled the face on the rogues' gallery wall. "That man is a terror-ist!" he yelled.

Mel Parry was on the half landing, passing the hostages along the chain, when he realized the man he had hold of was a possible terror-ist. Parry's mask had misted up, and he could not see the face clearly. "I immediately pushed him down the stairs to the soldier below me and shouted, 'Terrorist!'"

A voice from the upper floor yelled: "He's got a grenade!"

The cry was taken up further down the chain.

"There's one of the fuckers there," said John McAleese, pointing directly at Jassim, who now seemed to be "crouched, [as if] trying to protect his genitals."

Two soldiers clearly spotted the grenade in his hand.

Unable to get a clear shot, Pete Winner, the soldier halfway up the first flight, swung the butt of his machine gun with maximum force into Jassim's head as he passed and sent him flying down into the hallway.

Jassim was now sprawled on the marble floor.

"Terrorist! Grenade!" someone shouted.

Four men opened fire simultaneously, in a long, unbroken, deafening volley.

The grenade was lying on the fourth stair. The pin was still in it.

A postmortem examination found thirty-nine bullet wounds, and head wounds consistent with a blow from a rifle butt. "This man was really peppered," said the coroner.

Jassim died a few feet from the spot where he had murdered Abbas Lavasani.

19:32

Ahmad Dadgar was carried out by Tommy Palmer and Ginge Garmon, placed on a stretcher, and rushed to the waiting ambulance. Tom Morell was next out, barely able to stand. He was stretchered to the horse trailer at the front of the building, where a four-man SAS medical team cut away his charred clothing, applied burn dressings, and injected him with enough morphine to stun a pony. An SAS sergeant accompanied the wounded man into the trailer, bagged up his guns, and slipped away. Morell regained consciousness in a private room at St. Stephen's, wearing blue pajamas, with two drips in his arm. He could no longer feel his leg.

EVERY FLOOR HAD been cleared, the last hostage removed, and yet a gun battle still seemed to be raging inside the building. Colonel Michael Rose dispatched one of the troop commanders back into the embassy to find out what was going on. Hector Gullan and Colin "Clutchplate" Clapton followed, to gather some facts and figures for the politicians in Cobra. They did not linger long.

The intensity of the fire had turned the central void into a chimney. Paper, plastic fragments, and even shards of broken furniture swirled up through the middle of the building, borne on the ferocious upward draft of the inferno. The crackle of gunfire was caused by live rounds cooking off in the heat.

Word ran back up the line of troopers on the stairs: "Everybody out. The building is burning."

"THE SKY. THE SKY. I can see the sky," exclaimed Ali Tabatabai as he was ushered onto the lawn. "Thanks be to God."

Dogs were barking.

"How many gazelles are there?" someone shouted. Fifteen people were laid out on the grass, coughing and gasping.

"Who are the guys who rescued us?" Sim Harris asked the knees of a uniformed policeman. "Were they police or what?"

"Never mind who they are. You are out."

"Is Trevor out?"

"Yes, Trevor is fine. He's gone off with the police already . . ."

Moving from one prone hostage to the next, the clipboard organizer came to a young, dark-haired man wearing light-colored chinos and a jacket, lying among the four women. His wrists were securely cuffed, his face buried in the turf.

"What is your name?" he asked, pen poised. "Do you speak English?"

"Student," the man croaked, eyes streaming. "I am student."

A shout came from an upper window in Kingston House. One of the snipers was gesticulating and pointing at the man.

Harris turned his head to the other side and spotted Fowzi.

"He's one of them!" screamed Harris, forcing his face off the grass and craning his neck round. "He's one of the terrorists!"

The man with the clipboard ran over to Harris. "Are you sure? Are you positive he's one of the terrorists?"

"He's a terrorist, there's no doubt."

"You're Harris?"

"Yes," Harris exclaimed. "He's definitely one of them."

By now, two SAS men in black were standing almost on top of the last surviving gunman.

"Is he a terrorist or hostage?" one of them shouted at the nearest woman.

"Don't hurt him!" she screamed. This was almost certainly Shirazeh Boroumand, the secretary who had befriended Fowzi Nejad during the long nights of incarceration. "Don't hurt him. He's a nice boy."

According to witnesses, Roya and Nooshin shuffled over on their knees to surround Fowzi, forming a human shield. Despite his bound hands, Fowzi "clawed at the girl's sleeve and gripped tight."

"He's a terrorist," Harris shouted again.

Another SAS man leaned over the woman "and screamed into her face." "Is he a terrorist or hostage?"

"Don't hurt him," she sobbed. "Please don't hurt him."

Roya joined in: "Don't hurt him . . . He's my brother!"

Harris watched as the two SAS men seized Fowzi, "ripping his bound hands from the girl's shoulder," and bodily lifted him off the ground. "He was screaming with fright. Next to him, the girl was still sobbing."

As Fowzi was being dragged back in, John McAleese heard a woman hostage shouting, "No, no, please don't, he was really good to us . . ."

What happened next is still a source of uncertainty, and dispute.

19:33

Alan Parker, a police photographer, was snapping pictures from the kitchen of one of the flats in Kingston House, sitting on the drainboard with his feet in the butler's sink. He later claimed to have overheard the conversation between the two SAS men as they grabbed Fowzi Nejad.

"This bloke is one of the terrorists masquerading as a hostage; he's been identified by some of the others."

"Let's take the bastard back inside and shoot him, then."

Parker was at least thirty yards away and the SAS men were wearing gas masks, but he nonetheless claimed to have heard every word.

According to Parker, at this moment one of the men looked up, saw they were being observed, and pointed.

"We can't—he's already been photographed by that bloke at the window up there."

Parker was in no doubt that the SAS men intended to pull Fowzi back into the burning building and kill him. The women certainly thought his life was in imminent danger.

"The SAS picked me up and were going to take me back inside when the women and the other hostages stopped them," he said.

Senior SAS officers at the scene emphatically reject this version of events, insisting that the killing of a suspect, once disarmed and identified, could not and would not have been considered, let alone attempted. Michael Rose claims that in the final briefing to the assault team, he had said, "It would be helpful if at least one terrorist wasn't killed . . . because then we could interrogate them about what the whole thing had been about." No one else recalls the commanding officer saying this.

Tom MacDonald, by contrast, firmly believed that Margaret Thatcher wanted all the gunmen eliminated: "The message was that we had to resolve the situation and there was to be no chance of failure . . . The prime minister didn't want an ongoing problem beyond the embassy, which we took to mean that they didn't want anybody coming out alive. No surviving terrorists."

That standpoint was supported by John McAleese: "They're not going in there to take prisoners. You go in there, you see them, you're going to shoot them. And if you shoot them, you better kill them. Remember, a wounded animal is always more dangerous than a dead one."

Another SAS eyewitness told the BBC, "One of my team actually goes across and picks this guy up to separate him from the group and starts walking back toward the building with him . . . We weren't quite sure where he was taking him."

Pete Winner, the trooper who had clubbed Jassim down the staircase, said, "We were not part of society in that moment of time. We had created our own society within Number 16. Law of the jungle. Kill or be killed."

There is no conclusive evidence to support one or another of these diametrically opposed perspectives.

The police were also uncertain how to interpret those fleeting moments when Fowzi was identified as a gunman. Michael Colacicco, an anti-terrorist officer in the intel cell, debriefed some of the SAS afterward. They too described Fowzi being dragged away: "Whether it was to take him back in to finish him, or into custody, you'll never really know."

Whether or not there was ever any desire, intention, or attempt made by the SAS men to kill the last gunman, this much is certain: they did not do so.

The Ladies' Man was now unceremoniously seized by four SAS men and carted off, upside down, to be handed over to the police Special Patrol Group waiting behind the Ethiopian Embassy.

Never more than a dupe in a grim plot he did not understand, Fowzi Nejad had never mistreated the hostages. He tried to back out when it was already too late. He was naïve, amiable, and good-looking. He was also astonishingly lucky.

Ron Morris saw Fowzi being led away and went over to shake his hand. "Good luck, mate," he said. "Take care of yourself."

PETER DE LA BILLIÈRE removed the headphones and entered the Cobra meeting room. "Home Secretary," he said, addressing William Whitelaw, "I'm very pleased to be able to tell you that the assault has been largely successful. Some soldiers have been injured but not seriously. One more hostage has been killed, and others may be hurt. But five of the terrorists are dead, and the sixth has been captured."

The room erupted. "Tension snapped. Papers flew in the air. Everyone leaped up, shouting and laughing. A roar of talk broke out."

Whitelaw put a call through to Mrs. Thatcher, who was pulling up outside the Cabinet Office in her car, and passed on the "thrilling news" that "the SAS operation had been a complete and dramatic success, [which] said much for their professional skill and courage." Thatcher "breathed a sigh of relief" and headed for the Cobra meeting room. This was a deliberate understatement: a different outcome might have sunk her premiership before it was a year old, and she knew it.

Whitelaw could sense from her tone of voice just how anxious she had been for the preceding half hour. "I was struck," he said, "by the immense burden of responsibility imposed on a prime minister . . . I was the minister directly in charge, but she had to bear the ultimate responsibility."

Alcohol magically appeared from some bottom drawer in the Cabinet Office. "The Prime Minister and whiskey appeared almost simultaneously," observed Douglas Hurd. Glasses were filled, clinked, and drained.

The home secretary summoned his driver, and soon Whitelaw and de la Billière were hurtling toward Princes Gate, preceded by motorcycle outriders cutting a path through the light evening traffic.

FOUR FIRE ENGINES had been waiting a few streets away for the all-clear. Now they screeched into Princes Gate, and torrents of water were soon pouring into the embassy through the flaming windows, front and back. The freed hostages were hauled to their feet, escorted out the side gate to the gardens, and led onto a road lined with ambulances. After a final check by the man with the clipboard, their plasti-cuffs were each removed with a pair of scissors, and the convoy set off, sirens screeching, for St. Stephen's, where Ahmad Dadgar was already in the intensive care unit undergoing emergency surgery for multiple gunshot wounds. As they were being unloaded outside the hospital, Sim Harris waved cheerily to his BBC colleagues behind the waiting cameras.

THE NEWS RAN on a loop, increasingly celebratory in pitch. The British press was about to go entirely over the top, gripped by a rare but intense wave of national euphoria.

FOWZI NEJAD WAS driven to Paddington police station, handcuffed to two large SPG policemen, and accompanied by Mrs. Shadloi, the Arabic interpreter. "Will they kill me?" he asked her repeatedly. "Are they going to hang me?"

IN THE POLICE negotiating room at the top of the Montessori nursery school, Max Vernon found tears running down his face. "I was devastated. My biggest emotion was that I'd failed. Despite six days of negotiating, we hadn't had a peaceful end to the siege. Policemen don't cry, but I've got news for you."

JOHN DELLOW JOINED Michael Rose at the back of the building, to await the arrival of the home secretary. The fire was quickly brought under control. Dozens of policemen milled around, watching the fire hoses play against the charred facades of the embassy.

As the SAS climbed into the waiting vans, one of the soldiers paused and turned to the nearest policeman. "What happened in the snooker?"

Nine minutes earlier, Cliff Thorburn had sunk the pink ball with a fifty-one-point break to win the world title, a moment in sporting history watched on live television by nobody at all.

THE OPERATION ENDED officially at 19:34, and authority was transferred back from the SAS to the police, returning control from the military to the civilian powers. What William Whitelaw called "the twilight area between peace and war" was over, and the sun was starting to set over Princes Gate.

The SAS slipped away.

The home secretary appeared at Zulu Control at 19:54. Prince Andrew arrived one minute later.

Operation Nimrod had lasted just eleven minutes.

MARGARET THATCHER ATTENDED many functions and receptions in her capacity as prime minister, but she had never been to anything quite like the party that erupted at Regent's Park Barracks that evening.

Mrs. Thatcher arrived at 20:37, accompanied by Willie Whitelaw and her husband, Denis, to find the SAS in full victory celebration, already several cases into a stack of lukewarm Foster's lager, still wearing combat gear, faces streaked black, reeking of gas and smoke, shouting, laughing, singing. Each weapon that had been fired was handed over, to be bagged and tagged for the anti-terrorist police forensics unit. Amid the post-assault euphoria, gathering statements was impossible.

"Most of them appeared to have slightly ginger hair and ginger mustaches and bottles of beer in their hand," said Richard Hastie-Smith, the Cabinet Office official in charge of Cobra. "The state of excitement was something I've never seen in my life before. They were like a pack of hounds. The air was thick with testosterone."

Thatcher moved among them, oddly at ease among adrenalized men of war. Michael Rose introduced her to Tommy Palmer, his burned neck heavily bandaged. Apart from Palmer and Tom Morell, the only other SAS soldier injured that day was a trooper who had shot off the end of his own index finger with one of the shorter MP5s.

Hector Gullan scribbled some last laconic diary notes: "Superb work by Sqn [squadron]. Prime Minister saw us. Sqn party Sgts mess. Telephone and telegrams coming in. Only now beginning to realize exactly what we did. Parents over the moon!"

The low casualty rate was miraculous, Rose conceded.

Denis Thatcher fell into conversation with Tom MacDonald. "You let one of the bastards live," he shouted above the din, with a big grin.

In another corner of the packed room stood Janet Dillon, only now grasping the scale of the operation she had very nearly taken part in.

Whitelaw, nicknamed "Old Oyster Eyes," had tears running down his cheeks. As she posed for photographs with men in balaclavas holding guns, Thatcher also seemed tearful. But perhaps it was just the residual tear gas.

Just before 21:00, someone turned on a large television, and the men settled down to watch themselves for the first time. The news opened with a figure in black clambering across a balcony to plant explosives. At that moment someone with bouffant hair obscured the screen.

"Oi, fucking sit down at the front," shouted John McAleese, who wanted a clear view of his moment of anonymous fame.

The person with big hair obediently ducked out of the way.

No one ever spoke to Mrs. Thatcher that way. But who dares, wins.

AFTERMATH

At 03:00, on May 6, John Dellow formally closed down Zulu Control and brought the siege to an end, six days, fifteen hours, and thirty minutes after it had started.

Britain emerged from that tumultuous week a different place. The embassy siege changed the way the world saw the SAS, Margaret Thatcher, and terrorism. It also altered the way Britain perceived itself. The siege would come to be seen as a watershed moment, seared into public memory as permanently as JFK's assassination or the moon landings.

The British media celebrated the dramatic ending of the standoff in a paroxysm of patriotic fervor: VICTORY, trumpeted the headlines, PROUD TO BE BRITISH. Queen Elizabeth expressed "gratitude and relief" at the outcome. The episode cemented **Margaret Thatcher**'s reputation as an iron-willed leader, uncompromising and decisive, and her popularity rocketed. "Wherever I went," she said, "I sensed a great wave of pride . . . Telegrams of congratulation poured in from abroad: we had sent a signal to terrorists everywhere that they could expect no deals and could extort no favors from Britain." For several years, whenever her actions were particularly bold, newspaper cartoonists depicted Mrs. Thatcher abseiling down a burning building in combat gear.

"It was a triumph," declared John le Carré as politicians scrambled to extract every ounce of advantage from the moment. "That was the word everywhere. Not victory but triumph . . . It was a police triumph, it was Mr. Whitelaw's triumph, it was a triumph for Conservatism and

Mrs. Thatcher and foreign policy and domestic policy and fiscal policy and for the sunny spring of Mrs. Thatcher's new Britain." He summed up the national mood: "The Ayatollah may hate our guts and imprison our friends, but we are still ready to risk our necks to kill his enemies and spare him twenty of his faithful." The SAS was now "Mrs. Thatcher's Army." She sent them into war two years later to fight Argentina in the Falkland Islands, a battle some saw as an extension of the gung-ho spirit she had shown over the embassy siege.

With a hint of one-upmanship, Thatcher promised to turn "this superb operation in Britain to the best advantage for the Americans held hostage in Tehran." The Iranian government thanked Britain for liberating its diplomats, but flatly refused to release the U.S. hostages held in Tehran. In vain, Jimmy Carter pointed to "the difference in the responsibility assumed by the British government in protecting the Embassy of Iran compared with the Iranian condoning of the terrorist attack on our embassy." The remaining fifty-two captives inside the U.S. Embassy would not be liberated until January 20, 1981, minutes after Ronald Reagan was sworn in as president.

Tehran hailed the death of **Seyyed Abbas Lavasani** as an act of religious self-sacrifice. "He wanted to be a martyr for Islam. We are happy his wish was granted," said a government spokesman. "We do not mourn his death." Lavasani's body was flown back to Iran for burial, along with that of **Ali Samadzadeh**. Lavasani was buried in Behesht-e Zahra cemetery; Khomeini's mausoleum would later be built next to his grave. **Sadegh Ghotbzadeh** learned the hard way that revolutionary dictatorships have a way of consuming themselves: he was ousted as Iran's foreign minister four months after the siege, and then arrested on charges of plotting to kill Ayatollah Khomeini by conspiring with Israel, the Pahlavi regime, and the CIA. Tortured into a confession, he was sentenced to death by the military revolutionary tribunal and shot by firing squad in Evin Prison on September 15, 1982. A decade afterward, a Soviet defector revealed that Ghotbzadeh had been framed by the KGB.

The attack on the embassy was a cynical attempt by Saddam Hussein to destabilize neighboring Iran. The Iran-Iraq War erupted five months later. The opening shots of that brutal eight-year conflict, in which more than one million soldiers perished, were fired in London.

There is a direct historical link between the events in Kensington in the spring of 1980, the two Gulf Wars that followed, and the 9/11 attacks that took place in the United States in 2001. The cause for which the five Iranian Arabs died remains as obscure and unfulfilled today as it was in 1980. Iran's theocracy retains its ruthless grip on power.

In the days and weeks that followed the siege, an enormous washing-up operation got under way at Number 16 Princes Gate: taking away forensic evidence, dismantling the intel cells, winding up the telephone and CCTV cables, photographing the wreckage, extracting eavesdropping devices, recovering weaponry and ammunition, carrying out the bodies. One of the last soldiers to leave remembered a cupboard he had opened, on a whim, in the attics: "There were shelves of stunning Victorian clocks, just jam-packed. They must have been very expensive. Everything's burning down. I'm still in all my gear, and I go running up the stairs to see if I could save any of the clocks. But I couldn't get to the top of the staircase for the flames slapping down." The hostages could be saved but not the shah's clock collection. An engraved metal plaque reading THE ISLAMIC REPUBLIC OF IRAN appeared overnight in the Valhalla Bar at SAS headquarters in Hereford; eventually, just as mysteriously, it was returned. For more than a decade, the embassy stood empty and smoke-blackened, while Britain and Iran wrangled over who should pay for the damage. The Iranian Embassy formally reopened in 1993 after a £5 million refit. Britain contributed £1.8 million; in return Iran paid for damage to the British Embassy in Tehran sustained during the Revolution. Today, two armed British policemen stand guard outside the Iranian Embassy, twenty-four hours a day.

The SAS was catapulted overnight from obscurity to worldwide fame. The hostages had no idea, until it was all over, who had rescued them. Applications to join the regiment sharply increased. An internal Foreign Office memo rightly predicted that the successful outcome of the siege would prompt a flood of requests for the SAS to be lent to other countries to tackle hostage situations. The SAS's founder, David Stirling, praised a "marvelously professional performance," noting that the regiment was "immensely more sophisticated than in my day." The siege and its dramatic ending, broadcast live across the nation, was instantly absorbed into British folklore, and suffused with mystery and speculation, since most of the SAS team involved declined to speak about it. In 1994, a 190-foot rope used in the assault was bought by the Imperial War Museum.

Not all SAS officers were pleased by the notoriety. Peter de la Billière described how hundreds of young men appeared at army recruitment centers "apparently convinced that a balaclava helmet and a Heckler & Koch submachine gun would be handed to them over the counter, so that they could go off and conduct embassy-style sieges of their own." The siege spawned multiple documentaries, films, and books: fiction, nonfiction, and something in between. As Hector Gullan predicted, the assault had not gone entirely to plan: the gunmen and their captives were not where they were supposed to be, Tom Morell had almost burned to death, and two hostages had died. But the mistakes were forgotten in the jubilation. The regiment's reputation for muscular derring-do was set in stone and endures today, reinforced by macho television programs mimicking the selection process. "The Iranian Embassy siege was the worst thing that ever happened to the SAS," says Michael Rose. "The media and the politicians and the world noticed them, and started to build the myths and legends about them. Up to then, the SAS had been unheard of. They were jungle ruffians, as they were in the desert. The siege was the beginning of the end of that old SAS world. They were a public organization." Never again would the SAS be able to operate in the shadows. The regiment has struggled to balance secrecy with celebrity ever since.

The siege was one of the biggest and most costly operations ever mounted by the Metropolitan Police, requiring 5,000 meters of cable, more than 30 TV monitors, 20 tape recorders, 60 pencils, 20 rolls of Sellotape, 818 ballpoint pens, 1,098 sheets of graph paper, 1,900 envelopes, 20 wastebins, 4 easels, 4 blackboards, 60 industrial gloves, 400 plastic bags, 2 beds, 12 pairs of scissors, 44 blankets, 3 pencil sharpeners, 72 toilet rolls, 10 bottles of Tipp-Ex correction fluid, 2,000 plastic cups, and 30 plastic handcuffs. More than a hundred members of the police catering staff served a total of 20,600 meals to police officers, soldiers, firefighters, and ambulance workers (as well as the hostages and gunmen). The police alone consumed 40,000 snacks. The siege led to an

improvement in equipment. Every Diplomatic Protection Group officer was henceforth issued with a battery-powered locating device hidden in his uniform. Members of the SAS were equipped with fireproof
overalls, better holsters, helmets, and identifying armbands. Snipers complained they had spent time filling out surveillance forms when they
should have been watching the embassy; they were given Dictaphones.

In a report written six years after the siege, **John Albert Dellow**
offered a prescient warning: "TV coverage of the siege had shown the
increasing reach of technologies which might one day become a
weapon for the terrorists themselves." Immaculate in his uniform, uniform in his outlook, Dellow continued to serve as Scotland Yard's
troubleshooter-in-chief. Appointed head of the Criminal Investigation
Department, he investigated the Brink's-Mat gold-bullion robbery of
1983, stood in as acting commissioner for six months, and retired in
1991 with a knighthood. From then until his death in 2022 at the age
of ninety-one, he painted watercolors and polished his shoes every
Sunday. Looking back on the embassy siege, he insisted, "I have no re-
grets." This was not entirely accurate. Like those in the police negotiation team, he wished the story had ended bloodlessly. Dellow privately
lamented the messy, violent culmination to the siege, and carried a
knotty sense of mourning, buttoned up beneath his pristine exterior, for
the rest of his life. "We were dealing with gunmen dedicated and prepared to die unless they got what they wanted," he wrote. "At the end,
their only demand was for safe passage out of the country." And that
Dellow would not and could not give them.

Max Vernon ran the Metropolitan Police negotiation course from
1983 to 1986, traveled to the United States to study FBI siege tactics,
and ended his career as divisional commander in Woolwich, in Southeast London. He was haunted by a sense of failure. "I felt guilty about
my feelings for a long time," he explained. "It was like a huge, dense
cloud that dropped on me. A couple of the others were in the same
boat, but nobody said anything." Vernon died in 2021, still wondering
about the man he knew as Salim. "I would have liked to have met him,"
he said in his last interview.

David Veness went on to become one of the world's foremost
experts on international terrorism, running the Anti-terrorist Branch,

Special Branch, and both the Royal and Diplomatic Protection teams. Promoted to assistant commissioner of specialist operations, the highest-ranking officer responsible for counterterrorism in the United Kingdom, he was awarded the Queen's Police Medal, appointed Commander of the Most Excellent Order of the British Empire, and knighted in 2005, the year he became the United Nations' first undersecretary-general for safety and security.

Fred Luff was another to suffer lingering aftereffects. He checked into the police nursing home in Hendon, and was released after three weeks, a different man. "It certainly affected his mind," said his wife, Corrine. "After that, he was very fragile in his thinking. I would say he had a mental breakdown. It was the one thing in his career that affected him." Within a year, Luff left the force to pursue a new vocation as a missionary in Africa, bringing unbelievers into what he saw as the one true faith. He later became warden of St. Nicholas Church in Shepperton, Surrey.

Graham Collins of the Anti-terrorist Branch became detective inspector in 1983, specializing in the acquisition of technical intelligence. He left the Met in 2002 and now works as an independent cybersecurity adviser.

A special commemorative tie was issued to police officers who had taken part in the operation: it featured a prince's coronet above a five-bar gate, to represent Princes Gate.

Towfiq al-Rashidi, leader of the Group of the Martyr, had requested that his body be returned to Arabistan to lie alongside that of his murdered brother. Instead, the five dead gunmen were buried facing Mecca in a single, unmarked grave in Woodgrange Park Cemetery in East London. "They don't belong here," complained Pamela Stagg, a local resident. The area was sealed off by armed police on the day of the burials in case of demonstrations. But there were no protesters, and no mourners. In 2018, members of the exiled Ahwazi community erected a simple headstone, with the gunmen's real names carved in Arabic. In 2003, an Iraqi defector named Abid Hussein, a former Mukhabarat colonel, told *The Observer* that the Iranian Embassy operation had been run by the senior Iraqi intelligence officer **Fowzi al-Naimi**. "I was in special operations in Baghdad at the time and I saw

their files and their information," Abid said. An arrest warrant was issued for the Iraqi spy known as **Sami Muhammad Ali**. The Fox has
never been traced.

The terrorist mastermind **Abu Nidal** continued his campaign of
sponsored slaughter. In 1982, one of his assassins, accompanied by an
Iraqi intelligence officer, shot the Israeli ambassador Shlomo Argov in
the head as he was leaving the Dorchester Hotel in London. Argov survived but was disabled for life. Abu Nidal moved from Iraq to Syria,
and then on to Libya. He became close friends with Libyan leader
Muammar Gaddafi, with whom he shared a raging inferiority complex
and a taste for murder. Increasingly paranoid, he continued on his
bloody trail, while also claiming responsibility for atrocities he had
nothing to do with, including the Brighton Hotel bombing in 1984, the
IRA attack that almost killed Margaret Thatcher. Of the bombing of
Pan Am Flight 103 in 1988, he said: "We do have some involvement in
this matter, but if anyone so much as mentions it, I will kill him with my
own hands." Expelled from Libya, Abu Nidal returned to Iraq in 2002.
In August of that year, he was killed in a house belonging to the
Mukhabarat. Iraqi officials claimed his death was suicide, an assertion
undermined by his numerous gunshot wounds. Palestinian and most
Western sources believe he was killed on the orders of Saddam Hussein, who feared that Abu Nidal and his forces would turn against him
in the event of an American invasion. "He was the patriot turned psychopath," reported *The Guardian*. "He served only himself, only the
warped personal drives that pushed him into hideous crime. He was
the ultimate mercenary."

Four SAS soldiers were awarded the Queen's Gallantry Medal in
secret (as is special forces practice). These were 22 SAS's commanding
officer, Lieutenant Colonel (later General, Sir) **Michael Rose**, along
with Tommy Palmer, Mel Parry, and Tom MacDonald.

Tommy Palmer was commended for his "courageous example,
speedy reactions and determination to see his task through regardless
of the personal risk." The Scotsman saw action in the Falklands, where
he killed a local cow to provide steaks for his messmates. Palmer had
warned his wife, Caroline, that he would "never grow old." In February
1983, back in Northern Ireland, he was driving at speed to a covert

rendezvous when he skidded off the motorway and crashed. His body was thrown through the windshield and found fifty yards away. The trunk of the car was filled with weapons, but the exact nature of the operation has never been revealed. The Poacher was thirty-two. In 2023, Palmer Row was named after him in a housing development in Falkirk, near the children's home where he grew up.

Mel Parry's citation praised his "outstanding example of courage and cool, decisive leadership." In 1984, the leader of the balcony team joined an SAS expedition to scale Mount Everest from the Chinese side. He went on to invent a bulletproof shield modeled on an ancient Roman artifact, as well as the Parry Blade, a multipurpose survival knife: both are still in use by special forces around the world. After twenty-seven years in the SAS, he left the army in 1990 and went on to become a sought-after security consultant and an adviser to Swedish, Norwegian, and Swiss special forces. Parry died in 2023 at the age of seventy-six.

The quietest of the medalists, **Tom MacDonald** moved to New Zealand and settled on a remote farmstead in rural Oamaru on South Island, where he raised sheep, fished, skied, and seldom spoke about his role at the forefront of the battle for Princes Gate. His citation noted that his "speedy, courageous actions saved PC Lock." He died in 2019.

After several months of intensive skin grafting to his burned legs, **Tom Morell** fully recovered. For his role in Operation Nimrod he was awarded the George Medal, a step up from the Queen's Gallantry Medal. The citation read: "Without doubt the successful rescue of the majority of the hostages is very largely due to the outstanding effort, quick thinking, courage and personal example of SSgt Morell, who, regardless of his own injuries and the terrifying fire raging on the floor below him, continued to lead the team with coolness and decisiveness." The Fijian soldier retired to New Zealand with his English wife, Rose.

Peter de la Billière was promoted to general and awarded a knighthood, along with a host of other titles and medals, to add to his Distinguished Service Order and Military Cross. He was involved in planning for the Falklands War and served as commander in chief of British forces during the First Gulf War. Britain's most highly deco-rated soldier was embroiled in a different conflict when he defied official secrecy to publish his memoirs, a move that saw him temporarily shunned by the SAS.

Hector Gullan left the army in 2002, exchanged his short-back-and-sides for a bandanna and ponytail, and retired to Cornwall, where, with his Norwegian wife, he lives what he describes as a cracking life, kayaking, fishing, and brewing nettle wine. His verdict on the siege is pithy: "Five seconds the other way and it would have been a different story. It was a close-run affair. This is a risk business. If we had failed and the hostages had been killed—broadcast and televised live to the nation and the world—there would without doubt have been calls for the disbandment of the SAS. One could well ask if the Thatcher government would have survived. Yes, we were lucky. But then you earn your luck."

Having lost his taste for "hostile situations," **Sim Harris** left the BBC in 1982 after eighteen years as a sound recordist. He consulted Professor John Gunn about the psychological aftershocks suffered by most of the hostages. "The siege never goes away," he says. "To be honest I don't think I will ever fully recover." Harris worked in various television-management jobs and retired in 2011. He was best man at the first wedding of Chris Cramer, and together they wrote *Hostage!*, published in 1982. A grandfather of six, Harris continues to mix sound for his local theater group and church services.

Chris Cramer was the second hostage released, after Frieda Mozafarian, but perhaps the most adversely affected. He suffered post-traumatic stress disorder (a term coined the year of the siege), flashbacks, nightmares, claustrophobia, and fear of flying. But the trauma also altered his personality in positive ways. Gone was the aggressive, hard-driving Crusher Cramer. A gentler character emerged. He went out of his way to protect journalists on the front lines and showed particular compassion to colleagues in danger or distress. The experience "scared the hell out of me," he once said, "but at the same time it gave me the chance to find out a lot about myself." In 1996, he left the BBC after twenty-five years to move to Atlanta as managing director and executive vice president of CNN International, before taking up senior roles with Reuters TV and *The Wall Street Journal*. Cramer died of cancer in 2021 at the age of seventy-three. To the end of his life, he carried an unjustified millstone of shame for extricating himself early in the siege. "I know I'm a coward and I feel good about knowing it," he told the BBC, many years afterward. "People want to be tested in their lives and I was tested, and I failed that particular test. But I've passed many other tests, self-preservation being a very good one."

Mustapha Karkouti also bore what he called the "psychological scars." For several months he was unable to leave the house. But gradually, with the support of his wife, Faten, he emerged back into the world and embraced it with typical gusto. He became president of the Foreign Press Association in London and a member of Chatham House Council, worked for a year at the United Nations' Agency for Palestinian Refugees in Jordan, and continued to dispense his expertise on Middle Eastern politics on television, on radio, and in print. As he got older, his walrus mustache growing fatter and grayer, he remained an Arab to his heart, a Palestinian supporter in his soul, and British by choice: "London is my home and always will be." His connoisseurship of cigars, whiskey, and female beauty remained constant. Karkouti died of a heart attack in 2020 at the height of the Covid pandemic. Of all the hostages, he was the most sympathetic to the naïve and violent young Arabs who had kidnapped him. "They didn't know London's long history of fighting terrorism, didn't know about the IRA," he said. "If I am ever taken hostage again, I hope to God to be taken by professionals—much less stress."

Ron Morris returned to Battersea; his wife, Maria; and Gingerella the cat. After two days off, he resumed work as caretaker of the new, temporary Iranian Embassy, housed in the nearby Iranian Consulate. He recovered his replica guns, his life savings, and his moped, which had remained parked outside the embassy for the duration. It had been damaged by falling masonry from the balcony, so he swapped it for a Triumph and adopted a new hobby: membership of the South London Triumph Motorcycle Owners' Club. He was never late for meetings, and always made the tea. Morris's ordered life barely changed, and nor did the solid, simple, sturdy philosophy that had carried him (and others) through the ordeal. "I'm very happy to be out, but I'm sad it happened," he told Kate Adie the day after his release. "I'm not trying to be sensationalist." In October 1981, Morris was sacked, after "a new ruling by the Iranian government that non-Muslims could not be employed at embassies." He took a job as chauffeur at the nearby Syrian Embassy. Morris died of a brain tumor in 1993 at the age of sixty-one. "I wish that I could have come out of the embassy a hero," he once said, entirely unaware that he had done just that.

The Iranian diplomat **Gholam-Ali Afrouz** returned to Iran and became manager of Peyvand Publications, a publisher of books on child and young adult psychology.

Abdul Ezzati was appointed professor of Islamic philosophy at Tehran University.

Ali Asghar Tabatabai stayed in the UK, and was granted political asylum. "Rehabilitation was extremely difficult, yet how very grateful I was to be alive!" he later reflected. Searching for some spiritual meaning behind the distress he had suffered, he began reading *The Watchtower*, the Jehovah's Witnesses publication, and discovered what he called "an individual, personal God, with a loving purpose for mankind." Ali the Bank and his wife were baptized as Jehovah's Witnesses and never returned to Iran.

The day after the siege, the attractive face of the youngest hostage, **Nooshin Hashemenian**, was splashed across the front page of the *Daily Mirror*, with the headline BEAUTY IN THE SIEGE. The twenty-one-year-old secretary was depicted as the "Cheery Heroine" of the siege: "She kept the others calm. She built up a special relationship with the gunmen. She helped to save many of the others."

This was even truer of **Roya Kaghachi**, whose pivotal role in the siege has been overlooked by history. As she had vowed, Kaghachi quit her embassy job at the first opportunity and never worked for the Iranian government again. She gave no interviews and was not invited to testify in legal proceedings. She married and settled in Australia, where she still lives.

Shirazeh Boroumand had two children and moved to Spain. She visited Fowzi Nejad in prison and maintained contact for many years with the gunman whose life she had probably saved.

When **Ahmad Dadgar** arrived at hospital with multiple gunshot wounds, doctors warned that he had no more than a 5 percent chance of survival. To their astonishment, he made a full recovery.

The Pakistani-born journalist **Muhammad Hashir Faruqi** exhibited no ill effects after the siege and rejected all trauma counseling. He ran the Muslim magazine *Impact International* for thirty-five years, helped to launch the Muslim Council of Great Britain, became a trustee of Muslim Aid, and lived in a small flat in Kilburn until the end of his long life, at the age of ninety-two, in 2022. "He never expected any credit from anyone," said one of the journalists he trained. "He was collecting his credit from Allah."

Nawabzada Ghazanfar Ali Gul, the Pakistani tourist, missed his plane to Lahore, but, after being extensively interviewed by police, he finally flew home. A senior member of the Nawabzada family, the oldest political dynasty in Gujrat, Gul launched his political career in 1985. He was duly elected a member of the National Assembly of Pakistan and the Provincial Assembly of Punjab, and served as federal minister of Pakistan and adviser to the prime minister on political affairs. In 1997, Gul was attacked and injured in the city of Gujrat by an unidentified gunman riding a motorbike. In 2024, he stood again as a candidate for Pakistan's parliament.

Every year for many years, around the first May bank holiday, the hostages held a reunion, usually at Karkouti's home in Ealing, where they recalled the siege and discussed how it had changed their lives. Harris called the gatherings "a tangible and essential form of self-help on the long road to recovery."

A BBC duty reporter in May 1980, **Kate Adie** became a household name. Her coverage of the assault propelled her to a career on the front line of world news: she covered Fowzi Nejad's trial and went on to report from Tiananmen Square (with Chris Cramer as her manager), Bosnia, Northern Ireland, Tripoli, and Iraq, among other war zones. She became the BBC's chief news correspondent in 1989, a position she retained for fourteen years. A cartoon at the time of the Iraq War depicted two soldiers preparing for battle above the caption "We can't start yet . . . Kate Adie isn't here." The ITN team responsible for secretly filming the rear of the embassy won a BAFTA for its coverage. Contrary to popular myth, the presence of the hidden camera did nothing to jeopardize Operation Nimrod.

The siege was the first breaking news event to be broadcast live on every British television channel. Some viewers were furious. Mr. F. M. Chambers of Keele University denounced what he called the BBC's reprehensible decision to broadcast breaking news on a bank holiday, and composed an angry letter to *The Guardian:* "Why, when covering the world snooker final live on BBC2, did they interrupt this in the most crucial part of the match? It is quite intolerable."

Cliff Thorburn was ranked the world's number one snooker player in 1981, but in 1982 **Alex Higgins** won the world title back. In subsequent years Hurricane Higgins headbutted one official, punched another, threatened to have a rival player killed, and was stabbed three times by a girlfriend during a domestic spat. An alcoholic with an eighty-a-day smoking habit and a supreme snooker talent, he was diagnosed with throat cancer and died in 2010. Grinder Thorburn played his final competitive event in 2022 at the age of seventy-three, at the UK Seniors Championship in Hull.

At the Maudsley, **John Gunn**, CBE, developed the largest postgraduate teaching center in Britain for forensic psychiatry, and co-authored the definitive textbook on the subject. He is now emeritus professor of forensic psychiatry at the Institute of Psychiatry, King's College London.

Rebecca West moved back into Kingston House and penned a vivid account of the siege she had witnessed from her kitchen window. "It has fallen to my lot to be swept into the orbit of one of the most glorious episodes in British history, and my heart swells at the thought of the bravery of the SAS and police," she wrote in *The Daily Telegraph.* "The emotion is valid, for it was given to me, because the windows of my flat look down on the private garden of the Iranian Embassy, to contemplate the magnificent coolness of the police at a distance of 50 yards." Typically, she then swerved in the opposite direction: "Let me also say that this was also the most disgusting and humiliating experience of my life, and I regard it as essential that it never happens again." She complained bitterly about the displacement she and her neighbors had undergone, blamed the government for the bloody denouement by failing "to get in touch with certain ambassadors," and ended with an original and wholly impractical suggestion that Britain should "segregate all embassies in a diplomatic quarter" outside London, safe from terrorist attack. This diplomatic enclave, she suggested, could be located in "such quiet watering places as Southend [or] perhaps a cluster of high-rise abandoned flats in some Midland city." West died three years later at the age of ninety, following seven decades of literary output ranging from reportage to political commentary, essays, history, and novels. "Rebecca West was one of the giants and will have a lasting place in English literature," declared William Shawn, editor of *The New Yorker*. "No one in this century wrote more dazzling prose, or had more wit, or looked at the intricacies of human character and the ways of the world more intelligently." Dame Rebecca's article about the Iranian Embassy siege was her last news report.

ON THE EVENING of May 5, 1980, following six hours of interrogation, **Fowzi Badavi Nejad** was charged with murder.

"I haven't killed them," he told detectives.

The trial opened at the Old Bailey on January 14, 1981. Nejad pleaded not guilty to murdering Lavasani and Samadzadeh but admitted the other charges: conspiracy to murder, false imprisonment, and possession of firearms with intent to endanger life. Nejad claimed he had been asleep when Abbas Lavasani was killed and described how he had opposed the decision to start executing hostages. "Myself and Abbas rejected it," he told the court. "Salim Towfiq told us he would shoot us if we went against him. He had the power in the group. We had to obey him." He claimed that he had not witnessed the death of Ali Samadzadeh, the young Iranian press assistant, in the telex room. Iraqi intelligence officers had manipulated all of them into undertaking a doomed operation, he insisted. "I have been cheated in Iraq and I am repentant," he said. When he was shown photographs of his slain companions and the two dead hostages, he turned away. "I cannot look at the pictures," he said. "I am too upset."

"The final attack by the SAS was planned extremely well," the counsel for the crown observed. "They could have had no last-minute knowledge of the actual disposal of weapons by the terrorists . . . There doesn't seem much doubt the soldiers were shooting to kill. That's what soldiers are trained to do." But he added that any impression "of the SAS deliberately gunning down unarmed men who had surrendered [was] wholly misleading."

On the fifth day of the trial, Nejad dramatically changed his not-guilty plea, and instead pleaded guilty to manslaughter. The judge accepted that he had not killed anyone but stated that he had, nonetheless, taken part in an "outrageous criminal enterprise . . . in pursuance of a grievance against the government of [his] native country." Nejad was sentenced to life imprisonment.

In HMP Wellingborough he learned English and proved a model prisoner. The other inmates nicknamed him Fozzy. He sent letters of apology to the hostages. Some of these, in turn, signed a petition urging that after more than two decades in prison he should be liberated.

Nejad was finally released in 2008, having served twenty-seven years. In Iran, he still faced murder charges for the deaths of Lavasani and Samadzadeh. Tehran gave no assurances he would not be tortured and executed if repatriated. He was therefore allowed to remain in the UK, a decision described by Iran as "condemnable and indefensible."

Fowzi Nejad now lives in the UK.

The last remaining piece of the legal puzzle was to establish how, exactly, the five gunmen had perished and who, if anyone, was legally responsible. An inquest opened at Westminster Coroner's Court on February 3, 1981, as is usual in cases of sudden or unexplained death. The coroner, Dr. Paul Knapman, briefly ran through the events of the embassy siege for the benefit of the jury, adding, "In case you have been on a desert island."

Several of the SAS soldiers—including Morell, Parry, Pringle, Palmer, and MacDonald—gave written evidence under aliases. Two testified in court: Pete Winner (one of the ground-floor assault team identified only as "Soldier I") and Paul Sanford ("Soldier CC"). Some of the testimony from the Iranian witnesses was confusing and contradictory. The doorman Abbas Fallahi said that an SAS soldier had held Shaye's head under his arm and shot him at point-blank range, but both the forensic pathologist and ballistic expert stated that this was contradicted by the evidence, and impossible "without the soldier blowing his own arm off." Ali Tabatabai claimed that Jassim had been killed by a single shot to the head as he knelt, unarmed, facing the wall of the telex room—an assertion contradicted by evidence proving he had been shot thirty-nine times at the bottom of the stairs. Under cross-examination, some of the Iranian witnesses backtracked on statements they had made earlier and denied suggesting that the gunmen had been killed after clearly surrendering. The coroner put the confusion down to language difficulties, and noted that "the recollection of some of the hostages has been embellished or misinterpreted with the passage of time."

Knapman asked Winner if the SAS had been aware of the group's threat to blow up the building before the assault.

"Did you know whether it was booby-trapped?"

"No. It could have been," Winner replied.

"So you took a chance?"

"Got to, haven't you?"

As Winner finished giving testimony, a tall, dark-haired man rose from the public benches and asked to address the court. It was Ron Morris. "May I please shake hands with this gentleman after all he did for us?" he asked.

Surprised, the coroner agreed, and Morris rushed forward and shook Winner's hand.

Knapman instructed the jury to deliver one of four verdicts: justifiable homicide if the SAS had used reasonable, necessary, and proportionate force; unlawful killing if the SAS actions had been "totally unreasonable"; misadventure if the five gunmen had been killed by accident; and an open verdict if there was insufficient evidence to reach a decision.

The coroner concluded that Ron Morris's toy gun may have contributed to the death of one man, and his biscuits to another. But he made his own sympathies clear: "Imagine the confusion, the noise, and the terror as the SAS went in," said Knapman. "Imagine peering through the smoke and seeing the enemy and ask yourself whether it is reasonable to shoot first and ask questions afterward. The SAS took no chances." He was peeved when the jury took several hours to reach a decision. "I'm a little surprised it has taken you quite so long to come to your verdict," he snapped.

The jury returned unanimous verdicts of justifiable homicide in each case.

AN HOUR AFTER the siege ended, **Trevor** and **Doreen Lock** were reunited at St. Ermin's Hotel near Scotland Yard, where they checked in under a false name to avoid the press. Sir David McNee met Lock there, and promptly burst into tears. "His conduct throughout was just heroic," said the police commissioner. The newspapers embraced him with headlines like SIEGE HERO. Lock's fellow officers took up a collection and raised a thousand pounds to give the couple a "much-needed holiday." But Lock was no longer Trev the Barking Bobby. In Dagenham, people stopped him in the street to demand autographs. The Locks moved from their house to escape the media attention. In 1981, Lock was awarded the George Medal for "outstanding courage, sustained bravery, calmness and devotion to duty." Without him, the citation noted, "the hostages' lives might have been lost." Doreen kept the medal in her knitting basket. Later, Trevor donated it to the Metropolitan Police Museum.

Lock gave few interviews and shunned his own fame. He never made a penny out of his experience. "Selling my story would be like selling my soul," he said. Apart from occasional lectures to trainees on the hostage-negotiation team, he seldom spoke about his ordeal, and never in public. "I'm not an extrovert," he said. He transferred to the M11 Motorway Control Unit at Chadwell Heath, just north of Dagenham, and spent the rest of his police career quietly watching the cars go by, keeping doves in his spare time. The celebrity faded, but the trauma did not. Lock experienced nightmares and mood swings. Professor Gunn told him he was suffering from survivor's guilt. After more than four decades, he still cannot forgive himself for failing to save the life of Abbas Lavasani. He retired in 1992. Today Trevor Lock lives in Dagenham, with Doreen. Occasionally, on a bus or out shopping on the high street, he catches a whiff of someone wearing Old Spice: "Whenever I smell that aftershave, it all comes back to me." He still has the broken coffee cup he dropped when the gunmen stormed the embassy.

"I don't feel at all heroic. Thousands of men and women in the force would have acted exactly the same way," says the policeman who discovered accidental courage without looking for it, wanting it, or knowing what it was.

Trevor and Doreen Lock reunited, May 6, 1980. (From Alamy: PA Images)

The first hostage reunion, July 6, 1980. Back row, left to right: Ali Tabatabai, Sim Harris, Ron Morris. Front row, left to right: Ahmed Dadgar, Mustapha Karkouti, Muhammad Faruqi, Trevor Lock, Roya Kaghachi, Chris Cramer. (Courtesy of Sim Harris)

Margaret Thatcher poses with the SAS, December 1980. (From Sworders Fine Art Auctioneers)

The Queen's Gallantry Medal recipients. Left to right: Tommy Palmer, Mel Parry,
Tom Morell, Tom MacDonald, Michael Rose. (Courtesy of Bethan and Gail Parry)

SELECTED DRAMATIS PERSONAE

The Group of the Martyr

Towfiq Ibrahim al-Rashidi (alias Salim, alias Oan): lead gunman

Jassim Alwan al-Nasiri (alias Faisal): his deputy

Shaye Hamid al-Sahar (alias Hassan): gunman

Makki Hanoun: gunman

Abbas Maytham: gunman

Fowzi Badavi Nejad (alias Ali): gunman

Abu Nidal: terrorist mastermind

Fowzi al-Naimi: senior officer in Directorate 4 of the Mukhabarat, Iraqi intelligence

"Sami Muhammad Ali" (alias the Fox): officer in Directorate 4 of the Mukhabarat, Iraqi intelligence

Hostages

Iranian

Dr. Gholam-Ali Afrouz: chargé d'affaires, Iran's senior diplomat in London

Issa Naghizadeh: first secretary

Abdul Ezzati: embassy press attaché

Seyyed Abbas Lavasani: embassy deputy press attaché, member of the Revolutionary Guard

Ali Akbar Samadzadeh: embassy press assistant

Ahmad Dadgar: embassy medical orderly

Abbas Fallahi: embassy doorman

Roya Kaghachi: senior secretary to the chargé d'affaires

Frieda Mozafarian: secretary to the press attaché

Hiyech Sanai Kanji: embassy secretary

Nooshin Hashemenian: embassy secretary

Shirazeh Boroumand: embassy switchboard operator and secretary

Zahra Zomorrodian: embassy assistant telex operator

Vahid Khabaz: student journalist

Ali Asghar Tabatabai: banker

British and Other Nationalities

Chris Cramer: BBC news producer

Sim Harris: BBC sound recordist

Ron Morris: embassy majordomo

Trevor Lock: police constable, Diplomatic Protection Group

Mustapha Karkouti: journalist (Syrian British)

Nawabzada Ghazanfar Ali Gul: tourist, farmer, and politician (Pakistani)

Muhammad Hashir Faruqi: journalist (Pakistani British)

Police

David McNee: commissioner of the Metropolitan Police

John Dellow: deputy assistant commissioner, operations

Roger Bromley: chief superintendent, Diplomatic Protection Group

Fred Luff: police negotiator

Ray Tucker: police negotiator

David Veness: police negotiator

Max Vernon: police negotiator

Graham Collins: detective sergeant, Anti-terrorist Branch

Jeff Chippendale: detective sergeant, Special Branch

John Gunn: psychiatrist, professor of forensic psychiatry

SAS/Military

Peter de la Billière: director of special forces

Michael Rose: commanding officer, 22 SAS

Jeremy Phipps: operations officer, 22 SAS

Ian Crooke: operations officer, 22 SAS

Hector Gullan: officer commanding, B Squadron

Colin "Clutchplate" Clapton: yeoman of signals, B Squadron

Mark "Wingnut" Gilfoyle: lance corporal, Clerk, B Squadron

Janet Dillon: 14 Intelligence Company

Red Team (B Squadron)

Tom Morell: staff sergeant (second in command)

Simon "Squashball" McGregor: signaler

Peter "Ginge" Garmon: corporal

Tommy Palmer: lance corporal

Paul Sanford: trooper

Blue Team (B Squadron)

Rob Timson: staff sergeant (second in command)

Tom MacDonald: lance corporal

John McAleese: lance corporal

Ben Canon: trooper

Denis Pringle: trooper

Mel Parry: trooper

Pete Winner: trooper

Government

British

Margaret Thatcher: prime minister

William Whitelaw: home secretary

Peter Carington: foreign secretary

Douglas Hurd: foreign minister

Hayden Phillips: assistant secretary, Home Office

Richard Hastie-Smith: undersecretary, Cabinet Office

David Tatham: assistant head of Middle East Department, FCO

John Chilcot: principal private secretary to William Whitelaw

John Graham: ambassador to Iran

Iranian

Ruhollah Khomeini: ayatollah and supreme leader

Abolhassan Banisadr: president

Sadegh Ghotbzadeh: foreign minister

Ahmad Madani: governor of Khuzestan

ACKNOWLEDGMENTS

I am most grateful to the huge number of people who have helped to create this book. James Liddell provided invaluable research assistance: without his efficiency and determination, many of the sources and people vital to this story would have remained hidden. Once again, Cecilia Mackay has performed miracles of picture research. Susie Tempest, my brilliant assistant, kept the show on the road throughout. For the ninth time, Robert Hands read the manuscript, twice, and saved me from numerous howling errors. Roland Philipps, my dear friend, offered sage advice on the early draft.

My publishers and agents are the best any writer could hope for: Daniel Crewe, Alpana Sajip, Alex Muholland, Preena Gadher, Jane Gentle, Rose Poole, Emma Brown, and Donna Poppy at Viking Penguin; Kevin Doughten, Dyana Messina, Chantelle Walker, and Julie Cepler at Crown; Doug Pepper and Stephanie Sinclair at McClelland & Stewart; Jonny Geller, Viola Hayden, Atlanta Hatch, and Ciara Finan at Curtis Brown; St. John Donald, Jonny Jones, and Antony Joblin at United Agents.

I am greatly indebted to the many individuals who agreed to be interviewed; enabled me to interview others; or provided additional material, assistance, and support: Karim Abdian, Kate Adie, Wejdan Afravi, Nazy Amini, Alexandra Anisimova, Antonina Anisimova, Anton Antonowicz, Dana Awwad, Richard Ayre, Jo Barrett, Paul Barrett, Paul Bickley, Trevor Binnington, Malcolm Brabant, Daniel Brett, Jason Burke, Venetia Butterfield, Graham Cassidy, Sarah Clark,

Caro Cluskey, Michael Colacicco, Graham Collins, Bob Cox, Hannah Cramer, Maygol Dadgar, Alastair Davidson, Byron Davies, Peter de la Billière, Andrew Dellow, Khalil Delwani, Kathleen Dickson, Bryn Elliott, Ausaf Faruqi, Hafez Fazeli, Yaghoub Fazeli, Bob Fenton, Anna Ford, Charles Garraway, Charmine Gayle-Petrou, Malcolm Goldie, Brian Greenan, Paul Griffiths, Colin Grimshaw, Hector Gullan, Lilly Gullan, John Gunn, Mamal Hamidi, Fiona Hamilton, Maurice Harding, Andy Harries, Helen Harris, Simeon Harris, Sherry Houghton, Chris James, Paul Johnson, Juliana Jonklaas, Faten Karkouti, Shahla Karkouti, Talal Karkouti, Sandy Kaye, Alan Lees, Donna Leigh, Doreen Lock, Trevor Lock, Chris Lomas, Corrine Luff, Keith Lumley, James MacDonald, Eliza Manningham-Buller, Adrian Maybanks, Rose Morell, Tom Morell, Cherry Morgan, Oliver Morse, Alan Moss, Ammar Najarian, Aref Nasr, Doris Neville-Davies, Ken Neville-Davies, Cara Palmer, Darren Palmer, Shona Palmer, Bethan Parry, Gail Parry, Hayden Phillips, Jake Phipps, Sue Phipps, Caroline Probyn, Michael Rose, Richard Sambrook, Leyla Sanai, Graeme Shaw, Shobeir Shobeyri, Lindsay Siviter, Clare Smith, Shervin Tabatabai, David Tatham, Bill Taylor, Pamela Taylor, Stewart Tendler, David Veness, John Virgo, Barry Walsh, Chris Webb, Rachel Webb, Suzanne Williams, Zahra Zomorrodian. A number of others from the SAS and intelligence services made crucial contributions and appear with pseudonyms in this book, but they have asked not to be named. You know who you are, and how grateful I am.

Once again, my beloved children, Barney, Finn, and Molly, have steered me through another book with copious quantities of patience, good humor, and food.

A NOTE ON SOURCES

Most of the source material for this book is secret, pseudonymous, unpublished, or privately owned.

At the time of the siege in 1980, everyone still wrote on paper. This was particularly true of those in this story, an episode of such historical importance that some participants felt motivated to create their own records and testaments during the siege, immediately after it, or later. These are the source foundations for this book.

Sim Harris, John Dellow, and Hector Gullan each wrote contemporaneous diaries as the events unfolded, offering unique minute-by-minute records from the perspectives of the hostages, police, and SAS. Soon after the siege, Harris dictated a narrative of events while these were still fresh in his memory. Before his death, Mustapha Karkouti wrote an extraordinary 345-page manuscript titled "A Hostage's Tale." None of these works has been published, and I am hugely grateful to these individuals, and their families, for permission to quote from their writings.

While some eyewitnesses wrote complete manuscripts and memoirs, others made informal notes, and kept clippings, photos, or souvenirs in private archives that they have generously shared.

This book also derives from multiple interviews with living witnesses, including hostages, police, negotiators, journalists, intelligence officers, and the on-site psychiatrist. Some people inteviewed for this book have asked to remain anonymous for their protection.

Many of the surviving SAS soldiers who carried out Operation Nimrod were granted conditional express prior approval in writing by the Ministry of Defense to speak to me on the record. At their request, some of these participants have been disguised with pseudonyms in the text. All other interviewees are identified by their real names, with the exception of intelligence sources, who have not been identified. This work has not been authorized by the SAS.

Memories are malleable and fallible. Few events in modern British history are so heavily mythologized (and misunderstood) as the Iranian Embassy siege. Over the intervening years, many people have recounted or added to the story without being directly or even peripherally involved. As one SAS officer warned me when I was setting out on this project: "If everyone who claimed to be there at the time had really been there, the balcony would have collapsed under the weight." Some of the resulting legends, burnished by repetition, have proved extremely durable: for example, several eyewitnesses assured me, with absolute conviction, that one of the gunmen was killed by a single sniper shot fired from Hyde Park. This did not happen.

Two or more people can witness the same event but retain entirely different or contradictory recollections. After four decades, our memories become "true" to ourselves when they may, in fact, be inaccurate. We come to believe we have seen something we have only heard about. One of the challenges of this book has been to sift through the huge amount of remembered material, identifying those memories that seem to me most credible, consistent, and in agreement with other verified evidence. This means privileging some memories over others. A few interviewees may feel shortchanged.

Published material on the siege is vast in scale but variable in quality. Every British newspaper covered the story in depth, every day, for a week, and for months thereafter. Television reports (including student television) provided vivid on-the-spot coverage. Some of this journalism was inspired and accurate; some, comically bad. After the siege ended, *The Sunday Times* Insight Team and *The Observer* each published an "instant book," with the same title and identical cover images. Then the fastest books ever published in the UK, they landed in bookshops just eighteen days after the siege ended. Remarkable feats of high-speed

reporting, writing, and editing, these competing accounts, hastily com-
piled and incomplete, are invaluable "first drafts of history."

Several prominent individuals—including Margaret Thatcher, William Whitelaw, Douglas Hurd, David McNee, Hayden Phillips, and
Peter de la Billière—described the siege in their memoirs. In defiance
of SAS rules surrounding operational confidentiality, a few soldiers
have broken ranks over the decades to write about the siege, either
pseudonymously or under their own names. Some of these accounts
are insightful and useful; a few are self-serving and inaccurate. All published accounts are listed in the bibliography.

The Ahwazi community in the UK provided copious documentary
material, including a privately printed eighty-four-page pamphlet on
the siege, *Ambassadors of Martyrdom*, written in Arabic from the Arab
perspective immediately after these events.

Government records relating to the Iranian Embassy siege are
housed in the National Archives at Kew (FCO/8/3660/2/3 and
CAB/128/67/18). The military records on Operation Nimrod have
not been declassified, but some important additional material is held by
the National Army Museum.

Professor John Gunn wrote "The Psychiatrist and the Siege," a per-
ceptive article in *The Psychiatric Bulletin*, based on his experience at
Princes Gate. John Dellow's official 135-page report on the siege is the
definitive police account.

Despite repeated Freedom of Information Act applications, the
Metropolitan Police has declined to release its nine hundred pages of
records on the grounds that this declassification process would take
eighteen days to complete and "would impose a grossly oppressive burden on the Metropolitan Police Service." Luckily, policemen also tend
to retain documents, and much of this material is in private hands.

SELECT BIBLIOGRAPHY

BOOKS

Abrahamian, Ervand. *Khomeinism: Essays on the Islamic Republic.* Berkeley, CA, 1993.

Adams, James. *Secret Armies: The Full Story of the SAS, Delta Force and Spetsnaz.* London, 1988.

Adie, Kate. *The Kindness of Strangers.* London, 2002.

Algar, Hamid. *Islam and Revolution: Writing and Declarations of Imam Khomeini 1942–1980.* Berkeley, CA, 1981.

Amir-Moezzi, Mohammad Ali. *The Divine Guide in Early Shi'ism: The Sources of Esotericism in Islam.* New York, 1992.

Andrew, Christopher. *The Defense of the Realm: The Authorized History of MI5.* London, 2010.

Anonymous. *Ambassadors of Martyrdom: From Ahwaz to London.* Privately printed. Ahwaz, 1980.

Aslan, Reza. *No God but God: The Origins, Evolution and Future of Islam.* London, 2011.

Axworthy, Michael. *Iran: Empire of the Mind—A History from Zoroaster to the Present Day.* London, 2007.

———. *Revolutionary Iran: A History of the Islamic Republic.* London, 2013.

Bowden, Mark. *Guests of the Ayatollah: The Iran Hostage Crisis—The First Battle in America's War with Militant Islam.* London, 2007.

Brock, George, et al. *Siege: Six Days at the Iranian Embassy (The Observer).* London, 1980.

Clarke, Shaun. *SAS Operation: Embassy Siege.* London, 1994.

Collins, Frank. *Baptism of Fire: From SAS Hero to Spiritual Warrior.* London, 1997.

Curry, Bob. *The Psychic Soldier: The True Story of One Man's Psychic Journey from Childhood to the SAS and Beyond.* Charleston, SC, 2014.

Davies, Barry. *SAS Rescue Missions: From the Jungles of Malaya to the Iranian Embassy Siege 1948–1995.* London, 2019.

De la Billière, Peter. *Looking for Trouble: SAS to Gulf Command.* London, 1994.

Edwards, Aaron. *Agents of Influence: Britain's Secret Intelligence War Against the IRA.* Newbridge, Ireland, 2021.

Firmin, Rusty, and Will Pearson. *Go! Go! Go!: The SAS. The Iranian Embassy Siege. The True Story.* London, 2010.

Fisher, William, et al. *The Cambridge History of Iran.* Seven vols. Cambridge, 1968–1989.

Forsyth, Frederick. *The Day of the Jackal.* London, 1971.

Fremont-Barnes, Gregory. *Who Dares Wins: The SAS and the Iranian Embassy Siege.* London, 2009.

Gunn, John, and Pamela Taylor. *Forensic Psychiatry: Clinical, Legal and Ethical Issues.* London, 2019.

Harris, Sim, and Chris Cramer. *Hostage!* London, 1982.

Hastings, Max, and Simon Jenkins. *The Battle for the Falklands.* London, 1982.

Horsfall, Robin. *Fighting Scared.* London, 2002.

Hurd, Douglas. *Memoirs.* London, 2003.

Irving, Sarah. *Leila Khaled: Icon of Palestinian Liberation.* London, 2012.

Kennedy, Hugh. *The Prophet and the Age of the Caliphates: The Islamic Near East from the Sixth to the Eleventh Century* (A History of the Near East). London, 2004.

Khomeini, Ruhollah. *Islamic Government.* London, 1979.

King, David. *Six Days in August: The Story of Stockholm Syndrome.* New York, 2020.

MacWilson, Alastair C. *Hostage-Taking Terrorism: Incident-Response Strategy.* London, 1992.

McNee, Sir David. *McNee's Law.* Glasgow, 1983.

Moore, Charles. *Margaret Thatcher: The Authorized Biography,* vol. 1: *Not for Turning.* London, 2013.

Neville, Leigh. *European Counterterrorist Units 1972–2017.* Oxford, 2017.

Ochberg, Frank. *Post-traumatic Therapy and Victims of Violence.* New York, 1988.

Phillips, Hayden. *Boy on a Bicycle: A Mandarin's Memoir.* London, 2023.

Phillips, Russell. *Operation Nimrod: The Iranian Embassy Siege.* Stoke-on-Trent, 2015.

Ramsay, Jack. *SAS: The Soldiers' Story.* London, 1996.

Ryan, Chris. *The History of the SAS.* London, 2019.

Scholey, Pete. *The Joker: Twenty Years Inside the SAS.* London, 1999.

Scott Cooper, Andrew. *The Fall of Heaven: The Pahlavis and the Final Days of Imperial Iran.* New York, 2016.

Seale, Patrick. *Abu Nidal: A Gun for Hire.* London, 1992.

Strenz, Thomas. *Psychological Aspects of Crisis Negotiation.* London, 2005.

Sunday Times Insight Team. *Siege! Princes Gate, London, April 30–May 5: The Great Embassy Rescue.* London, 1980.

Thatcher, Margaret. *Margaret Thatcher: The Downing Street Years.* London, 1993.

Whitelaw, William. *The Whitelaw Memoirs.* London, 1990.

Winner, Pete, and Michael Paul Kennedy. *Soldier "I": The Story of an SAS Hero.* Oxford, 1989.

Wright, Peter, and Paul Greengrass. *Spycatcher: The Candid Autobiography of a Senior Intelligence Officer.* London, 1987.

ARTICLES

British Ahwazi Friendship Society. "Report: Human Rights and the Ahwazi Arabs." London, 2007.

Draper, Ben. "The Iranian Embassy Siege of 1980: A Historical Case Study." MA dissertation, Queen Mary College, University of London. London, 2012.

Grob-Fitzgibbon, Benjamin. "Those Who Dared: A Reappraisal of Britain's Special Air Service 1950–1980." *International History Review* 37, no. 3 (2015).

Gunn, John. "The Psychiatrist and the Siege." *Psychiatric Bulletin* 17, no. 3 (March 1993).

Hetteh, Abdulrahaman. "Political History of Ahwaz." *Journal of Iranian Studies* 7, no. 2 (2023).

Johnson, Hugh, and Iain West. "The Iranian Embassy Siege." *Medico-Legal Journal* 51, no. 4 (1983).

Tabatabai, Ali Asghar. "Surely I Must Die," *Awake!* 65, no. 19 (October 8, 1984).

Veness, David. "Protecting Against Unconventional Attack." *RUSI Journal* 143, no. 6 (1998).

———. "The Fight Against Terrorism: Achieving a New Balanced Normality." *RUSI Journal* 148, no. 4 (2003).

INDEX

ABOUT THE AUTHOR

BEN MACINTYRE is a writer-at-large for *The Times* (UK) and the bestselling author of *Agent Sonya, The Spy and the Traitor, A Spy Among Friends, Double Cross, Operation Mincemeat, Agent Zigzag, Rogue Heroes,* and *Prisoners of the Castle,* among other books. Macintyre has also written and presented BBC documentaries of his work.